World Media Ethics

Cases and Commentary

Robert S. Fortner and P. Mark Fackler

WILEY

Registered Offices
John Wiley & Sons, Inc., 111 River Street, Hoboken, NJ 07030, USA

Editorial Office
1606 Golden Aspen Drive, Suites 103 and 104, Ames, IA 50010, USA

For details of our global editorial offices, customer services, and more information about Wiley products visit us at www.wiley.com.

Wiley also publishes its books in a variety of electronic formats and by print-on-demand. Some content that appears in standard print versions of this book may not be available in other formats.

Library of Congress Cataloging-in-Publication Data is available for this title
Hardback ISBN: 9781118989999
Paperback ISBN: 9781118990001

Cover image: nito100/iStockphoto

Cover design by Wiley

Set in 10/12pt WarnockPro-Regular by Thomson Digital, Noida, India

Printed in Singapore by C.O.S. Printers Pte Ltd

1   2018

Contents

Contents

Preface

The genesis of this book was a course taught at the American University in Bulgaria in the fall of 2011. When Robert arrived on campus, the text for this course had already been ordered. It was one of the standard media ethics texts used in U.S. journalism and media programs. It included some case studies from outside the United States, but most were domestic. As the course progressed it became clear that the situation of most students enrolled was significantly different than in the United States, and the case studies were of limited value in those contexts.

Many of the students had already worked in media organizations as interns, some as part-time employees, some as volunteers. They began to bring their experiences to Robert for advice. One student had been an intern in a Moscow television station. She was expected to have sex with any foreign visitors to the station and her female supervisor, when she objected to that expectation, told her, "It's just sex. What's the big deal?" She left her internship. Another student thought there was a story in an encounter in a Sofia hospital where she had been told by a horrified visitor that there was a corpse in the women's toilet. Her idea was turned down by the editor who told her, "There's no story there. That happens everywhere." When she followed up anyway, she discovered that this was a common practice because the hospital didn't want anyone pronounced dead to "wake up" in the morgue, so their bodies were left for some time in the toilets to make sure they were actually deceased. A third student was told she needed to be part of a sting operation targeting casinos that allowed underage children to gamble. She was asked to play the part of a child. She objected. So she was told to recruit an actual child. Again she objected, telling the producer that casinos were run by known mobsters, and playing such a role, or recruiting someone to do so, could put their lives in danger once the story aired. She was fired.

Many students came from countries, such as Georgia, Belarus, or Turkmenistan, that had strict controls over the press, and / or had media owners who cozied up to the political powers such that they could do what they liked, without consequence, or who were targeted by political elites for adverse reports and whose employees were often beaten up or jailed for stories. One student's mother had to flee Kyrgyzstan when her extended family was threatened as a result of her reporting on a labor strike that had been brutally put down by the military.

Using a text that emerged from an environment of independent ownership, professional commitments, and a guaranteed free press became increasingly problematic. Ethics in a "free" versus a corrupt, controlled, or amoral environment seemed to Robert a stretch too far. These students' experiences were merely one type of experience outside the zone of a free press. Experiences both Mark and Robert have had in other contexts, from Europe to the Middle East and North Africa, sub-Saharan Africa, Latin America, and Asia, culminated in the decision to write this book.

1

Introduction: Contexts for Ethical Decision-Making

Ethics is not practiced in a vacuum. Choosing how to act occurs in particular contexts that exert various kinds of pressure on those making choices. So we will begin this book with attention to the various aspects of society and culture that affect the ethical choices made within them. Although we are presenting these as separate entities, it will become clear in the reading that they are so intertwined that it is difficult to speak of them separately. The value of doing so is to highlight them as important considerations. Once our initial analysis is complete, we will be able to show how various ethical perspectives relate to them, and then provide comments on how ethical decisions might reasonably be made within complex contexts.

Each of the following characteristics of societies and cultures forms a part of the overall context of moral choice. This differs not only from society to society, but from individual to individual. Some people in a society make choices based in large measure on religious commitments. Others are driven by the perceived demands of media technology or professions, and still others by ideological commitments. To fully understand the choices made, then, it is necessary to give some thought to how each of the following contexts may impact on them. We do not mean that ethics is relative, but that it is situational. People of goodwill may, within a given socio-cultural context, come to different decisions. Are all decisions equally ethical? We would say "no," but to evaluate the ethics of choice it is useful to understand the context within which choices are made. Then we will have the basis for conversation as to whether a decision can be defended on ethical grounds.

Does the "Global Village" Imply a Global Media Ethics?

The first hurdle to overcome when thinking about global media ethics is the belief that a global village exists. It doesn't. There are markers of its existence, to be sure, but they are misleading, especially for those who see them from a Western perspective. Since the nineteenth century, the so-called century of progress, Western pundits and the popular media have touted the role of new communications technologies in "shrinking" the world, annihilating time and space, and allowing for universal connectivity for the world's peoples. The world wars of the twentieth century did little to dampen the enthusiasm, for global connection and expectations rose to new heights with the arrival of satellite communication, global media networks, and real-time reports from far-flung regions via, first, satellite telephony and then video feeds. The arrival and rapid spread of the internet continued the trend. The final burst of expectation (so far) was unleashed by the development of mobile smartphones using broadband systems and wireless capability. It seemed that all the barriers that had prevented global universal communication had been overcome by technological progress.

World Media Ethics: Cases and Commentary, First Edition. Robert S. Fortner and P. Mark Fackler.
© 2018 John Wiley & Sons, Inc. Published 2018 by John Wiley & Sons, Inc.

It is not difficult to find claims that the global village has arrived. The International Monetary Fund trumpeted its arrival in September 2012 (Mahbubani, 2012, p. 1). Kishore Mahbubani claimed the milestone that justified this claim was that teledensity had reached the point that people had "become interconnected at a level never seen before in history," and that such technology (mobile telephones and the internet) had generated global convergence that, along with education, had improved human lives (Ibid.).

The problem with such claims is that they ignore more than they reveal. There is little doubt that connectivity among people is more widely distributed, and used in greater measure, than ever before. In 2014 the International Telecommunication Union (ITU) estimated that there were 6.9 billion mobile-cellular subscriptions around the world, nearly equal to the total population of the planet. However, somewhat fewer than three billion people had access to the internet, with access in developing countries reaching only 32% (ITU, 2014). The main reason for the difference is the much lower access to mobile broadband internet services in the developing world where wired infrastructure is not available.

Related to this difference in access to technology is the problem with seeing all connections as equally capable of accessing content. For instance, although the teledensity in the continent of Africa has increased several times over in the past decade, much of this development has provided only the barest connection to people. In Ivory Coast, for instance, 3G+ mobile coverage in 2014 was limited to 10 urban areas, and those that were connected to these systems, although they could access the internet, could see YouTube content at only 240p, the site's minimum resolution, while the more highly developed infrastructures in other countries allowed for 1040p HD (high-definition) connections. Rural areas of Ivory Coast were still without any broadband coverage at all, limiting use of mobile telephones to voice and SMS (text). On many of the islands in the Pacific, including those that are part of the Philippines and Indonesia, the only television available is through satellite delivery, and then only when generators are used to provide the power for connection. In mountainous areas, such as Nepal, the same situation applies and even radio is problematic since the most prevalent system employed is frequency modulation (VHF/FM), which uses only line of sight signals that are easily blocked by the terrain. The absence of a power grid also makes people dependent on expensive batteries that can only be replaced by trekking often long distances into towns on treacherous footpaths. Such circumstances make talk of a global village more of a fantasy than a reality.

Besides such access issues, many other obstacles continue to frustrate efforts to think of the world as a global village. People who have the good fortune to see films or television programs made in other countries, for instance, rarely see the reality of people's lives. Television does not thrive on careful documentaries of the lives of ordinary people living ordinary lives. Typically, actors portray others and, in so doing, interpret their scripts according to preconceptions that may have no firm foundation in the ordinary social, cultural, or economic lives of those they purport to represent. Many programs, regardless of source, are formulaic indigenized versions of programs that have attracted audiences in other countries. Often they become caricatures of the original, because the premise of the formula was culture-bound and those in the knock-off have altered their personas to qualify for the program. These two realities are "thin," barely scratching the surface of authentic portrayal. Even "thicker" programs, such as carefully crafted documentary approaches, are the perceptions of single filmmakers of "the other"; few to none are actually produced by those indigenous to the community portrayed.

So, despite the growth of global telephony, wired and wireless internet services, and widespread distribution of cultural products, the claim of a global village is actually a chimera – at best less than half the world's population could be said to be within range of this ideal. But despite the lack of a single media environment – a truly global village – there are still good reasons to think of ethics in a global perspective. Increasingly citizen reporters, bloggers, tweeters, and YouTube video producers seek global audiences. From #BringBackOurGirls to propaganda and recruitment videos produced by ISIS (Islamic State of Iraq and Syria),[1] media producers – amateur and professional – are appealing both to political establishments and to the global public sphere. The same is true of those who parody terrorists in the Middle East in their own viral videos, some using music videos or Lego figures (Zahriyeh, 2015).

The Political-Economic Context of Global Media Ethics

Although there are various political and economic relationships that bind countries together through international conventions and organizations, free trade agreements, trade pacts, and technological connections via fiber optic undersea cables and satellites, such relationships are only operable so long as the countries so bound find them to be in their own best interests. They are all subject to the sovereignty claims of the signatories. All international conventions must be ratified by individual countries to have authority within them. Countries may take reservations when signing to indicate their intention not to be bound by certain aspects of them. Trade pacts can be abrogated, alliances broken, connections shut off at borders. They can also simply be broken when considered inconvenient. There is no universal method of enforcing such agreements or connections.

Political economy is concerned with the moral or ethical results of political and economic practices. Since these practices differ from one country to another, the contests that exist between efforts to reveal (practiced by media practitioners) and those to conceal or control, also differ. Several different political and economic configurations within countries affect both the context for ethical decisions and the fragmentation of the "global village." Many countries have constitutional, regulatory, or philosophical commitments to free expression, although actual compliance with them is problematic. For instance, questions were raised in the United States as a result of the Obama administration's efforts to uncover leaks claimed to compromise national security, and in Britain as a result of both leaks and a hacking scandal that resulted in prosecutions of staff members of the now-closed *News of the World*. There have been official efforts to shut down Twitter in Turkey, China has restricted websites that raised moral issues by publishing pornographic images (including bare-breasted female anime characters), and in India the court found that the publication of an academic book (available in other countries for some time) in Hindi could foment religious unrest. In Fiji two journalists received death threats for their reports about a cancelled live television debate between the leading contenders for the post of prime minister. Iran and Russia have been developing their own internet that restricts access to connections outside their own countries and China has established the so-called "Great Firewall" to accomplish the same ends.

In addition, conflicts in various countries have led not only to arrests of journalists and bloggers, but also to denials of entry and manhunts of Russian journalists in Ukraine; expulsion and denial of entry to journalists in Yemen; prosecution of Al-Jazeera journalists in Egypt as terrorists; murders of journalists in Pakistan by Taliban factions (as well as expulsion of Indian journalists) and in the Philippines by Marxist-inspired separatists; street protests against restrictions on journalists in Venezuela; and rewritten laws governing expression in Kenya, Russia, and Libya (although overturned by the Libyan Supreme Court), among many other happenings. Many journalists, videographers, photojournalists, and filmmakers have also died covering the Syrian, Sudanese, and Congolese civil wars, in the Palestinian territories, and in ongoing sectarian conflicts in Iraq and Afghanistan. Many others have found themselves kidnapped or "detained." The Committee to Protect Journalists (CPJ), for instance, lists 1,054 journalists killed since 1992 (617 of them "with impunity"), and 211 journalists in prison in 2013 (cpj.org). And in Europe a non-governmental organization (NGO) called the

European Initiative for Media Pluralism began registering in different countries in the effort to collect signatures to create a new European Commission directive to fight against media monopoly, seeking to "enshrine the severance of ties between media, business and politics in the different media states in a lawful manner on an EU [European Union] level" (Novinite.com, 2014). All of these realities influence the perceived relevance and practice of ethics by media practitioners.

The Cultural-Religious Context of Global Media Ethics

The religious fragmentation of the planet is well documented, but even the division of religion into Christian, Islamic, Buddhist, Hindu, Jewish, Shinto, or "traditional" groups fails to capture the differences that actually exist. There are many variations within each of these groups, some so severe that it is sometimes difficult to see them as part of the same tradition. In addition to the obvious divisions, say between Catholics and Protestants, or Shia and Sunni Muslims, there are many other subgroups and "heretical" sects that could be identified. There are also humanists, non-believers, cultural adherents (or nominal believers), and those who say they are spiritual but not religious. The implication of this fragmentation is that "religious" bases for moral choice abound. Morality is a broad concept. It is, as Bernard Gert defined it, "an informal public system applying to all rational persons, governing behavior that affects others, and has the lessening of evil or harm as its goal" (quoted in "The definition of morality," 2011). This generic definition of the term does not suggest where any individual's sense of morality is grounded. For the billions of people on the planet who adhere to a religious tradition, however, there is a connection between their faith's requirements for behavior and its adherents' sense of morality. Although not all religions have scriptures (or holy books), all do have parents and teachers (including priests, imams, and gurus, among others) who pass along moral prescriptions to those who are either born into, or choose to follow, the tradition. As Paul Bloom (2012, p. 184) puts it: "Through holy texts and the proclamations of authority figures, religions make moral claims about abortion, homosexuality, duties to the poor, charity, masturbation, just war, and so on. People believe these claims because, implicitly or explicitly, they trust the sources. They accept them on faith."

Of course, the requirements of each faith differ, sometimes profoundly, from each other. What one faith considers a necessary moral requirement, another doesn't deal with at all. Despite the clear relationship between Judaism and Christianity, for instance, the moral expectations for the treatment of debt, or the appropriate response to insult, differ. And, as suggested above, those within a particular tradition can have quite different ideas about abortion, capital punishment, or the treatment of the poor. Nevertheless, religion remains an important source of moral thought among the world's religious people.

Not only are people divided by religious commitments, there are also cultural divides to consider. Cultural divides, whether defined by tribe, clan, ethnicity, race, or visions of history, can even trump common moral commitments within religious traditions. Christians in Rwanda were both victims and perpetrators in the 1994 genocide. Sunni Muslims kill Shia Muslims in Iraq. Israeli Jews disagree profoundly about what to do to gain peace in the Middle East. Hindus judge one another more on the basis of caste than common faith. It sometimes seems too easy to ignore religious proscriptions on behavior when acting in response to propaganda or to historical inequities or atrocities. Death is not necessarily a function of hatred between nation-states. Robert Kaplan (1996, p. 8) reminds us that "of the eighty wars since 1945, only twenty-eight have taken the traditional form of fighting between regular armies of two or more states. Forty-six were civil wars or guerrilla insurgencies. . . . The fighting in the Balkans, in the Caucasus, and elsewhere suggested that this anarchic trend was proliferating."

The Professional Context of Global Media Ethics

Media practitioners function in quite different professional contexts around the globe. In some countries, and notably in the United States, there are no requirements of any kind before a person can work in the media, including journalism. Requiring any education, credentials, examination, registration, or endorsement is seen as anathema to the U.S. Constitution's First Amendment guarantee of a free press (with the press including all forms of media work). However, in many cases press credentials issued by a government or other agency (such as a local police force or organizing committee) are required for access to particular events or venues.

Other countries, however, do require some basic qualifications, especially for journalists. In Brazil, for instance, practicing as a journalist required a university degree in journalism and registration with the Labor Ministry from 1969 until the Supreme Court of Brazil abolished it in 2009 (see Lago and Fernandez, 2011). Nine other Latin American countries continue to have similar requirements (Kirtley, 2010). In Italy a journalist must have a university degree, pass an entrance examination given by the professional Order of Journalists, and be a member of the Order. In France the National Union of Journalists recommends that would-be journalists attend a certified university program in journalism, although it is possible to enter the profession without such a degree. It is more difficult, however, absent the degree, to be employed at more prestigious media organizations. In Portugal, there are no university degree requirements, but – practically speaking – anyone who desires employment as a journalist would do well to have one (Fidalgo, 2008).

"In a small number of countries," according to Article 19 (an international free expression monitoring and advocacy organization), "the law provides for the possibility of temporarily, or even permanently, stripping an individual of the right to practice journalism or other media professions." Since licensing, per se, is impermissible under international law when exercised by a government authority, this "power is exercised by courts as a sanction in criminal proceedings." Several Kyrgyz journalists "were barred from practicing journalism for 18 months" when they were convicted of libeling the director of a state-owned gold-mining company in 1997 (Article 19, n.d.).

In Timor-Leste veteran journalist José Belo protested a new media law that he warned would signal the death of Timorese journalists' spirits due to its restrictions on who could or could not operate as a journalist, stipulations on information access, and government control of the regulating press council body (Robie, 2014). And in China, before any trial determined guilt or innocence, accused journalists were required, by mid-2014, to confess their "crime" on national television:

> For the second time in a week, a Chinese journalist . . . has appeared on China's state-owned broadcaster, confessing to alleged crimes. "I have made up things that are not facts," said . . . Xiang Nanfu, a frequent freelance contributor to New York-based Chinese language website Boxun.com. "My behavior has had a very bad impact. I realize that I have smeared the ruling party and the government."
>
> *(Roberts, 2014)*

Practicing media work, in other words, occurs in a variety of professional contexts – some defined by unions, some by court mandate, some by censorship, some by law, some by educational requirements, and some by unspecified, but widely known, expectations.

The Moral Context of Global Media Ethics

It is a mistake to assume that the basic moral commitments in one society are identical to those in another. Although there are some basic universals, such as prohibitions against taking the life of another, respecting the other's human dignity, not harming the innocent, and truth-telling, adhering merely to these four proto-norms, as Clifford G. Christians and Michael Traber (1997) call them, provides only a "thin" ethics. What we mean is that, although these four commitments are essential, they are also of limited use in making moral choices in media work. By definition universal values are applicable across all societies and cultures. They also apply equally to those in media as much, or as little, as they apply to other professionals, tradesmen, laborers, or stay-at-home mothers. They are not unique to media workers who are unlikely to be in situations where they would have to choose whether or not to take a life or harm the innocent, if such demands are interpreted in the context of people's usual material existence. Media workers, however, especially those in the entertainment or culture industries, may face these issues in productions where violence is part of the story, calling for symbolic deaths, torture, rape, or beatings, or where people are symbolically dehumanized, but these choices are on a different order than those made in everyday life. They are depictions – sometimes justified, sometimes not – but the violence or dehumanization affects characters portrayed by actors, not actual people.

We find it useful to start with universals, however, as they are foundational. They are necessary, but also insufficient, for the moral character of societies is not entirely – perhaps not even primarily – universal. For instance, U.S. television programs contain much more violence than those in most of the rest of the world. This violence, too, is more explicit than the artful portrayals in Asia or those that are left to the imagination by European television producers. European television, however, does not shy away from scenes with fully nude actors, a production choice that is simply not made in U.S. or Asian programs (at least on readily accessible on-air channels). In Russia and several African countries, and most notably in Uganda, the media must tread lightly when reporting, or including in entertainment programs, information that would be considered homosexual "propaganda" or advocacy – again on moral grounds. In some countries, too, notably those with large populations of Muslims, not only is nudity prohibited, but also any programming that is considered blasphemous, something not avoided in U.S. or European programs. In China, media products, including social media, are prohibited from questioning the legitimacy of the Communist Party – often for "moral" reasons. It is difficult in some cases for Chinese journalists to pursue stories of corrupt officials.

For example, Xinran (2002, chapter 1) was a presenter for the Chinese state radio service and received a letter from a young village boy pleading for intercession for a young girl who had been purchased by an old man to be his wife. The boy suspected she had been kidnapped. Xinran contacted the local police and one policeman reluctantly agreed to help, although he told her, "'In the countryside the heavens are high and the emperor is far away.' In his opinion the law had no power there." She went to the village with the police, who freed the girl whose family lived 22 hours away by train. They had been searching frantically for her. "I received no praise for the rescue of this girl, only criticism for 'moving the troops about and stirring up the people' and wasting the radio station's time and money. . . . Just what was a woman's life worth in China?" In many countries this would be considered a moral issue – but not by officials in China.

In 2015 in Saudi Arabia a cartoonist was sentenced to death for apostasy, the result of filming himself tearing up a copy of the Koran and hitting it with his shoe (a sign of disrespect in the Middle East) (Spencer, 2015). This would be seen in many countries as freedom of expression, even if distasteful, but in most Middle Eastern countries such behavior is punishable by execution.

It also seems clear, despite the existence of universals, that a people – defined by tribe, clan, ethnicity, or race – can find ways to avoid, at least in their own minds, the approbation that might otherwise attach to them for immoral actions. Serbs found ways to legitimize ethnic cleansing, radical Hutus to legitimize genocide (see Fortner, 2006). As Martha Minow (1998, p. 11) put it: "At a societal level, as the recent conflicts in Bosnia and Rwanda have only too vividly demonstrated, memories, or propaganda-inspired illusions about memories, can motivate people who otherwise live peaceably to engage in torture and slaughter of neighbors identified as members of groups who committed past atrocities. The results can be devastating, escalating intergroup violence. Mass killings are the fruit of revenge for perceived past harms." More recently, Dinka and Nuer tribesmen in South Sudan, Syrians, Ukrainians (including ethnic Russians), and Egyptians have engaged in mass violence against countrymen using a variety of justifications. The list of atrocities continues to lengthen. Despite universals, moral contexts vary and can justify to perpetrators sometimes unspeakable atrocities.

The Legal Context of Global Media Ethics

Some countries operate under a clearly defined rule of law. This means, as the World Justice Project puts it, that (1) the government and its officials and agents as well as individuals and private entities are accountable under the law, (2) laws are clear, publicized, stable, just, and are applied evenly to protect fundamental rights, (3) the process by which laws are enacted, administered, and enforced is accessible, fair, and efficient, and (4) justice is delivered in a timely manner by competent, ethical, and independent representatives who are of sufficient number and adequately funded, and reflect the makeup of the communities they serve ("What is the Rule of Law?," 2014). In other words, all persons or institutions are subject to laws equally applied within a society, regardless of status, or economic/political significance. The principle of rule of law is "at the heart of the United Nations' mission," embedded in its Charter ("United Nations and the Rule of Law," 2014).

The World Justice Project has ranked 99 countries, based on nine factors and 47 sub-factors, using surveys provided both to local experts and to general publics, on the rule of law. Its analysis concluded that the rule of law was strongest in Denmark, Norway, Sweden, Finland, and the Netherlands, and weakest in Cameroon, Pakistan, Zimbabwe, Afghanistan, and Venezuela. In general, sub-Saharan African countries fared worst, and European countries, New Zealand, and Australia fared best, as groups. Some representative rankings include: Canada 11, Japan 12, South Korea 14, Hong Kong 16, the United States 19, Malaysia 35, South Africa 40, Indonesia 46, Mongolia 51, Vietnam 65, India 66, Egypt 74, China 76, Russia 80, Kenya 86, Myanmar 89, and Bangladesh 92 ("WJP Rule of Law Index," 2014).

Respect for and application of the rule of law by all parties in society – including government and corporate leaders, media professionals, educators, and other professionals – provides a basic platform for resolution of disputes, justice for both criminals and victims, and a foundation for civility and trust. Ethical practices are enabled by such commitments and practices.

But ethics and law are not identical. Laws can be just but still immoral. As the American jurist Thane Rosenbaum (2005, p. 22) puts it: "what passes for justice in America is often immoral justice – a resolution that makes sense legally and can be explained and justified by judges, lawyers, and law professors simply by conforming, in a very formalistic sense, to precedent and procedure, but ultimately feels emotionally and morally wrong to everyone else. Justice that doesn't feel just, but instead feels like a colossal misnomer." Expanding on this, he provides this example: "But to stand apart from the crowd, and stand up for friends and neighbors – even if they are strangers – to oppose governmental authority when it lacks moral authority, to rescue fellow men from danger, may be the right thing to do morally, even if it's not reasonable to do so" (Ibid., p. 29).

Traditional practices can warp the application of law, or even overwhelm it. In West Africa, for instance, the traditional practice of "dash" (gift-giving for services rendered) provides incentive for people to rise to power and to rain gifts on those who assisted in their rise: "The bigger the man, the bigger the 'dash' for the favour received. The 'Big Man' became an accepted feature of West African life, a patron fostering his followers by his fame and fortune" (Meredith, 2005, p. 172). Since the loyalist followers tended to be from the Big Man's own tribe or clan, this tradition made it seem acceptable, in many cases, for him to shower largesse within these circles – as well as to engender resentment from other tribes or clans that would then rebel, leading to decades of instability.

Operationally, such a tradition meant that certain people would be favored for government contracts, or licenses to operate mining, import-export, or agricultural enterprises (cocoa or sugar cane growers, etc.), leading to narrow concentrations of wealth (see Ibid., pp. 278, 686). This wealth could either be legitimate or ill-gotten, depending on the particulars.

Such practices are not restricted to West Africa. Payments for "services rendered" exists in many parts of the world in the form of purchased news stories or favorable coverage in otherwise legitimate coverage. One study of the situation in India (Sharma, 2013, p. 9) linked the practice of purchasing positive media coverage with a rising level of organized and institutionalized corruption. Sanjay Kumar wrote about this problem as long ago as 2010:

> Following last year's elections in Maharashtra, allegations surfaced that the local media had taken thousands of dollars from politicians in return for publishing favourable news stories about them. And, in a panel discussion at the Ramnath Goenka Awards [India's awards for excellence in journalism], executives from India's leading media accepted the sad truth that such media payments are indeed commonplace today. Arun Shourie, an eminent journalist and politician from the right wing Bhartiya Janata Party, accused the media of adopting the "politics of silence" over this issue, arguing that broadly speaking, there was little internal debate or introspection among the nation's media houses. According to Star News CEO Uday Shankar, the main reason is (perhaps not surprisingly) the significant amounts of money that media houses are earning from paid news.
>
> *(Kumar, 2010)*

In this case the initiation of such paid relationships came from the press itself, not from those seeking favorable coverage.

Julie Moos (2010), writing for the Poynter Institute about the situation in the United States, says that "journalism organizations that once refused to pay sources now write them large checks for access to information. They label these payments 'licensing fees,' and in return they receive photos, video, emails, or cell phone records. In the process, they lose credibility and simultaneously strengthen the market for checkbook journalism." Quoting Paul Friedman, then senior vice president at CBS News, she continued: "If we all drew a line again, maybe we could stop this . . . But that's probably hopelessly naïve. It's out of the bottle."

Economics, Acquisition, and Materialism in Global Media Ethics

Although many of the media systems set up around the world during the twentieth century followed the public service model pioneered by the British Broadcasting Corporation (BBC), most media in the twenty-first century have adopted a commercial model with their activities directed by commercial considerations – achieving a profit. However, profitable media organizations have also become more difficult to sustain. This has resulted, sometimes, in successful non-media entrepreneurs, such as Jeff Bezos of Amazon and Pierre Omidyar of eBay, investing in media properties or in the continuing development of multinational media conglomerates, such as News Corporation (owned by Rupert Murdoch). In 2001 seven multinational corporations dominated the global media market. These were Disney, AOL-Time Warner, Sony, News Corporation, Viacom, Vivendi, and Bertelsmann (McChesney, 2001). By 2015, however, indicative of the rapid changes in media-related technologies, the world's largest media corporations included Comcast, Disney, 21st Century Fox, Time Warner, Time Warner Cable, DirecTV (later purchased by AT&T), WPP (a UK-based company), CBS, Viacom, and BSkyB (Le, 2015). All of them operate on a for-profit basis.

What this means is that, for them to flourish, they must either charge for access to media material, or they must sell access to audiences to their advertisers, or both. The result is an increasingly materialist alternative to traditional culture and lives increasingly dominated by personal acquisition of goods. The consequences?

> Using statistics and psychological tests, researchers are nailing down what clerics and philosophers have preached for millennia: Materialism is bad for the soul. Only, in the new formulation, materialism is bad for your emotional well-being. In recent years, researchers have reported an ever-growing list of downsides to getting and spending – damage to relationships and self-esteem, a heightened risk of depression and anxiety, less time for what the research indicates truly makes people happy, like family, friendship and engaging work. And maybe even headaches. "Consumer culture is continually bombarding us with the message that materialism will make us happy," said Tim Kasser, a psychology professor at Knox College in Illinois who has led some of the recent work. "What this research shows is that that's not true."
>
> *(Goldberg, 2006)*

The Bahai author Abdu'l-Missagh Ghadirian says that materialism is devastating both to society and to individuals; it creates a moral dilemma – unbridled accumulation of wealth or response to economic injustice and corruption:

> Materialism in moral terms . . . can have destructive consequences and may permeate society as a form of social dysfunction. It is an acquired condition and state of mind which develops as a result of a number of factors, including materialistic education, parental attitudes and socio-cultural influences. To remedy this condition, a reconstruction of society's mindset and attitude toward the accumulations of wealth and greedy attachment to it is needed, through a consciousness of and belief in intrinsic moral values and the spiritual reality of existence which transcend dependence on material wealth as a lifestyle.
>
> *(Ghadirian, 2010, p. x)*

Politics and Face-Saving in Global Media Ethics

Politics is practiced differently in societies around the globe. We do not mean by this that some are representative democracies, others parliamentary democracies, or autocracies, dictatorships or monarchies, although these exist. More significant than the type of government, however, are the practices of politics. An autocracy, for instance, can be authoritarian or benign. A democracy can be inclusive or exclusive – simply by declaring some residents to be *persona non grata* when it comes to basic rights or claiming the benefits of citizenship. Simply labeling a government is insufficient to understanding how it works, seeks, and maintains legitimacy, deals with dissent, or what it allows by way of access to communication systems or content.

There is an important dimension to politics that reflects cultural values and demonstrates a dimension of moral choices in society. This is the notion of face. In their study of politeness in politics in the United States, Dailey, Hinck, and Hinck (2008, p. 13) argue that debates between candidates represent a clear clash of images that include both positive and negative face. Even the ritualized nature of these debates, and thus criticisms of their artificiality, do not reduce their value. Candidates who refuse to debate, they say, "risk losing political face." But the stakes are different for each participant. Sometimes balance is expected, while in others, "audiences might be expecting one candidate to show a greater degree of aggression or support" (Ibid.). What matters is whether the face expressed, or defended by a candidate, accords with the expectations of him or her by the audience.

No political candidate (or any other individual, for that matter) is without flaw. This makes face-saving a continual issue as information is uncovered, distributed, or interpreted in various ways. To protect face requires one to be continually on-guard. It can also mean dissembling, or contorting, the truth, sometimes in fantastical ways, to protect face. The more deeply the idea of face is interwoven in culture, the more problematic ethics may be within that context.

One historic encounter between the United States and the Soviet Union in 1962 over missile launchers in Cuba raised the possibility of a nuclear exchange when the United States blockaded Cuban ports. The rhetoric ratcheted up between the two superpowers. But eventually, if war was to be avoided, it became necessary for the two countries – and their respective leaders, John F. Kennedy and Nikita Khrushchev – to save face. Stella Ting-Toomey (1990, p. 80) explained that these two leaders searched for ways that would allow them to retain both personal and national honor in the effort to de-escalate the conflict. In 2014, in another dispute between the United States and Russia, RIA Novosti claimed, based on opinions of Russian experts, that U.S. vice president Joe Biden visited Ukraine "to explore the possibilities for Washington's face-saving exit from its foreign policy catastrophe" ("Biden to test US face-saving retreat plan for Ukraine," 2014). As Brown (1977, p. 275) puts it: "Among the most troublesome kinds of problems that arise in negotiation are the intangible issues related to loss of face. In some instances, protecting against loss of face becomes so central an issue that it swamps the importance of the tangible issues at stake and generates intense conflicts that can impede progress toward agreement and increase substantially the costs of conflict resolution."

The United States is what is referred to as a "low-context" culture. In such cultures the communication is more direct and there is relatively little concern with non-verbal cues. Many other societies, however, are "high-context" cultures, especially those in Asia, Latin America, and the Middle East. Face is a more serious issue in these parts of the globe.

In Thailand, Krisana Kitiyadisai (2005, p. 18) writes: "conflict avoidance or non-confrontation can be disastrous as it results in 'losing-face' ('siar-na') by either side of the conflict. 'Face' represents one's social and professional position, reputation and self-image, so that a loss of face is to be prevented or avoided at all costs – which further means that face-saving or 'koo-na' has to be instigated at critical junctures."

Similarly, in China politics is often driven by the perceived necessity for saving face. Xing Lu (2000, pp. 11–12) says that accusations from the West about human rights violations in China are often met with countercharges, a strategy based on ignoring the accusation and responding with threats: "These are, in fact, face-saving strategies. Instead of arguing against the actual charges, China chose to counterattack, ignore, and pose new threats." Another similar strategy, he says, is to disregard the premise underlying the attack and then direct attention to a different set of variables and situations:

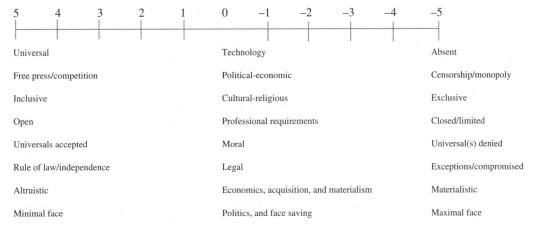

Figure 1.1 Ethical context factors (see text for details).

"For example, according to [Mao's principle of bu bi ran (probability)] instead of responding to human rights violation charges from the U.S., the Chinese government countercharges the U.S. with racial discrimination of its own citizens. This approach may not appear logical, but it recognizes the complexity and intricacy of argumentation. Such a strategy is employed by the Chinese government as a means of face saving" (Ibid., p. 12).

Section Summary

We have covered eight dimensions of societies that can help distinguish one from another and that have implications for the practice of ethics. One way to think of these dimensions is as a set of scales, each numbered from five to zero (center) and then again from zero (center) to five (see Figure 1.1). The closer a society adheres to the left side of any of these factors, the more amenable it is to ethical choices; the closer to the right, the more poisonous the context for ethical choice. But even when all the factors are far to the right, ethical choices can still be made. Ethics is more likely to face opposition, however, and those making ethical choices will be battling against various societal expectations when compared to those making choices on the left-hand side. The opportunity to act ethically is more obvious on the left side, but merely operating within such a welcoming environment does not guarantee that ethics will govern choice. There are both different philosophies of ethics and the different purposes of media work to consider. We will take up philosophies in the next two chapters. First, however, we will focus on the reasons for, and expectations of, media workers – their purpose in society.

Freedom of the Press

The Anglo-American ideal of a free press, founded in post-Enlightenment political philosophy and enshrined most clearly in the United States' First Amendment to its Constitution (part of what is referred to as the Bill of Rights), has gradually become a near-universal ideal around the world. The original impetus for a free press arose during the era of monarchy (political and religious), in which both sedition and blasphemy were highly controlled through censorship and licensing, with penalties for violations ranging from fines, to imprisonment and execution. Elites were in control. Rational arguments against strict control were originally raised by John Milton, who argued that suppression of ideas was nonsensical unless the suppressor could be absolutely certain in his opinion – impossible in Milton's view. This was perhaps not so obvious to the elites in control, many of whom clung to the idea that they were God's appointed rulers. But such arguments did find resonance in the small, but growing, business community that depended on information for their success. Many of them were part of the minority of literate citizens who could see the value of a free press to their own livelihoods. These citizens were the core of what Jürgen Habermas would call the public sphere.

The American and French Revolutions claimed rights for the common people that had been suppressed during the previous autocratically dominated centuries when most people did not count. The idea of "one man, one vote" took on a reality that required an informed citizenry. Freedom of the press took on a new urgency, reinforced by John Stuart Mill's robust defense of its necessity and by the fact that, by about 1850, a majority of people in Western societies were literate (see Fortner, 2013). The need for accurate and up-to-date information was made obvious, too, by the developments in print, film, and radio propaganda in the First and Second World Wars. When the European colonial empires began to disintegrate after the Second World War, with these new societies often heavily influenced by the practices of former colonial rulers, it was common for freedom of the press to be assumed, although economic realities and political instability usually meant state-controlled radio, and later television, systems were developed. Eventually most of these succumbed to new economic realities, massive foreign debt, and slow development, leading to private and commercial ownership of broadcasting.

This all-too-brief and generalized history suggests a central axis in considering the value of a free press: the control of information. Government or corporate elites have attempted to control the distribution of information by requiring licenses for media organizations, licensing media workers, censoring the distribution of information, and using civil law statutes. Additionally, they have influenced the flow of information by engaging in propaganda (including both truthful and false advertising and public relations), funding, creating, and distributing films and radio and television programs, running disinformation campaigns, copyrighting and trademarking intellectual products, dumping products at prices far below their value to establish footholds in new markets, buying up competitors, using national security or proprietary information labels, or even denying any knowledge of information sought by others. Although such tactics may from time to time affect the activities of media organizations – most of which are corporate entities – the real effect of such practices is to influence the interpretation of what a free press is. During the Cold War (1946–1991) Western nations famously argued that there was no free press in the Soviet Union and its client states since the Communist Party controlled the distribution of information. The Soviets and their allies responded in kind, saying there was no free press in the West as its media were controlled by corporate owners that would only publish what was in their own economic interests.

In the twenty-first century countries around the world have embraced the idea of a free press. There are some exceptions, such as North Korea and Cuba (although Cuba began to open up in 2016), and there are also multiple criticisms of the People's Republic of China, Malaysia, East Timor, Brazil, Egypt, Ukraine, Russia, Pakistan, Nigeria, Rwanda, Somaliland, South Sudan, Serbia, Hungary, Turkey, Iran, and many others when it comes to actual practices concerning the free press. The United States and the United Kingdom have also been heavily criticized, the former for their treatment of journalists reporting based on leaked information and latter for the creation of an independent commission as a result of the hacking scandal in that country. Reporters without Borders' annual *World Press Freedom Index*, which ranks the countries of the world on their degree of press freedom, ranked Eritrea, North Korea, Turkmenistan, Syria, China, Vietnam, Iran, Sudan, and Laos at the bottom of its index of 180 countries in 2016 (www.rsf.org).

A free press, along with free expression, are seen by its advocates both as a necessity for democracy and as a basic human right. Index on Censorship's Senior Advocacy Officer, Melody Patry, said in May 2014, for instance, that "free expression is the foundation of a free society. Enabling journalists to report on matters without the threat of censorship or violations against them means promoting the right to freedom of expression and information, which is a fundamental and necessary condition for the promotion and protection of all human rights in a democratic society" (Kirkland, 2014). Indonesia's Melani Indra Hapsari, responding to a query from the Southeast Asian Press Alliance, wrote in the same month that "every country needs press freedom. [The] Press is the watchdog of government. I can't imagine how I can work without press freedom. . . . Journalists must work in press freedom to freely report good and bad news including news about government corruption, bad policy, or other important things that the audience needs to know. Press freedom brings benefit for the country and region. It encourages democracy, good governance, and good society" ("Southeast Asian journalists speak out for press freedom," 2014).

The United Nations has taken up the debate on the status of a "right to communicate" several times since 1974. Although no formal instrument has been ratified guaranteeing such a right, various resolutions have been drafted, discussed, and adopted by various organizations, including the United Nations Educational, Scientific and Cultural Organization (1974), and the MacBride Commission (1980), along with ad hoc resolutions such as the People's Communication Charter (1993), the Universal Communications Rights Charter (1994), the Vdeazimut Declaration of Capetown (1998), the Tash Resolution (1992, 2000), and the Draft Declaration on the Right to Communicate (2003), among several others. Article 19 has defined the right to communicate, "in its widest sense, as 'the right of every individual or community to have its stories and views heard'" (Right to Communicate," 2002"). This claimed right is not restricted to the news media (what is often called "the press"), but to all forms of expression used by individuals, communities, and organizations. For example, in 2014 the Tibetan filmmaker Dhondhup Wangchen was released from a Chinese prison after six years of incarceration for making a film, *Leaving Film Behind*, which the Chinese government claimed was subversive and incited separatism for the region. Matteo Mecacci, president of the International Campaign for Tibet (ICT), welcomed his release: "Freedom of expression is a universal right and must be exercised by all citizens" (Coonan, 2014a).

The foundational declaration undergirding these various conversations and concerns is the Universal Declaration of Human Rights adopted in 1948 soon after the creation of the United Nations. Article 19 of this declaration states that "everyone has the right to freedom of opinion and expression; this includes freedom to hold opinions without interference and to seek, receive and impart information and ideas through any media and regardless of frontiers."

The Universal Declaration was adopted after vigorous lobbying by former U.S. First Lady Eleanor Roosevelt. It was a product of its time, adopted shortly following the end of the Second World War – a war waged not only militarily but through propaganda – and by warring countries that were largely a product of the Western Enlightenment tradition. The various statements that followed it were likewise heavily influenced by Western nations committed to free expression and convinced that only by guaranteeing it would the democracy they had fought for in the mid-twentieth century be spread throughout the world. Adherence to the principle, however, has always been problematic, largely because of different interpretations of "human rights." Asian nations, for instance, "reject outright the globalization of human rights and claim that Asia has a unique set of values, which . . . provide the basis for Asia's different understanding of human rights and justify the 'exceptional' handling of rights by Asian governments" (Li, 2001, pp. 397–398). They are not part of what Charles Taylor (2001, p. 411) has called "the Western Rights tradition."

If nations are unable to agree about the centrality of communication to human rights, this creates a problematic reality for those who work in communication professions. On what basis should they argue for a special status for their work on behalf of people, whether to inform, entertain, or interact? The answer to this quandary, we think, is an emphasis on social responsibility. Regardless of the sort of society that people live in, or what cultural or legal philosophy undergirds their society, everyone can agree, we propose, that media organizations and practitioners should have a responsibility to the society they ostensibly serve. What does this entail?

Social Responsibility

Merely to affirm rights without the expectation of responsibility is to accept only what Isaiah Berlin in (1958/2002) referred to as "negative liberty." It is freedom *from* – from government intrusion, prosecution, censorship, and so on. There is, however, another sort of liberty: positive liberty. This is freedom *for* – freedom to accomplish some positive outcome. For media work this is the sort of freedom that social responsibility theory advocates, and one of the animating ideas of this book. Although this theory has its roots in the early twentieth century, its most powerful advocate was the Commission on Freedom of the Press, chaired by Robert Hutchins in the United States in the late 1940s. This Commission (often referred to as the Hutchins Commission) released its report, *A Free and Responsible Press*, in 1947. This report was of course written to address the situation only in the United States, so after outlining the Commission's conclusions, it will be necessary here to address two other issues: first, does it apply to other contexts, and second, has the development of media technology made its conclusions obsolete? But first we will examine the report itself.

The Commission concluded (Hutchins Commission, 1947, p. 1) that freedom of the press was in danger for three reasons. First, although it had become more important to the people, the percentage of people who could express their ideas and opinions through the press had declined; second, those who had access to the press had provided inadequate service to society; and third, the owners of the press had "engaged from time to time in practices which the society condemns and which, if continued, it will inevitably undertake to regulate or control." These problems were nearly unique to the United States at that time. Most countries had state-controlled media and most countries that are part of the world today did not yet exist. The problems reflected the reality of private ownership of the media and the traditional suspicion of the government that is part of the American ethos.

The Commission also recognized the continuing threat of totalitarianism ("We cannot suppose that the military defeat of totalitarianism in its German and Italian manifestations has put an end to the influence and attractiveness of the doctrine"; Ibid., p. 4), and the new danger of total annihilation ("universal catastrophe") made possible by the atomic bomb (Ibid.). What was required of the media was assistance in helping "create a world community by giving men everywhere knowledge of the world and of one another, by promoting comprehension and appreciation of the goals of a free society that shall embrace all men" (Ibid.).

The Commission acknowledged that a free press was essential to political liberty and that civilized society "must guarantee freedom of expression, to the end that all adventitious hindrances to the flow of ideas shall be removed" (Ibid., p. 6). The government must refrain from intervening to control the press and those who owned the press must operate responsibly: "The complexity of modern industrial society, the critical world situation, and the new menaces to freedom which these imply mean that the time has come for the press to assume a new public responsibility" (Ibid., p. 17). Using terminology that Berlin would later take up, the Commission said that "freedom of the press means freedom from and freedom for. The press must be free from the menace of external compulsions from whatever source. . . . The press must be free for the development of its own conceptions of service and achievement. It must be free for making its contribution to the maintenance and development of a free society. This implies that the press must also be accountable" (Ibid., p. 18).

What society required from the press, the Commission said (Ibid., pp. 20–21), was, "first, a truthful, comprehensive and intelligent account of the day's events in a context which gives them meaning; second, a forum for the exchange of comment and criticism; third, a means of projecting the opinions and attitudes of the groups in society to one another; fourth, a method of presenting and clarifying the goals and values of the society, and, fifth, a way of reaching every member of the society by the currents of information, thought, and feeling which the press supplies." Specifically, the Commission said:

> "The first requirement is that the media should be accurate. They should not lie." (p. 21)
>
> "The second requirement means that the great agencies of mass communication should regard themselves as common carriers of public discussion." (p. 23)
>
> Third, "the images repeated and emphasized [should] be such as are in total representative of the social group as it is. The truth about any social group, though it should not exclude its weaknesses and vices, includes also recognition of its values, its aspirations, and its common humanity." (pp. 26–27)
>
> Fourth, "the agencies of mass communication are an educational instrument, perhaps the most powerful there is; and they must assume a responsibility like that of educators in stating and clarifying the ideals toward which the community should strive." (pp. 27–28)
>
> Finally, "the amount of current information required by citizens in a modern industrial society is far greater than that required in any earlier day. [Leadership chosen freely by citizens] does not alter the need for the wide distribution of news and opinion." (p. 28)
>
> *(Hutchins Commission, 1947)*

The Commission recognized the technological revolution in media that had opened up new channels for communication (Ibid., pp. 30–36). However, despite this, it said "the number of units has declined" (Ibid., p. 37). Concentration of ownership and media monopolies were increasing: "Monopolistic practices, together with the cost of machinery and the momentum of big, going concerns, have made it hard for new ventures to enter the field of mass communication" (Ibid., p. 49). Finally, the press's performance was problematic: "The news is twisted by the emphasis on firstness, on the novel and sensational; by the personal interests of owners; and by pressure groups" (Ibid., p. 68).

Social Responsibility in a Global Context

The Commission's report was clearly a post-Enlightenment document, which leads to the issue of whether its expectations of the media have any useful applications in other contexts. As we have seen, the post-Enlightenment expectation of free expression has found endorsement more globally – although not universally – but has the expectation of socially responsible free expression also found endorsement?

Although it may not be the type of endorsement sought, it is clear that many countries have used the expectation of a socially responsible media to their own advantage in an effort to exercise social and political control. The Egyptian prosecution of Al-Jazeera journalists for their presumed support of the Muslim Brotherhood, and thus aiding terrorists, is one example. The Iranian government's shutdown of Twitter, Instagram, and Facebook is another. In Pakistan at a meeting organized at Punjab University, Dr. Mehdi Hassan claimed that media reports should not be biased, misleading, or false, while other participants in the conference said that news stories should be reported accurately and only after verification (Pakistan Today, 2014). In Zimbabwe Deputy Minister of Information, Media and Broadcasting Services Supa Mandiwanzira told delegates at a World Press Freedom Day that "press freedom comes from responsible journalism and that is what we expect from media practitioners" ("Media reform needs wide consultations – Mandiwanzira," 2014).

In China the government watchdog banned the television programs "The Big Bang Theory," "NCIS," "The Good Wife," and "The Practice" (all U.S.-made shows) because it claimed these programs violated Article 16 of state regulations on internet audiovisual products. This Article prohibited programs that "harm the nation's reputation, [and] mislead young people to commit crimes, prostitution, gambling or terrorism" (Coonan, 2014b). In Ghana the Executive Director of Africa Centre for Energy Policy, Dr. Mohammed Amin Adam, called on journalists to hold the government there accountable for its disbursement and use of the nation's oil revenue: he urged them to hold all stakeholders involved accountable by engaging in investigative research to assure transparency and accountability (Tandoh, 2015). In the United Kingdom, a new media oversight commission has been established in the wake of the hacking scandal in which media were hacking into mobile telephone accounts in the quest for stories.

All these examples demonstrate that the expectation for social responsibility is more general than particular to the United States.

Social Responsibility and Technological Change

The second issue requiring attention is that of technological change. When the Hutchins Commission wrote its report the dominant media were print and radio. Their influence, however, has waned with the arrival of television, the internet, and Web 2.0. So are the claims about consolidation and monopolization of information as the Commission saw them in 1947 still true 70 years later?

The development of the internet has not only provided access for hundreds of millions of people around the world to news and entertainment materials they could never have retrieved before, but also provided unparalleled ability for them to create their own content: videos on YouTube, music on SoundCloud, opinion blogs on Blogger, WordPress, and Tumblr, personal interests on Pinterest and news on Facebook, business or personal messages on email or SnapChat, news reports on CNN and MyNews, and so on. This would seem to suggest that the bottleneck that limited expression to a few in the 1940s has been broken. To a degree, this is true. However, the penetration of the internet globally is barely over 50% of the global population in 2016, and of these global users the top 20 countries provided 55% of the total number of users.[2] The penetration of mobile telephones is far higher, at 93% of the global population, but the slow speeds of service and general lack of infrastructure means that far less than half of these users can access the internet. While the internet penetration in North America is 81% and in Western Europe 78%, the penetration in Central America is only 34%, in Africa 18%, and in South Asia 12%. The worries of 1947, in other words, are still relevant in large parts of the world.

In addition, even in societies that have high percentages of their populations connected to the internet, or who can access satellite television or local radio, or who own mobile telephones useful for various purposes, there continues to be the issue of systems-ownership. Many newly connected

Facebook users in the developing world, for instance, don't understand the undergirding economic profit system that drives its services. They haven't been introduced to surveillance activities, threats to privacy, or the monetization of their "eyeballs." They think of it as a "free" system for connection, not one that wrings profit from virtually every choice they make. All systems that provide some form of connectivity to people exact a price for it, and in many cases that price is not known until long after decisions are made by users and then it's too late to effectively withdraw. People are lured into use without the requisite knowledge to resist.

The second aspect of the Hutchins Commission's critique was concentration of ownership. The fewer media owners there were, it reasoned, the less freedom of expression would exist. The concentration the Commission feared has only strengthened in the past 70 years. In 2010 Timothy Wu concluded that "most of the phone system was back in the hands of Bell, and its competitors were being steadily run down. A gang of conglomerates comfortably controlled film, cable, and broad-casting. And while this new order was by no means absolute, the industrial concentration had reached levels not seen since the 1950s" (Wu, 2010, p. 255). He also wrote that the concept of net neutrality, which required that all traffic, from whatever source, have equal access to bandwidth, was under siege by corporations such as Google and Apple, finally concluding that, despite Apple's carefully cultivated reputation as an innovator, its devices "are a betrayal of the inspiration behind that pathbreaking device [the original Apple II], which was fundamentally meant to empower its users, not control them" (Ibid., p. 292).

Although Wu's analysis was restricted to the United States, it is not difficult to find others who have reached similar conclusions elsewhere:

> Net Neutrality is digital freedom. Mandating it is vital. Unrestricted online access is the only way to stay informed. It's a vital source for real information. It's free from state or corporate control. It's been this way so far. Public interest groups want it preserved. Everyone has the right to demand it. It's too precious to lose. Giant telecom and cable companies want control. They want toll roads established. They want higher priced premium lanes. They want unrestricted pricing power. They want license to steal. They want content restricted. They want the right to censor. They want dissent crushed. They want independent thought eliminated. They want digital democracy destroyed. Net Neutrality denies them. They spent enormous amounts contesting. They want total Internet control.
>
> *(Centre for Research on Globalization; Lendman, 2014)*

> "Western dominance is one of the biggest challenges for developing nations," says Alice Munyua, a researcher and policy development expert, representing Kenya and Africa on forums such as ICANN [Internet Corporation for Assigned Names and Numbers]. "It is a big concern for African governments and stakeholders, and not just because of how the internet is governed, but how it is developed from a commercial and technical perspective," she said. "There is a feeling that we are not able to participate or contribute effectively because of the lack of capacity, skills and resources, so there's a digital divide in terms of access, but also in appropriating the internet for our own development."
>
> *(Kiss, 2012)*

In many respects, then, despite the enormous technological changes that have affected media since 1947, the situation remains basically the same.

Discussion Questions

1 It has long been an article of faith in Western nations that a free press is necessary for democracy to thrive. Is this true or can democracy thrive in situations where the press is owned by, or heavily censored by, the state?

2 Does corporate control of the media guarantee freedom of expression? Does it enable the "watchdog function" of the press, or merely create new concerns for free expression?

3 Does social responsibility matter when it comes to the operations of media companies? Can they be trusted to exercise it?

Notes

1 ISIS is also referred to as ISIL (Islamic State of Iraq and the Levant) and the Islamic State (or Caliphate as its adherents contend), and indigenously Da'ish.
2 http://www.internetworldstats.com/top20.htm. Accessed February 11, 2017.

2

Philosophical Perspectives on Ethical Decision-Making: The Individualist Traditions

Introduction

We argued in Chapter 1 that media workers should make decisions in a socially responsible manner. However, responsibilities vary from one society to another. In Western societies it would seem irresponsible to squander opportunity – claims of this sort usually accompany discussions of unemployment, welfare, and poverty. But in societies where a more collectivist approach to relationships is practiced, people would think it irresponsible not to care for another who lost a job or became disabled. In rural Nepal, for instance, members of the high Brahmin caste may sometimes care for members of the lowest caste Dalits when they are disabled – people they would have little to do with otherwise.[1]

Both Christianity and Islam call for charity to those in need as well. Such expectations and practices may result in the conclusion that this is merely human decency at work. This might be acceptable, if it were not for the multiple examples of ethnic cleansing, genocide, sectarian violence, tribal warfare, racism, and other forms of exclusion or atrocity that also seem so human in their origins. If it is responsible to take care of others, is it likewise responsible not to do so – depending on the society in which a person lives? We might ask what the socially responsible thing to do was in Rwanda in 1994 when that country's genocide occurred. Were the so-called "moderate Hutus" who refused to partake in the violence socially responsible, or were those who did join in at the call of their community? Were Hutus who hid their Tutsi neighbors being socially responsible, or the Dutch who hid Jews from the Nazis? Or Serbs who hid Bosnians, when those in power said otherwise?

Of course not, we say. Clearly engaging in the slaughter of the "other" cannot be seen as socially responsible. All such acts are immoral. But then the question is – why? What makes these acts immoral? As we mentioned in Chapter 1, the universal of the sacredness of life would condemn such behavior. True enough. But this is thin – easily discarded in the heat of the moment, in the society that excludes certain people from the community as "vermin," "cockroaches," or "dogs" (see Fortner, 2006). In such societies where the media are means to stir up hatred, encourage bloodlust, or create scapegoats, especially at the behest of government authorities, is it the state that should be condemned for atrocities or the media that carry out its demands?

Sources of Moral Action

Morality is concerned with right action. A moral choice is one that requires a person to make a decision between right and wrong, good and evil. People draw on a variety of sources to inform those choices. Such sources include religion, philosophy, ideology, principle, "common" sense, or a code of

World Media Ethics: Cases and Commentary, First Edition. Robert S. Fortner and P. Mark Fackler.
© 2018 John Wiley & Sons, Inc. Published 2018 by John Wiley & Sons, Inc.

ethics adopted by a profession or organization. People learn about such possibilities at home, in religious training, at schools and universities, or when they enter a particular profession or accept a position at an organization – including media businesses, non-profit or charitable organizations, or even as volunteers for short- or long-term periods. They also learn them from the expectations provided by commitment to ideological perspectives or by emulating others whom they identify as role models. There is no single source for right action, just as there is no limit to the bad actions that people may commit.

After the end of the Second World War two events occurred in Germany that tested the issue of responsibility for the atrocities committed, especially in the concentration camps where millions died at Nazi hands. The first was the Nuremberg Trials of war criminals. It was here that the principle of individual responsibility for atrocities was affirmed, especially in the trial of Alfred Jodl, who was chief of the National Defense Section of the High Command of the German Armed Forces. Jodl claimed during his trial that he had to obey Hitler, since he was a soldier pledged to obey the chief of state. His defense was rejected by the International Criminal Tribunal and he was hanged (Austin, n.d.).[2] This question of responsibility was also taken up when Adolf Eichmann was abducted in Argentina by the Mossad (the Israeli intelligence agency) and taken to Israel for trial for his role in the Holocaust. Eichmann had been the head of the "Jewish Section" of the SS – "He was the prototypical behind-the-scenes mastermind, an unscrupulous bureaucrat who never killed anyone with his own hands" (Wiegrefe, 2011). Eichmann himself "did his *duty*, as he told the police and the court over and over again; he not only obeyed *orders*, he also obeyed the *law*" (Arendt, 1992, p. 135). He also claimed that he had lived his entire life obeying the moral precepts of Kant, but as Hannah Arendt put it, "This was outrageous, on the face of it, and incomprehensible, since Kant's moral philosophy is so closely bound up with the man's faculty of judgment, which rules out blind obedience" (Ibid., p. 136). Eichmann did admit, however, that when he was charged with carrying out the Final Solution, he "had ceased to live according to Kantian principles," and "had consoled himself with the thought that he no longer 'was master of his own deeds,' that he was unable 'to change anything'" (Ibid.). He was convicted and hanged. His obedience to law and performance of his duty as a soldier were insufficient justifications for his actions.

The second event was a series of lectures that the German philosopher Karl Jaspers began delivering around Germany almost immediately after the conclusion of the war. The question he addressed in these lectures was German guilt. Jaspers proposed a fourfold typology of guilt. First was criminal guilt, limited to those who broke natural and international law; second was political guilt, which applied to all citizens of a modern state; third was moral guilt that would be suffered by anyone whose personal responsibility for actions would trouble his own conscience; and fourth was metaphysical guilt, a guilt "that can encompass an otherwise innocent person in whose presence or with whose knowledge crimes were committed" (Koterski, 2001, p. x). Jaspers (2000, p. 16) counselled those who heard him that "no one is guiltless." He claimed that "we Germans are indeed obliged without exception to understand clearly the question of our guilt, and to draw the conclusions. What obliges us is our human dignity. . . . The guilt question is more than a question put to us by others, it is one we put to ourselves. The way we answer it will be decisive for our present approach to the world and to ourselves. It is a vital question for the German soul" (Ibid., p. 22). He recognized, however, that moral judgments could not be levied against a group, but only against individuals, and that "there is no such thing as a people as a whole" (Ibid., p. 35). But, he argued, there were various reasons for Germans to think of themselves as guilty even if they had not actively participated in the war crimes being adjudicated at Nuremberg, and even if they were unaware of the atrocities perpetrated by the Nazi regime:

> First, anyone who pledged "loyalty to threatening bodies like the Gestapo, [or who gave] the Hitler salute, [who attended meetings] – who among us in Germany was not guilty of that, at one time or another." (p. 58)

Second, speaking of guilt incurred by false conscience, he claimed: "our duty to the fatherland goes far beneath blind obedience to its rules of the day. The fatherland ceases to be a fatherland when its soul is destroyed. The power of the state is not an end in itself; rather, it is pernicious if this state destroys the German character." (p. 59)

Third was inner assimilation of the idea that not everything done was evil – "there was some good to it" – but, Jaspers said, if the principle is evil, "everything is evil." (p. 61)

Fourth was self-deception, the argument that National Socialism would be dispensed with when the Führer died at the latest, but in the meantime assimilating the party's "inhuman, dictatorial, unexistentially nihilist essence." (p. 63)

Fifth was the guilt of inaction of passivity, which "knows itself morally guilty of every failure, every neglect to act whenever possible, to shield the imperiled, to relieve wrong, to countervail." (p. 63)

Lastly was "running with the pack" to carry out normal life, a decision that evinced "the lack of absolute solidarity with the human being as such – an indelible claim beyond morally meaningful duty." (p. 65)

(Jaspers, 2000)

If Jaspers was correct, there is little room for media professionals (or any citizen, for that matter) to evade responsibility for what a state does.

To put this differently: The first requirement for ethical choice is to decide if it matters whether behavior follows moral precepts (from whatever source) or it doesn't. Ayn Rand (1964) puts the issue this way:

The first question is not: What particular code of values should man accept? The first question is: Does man need values at all – and why?

[. . .]

Man has no automatic code of survival. He has no automatic course of action, no automatic set of values. His senses do not tell him automatically what is good for him or evil, what will benefit his life or endanger it, what goals he should pursue and what means will achieve them, what *values* his life depends on, what course of action it requires. His own consciousness has to discover the answers to all these questions – but his consciousness will not function *automatically*.

The Danish philosopher Søren Kierkegaard (1987, p. 169) takes a similar position, writing, "rather than designating the choice between good and evil, my Either/Or designates the choice by which one chooses good and evil or rules them out." In other words, before a person can decide whether to do good or evil, s/he must decide that the distinction between these two opposites actually matters. To Kierkegaard the antithesis of deciding that good and evil matter is the decision to live aesthetically – to seek only what is pleasing to one's self.

Once the decision is made to consider the good or evil of one's actions, the next problem is to determine what is good and what is evil. This is a moral issue. Moral acts lead to good, immoral acts lead to evil. This is where the moral universals (or proto-norms) mentioned earlier (preservation of life, protection of innocents, truth-telling, and non-violence) may be invoked. Following such precepts would provide a normative condition for life:

Among those who use "morality" normatively, all hold that "morality" refers to a code of conduct that applies to all who can understand it and can govern their behavior by it. In the normative sense, morality should never be overridden, that is, no one should ever violate a moral prohibition or requirement for non-moral considerations. All of those who use "morality" normatively also hold that, under plausible specified conditions, all rational persons would endorse that code.

("The definition of morality," 2011)

Several ethical theories provide guidance to making this choice between good and evil. Some emerge from religious convictions based on sacred texts, while others are the result of philosophical or ideological speculations or examinations of the human condition. The normative ethical traditions in the West are typically categorized under four traditions: deontology, utilitarianism, virtue, and contractual ethics (see Darwall, 2003). Expanding our scope to global ethics, however, requires a more comprehensive consideration of relevant traditions.

We are approaching ethical traditions by dividing them into two categories. The first category contains those traditions that put the responsibility for ethical choice primarily in the hands of individual persons. These traditions assume that choice is individual and that choice is based on the application of rationality, or logic, to problems as they arise. This chapter will provide an outline of these traditions and some cases to use in evaluating them. The next chapter will outline the second category, which contains those traditions that recognize the important role played by communities in ethical choice. Although people in this category must also choose, they do so by making that choice with an eye toward the consequences of choice not only for themselves or others immediately affected by the choice, but also for the flourishing of others in the community. The community, in other words, transcends the individual. We will refer to the ethical traditions of the first sort as individualist ethics and of the second sort as collectivist ethics.

There are two issues raised by this distinction between individualist and collectivist ethics. First is the issue of motive. People may choose a particular course of action based on what they think will have the best results for themselves. But they may choose, too, based on what they think is best for others. In the first case the person acts out of self-interest; in the second, out of altruistic motives. Self-interest motives are probably better understood using post-Enlightenment ethical perspectives. In Rand's "objectivist ethics," selfishness is a virtue:

> In popular usage, the word "selfishness" is a synonym of evil; the image it conjures is of a murderous brute who tramples over piles of corpses to achieve his own ends, who cares for no living being and pursues nothing but the gratification of the mindless whims of any immediate moment. Yet the exact meaning and dictionary definition of the word "selfishness" is: concern with one's own interests.

(Rand, 1964, p. 5)

Selfishness implies both a consideration of one's own interests and how best to achieve them, and the application of logic to the issue: ethics based in the post-Enlightenment values of individualism and rationality. In more community-based ethical traditions, while rationality comes into play, the role of the individual is subsumed under the interests of the collective.

Second is the issue of universality of ethical decisions. The notion of proto-norms suggests that these widely accepted universals not be violated by either individual or community choice. Accepting this claim circumscribes some ethical traditions more than others. Utilitarianism, for instance, argues for the "greatest good for the greatest number." It is possible that the greatest number of people will be assisted, however, by choices that violate one or more of the proto-norms, even when the rights of minorities are protected from the will of the majority, as John Stuart Mill proposed. Or it is equally possible that the greater good (as defined by community values) would be best served by a decision that could not serve as a universal commitment due to unique circumstances. In the Western tradition, deontological ethics as proposed by Immanuel Kant argues that any decision must apply in all circumstances and to all choices. But other traditions in the Western ethical canon do not make such claims. Thus universality remains problematic philosophically.

Individualist Ethical Traditions

Deontological Ethics

Deontological ethics argues for action based on the duty to obey principles or rules. It assumes that people have certain duties to others, such as "do no harm." The philosopher most closely associated with the deontological perspective is Immanuel Kant, and the overriding principle he is famous for is the categorical imperative. Such an imperative is inviolate. It brooks no exceptions. It is what is right, regardless of the consequences that may result from acting on it. As Ralph Walker (2012, pp. 145–146) puts it, "categorical imperatives . . . command us absolutely, by telling us what morality requires, and morality may very well require that we should override our non-moral aims and inclinations." Duty trumps all. Kant's perspective on ethics owed much both to his Lutheran upbringing and belief and to the elevation of rationality during the Enlightenment. In some respects his efforts can be seen as an attempt to merge faith (or at least his belief in God) and rationality, which the Enlightenment in many respects had sought to use as a replacement for faith. Christian ethics, by and large, is based on Kant's deontological approach, and the universality of both duty and principle in determining behavior.

Kant also made two other important claims in ethics. First, he said, people should always be treated as ends, never as means. This means that human beings could never be used as a means to an end regardless of the value of that end. They are inviolate.

> The moral law we arrive at through the exercise of our will requires that we treat humanity – in our own person and in others – never only as a means but as an end in itself. Although this moral requirement is based on autonomy, it rules out certain acts among consenting adults, namely those that are at odds with human dignity and self-respect.
>
> *(Sandel, 2009, p. 108)*

As Derek Parfit (2011, p. 154) explains: "According to Kant's best-loved principle, often called the Formula of Humanity: We must treat all rational beings, or persons, never merely as a means, but always as ends. To treat people as ends, Kant claims, we must never treat them in ways to which they could not consent." If they were not so, there would be no reason to worry with universalism. When one person, or group of people, can be treated differently from others to achieve some good end, then universalism fails, and ethics fails.[3]

Second was Kant's insistence that rationality was not a function of subjectivity. It was independent of the person making choices, who by definition would be unable to separate his own interests from those of others when making a decision. Rationality had to be inviolate and universal. Again, Walker (2012, p. 144): "the Moral Law is a fundamental principle of reason: of pure practical reason. It binds all human beings, not because of any contingent facts about human nature. It binds human beings because they are rational, and it equally binds whatever other rational beings there may be. Its status is similar to that of logical laws, which are basic laws of pure theoretical reason; and it is known in the same way, *a priori*, independently of experience."

Utilitarian Ethics

Utilitarian ethics, in contrast, is concerned only with the consequences of choice. The morality of any act depends only on its results. The famous dictum of utilitarianism is that moral choice is a calculation of what will achieve greatest good for the greatest number. It balances both the number of people affected, either for well or for ill, and the amount of good or bad they experience. Only then, based on this calculation, can a person know whether his actions are good or bad. The utilitarian approach to ethics was originally proposed by Jeremy Bentham and then argued in altered form by John Stuart Mill.

This approach to ethics is directly at odds with Kant's. Utilitarianism "says the morality of an action depends solely on the consequences it brings about; the right thing to do is whatever will produce the best state of affairs, all things considered. [Kant argues] that consequences are not all we should care about, morally speaking; certain duties and rights should command our respect, for reasons independent of social consequences" (Sandel, 2009, pp. 30–31). The questions, then, taking these two approaches are: is morality a matter of counting lives and weighing costs and benefits, or are certain moral duties and human rights so fundamental that they rise above such calculations? As Mill himself put it: "The creed which accepts as the foundation of morals 'utility' or the 'greatest happiness principle' holds that actions are right in proportion as they tend to promote happiness; wrong as they tend to produce the reverse of happiness. By happiness is intended pleasure and the absence of pain; by unhappiness, pain and the privation of pleasure" (1871, reprinted in Hayden, 2001, p. 137).

"And if certain rights are fundamental in this way – be they natural, or sacred, or inalienable, or categorical – how can we identify them? And what makes them fundamental?" (Sandel, 2009, p. 31). Bentham's and Mill's doctrines were that the task of morality itself was to maximize happiness, to assure that pleasure outweighed pain (see Ibid.).

Testing these two approaches to ethics can be accomplished by applying them to specific situations. In this book we will do that by using case studies. These are situations where media professionals were called upon to make difficult choices and to defend those choices to others. The first case here could be approached using either deontological or utilitarian ethics. What difference would it make, if any, to apply these two perspectives?

Case 2.1: Humanizing "Terrorists?"

On June 12, 2014, three young Israeli settlers disappeared from the Israeli-controlled part of the West Bank. This abduction raised issues about the Israeli presence in the West Bank, the possible complicity of Hamas (a Palestinian political and military group), what Israel could or would do to free the young men, and whether Israel's response would trigger a renewal of the Intifada. A week following the abduction Hamas spokesman Sami Abu Zuhri claimed that "Israel is conducting a large-scale military operation against Hamas and the Palestinian people. The ongoing air raids in the Gaza Strip constitute a dangerous escalation" (Al-Ghoul, 2014). Another week later Batya Medad (2014), writing for the blog Jewishpress.com, said that there was good news: Israeli Channel Two News had reported that the Israeli Defense Force (IDF) now had a major lead into the identity of the kidnappers. But he also objected that, since the media had had the information about this lead for several days prior to its report, "they had prepared a terribly sympathetic, humanizing piece about [the kidnappers] featuring one of the wives, who looked young, beautiful and innocent crying that she didn't believe her husband was guilty. [Her husband's father] firmly denied that his *darling* son could be involved." Later the three abducted young men were found dead (accusations were made that they had actually been murdered by Israelis themselves to provoke Palestinians) and a Palestinian teenager was burned alive in reprisal. Six Israelis were arrested for that crime.

Commentary on Case 2.1

Kant and Mill would have quite different responses to this situation. Their judgments about its ethics would result from quite different considerations of the facts. Kant would insist that kidnapping is wrong in principle. But he would also argue that demeaning those accused (but not yet proven guilty) of the kidnapping – and especially their relatives – should nevertheless not be demonized since this would deny their humanity. In addition, he would object to the use of one kidnapper's wife and father as means to demonize (by his sarcastic tone) that kidnapper. Mill would insist that this volatile situation should be weighed carefully, taking into consideration the likelihood that those kidnapped would lose their lives, that the kidnappers would be falsely accused or face the trial of public opinion illegitimately, that the IDF would over-react, that any response of the IDF would result in a reignited Intifada (widespread resistance to the IDF in situ, rocket attacks or suicide bombs in Israel). What action would lead to the maximum pleasure and the minimum pain?

But there is also the issue of the media here. First is the report of Israeli Channel Two that included interviews with relatives of one of the accused kidnappers: Was its report ethical? Should it have included such content? Second is the blog post response: Is objecting to the "humanization" of "terrorists" ethical?

Virtue Ethics

Virtue ethics emphasizes moral character. In the West this approach is traceable to Aristotle and in the East to Confucius. Rosalind Hurthouse (2009) explains that although the approach was eclipsed by both deontological and utilitarian ethics after the Enlightenment until the late 1950s, it was reinvigorated by the work of G.E.M. Anscombe (1958):

> [Anscombe] crystallized an increasing dissatisfaction with the forms of deontology and utilitarianism then prevailing. Neither of them, at that time, paid attention to a number of topics that had always figured in the virtue ethics tradition – virtues and vices, motives and moral character, moral education, moral wisdom or discernment, friendship and family relationships, a deep concept of happiness, the role of emotions in our moral life and the fundamentally important questions of what sort of persons we should be and how we should live.
>
> *(Hurthouse, 2009)*

What are the virtues? Virtues may include a variety of qualities. For instance, your friends probably expect loyalty from you – they would consider that a virtue. Other virtues could include charity, courage, creativity, compassion, diligence, empathy, hope, humility, justice, patience, or wisdom. In religious terms, faith would be a virtue, or obedience, or stewardship. Any quality that expresses the best that human beings are capable of achieving would be a virtue. And these virtues are often contrasted with vices or sins, such as the so-called "seven deadly sins" in Catholic theology: anger, envy, gluttony, greed, lust, pride, and sloth.

Virtues can be cataloged in several ways. In Aristotle's day the cardinal virtues were prudence, temperance, courage, and justice. The Apostle Paul in the New Testament of the Bible articulated the theological virtues of love, hope, and faith. And the seven virtues that are antidotes to the seven deadly sins were humility, kindness, abstinence, chastity, patience, liberality, and diligence. There are, in other words, a variety of virtues for a variety of circumstances, or emerging from a variety of perspectives. There may be at least 60 virtues that have been promoted by different authors since the time of Aristotle.

Aristotle is sometimes referred to as the creator of the "golden mean," an argument in favor of moderation, the result of the lists of virtues he provided in both the *Eudemian Ethics* and *Nichomachean Ethics*. In the *Eudemian Ethics* he provided a diagram of opposites, such as wastefulness vs. meanness (mean here referring to pecuniary matters, not attitude), or stiff-neckedness vs. subservience. His golden mean in the first case was liberality and in the second dignity. Such an approach is "a philosophically interesting way of cashing out two well-known Greek proverbs: Solon's *mêden agan*, 'nothing to excess', and Cleobulus' *metron ariston*, 'moderation is best'" (Chappell, 2012, p. 63).

The virtues Aristotle identified were "by definition those character-traits that promote overall well-being" (Ibid., p. 58). But such traits were not something that he proposed be taught, or striven for. Rather they were the result of good character, something he thought could not be taught. His view of virtue and character were also intrinsic to his definition of "pleasure." He was not in favor of "hedonistic utilitarianism" (what Mill and Bentham proposed later), but pleasure that would result from good character, character "that tends to produce what we all agree is pleasure" (Ibid., p. 56). Those who had bad character would identify pleasure, he argued, quite differently than those of good character: "For Aristotle, there is a fundamental connection between virtue and pleasure: between what we find enjoyable or not and whether we are called good people or not" (Ibid., p. 53). This good character was something that would be learned by living within families and communities, realizing what was good in "habituation" and then forming one's own character. The moral quality of one's context was the foundation of character.

A second important aspect of Aristotle's approach to virtue is that he saw virtues as teleological. This means that, in order to know what constituted good character, one had to figure out the purpose or essential nature of the social practice that was exhibited by a person with such character. What did the trait accomplish, and was what it accomplished good in its social context? So, for instance, we could ask, what is the purpose of justice, or of dignity? If the essential quality of justice or dignity was good, then practicing them would be good as well, and a person who exhibited such virtues would be honored or rewarded in the society (see Sandel, 2009, pp. 149–150). The more people who had such virtues, the more their community would provide a context for continuing character development.

We are discussing Aristotle here within the context of individualistic ethics since he recognized the necessity of each person coming to his or her own conclusions in facing moral quandaries. But we must say that, as the last couple of paragraphs implied, he also recognized the important role played by community in raising people of good character.

Contractual Ethics

Contractual ethics is based on the idea that all people live under a type of social contract that makes society possible. There have been a variety of approaches to such ethics, beginning with Thomas Hobbes and including Jean-Jacques Rousseau and John Locke. More recently a variant of contractual ethics was proposed by John Rawls. Some aspects of contractual ethics were also represented in some of the Socratic dialogues, especially in *The Republic*. Hobbes took the position that political authority and obligations to it were based on the self-interests of equal individuals in a society and that no one, regardless of lineage (or royal lines), had any special claim to rule. The starting point for contractual ethics was an imagined state of nature where force ruled. Any society that developed from this state had to be based, Hobbes thought, on conventions about how people were to live together without rule by the law of the jungle. Civilization emerged as a result of these conventions.

John Locke, whose ideas were especially significant in the thinking of the founding fathers of the United States (especially Thomas Jefferson and James Madison), also began his argument in the state of nature, but unlike Hobbes, thought of that state as only pre-political, not pre-moral. He was also not as individualistically inclined, and recognized that there were some conjugal relationships, such as families, that agreed to care for children together.

Jean-Jacques Rousseau's position was closer to Locke's than Hobbes', and he had an idealized theory of social contract that emerged as populations increased in number and found it essential to create communities. But living in proximity in a community also gave rise to comparisons among its residents, which resulted in competition, vanity, greed, and recognitions of inequality. The development of private property created conditions of discord and increased distinctions and inequalities among people, leading to the development of social classes and subsequently the need to contract for equality among people.[4]

John Rawls' (1971) approach to the social contract sought to take accomplishment or status out of the equation when people were engaged in determining the most ethical response to a particular situation. He proposed that decisions between right and wrong had to be made behind a "veil of ignorance" where none of the relevant parties could know, in the end, how they would fare as a result of the decision. He agreed with Kant that people were capable universally of deciding what was right and wrong, but that their position in society blinded them in the search for the right or good. He objected to utilitarianism. On this issue Sandel writes:

> [O]nce the veil of ignorance rises and real life begins, we don't want to find ourselves as victims of religious persecution or racial discrimination. In order to protect against these dangers, we would reject utilitarianism and agree to a principle of equal basic liberties for all citizens, including the right to liberty of conscience and freedom of thought. And we would insist that this principle take priority over attempts to maximize the general welfare. We would not sacrifice our fundamental rights and liberties for social and economic benefits.
>
> *(Sandel, 2009, p. 123)*

Therefore, the answer had to be in a guarantee of impartiality so that no one's particular circumstances could influence his or her decision. All distinctions, from race and gender to reputation and power, had to be eliminated so that a true decision could be made (see Friend, 2004).

Humanist Ethics

Frederick Edwords, Executive Director of the American Humanist Association, while recognizing that there are "religious humanists," nevertheless writes:

> [H]umanism teaches us that it is immoral to wait for God to act for us. We must act to stop the wars and the crimes and the brutality of this and future ages. We have powers of a remarkable kind. We have a high degree of freedom in choosing what we will do. Humanism tells us that whatever our philosophy of the universe may be, ultimately the responsibility for the kind of world in which we live rests with us.
>
> *(Edwords, n.d., p. 3)*

Paul Kurtz (1980, p. 11) claims that "humanists by and large are secularists. They are committed to free thought and to the view that ethical values are relative to human experience and needs." The ethical commitments of humanists, as Kurtz puts it (Ibid., p. 15), are to freedom and social progress, although he admits that humanists are as likely to be immoral, nasty, deceitful, prideful, or moved by lust, fame, or power as anyone else: "There is no moral exclusivity for any one philosophical, religious, or ideological party." Corliss Lamont (1949, p. 273) said that the chief end of humanist ethics "is to further this-earthly human interests on behalf of the greater happiness and glory of man. The watchword of Humanism is service to humanity in this existence as contrasted with the salvation of the individual soul in a future existence and the glorification of a supernatural Supreme Being. Humanism urges men to accept freely and joyously the great gift of life and to realize that life in its own right and for its own sake can be as beautiful and splendid as any dream of immortality."

Kurtz argues that a "humanistic ethic of freedom" is insufficient in itself – it must have a "theory and practice of moral education" and "a set of *prima facie* ethical principles that should have a claim upon our action" (Kurtz, 1980, pp. 16–17). These principles, he explains, should include those that are the most basic and commonly shared "as the fabric of the community and the basis of human relationships: truth, honesty, sincerity, trust, kindness, generosity, friendship, sharing, concern for others, et cetera" (Ibid., p. 19). Kurtz distinguishes between relativism and situationalism – relativism assumes that there are no extant principles that should prevail in every case, while situationalism recognizes that there are such principles although applying them in a particular situation depends on circumstances. "We need," he says, "to consider the *prima facie* ethical principles that are relevant. Our actual duties, obligations and responsibilities will depend upon the situation and the social milieu in which we live" (Ibid., p. 24). Of course, the problem that anyone faces in trying to do the right thing is that, as Michael Ignatieff (1984) puts it, "Beneath the social there ought to be the natural. Beneath the duties that tie us to individuals, there ought to be a duty that ties us to all men and women whatever their relation to us. In fact, beneath the social, the historical, there is nothing at all. . . . There is no such thing as love of the human race, only the love of this person for that, in this time and not in any other." Which brings us to the perspective of postmodern ethicists.

Liberation Ethics

Liberation ethics emerged from liberation theology that was birthed in a grass-roots movement within the Roman Catholic Church in Latin America in the early 1960s (Schubeck, 1993, p. xvi). It was a response in faith "within the struggles of oppressive living conditions" (Ibid.). This theological perspective demands preference for the poor in evaluating national economic policies and functions as a "genuinely transformative theology that calls upon people to work for a just society" (Ibid., p. xix). As Schubeck puts it, liberation theology's original contribution to Christian ethics was its "insistent integration of theology and lived faith, of contemplation and action, and of ethical theory and prophetic practice" (Ibid., p. xx).

Although liberation theology, and the ethics it engenders, has been criticized as being too Marxist in orientation (making class warfare ethically normative in the view of the current Pope), theologians and ethicists within the tradition have argued that "Christian ethics should first concern itself with the ethos and power structures of society that shape moral norms and ethical reasoning" (Ibid., p. 11; see also Dussel, 2003, chapter 1). One cannot assume, for instance, within a society shaped by the dominance of economic elites and oppression of the poor, that the understandings of natural law that have undergirded traditional Christian understandings of ethics have not been tainted by such society. Instead, they say, "moral judgments depend upon a vision of the good and just society within which decisions based on justice are to be made" (Schubeck, 1993, p. xxi). Fatalistic acceptance of one's lot in life is not part of the ethics of liberation – rather it intends to inculcate a perspective that convinces people to assume active control over their own lives (Ibid., p. 59). Although the ethics of liberation are concerned with the context of ethical choice – the judgments that must be made about the value of culture and politics – it is also primarily concerned with "the survival and well-being of the self, the human being as a self-conscious, cultural, and responsible" entity (Marsh, 2000, p. 54).

Perhaps the most significant difference between liberation ethics and more traditional Christian ethics is the assumption about the source of ethics itself. In liberation ethics "the judgment or ideological suspicion does not flow from moral reasoning, as in a natural law or deontological argument [sources of traditional Christian ethical development], but from a moral intuition based on experience of negative or oppressive situations. These suspicions must be tested, however, to confirm whether one's intuitive judgment is supported by evidence," and subsequently by social analysis and scripture (Schubeck, 1993, p. 68).

Postmodern Ethics

One of the essential perspectives of postmodern theory is that meta-narratives or "grand narratives" are no longer relevant. This perspective also is part of the discussion of ethics within a postmodern paradigm. Zygmunt Bauman (1993), for instance, tries to explain how ethics has had to change with the movement from tradition to modernity to postmodernity. In traditional life, one did "right" merely by following the precepts of the community, which were based on a common belief-system. "Wrong" was whatever deviated from the norms of community life. Modernity led to a breakdown of this way of life as the church became either ineffective or "extinct" (Ibid., p. 6). The moral thought of modernity, he said, "was animated by the belief in the possibility of a *non-ambivalent, non-aporetic ethical code*" (Ibid., p. 9). This code was to provide a clear, non-contradictory, set of rules for life that would replace those of the belief – but they never arrived. Human beings are "morally ambivalent: ambivalence resides at the heart of the 'primary scene' of human face-to-face" (Ibid., p. 10). He claims that individual human beings must be responsible for moral choice apart from the plague of relativism that affects the moral codes of modernity which, despite their claim to universality, are, in fact, parochial, enforced by "institutional powers that usurp ethical authority" (Ibid., p. 14).

Because modernity in the West had delegitimized the authority of the church for its "ignorance" of what was truly universal about humanity, and had replaced it "with the yet more radical and uncompromising claim for universal validity" (Ibid., p. 25) it was necessary that people be convinced that it was a rational choice to do good – as the "moral enlighteners" taught (Ibid., p. 27). What then occurred was that multiple institutions were created to enforce (through coercive sanctions) the "codes" that emerged as the containers of moral action (see Ibid., pp. 28–29). Bauman goes on: "In a shorthand form, this duality of measures is expressed as the quandary of, on the one hand, intrinsic desirability of free decision-making, but, on the other, the need to limit freedom of those who are presumed to use it to do evil. You can trust the wise (the code name of the mighty) to do good autonomously; but you cannot trust all people to be wise" (Ibid., p. 30).

But postmodernists reject universals: "Human reality is messy and ambiguous – and so moral decisions, unlike abstract ethical principles, are ambivalent. . . . [W]e demonstrate day by day that we can live, or learn to live, or manage to live in such a world, though few of us would be ready to spell out, if asked, what the principles that guide us are, and fewer still would have heard about the 'foundations' which we allegedly cannot do without to be good and kind to each other. Knowing that to be the truth (or just intuiting it, or going on *as if* one knew it) is to be postmodern. Postmodernity, one may say, is *modernity without illusions*" (Ibid., p. 32). One such jettisoned illusion is that of "unemotional, calculating reason. Dignity has been returned to the emotions; legitimacy to the 'inexplicable', nay irrational, sympathies and loyalties which cannot 'explain themselves' in terms of their usefulness and purpose" (Ibid., p. 33).

Nihilist Ethics

Some postmodern philosophers, such as Jean-Francois Lyotard and Jacques Derrida, are accused of advocating a nihilist philosophy, but as nihilism itself claims to be a universal truth, which postmodernism denies on its face, clearly there are differences in the two approaches. One philosopher who does seem to have a nihilist ethic is Günther Anders. According to Paul van Dijk (2000, p. 33), Anders complained "that much of what constituted the idea of humanism until far into the nineteenth century has been lost through the process of industrialization and technology." To Anders, "the state of the human being, life in general, seems to have become an antiquated form of life, when measured against the immanent tendencies of the technical achievements of the twentieth century" (Ibid., p. 34). Anders' "negative anthropology" is actually based on human achievement: "the very triumphs of human beings cause them to disappear" (Ibid., p. 35). This is not due to abuse or mistake, but success and triumph. The more success human beings have, the less significant they become – the more enmeshed in the "all-encompassing industry, raw material for a production machinery that has become self-sufficient" (Ibid.).

Gianni Vattimo (2003, p. xv) defines nihilism "in the sense first given by Nietzsche: the dissolution of any ultimate foundation, the understanding that in the history of philosophy, and of western culture in general, 'God is dead,' and 'the real world has become a fable.'" To a nihilist there is no point in trying to discover ethical universals, or even a universal humanism, since people can only understand or make meaning within their own cultural milieu: "When western philosophy realizes this, it becomes nihilistic; it acknowledges that its own argumentative process is always historically and culturally situated, that even the idea of universality is 'grasped' from a particular point of view" (Ibid., pp. xv–xvi).

Vattimo's explanation of the nihilist perspective, based on his reading of Nietzsche, is similar to Plato's reading of the idea of Thrasymachus, who, according to Plato, was a "man who believes that, since the sense of all moral terms is determined by the social and political context in which they are uttered, it is only fools (and especially fools duped by those more astute in the 'propaganda' struggle) who take them seriously in the sense of believing themselves to be not merely imprudent in breaking the rules and acting 'unjustly,' but objective evil-doers" (Rist, 2002, p. 15).

In other words, a nihilist would argue that all ethical commitments are so much hot air. They have no substance, no anima. Therefore, there is no real point in arguing in favor of an ethic, whether of justice, goodness, love, or whatever, as whatever our perspective is has been conditioned (or warped) by our own culture to the point that we are incapable of thinking outside that box of meaning and perhaps, even more rudely, outside our own fantasy of ethics – shared only within our own head.

Often it is necessary for people to approach an ethical issue from several different points of view. This can be particularly difficult when that issue emerges from a culture or society whose foundations are significantly different from one's own. The ability to see facts from another's perspective, however, is a mark of ethical maturity. With that in mind, consider the following case, which pits two perspectives that are fundamentally at odds with one another. What should you do when being ethical can also mean to be judged unethical from different points of view?

Case 2.2: Aliaa Maghda El-Mahdy

The Arab Spring of 2011 resulted in the resignation of Hosni Mubarak, president of Egypt. A military government took over and promised elections. After several months cracks appeared in the relationship of the Muslim Brotherhood (a formerly banned Islamic political party), the more liberally minded opposition, and the military government. Coptic Christians were attacked, protested, and were repulsed by government troops, whom they had depended on to protect their minority rights. People began to protest again, demanding an end to military rule. Tahrir Square once again filled with protesters, but the military seemed unbending. Some began to wonder whether they would actually relinquish power voluntarily.

Aliaa Maghda El-Mahdy was a 22-year-old student at the American University in Cairo. She had only joined the original Tahrir Square protests near their very end and had to drop out of the university when her parents threatened not to pay her tuition and fees. She had moved in with her boyfriend, but as an "atheist" began to feel the constraints of the conservative Muslim culture and social mores that defined Egyptian society, especially since it did not appear that this would loosen up and provide the freedom that she and many other young people had longed for in deposing Mubarak.

She decided to mount her own protest, by posting a nude photo of herself, wearing only stockings, flats, and a red ribbon in her hair. She took the photo using her own camera with a timer and posted it on Facebook in November 2011. Facebook removed it and her boyfriend offered to post it on his blog. When he did so in mid-November the "explosion" was heard around the world. Her nude photo was reprinted in various ways on multiple web and blog sites. The boyfriend's blog began to get hits that quickly reached into the millions, and people from across the planet began to weigh in on her action, both in favor of, and opposed to, the nature of her protest.

She continued her protest later by appearing with other female activists (all topless) in front of the Egyptian embassy in Berlin. One woman in this protest had "There will be millions of us" written across her chest. Another's chest said "Woman's spring is coming." El-Mahdy's body was adorned with Arabic script. She, along with another of the women, had red handprints on her torso. In this protest and others at the Louvre in Paris and in Stockholm, where she and Femen activists stood naked in the snow, they held black props purporting to be the Torah, the Bible, and the Koran to protest both religious oppression and the new Egyptian constitution.

Commentary on Case 2.2

El-Mahdy's protest using social media not only offended the Islamic principle of modesty, but also raised political issues as both the pro-democracy and Muslim Brotherhood advocates condemned it for fear that her bold statement would adversely affect their candidates' vote count in the upcoming parliamentary election. There was no question that the protest attracted massive attention, although its avowed purpose – to demand the freedom that the Arab Spring had represented – was not met. She sparked a new Twitter trend (#nudephotorevolutionary) and said of her photo: "I am not shy of being a woman in a society where women are nothing but sex objects harassed on a daily basis by men who know nothing about sex or the importance of a woman. The photo is an expression of my being and I see the human body as the best artistic representation of that" (Carville, 2011). As she continued her protest all pretense to modesty disappeared. The protest attracted other women who objected to the treatment of women in different societies. A large group of Israeli women, in solidarity with El-Mahdy (notable in itself in this troubled part of the world), posed topless to demonstrate their support (see Figure 2.1). But many Middle East news services and bloggers emphasized the shock and outrage that her posting had elicited, especially in Egypt. Are such protests, which have also been seen in other countries led by the Ukrainian Femen group, an ethical way to highlight oppression of women by men, or the unequal treatment under the law or religion of the two sexes? Should they be judged by their effectiveness in creating change, or is the achievement of solidarity or the symbolic representation of unequal treatment sufficient to justify their action – ethically speaking?

Figure 2.1 Israeli women pose topless in "Homage to Aliaa El Mahdi."

Free speech advocates would likely applaud El-Mahdy's post, while those who advocate social responsibility, especially in a volatile situation with possible consequences for parliamentary candidates, likely would not. Is this an issue where politics is more significant than ethics, or morality (Islamic sensibilities) more significant than legitimate protest? What would the various ethicists seeking justice have to say about her protests? Should the will of the majority prevail here? Or, as the postmodernists and liberationists would have it, are the obvious moral issues passé, or somehow made irrelevant by the necessity of bold action for change?

Conclusion: Reconciling Different Perspectives?

There are significant differences among these different approaches to ethics. But there are some compatibilities, too. Derek Parfit argues, for instance, that the Golden Rule (do to others what you would have done to yourself) and Immanuel Kant's Universal Law are similar in two respects: "In their best forms, both principles appeal to claims about what it would be rational for people to choose. And both principles assume that everyone matters equally, and has equal moral claims" (Parfit, 2011, p. 249). Although he admits there are various legitimate objections to the Golden Rule, when compared to Kant's Consent Principle and the Impartial Observer Formula, in the end it "may be, for practical purposes, the best of these three principles. By requiring us to imagine ourselves in other people's positions, the Golden Rule may provide what is psychologically the most effective way of making us more impartial, and morally motivating us. This may be why this rule has been the world's mostly [sic] widely accepted fundamental moral idea" (Ibid., p. 251). However, Kant's claims about universality, Parfit suggests, if it appealed to principles and to what everyone could rationally will to occur, would become a form of contractualism and his formula for choice would be: "everyone ought to follow the principles whose universal acceptance everyone could rationally will." This might be "the supreme principle of morality" (Ibid., p. 259).

Parfit then examines the moral claims of contractualists (especially John Rawls), utilitarians, and consequentialists, finding faults with the logic underlying both approaches (and their variants), and suggesting that what they add to Kant's contractualist formula might lead to a restatement in which Kantians could claim: (1) everyone ought to follow the principles whose universal acceptance everyone could rationally choose, or will; (2) there are some principles whose universal acceptance would make things go best; (3) everyone could rationally will that everyone accepts these principles; (4) these are the only principles whose universal acceptance everyone could rationally will, and thus (5) these are the principles that everyone ought to follow (Ibid., p. 294).

Parfit then explains what can allow deontology, contractualism, and consequentialism to co-exist without the assumed deep disagreements that many believe separate them:

> Of our reasons for doubting that there are moral truths, one of the strongest is provided by some kinds of moral disagreement. Most moral disagreements do not count strongly against the belief that there are moral truths, since these disagreements depend on different people's having conflicting empirical or religious beliefs, or on their having conflicting interests, or on their using different concepts, or these disagreements are about borderline cases, or they depend on the false assumption that all questions must have answers, or precise answers. But some disagreements are not of these kinds. These disagreements are deepest when we are considering, not the wrongness of particular acts, but the nature of morality and moral reasoning, and what is implied by different views about these questions. If we and others hold conflicting views, and we have no reason to believe that *we* are the people who are more likely to be right, that should at least make us doubt our view. It may also give us reasons to doubt that any of us could be right.
>
> *(Parfit, 2011, p. 304)*

Parfit then concludes that there are no deep disagreements: "These people are climbing the same mountain on different sides" (Ibid.).

Discussion Questions

1 Do people have an innate sense of right and wrong, as several of these theorists argue? If so, where would that sense come from?

2 Can right and wrong be defined in advance, or is it a matter of the consequences of choice? What are the results for justice using these two approaches?

3 What are the virtues that people should possess if they are to act ethically?

4 When it comes to deciding between right and wrong, what difference does it make, if any, that a person is male or female, black or white, famous or unknown? Does it matter? Should it matter?

5 Is Parfit correct in claiming that different approaches to ethics are efforts to reach the same right decisions, only using different approaches to arrive?

Notes

1 Robert saw this for himself in Eastern Nepal when conducting research for a local hospital. He spent time living near a Brahmin man who cared for a local disabled Dalit man and paid the expenses for his only daughter to attend university in Kathmandu.

2 The radio broadcaster Hans Fritzsche was acquitted for his dissemination of information and propaganda, since it could not be demonstrated that he had originated any of the materials broadcast and since the media were under tight control by Goebbel's Ministry of Propaganda (Goebbels himself committed suicide in Hitler's bunker on April 30, 1945). Julius Streicher, however, who was editor-in-chief of the anti-Semitic paper *Der Stuermer*, was convicted and hanged. These were the only two media figures tried at Nuremberg.

3 Parfit does not wholly accept Kant's objection to using people as mere means to an end, arguing that doing so may, in some cases, actually result in a positive outcome for the other and thus could not be considered wrong (see Parfit, 2011, pp. 177–188).

4 This discussion of contractual theory is a condensation of the entry for "Social contract theory" in the *Internet Encyclopedia of Philosophy* (Friend, 2004).

3

Philosophical Perspectives on Ethical Decision-Making: The Collectivist Traditions

Introduction

Societies where collectivist ethics are more prevalent than in the industrialized West may appear to have an easier task in achieving socially responsible media practices. But these societies have their own problems to solve, from tribal warfare and the exclusion of indigenous peoples in thinking about the collective, to language fragmentation, religious conflict, authoritarianism, and massive populations whose very existence can sometimes make life seem cheap. Protections afforded to all through the protection of one may not have much purchase in such situations. While elevation of the individual can often seem to denigrate group identity and social responsibility, so can collectivist notions that fail to recognize the oppressive weight of the majority and the exclusion of the other.

The collectivist traditions do not strip responsibility for ethical decisions away from the media workers who practice within them. However, they do change the dynamic of these choices. Instead of individuals being solely responsible for the choices they make, the collectivist traditions spread responsibility across the community that adopts and maintains the values that individuals within them are expected to exhibit. If unethical choices are made by these individuals on the basis of the collectively enforced ethics, then the community itself is culpable and not merely the individual. Depending on the society this culpability may also taint larger groups, such as clans or tribes. An unethical decision is a community decision and thus betrays all, not merely the individual who, in the Western mind, would be individually blamed. So there is much potential in such cases for the "collective guilt" that Karl Jaspers lectured about – and that was discussed in Chapter 2 – to be manifest.

Communitarian Ethics

Alasdair MacIntyre spent a great deal of time in his 1981 book, *After Virtue* (now in its third edition, 2008), providing a detailed examination and objection to the present status of ethics. He objected both to the notion that there are ethical universals that apply to all societies without exception and to the development of a modern sense of ethics he said was driven by "emotivism," a "doctrine that all evaluative judgments and more specifically all moral judgments are *nothing* but expressions of preference, expressions of attitude or feeling, insofar as they are moral or evaluative in character" (MacIntyre, 2008, p. 12).

MacIntyre's analysis has led to the application of communitarian ethics, in which each individual community – based on tribe, clan, nation, or linguistic group – would interpret its own needs and apply ethical virtues within its own context. MacIntyre admired Aristotle, and in this sense, he provided a more

World Media Ethics: Cases and Commentary, First Edition. Robert S. Fortner and P. Mark Fackler.
© 2018 John Wiley & Sons, Inc. Published 2018 by John Wiley & Sons, Inc.

nuanced and recent application of virtue ethics. Virtues, however, can differ from one community to another, for what matters is not how well they accord with a sense of universals but rather how well they function as a moral consensus within that society, that allows it – as a whole – to flourish.

Charles Taylor (1989) explained why MacIntyre's conclusion justified communitarianism as an ethical perspective. Taylor was concerned about the relationship of morality, language, and identity. He argued that people could only understand their identity within a language community that established the terms of reference (or framework as Taylor called it) within which people could construct their personhood. "My identity is defined by the commitments and identifications which provide the frame or horizon within which I can try to determine from case to case what is good, or valuable, or what ought to be done, or what I endorse or oppose. In other words, it is the horizon within which I am capable of making a stand" (Ibid., p. 27). "To know who you are is to be oriented in moral space" (Ibid., p. 28), and the dimensions of this space are determined by one's community – not by universal principles. "One is a self only among other selves. A self can never be described without reference to those who surround it" (Ibid., p. 35). The selves that surround us and with whom we have discourse constitute, Taylor wrote, a web of interlocution (Ibid., p. 36). Even those who had prophesied against their own community (as Old Testament prophets had often done) did so (took a heroic stance) within the foundational discursive environment of that community that allowed others to understand the condemnation: "Taking the heroic stance doesn't allow one to leap out of the human condition, and it remains true that one can elaborate one's new language only through conversation in a broad sense, that is, through some kind of interchange with others with whom one has some common understanding about what is at stake in the enterprise" (Ibid., p. 37).

Clifford Christians, writing the introduction of *Ethics for Public Communication* (Christians, 2012, p. ix), says that communitarianism "stands for a theory of persons and goodness that relocates your center from self to the space between selves, from me to us, from your mind as the focus of identity and being to the relationships you have with others as the centerpiece. Communitarians believe that you have to look away from yourself to understand yourself. Good comes through relationships, not from assertions or moral claims conceived or adopted by your own persona."

Christians goes on to explain (Ibid., p. xiv) that abandoning the Western ethical canon meant also jettisoning a monocultural perspective. To replace it was a more "multicultural, gender inclusive, and transnational" system – communitarianism – that would acknowledge the power embedded in the everyday lives and activities of people in relationship. It would reimagine the role and distribution of power within communities, provide superior attention to the role of communication in binding and maintaining relationships (shades of John Dewey and Robert Park), and hold media organizations accountable both to universal values and to particularist community norms. Although Christians continued to acknowledge the role of Enlightenment commitments (Ibid., p. xv), he also acknowledged the ethical approaches that emerge from other non-Western traditions and that have powerful claims to make in the realm of ethics. Several of these will be discussed in this chapter.

Buddhist/Shinto Ethics

"The morality found in all the precepts [of Buddhism] can be summarized in three simple principles: 'To avoid evil; to do good; to purify the mind.' This is the advice given by all the Buddhas" (Thera, n.d., n.p.). What the Buddha offered people who followed the ethical system proposed was similar to what Aristotle proposed: happiness (de Silva, 1993, p. 60). The claim was that "a life of pure pleasure by its inner nature ends up in boredom and dissonance, and interferes with the healthy functioning of family and community life. The Buddha condemned pure hedonism on psychological and ethical grounds.

The Buddha was also critical of some materialists who did not believe in an afterlife and thus supported a hedonistic lifestyle without any moral values" (Ibid.).

The Buddha argued that every human action had a result, and every action had a cause. Causes that were rooted in such things as greed, hatred, or delusion would result in bad actions – and thus bad results – while those that emerged from liberality, compassion, or wisdom would result in good actions – and, again, good results (Ibid., p. 61). This, of course, we would refer to as motive – what compelled or encouraged a particular action. The Buddha did not limit evaluation of actions merely to motive, however, but included the way the act had to be performed, "the manner in which it is done and the consequences," as well: "In this sense this is a consequentialist or a teleological ethics" (Ibid., pp. 61–62). De Silva continues his examination of Buddhist ethics with this explanation: "Buddhism may be described as a consequentialist ethic embodying the ideal of ultimate happiness for the individual, as well as a social ethic with the utilitarian stance concerned with the material and spiritual well-being of mankind. In keeping with this stance, Buddhism also has a strong altruistic component, specially embodied in the four sublime virtues of lovingkindness, compassion, sympathetic joy and equanimity" (Ibid., p. 62).

There are different schools of Buddhism, including Theravada, Mahayana, and Vajrayana. The basic precepts of Buddhism require that adherents refrain from (1) destroying living creatures, (2) theft, (3) sexual misconduct, (4) incorrect speech, and (5) taking alcoholic drinks and drugs that lead to carelessness ("Western and Asian Ethics: Introduction," n.d., p. 7). In Theravada Buddhism, on both Buddhist Sabbath and festival days, priests remind the laity that they are to refrain from three additional acts: (1) eating after noon, (2) dancing, singing, music, entertainments, wearing garlands, using perfumes, and beautifying the body with cosmetics, and (3) lying on a high or luxurious sleeping place (Ibid.). In addition to these "thou shalt nots," Buddhists are to practice positive virtues such as reverence, humility, contentment, gratitude, patience, and generosity. All of these flow from the four sublime virtues (Ibid., p. 8). "Morally speaking, Buddhist 'civil society' is based on the sense of 'civility' that human beings owed one another. That sense of 'universal indebtedness' is expressed in the formula that, in some conceivable past life, we are all related, such that 'every man is my father or brother; every woman my mother or sister.' For the care we once received in that life, we owe them all eternal gratitude" (Lai, 2002, p. 164).

Similar to Buddhist ethics are the ethics of Shintoism, a Japanese tradition. Sannō-ichijitsu Shinto is a cult, or denomination, of Buddhism so that "'the seeds of the Buddha's teaching never cease,' i.e., as a supportive tool of (Tendai) Buddhism" (Scheid, 2002, p. 300). But Shintoism became an ideological tool in the hands of political authority, and thus separated from Buddhism, although its beliefs – somewhat modified by association with Confucianism – were largely the same (Ibid., p. 302). "The Japanese characters used to write *Shinto* come from the Chinese based kanji: *shin/kami* (divinity), and *to/michi* (way). Hence, the word has come to mean the divine way, or more simply the way" (Teasdale, n.d., n.p.). As Teasdale explains: "Indigenous to Japan, Shinto arose in the eighth century. One school related Shinto to the religions of Buddhism and Confucianism. Shrines were constructed alongside Buddhist temples, and homage was paid to divine *kami* or spirits. The second school practiced Shinto through daily attitudes and creeds. This division of Shinto can easily be broken into three categories: ethics, etiquette, and aesthetics. While Shinto as a strict religious practice has substantially dwindled, the attitude based Shinto continues to be found at the root of Japanese culture" (Ibid.). Like Buddhism, Shinto ethics emphasizes an individual's responsibility to both heaven and the community. A person who carries out these responsibilities is said to have a "beautiful heart" (Ibid.).

In terms of actual ethical behavioral guidelines, however, there are no formal commands. As Woodard (1962, p. ix) puts it, "there are very few people, Japanese or foreign, who understand Shinto thoroughly and are able to explain it in detail. . . . [T]here are many things which cannot be clearly explained because in some areas there is still no certain knowledge."

What does exist are individual points of view. "Except for the relatively short three-quarters of a century of regimentation after the Meiji Restoration, when there was an artificial, government-created authoritative interpretation of Shinto, there has not been any large body of interpretation that is generally accepted" (Ibid.). Part of the reason for this is that Shinto has no founder or prophet, and no scared scriptures (Ono, 1962, p. 3).

These collectivist positions suggest that civility and moderation are ideals that should govern people's behavior. Such ideals suggest that news reports that dwell on the details of violent crime would be considered unethical, or that the violence contained in various forms of entertainment should be considered out of bounds as it would violate the idea of moderation. Civility, too, would not result from either violence (physical or verbal), threats, coarse language, or any other forms of mistreatment of either individuals or fictional characters. Some of the mystical martial arts films from Asia may express aspects of these ethical traditions, even if inconsistently.

Confucian Ethics

Chinese ethics are the result of several strands of thinking, including the thought of Confucius and ideas adopted from Buddhist ethics (Hsieh and Hsieh, 2010, p. 248). Perhaps one of the greatest differences between Confucian ethics and Western ethics concerns the issue of individual rights. Unlike Western philosophies, which are founded on the idea of equal enforcement of individual rights – without favor or prejudice – Confucianism "does not recognize or place central importance on rights" (Ihara, 2004, p. 22). But the lack of attention to rights in Confucianism does not mean, Craig K. Ihara argues, that it cares little for the concept of human dignity. However, China has a "rich and distinctive" philosophical heritage based in Confucianism so, while Confucianism does not vest the dignity of persons in their individual rights, it does champion their intrinsic value as human beings, irrespective of the rights they may or may not have (Hansen, 1983, p. 73; Ihara, 2004, p. 25). David B. Wong refers to this commitment as "community-centered moralities" as opposed to "virtue-centered moralities" (Wong, 2004, p. 33). The advantage of this approach, as Seung-hwan Lee has put it, is that "the good of the community always precedes individual good" (quoted by Wong, 2004, p. 34). In this respect, Chenyang Li (2002) argues, there are similarities between the "jen ethics" of Confucianism and the care ethics of feminism.

Confucian ethics is based on aphorisms contained in *The Analects*, collected dialogues and exchanges remembered by his disciples (similar to what we know of Socrates' dialogues reported by Plato). *The Analects* contain "no explicitly prescriptive *ought*-statements. For Confucius the basic role of all language is to guide our acts (Hansen, 1983, p. 70). The way to learn how to live in families and societies, and thus how to act appropriately toward others, was to study the classics of Chinese literature that contained right behavior. From such study people would learn the various roles they would be called upon to play in society – they would then know how to play such roles appropriately. People would improve their behavior, too, as they interpreted the instructions contained in the literature and applied it, thus learning and practicing together (Ibid., p. 71). Confucius "bases his explicit normative system on roles. He does not assign a normative value to persons apart from their social relationships. All your duties are duties of your station towards other socially described persons or things. . . . This leads Confucianism to characterize itself as a system of 'partial' or 'graded' love. We deal with people qua 'mother,' 'neighbor,' 'mentor,' 'daughter'. Contrast this with the Kantian respect for individuals as bare persons or agents" (Ibid., p. 72). Wei-Ming Tu, writing about the five relationships in Confucian humanism, says that people's moral education was a function of self-cultivation within communal acts undertaken within primary human relationships of family, community, state, and world. Without self-cultivation within these communal relationships a person could become "humane or fully human" (Tu, 1998, p. 121).

All five of the relationships discussed (including a person's relationship with the self) were to function according to "three bonds," hierarchies of rulers over ministers, fathers over sons, and husbands over wives. "Obviously, the Three Bonds, based on dominance/subservience, underscore the hierarchical relationship as an inviolable principle for maintaining social order. The primary concern is not the well-being of the individual persons involved in these dyadic relationships, but the particular pattern of social stability which results from these rigidly prescribed rules of conduct" (Ibid., pp. 122–123). Although "virtue takes precedence over rank and age" in the Confucian order of things (Ibid., p. 128), putting emphasis on age as supreme in the village was "a deliberate attempt to build an ethic on a biological reality. The reason that 'filial piety' (*Hsiao/xiao*) and brotherly love (*t'i/ti*) are considered roots (*pen/ben*) for realizing full humanity is partly due to the Confucian belief that moral self-cultivation begins with the recognition that biological bondage provides an authentic opportunity for personal realization" (Ibid.).

Jen ethics in the Confucian scheme "means benevolence, humanity, mercy, charity, magnanimity, and kindness. To Chinese people, Jen is directed toward people and is the ethical principle by which the individual rightfully builds relationships. . . . It also includes concepts of philanthropy, love, love and justice, and benevolence and generosity" (Hsieh and Hsieh, 2010, p. 255). Although many of these terms are used as virtues in Aristotelian ethics, in the Confucian system they are social virtues learned within the contexts of family, community, and relationship with others while taking on and perfecting behavior within assigned roles.

Feminist Ethics

Feminist ethics developed from the work of educational psychologist Carol Gilligan. She contrasted the different ways male and female adolescents responded to ethical issues, and from her observations developed the contrast between what she termed "justice ethics" and "care ethics." She argued that the trajectory of Western philosophy was confined to justice ethics, which ignored the different reality of women's lives. The same was true, she said (Gilligan, 1982/1993, p. 2) of psychological theorists, who implicitly adopted the "male life as a norm, [and] tried to fashion women out of a masculine cloth. . . . In the life cycle, as in the Garden of Eden, the woman has been the deviant." The significance of psychological development, in her view (Ibid., p. 4), was that "for boys and men, separation and individuation are critically tied to gender identity," while this was not the case for girls and women. She concluded: "Since masculinity is defined through separation while femininity is defined through attachment, male gender identity is threatened by intimacy while female gender identity is threatened by separation. Thus males tend to have difficulty with relationships, while females tend to have problems with individuation" (Ibid.).

The significance of the differences originally claimed by Gilligan was put in a more philosophical vein by Virginia Held (2006). She introduced her book by writing that the "ethics of care is a distinct moral theory or approach to moral theorizing, not a concern that can be added to or included within other more established approaches, such as those of Kantian moral theory, utilitarianism, or virtue ethics. The latter is the more controversial claim, since there are similarities between the ethics of care and virtue ethics. But in its focus on relationships rather than on the dispositions of individuals, the ethics of care is, I argue, distinct" (Ibid., pp. 3–4). And Margaret Walker (2007, p. 57) concluded that feminist critiques of ethics were centered on gender and other biases implicit in the "authoritative representations of morality in canonical and contemporary works of the Western tradition of philosophy." She went on:

> A great deal of feminist criticism alleges gender bias in the *content* of such theories. Pre-occupation with equality and autonomy, uniformity and impartiality, rules and reciprocity fits voluntary bargaining relations of nonintimate equals, or contractual and institutional relations among peers in contexts of impersonal or public interaction. . . . It slights relations of inter-dependence centered on bonds of affection and loyalty whose specific histories set varying terms of obligation and responsibility. It obscures the particularity of moral actors and relations by emphasizing universality, sameness, and repeatability, excluding or regimenting emotional experience. Ignoring or slighting continuing relationships of intimacy and care, these views feature abstract problem solving to the neglect of responsive attention to actual others.
>
> *(Walker, 2007, p. 58)*

Hindu Ethics

Hindu ethics, according to Roy W. Perrett (1998, p. 2) is a consequentialist system. In that respect it is most like utilitarianism. Hindu ethics, explains Perrett, includes "a set of first-order moral precepts, a consequentialist theory of the right, and a theory of the good." These ethics developed along with Indian culture, however, and were not merely philosophically or intellectually developed, but interwoven with the "social and political structures forged over a vast period of time" (Bilimoria, 1993, p. 43). Thus, *dharma*, or "duty," has many different meanings, including righteousness, truth, right, justice, morality, and so forth, and is understood within the "social and moral regulations" that apply for each of the different groups comprising the Hindu social system, as well as providing some universal duties that apply to all (Ibid., p. 46). In addition Hindu thought provides four cardinal virtues: non-injury, giving, truthfulness, and non-attached action (Hindery, 1996, p. 27). There were also four cardinal vices: injury to any sentient being, too much ego, delusion – "thinking of this world as finally real instead of illusory" – and lack of self-restraint or application (Ibid.).

Because there is no single sacred text in Hindu thought, and those that are the oldest scripts are actually poems (providing the earliest Vedic perspectives on behavior), Hindu ethics has been open to many interpretations (see Pappu, 2004, p. 155). This is further complicated by the assumptions within Hinduism that "class is of divine origin or part of the very nature of the cosmos" (Hindery, 1996, p. 42). "The linkage of *dharma* and *karma* (action-effect) has the following consequences: there are no 'accidents of births' determining social inequities; mobility within one lifetime is excluded; one has one's *dharma*, both as endowment and as a social role" (Bilimoria, 1993, p. 47). The result of such perspectives – which is the basis of the caste system within Hindu thought – are "foundations for racial prejudice . . . sexual differentiation and sexual slavery, if not slavery in general" (Hindery, 1996, p. 42). As Pappu (2004, p. 156) puts it, Hindu ethicists distinguish between "(1) *sadharana* dharmas, or duties pertaining to persons-qua-persons, without reference to their station in life or their particular circumstances, and *vishesha* dharmas or relative duties, that is, duties pertaining to one's station in life and life stations." *Sadharana* dharmas include "duties such as nonviolence (ahimsa) and concern for the welfare of all creatures" (Ibid.). Hindu ethics should be understood, then, as "a set of norms, ideals, and a way of life developed by the Hindus. Some of these norms are universal and applicable to all human beings, but other norms are applicable only to followers of Hinduism" (Ibid., p. 157).

The universal ethical *dharmas* of Hinduism emerge from "the doctrine of *puhusharthas*, or 'human aims,' around which the Hindu system of values revolves" (Ibid., p. 156). There are four puhusharthas: wealth and power, desire (especially sexual desire), morality and virtue, and liberation. "[C]onceptions of good and right should be discussed in Hinduism in the context of their conception of the good life, because good life is wider than morally good life. Therefore, puhusharthas enunciated in the Hindu ethics examine 'the good' and the 'good life,' of which dharma is the moral good and moral rightness" (Ibid., p. 158). Hinduism, however, does not provide prescriptions concerning what is or is not allowed as behavior to achieve these goods. They are actually reasons to explain human actions in the effort to achieve a good life.

The ultimate puhushartha is *moksha*, or liberation. "As a transcendental good, moksha is variously conceived as merging oneself with brahman (the absolute), realizing one's self, attaining heaven, and so on. In its empirical dimension, moksha implies *liberation from* the very desires for wealth and power that human beings seek" (Ibid., p. 159). The ethical person, then, is one who seeks a way to renounce wealth, power, and desire, or what we may call self-gratification.

Other than feminism, the collectivist ethical traditions outlined above are Asian in origin. But Asia is not the only source of such perspectives. Africa, too, has contributed several collectivist perspectives that have been practiced for centuries on the continent. They are not as well articulated as those in Asia because they have been carried, and applied, in cultures dependent on oral tradition. One that does have a written history is *Ma'at*, a "fundamental, pervasive and enduring element in ancient Egyptian civilization and an inclusive and defining cultural category" (Karenga, 2004, p. 5). Others include the Zulu concept of *ubuntu*, the Yoruba notion of *iwa*, the Dinka idea of *cieng*, and the idea of *palaver*. We will examine these below.

Ma'at

Ma'at has been defined in many different ways, depending on the focus of the particular scholar, but the many interpretations coalesce around the idea of an "interrelated order of rightness, including the divine, natural and social" (Karenga, 2004, p. 7). It is the "foundation and order of the world" (Ibid., p. 6). It was present at the creation of the world and personifies order, rightness, truth, and justice, among other things (Ibid., p. 8).

Herodotus named the Kemetic people as the most religious people in the world. Ma'at was the moral ideal of Kemetic society (meta-religion.com). It was also the name of the God worshipped in many forms within the society. Individuals within the society exercised conscience within relationship with others, such that what one thought of oneself was based substantially on evaluation of one's behavior by significant others, making Kemet essentially a communitarian society (Ibid., p. 8). What was required of people was that they be in harmony with the divine or created order (similar to Hinduism). The idea of Ma'at was that it united God, society, nature, and universe (Ibid., p. 9). By uniting these four elements, peace and harmony could be achieved. "Ethically this has meaning in that it becomes the task of king and members of society to uphold this Maat-grounded world, which is essentially good, and to restore and recreate it constantly. It is in this context that Maat expresses itself as an ongoing ethical project" (Ibid., p. 10). Thus the essential meaning of Ma'at is *"rightness in the spiritual and moral sense in three realms: the Divine, the natural and the social. In its expansive sense, Maat is an interrelated order of rightness which requires and is the result of right relations with and right behavior towards the Divine, nature and other humans.* As moral thought and practice, *Maat is a way of rightness* defined especially by the practice of the Seven Cardinal Virtues of truth, justice, propriety, harmony, balance, reciprocity and order. Finally, as a foundation and framework for the moral ideal and its practice, *Maat is the constantly achieved condition of and requirements for the ideal world, society, and person*" (Ibid.; italics in original).

Ubuntu

The idea of ubuntu is "enshrined in the Zulu maxim *umuntu ngumuntu ngabantu*, i.e. 'a person is a person through other persons'" (quoted by Louw, 1998, n.p.).[1] It describes human beings as achieving their human-ness in relationship rather than as individuals. It is a concept that had application in southern Africa among many tribes, including the Shona, Xhosa, and Zulu. "Ubuntu directly contradicts the Cartesian conception of individuality in terms of which the individual or self can be conceived without thereby necessarily conceiving the other. The Cartesian individual exists prior to, or separately and independently from, the rest of the community or society. The rest of society is nothing but an added extra to a pre-existent and self-sufficient being" (Ibid.; see also Christians, 2004).

Ubuntu is "essentially an African philosophy of life, which reflects the African approach and worldview when considering cultural, social and political aspects of life" (Justice Mokgoro, paraphrased by Olinger, Britz, and Olivier, 2005, p. 4). Under this philosophy all human beings are equal, sharing a basic brotherhood and having the right to life. Ubuntu assumes that ultimate meaning and purpose will be found not by individuals seeking their own way, but by people in relationship acting within communities. There is no self-centeredness, but other-centeredness (see Ibid., p. 5). The core values of ubuntu include *communalism* ("the interests of the individual are subordinate to the group"), which, in turn, includes collective solidarity ("individuals will focus their interests, activities, and loyalties of their own accord, in line with the group's cause and well-being"), and collective thinking ("individual members cannot imagine ordering their lives individualistically without the consent of family, clan or tribe"), *interdependence* ("man exists in a social cluster and has an interpersonal nature, a nature dependent on others to help define and distinguish"), *humanness* ("warmth, tolerance, understanding, peace, humanity"), *caring* ("empathy, sympathy, helpfulness, charity, friendliness"), *sharing* ("unconditional giving, redistribution, open-handedness"), *respect* ("commitment, dignity, obedience, order"), and *compassion* ("love, cohesion, informality, forgiveness, spontaneity") (Ibid., pp. 6–7). Many of these aspects of ubuntu would mirror those of feminist ethics in the West.

Ubuntu is tied to the very idea of people's personal identities, but these identities are seen as grounded in community, indeed inseparable from it. "Desmond Tutu in an interview remarked, 'In our understanding, when someone doesn't forgive, we say that person does not have *ubuntu*. That is to say he is not really human.' Not to have *ubuntu* – love, forgiveness, generosity – . . . , then, is viewed as a moral deficiency. This is true, in part, because of the context of community in South Africa and the qualities of moral character that flow from this more communitarian way of being" (Bell, 2002, p. 89).

Iwa

Iwa is a Yoruba concept and has to do with ethical behavior and approved conduct. Ethics "relates to the norms that govern human behavior, on the one hand, and the behavior of the supernatural beings in their relationship with humans, on the other. As the above suggests, it is not only humans that have to be ethical: the gods do, too. The term 'iwa' (moral character) is attached in Yoruba philosophical discourse to a variety of other terms, all of which refer to ethical behavior and conduct" (Bewaji, 2006, p. 399). Those who do not act as they ought, or are expected to, are said to have a moral blemish (*abuku*). "Human beings with moral blemishes are deformed by the blemish, and will, for instance, be shy, as a consequence, to raise their voice in public to participate in the discussion of community affairs. In fact, to have such a blemish is to be unworthy of communion with one's peers or of holding a responsible office in the community" (Ibid., p. 400).

The significance of this exclusion (or, we might say, "excommunication") can be seen in the fact that Yoruba culture is largely oral. Exclusion is thus a statement about a person's honesty and reliability in a situation where the primary source of information is other people. "Knowledge of another person's moral character is said to be obtained, most reliably, from observing (firsthand) their behavior (*isesi*). And in Yoruba discourse behavior conventionally extends to 'what they say' and 'what they do,' which also pretty much corresponds to the standard Western notions of verbal and non-verbal behavior. . . . [T]he point is that a person's verbal and non-verbal behavior are construed as firsthand evidence (*imo*) of their moral character" (Hallen, 2004, p. 301).

Cieng

"*Cieng* places emphasis on such human values as dignity, integrity, honor, and respect for self and others, loyalty and piety, compassion and generosity, and unity and harmony . . . Good *cieng* is opposed to coercion and violence, for solidarity, harmony, and mutual cooperation are more fittingly achieved voluntarily and by persuasion" (Francis M. Deng quoted in Twining, 2007). "At the core of *cieng* are the ideals of human relations, family and community, dignity and integrity, honor and respect, loyalty and piety and the power of the word. *Cieng* is opposed to coercion, and, instead encourages persuasion and mutual cooperation" (Deng, 2007). It is so significant within the Dinka cultural tradition that it "has the sanctity of a moral order not only inherited from the ancestors, who had in turn received it from God, but is fortified and policed by them. Failure to adhere to its principles is not only disapproved of as antisocial, but more importantly, as a violation of the moral code that may invite a spiritual curse, illness and even death depending on the gravity of the violation. Conversely, a distinguished adherence to the ideals of *cieng* is expected to receive material and spiritual rewards" (Ibid.).[2]

"The anthropologist Godfrey Lienhardt wrote: 'The Dinka ... have notions ... of what their society ought, ideally, to be like. They have a word, *cieng baai* (*baai* meaning family, village, tribe or country), which used as a verb has the sense of "to look after" or "to order," and in its noun form means "the custom" or "the rule."' Father Nebel, one of the earliest Catholic missionaries to work among the Dinka, translated morals as 'good *cieng*' and benefactor as a man who knows and acts in accordance with *cieng*" (quoted by Deng, 1998). Every person in Dinka society has a "deep sense of worth and dignity." Also, "While the Western value system is largely premised on property relations, that of the Dinka is based on kinship, property and welfare ties that complement this shared value system. To Dinka youth, cattlewealth has an aesthetic significance far above its material value. When a man comes of age in his late teens and is initiated into adulthood through the age-set system, he becomes known as *adheng* (gentleman) and his virtue is *dheeng* (dignity)" (Ibid.).[3]

Another Sudanese tribe, the Nuer, also use the word *cieng*. Its basic meaning is "village." "If you ask a Lou man what is his *cieng* you are asking him where he lives, what is his village, or district. Suppose that he replies that his *cieng* is *cieng* Pual. You can then ask him what his *cieng* forms part of, and he will tell you that it is a part of *cieng* Leng, giving the name of a tertiary tribal section. If you continue to interrogate him he will inform you that *cieng* Leng is part of *cieng* Gaatbal, a secondary tribal section, and that *cieng* Gaatbal is a division of the Gun primary section of the Lou tribe" (Evans-Pritchard, 1940, pp. 204–205). Although the Dinka and the Nuer are both large tribes in southern Sudan, their use of this term is clearly different – although related. The Nuer do not attach the same ethical significance to the term as the Dinka.

Palaver

"The village palaver forms a foundation stone of African civil society and is a very interesting form of local democracy. The very nature of village life yields many such critical dialogues" (Bell, 2002, p. 112). These dialogues might concern property disputes (which would involve the elders) or a community crisis or illness (which might result in a call to a diviner, prophetess, or healer for explanations to the council).

> The village palaver or council model in many parts of Africa is a model of free discourse for the purpose of making good judgments and for doing justice for individuals and the community. These narrative situations force dialogue and give rise to human reflection, and they are far from uncritical. Each dialogical situation has earmarks of the Socratic enterprise; each is formative of the values characteristic of that community; each reflects the existential texture of human life; each dialectically serves to move a community from injustice to justice, from wrong to right, from brokenness to wholeness, from ignorance to truth. As each community revaluates its life in terms of new external factors, it can critically evolve its traditions to meet modernity.
>
> *(Bell, 2002, p. 113)*

The idea of the palaver suggests that the wisdom needed to solve problems, including ethical problems, is collective, not individual. The palaver calls for critical and reflective thought where all members of the community question themselves and their motives for the positions taken in disputes, proposing solutions to problems, or arguing for particular approaches in ethically charged matters. The approach taken is one that is "sanctioned by the ancestors" (Ibid., p. 116). Leaders, or Nzonzi, handle the language used in the palaver, assuring "that it does not degenerate into violent antagonism" (Ibid.). Bell describes the Nzonzi as akin to Socratic midwives, "guiding the palaver to just and wise conclusions. . . . The palaver clearly reflects a philosophical situation – it reflects a real critical effort on the part of its participants to resolve its common dilemmas. Furthermore, like the Ashanti, consensual model of community governance, the village palaver in central Africa is an exceptionally democratic form of local governance. In the palaver can be found a rich source for philosophical reflection in the African context that critics of orality, like Hountondji, underplay and at times scorn even though they lay claim to a form of philosophical reflection of a Socratic nature. These are more than just 'philosophical fragments from our oral tradition.' They are the self-expressed forms of life of Africans; they are embedded forms of rational discourse that democratically order their lives" (Ibid.).

Essentially the palaver is "open, communal discourse. Therefore African ethics is essentially communitarian, unlike Western ethics, which tends to be rationalistic and discursive, or Christian/Catholic ethics, which is based largely on natural law. Recognition of relatedness is important for proper appreciation of how Africans make moral judgments. 'African ethics . . . is concerned with the visible community for the discernment and laying down of norms and for ethical conduct as a whole.' This sense of relatedness goes beyond the concrete visible community to embrace the dead as well. . . . Black Africa, in principle and in fact, rejects the Cartesian *cogito ergo sum* in favor of *cognatus sum, ergo summus* (I am known, therefore we are) as decisive for moral thinking" (Odozor,

2008, quoting Benezet Bujo). Palaver ethics is consensual, denies the right to anyone to impose any particular set of virtues on others as culturally conditioned, and insists that the local culture must be decisive in determining right courses of action.

Although all these collectivist approaches to ethics aim to preserve communities and assure the continuity of applying their values when threats arise, some conflicts make such commitments quite difficult. How should they approach and determine positive results – such as in the following situation?

Case 3.1: Western Reportage of African Conflict

In July 2014 Nigeria's Ambassador to the United States, Adebowale Adefuye, testified before the U.S. Congress about the security of his country in the wake of the kidnapping by Boko Haram of several hundred Chibok girls. The kidnapping had ignited protests both in Nigeria and around the world, the United States had sent intelligence and logistical support to the Nigerian army, and Michelle Obama had become involved in a Twitter campaign asking for the return of the girls. Nigeria had increasingly been defined by the Western media as unsafe. In his testimony Adefuye claimed that Western media were misleading the world "with false and unfair reports about the security situation in Nigeria," and "blowing the situation out of proportion." He continued that "Nigeria believed in the freedom of the press, [but] that this did not mean that the western media should hide under the indulgence to create an atmosphere that was making the entire world believe that Nigeria was totally unsafe. 'All the reports from the foreign media are very untrue and unfair to the Nigerian government, and, for this reason, I challenge everybody here to go to Nigeria and you will discover that the situation is not as bad as portrayed by the international media organizations'" (Oladeji, 2014). As mentioned, the United States did send intelligence support to Nigeria to assist its government in finding the girls, and various reports followed that contradicted one another, reporting the girls' situation and continuing threats to the community where the girls had lived. Five months later none of them had been rescued. Even two years later many of these girls had still not been found, although the Nigerian government claimed that Boko Haram was no longer a threat.

Commentary on Case 3.1

For much of the world the Western press plays a disproportionate role in defining the reality of distant events, and when it comes to reporting on the developing world it has long been accused by the academic community of only being interested in "coups and earthquakes." This testimony called out the Western press for its sensationalism and lack of veracity in reporting about a potentially lethal situation for the kidnapped girls and for generalizing the lack of adequate security in one part of Nigeria to the whole country. This raises several issues. First, given its dominant role in defining reality for people about distant events, does the Western press thereby have a greater responsibility than the local press in such situations? Second, how should the idea of fairness be applied when there are so many different interests involved (the Nigerian government and military, the U.S. military and intelligence community, the girls who were kidnapped, Boko Haram itself, the First Lady, etc.)? Is it possible to provide a socially responsible, balanced, and fair account of such events "in a context which gives them meaning" when information is fragmentary, conflicting, and distant without portraying some party or parties unfairly, given limitations of space and time for such reports? And which perspective on ethics (collectivist or individualist) is likely to be most helpful in evaluating such situations? Should only African perspectives apply to Africa, Asian ones to Asia, Western to the West?

(We return to this case in a different context in Chapter 4 – see Case 4.2c.)

Differences in Religious Ethical Perspectives

We have dealt with some religiously based ethical perspectives earlier in this chapter, but there are two others that are not only significant but also seen as in conflict: the Judeo-Christian and Islamic traditions. One characteristic that defines them is that they are monotheistic, rather than polytheistic or a-theistic. Let us now discuss these perspectives.

Judeo-Christian Perspectives

"No one definition of Jewish ethics is possible," writes Menachem Kellner (1993, p. 82), "since there are so many varieties of Judaism." Nevertheless it is fair to say that Judaism is concerned with ethics and the treatment of the other, although there is no biblical Hebrew word for "ethics" (Ibid., p. 84). Joseph Telushkin (2006, p. 1) goes so far as to say that "God's central demand of human beings is to act ethically." Kellner (1993, p. 84) remarks that "one of the basic contributions of Judaism to the Western religious tradition [is] that one worships God through decent, humane, and moral relations with one's fellows . . . In other words, whatever morality might be, its basis is in God's will."

"Jewish ethics focuses upon how human beings can live out their lives in the awareness of their having been created in the image and likeness of God" (Sherwin, 1999, p. 1). Judaistic ethics are not fatalistic, but presume that humankind has moral volition. "For biblical religion, human action is not rooted in tragic necessity or predetermined fate, but in the free exercise of the God-given and God-like expression of the moral will" (Ibid., p. 3). In fact, in Jewish thought it is this moral choice that distinguishes human beings from animals (Ibid., p. 4).

The essence of Judaism has four components (Telushkin, 2006, p. 10). First, "what is hateful unto you, do not do to your neighbor." Second, this command is the whole Torah. Third, "all the rest is commentary." And fourth, all deserves to be studied, even should it take a lifetime. Telushkin goes on:

> The Rabbis understood the prophet Isaiah as seeking to discover the essence of Judaism. Thus, in an oft-quoted talmudic passage (Makkot 24a), the Rabbis conjecture that Isaiah condensed (or summarized) the Torah's 613 commandments into six principles of behavior:
>
> - practicing righteousness
> - speaking truthfully and fairly
> - spurning dishonest gain
> - refusing bribes
> - closing your ears to blood (this obscure working seems to refer either to not associating with anyone plotting violence, or avoiding any discussions that might lead to violence)
> - closing your eyes from seeing [that which might lead to] evil.
>
> According to Isaiah, a person who fulfills these six principles, "will dwell on high" (33:15–16); i.e., be rewarded by God. The Talmud follows this discussion with another passage which insists that Isaiah summarized the whole intent of Torah law into two principles:
>
> - Do justice (i.e., act fairly).
> - Perform acts of righteousness (alternatively "charity") (Isaiah 56:1).
>
> *(Telushkin, 2006, p. 16)*

Two other recent Jewish writers who have had much to say about the nature of the "other" are Martin Buber and Emmanuel Levinas. Buber (1986, p. 20) argued that all human beings can deal with others either as "things" – its, hes, shes – or as thous. "When Thou is spoken, the speaker has no *thing*; he has indeed nothing. But he takes his stand in relation." So in the I-It situation, man is in the world. He encounters things – houses, cars, work, and people –moving through his day. But in the I-Thou situation, man is in relationship – connection, intimacy. This could occur, Buber said, whether a person encountered a tree, another person, or a spiritual being (Ibid., pp. 22–23). It was not, then, a question of whether or not the other existed, but the way that humans encountered them and included them in their lives that mattered.

Levinas was concerned with the issues raised by encountering "the other." Each person in such an encounter is alien to the other. Even those who are intimates come together having experienced life and made meaning apart from the other and thus have a certain taint of alienation. The question was, given this everyday situation, how one could encounter the other without using him or her for one's own purposes: "How can I coexist with him and still leave his otherness intact?" (Wild, 1991, p. 13).

This can only be achieved by language: "This means that I must be ready to put my world into words, and to offer it to the other. There can be no free interchange without something to give. Responsible communication depends on an initial act of generosity, a giving of my world to him with all its dubious assumptions and arbitrary features" (Ibid., p. 14; see also Peperzak, 1993, p. 19). "The whole of my concrete – corporeal, sensible, kinetic, emotional, contemplative, striving – existence is determined by my orientation toward the 'other': I am demanded, disposed, obsessed, and inspired" (Ibid., p. 26). Levinas' focus is on the intersubjectivity of people encountering one another, not merely those with which we share an intimacy in love, but all others. "A general care for all human others whose face and word I cannot perceive personally" is imposed (Ibid., pp. 30–31).

In one widely read book on Christian ethics Paul Ramsey began by saying that "Biblical writers do not view ethics naturalistically as rooted in human nature or in the social environment, or abstractly in terms of some generalizations about human values. They view ethics theologically as rooted in the nature and activity of God" (Ramsey, 1950, p. 1). Thus, he argues, the three qualities of justice, righteousness, and mercy can never be legitimately separated (Ibid., p. 9) and their meaning is derived not from anything human beings devise to define them, but from "the measure of God's righteousness" (Ibid., p. 12).

The principle *par excellence* of Christian ethics, Ramsey writes, is to "discover the neighbor. Not that we should do to others as we would be done by, or merely love our neighbors as ourselves . . . but that we should love our brothers as Christ who laid down his life for his friends and for those predestined to be his disciples . . . or love our neighbors as Christ who, while men were yet sinners [separated from God] and his enemies, for their sakes emptied himself of all self-concern and himself did not grasp at being equal to God" (Ibid., p. 21). Such a statement moves beyond what has been called the "Golden Rule" to something greater and more profound – that ethics calls for people to go beyond what others do for them, to empty themselves for the sake of the other. Ronald Preston explains the difference this way: Citizens of the Kingdom of God should conduct themselves

> at the level of "natural" morality, for instance, [respecting] the Golden Rule, "Always treat others as you would like them to treat you" (Matthew 7:12), which is found in some form in other ethics, and which can be taken at different levels provided one is consistent between oneself and others. Some of Jesus' words appear to follow "natural" human judgements in offering rewards for good conduct and threatening penalties for bad . . . But the distinctive feature of Jesus' ethical teaching is the way it radicalizes common morality.
>
> *(Preston, 1993, p. 95)*

This radicalization includes such demands that there be no limit to forgiveness, that Christians love their enemies, that there be no restrictions on the care of neighbors, and that people have no anxiety over their material or physical situation, but rather trust in God to provide for their needs. "His ethics is very different from an everyday ethic of doing good turns to those who do good turns to you; that is to say an ethic of reciprocity" (Ibid.).

Dietrich Bonhoeffer – after beginning his book on ethics with the statement "The knowledge of good and evil seems to be the aim of all ethical reflection" – goes on to say that "the first task of Christian ethics is to invalidate this knowledge" (Bonhoeffer, 1955, p. 21). "In the knowledge of good and evil," he says, "man does not understand himself in the reality of the destiny appointed in his origin, but rather in his own possibilities, his possibility of being good or evil. He knows himself now as something apart from God, outside God. The knowledge of good and evil is therefore separation from God" (Ibid., pp. 21–22). Thinking that the knowledge of good and evil is the primary concern of ethics, for Bonhoeffer, was prideful, the extension of the hubris of the Garden of Eden (see Ibid., p. 23). What mattered was, rather, the knowledge of God and God's will.

Christian ethical thought has been central to many of the theories of ethics developed within Western culture, especially that of Kant and many humanists. The relationship is easy to see as Norman L. Geisler (2010, p. 15) explains Christian ethics as a "form of divine-command position. An ethical duty is something we ought to do. It is a divine prescription." Of course there have been many interpretations, or takes, on Christian ethics from various threads of Christianity (Catholic, Lutheran, Reformed, Anabaptist, Pentecostal, and so on), but the above should suffice for our purposes.

Islamic Perspectives

The word "Islam" in Arabic means surrender or submission and the religion of the same name is one of submission of one's own will to the will of God (Matthewes, 2010, p. 65). Like Christianity, Islamic ethics functions under a "divine-command" position. Muslims are to act, and to choose, according to the will of God (Hourani, 1985, p. 24; al-Attar, 2010, p. 12). They exercise reason to understand that will, choosing what is permitted (*halāl*) and avoiding what is forbidden (*harām*) (Ibid., p. 14). "Throughout its pages, the Qur'ān assumes human beings can discern God's claim on them by the use of 'reasoning' from signs and 'thinking' or 'reflection.' Muslims are urged to reflect and consider, on the assumption that reflection is a means to moral knowledge" (Reinhart, 2005, p. 246).

There is a tension, however, in Islamic ethics between the expectations of behavior by believers and actual instructions about how to do right (Ibid., p. 248). Reinhart explains: "the Qur'ān requires one to act well, and very occasionally specifies in some detail what good is. More often it simply exhorts the Muslim to do the good without further information. This created the expectation of detailed prescription without satisfying that expectation." Charles Matthewes (2010, p. 65) says that "there is a great danger of thinking of Islam as a totalizing system of doctrines; in fact it was historically quite adjustable to cultural contexts. It is deeply diverse, because the core of the tradition is fundamentally quite spare."

There is no "Golden Rule," for instance, in Islamic tradition. Since Muslims do accept the Torah, however, as an expression of God's revelation, such expectations, by extension, would be applicable to Muslims – as would Christ's injunctions for behavior based on his status as a prophet (see Ibid., p. 67). These expectations, however, are not included in the Koran itself. "Ethicists looking for a Golden Rule definition of the good, or a utilitarian definition, or indeed any definition at all will search in vain. Rather, the Qur'ān assumes that its hearers, certainly in the context of the 610–32 CE period of its revelation, would know the good from the not-good" (Reinhart, 2005, p. 248).

Muslims are expected, of course, to provide alms to the poor and to show their devotion to God through daily prayer and observance of Ramadan, among other requirements. The ethic of alms-giving is the equivalent of care expected of both Christians and Jews by their respective scriptures. All three monotheistic traditions also require attention be given to God – Jews through observance of the Sabbath and celebration of the Passover (among others) and Christians through the sacraments (baptism, Eucharist, and so on) and attention to Christ's birth, passion, and death during Lent leading to Easter.

In the Islamic ethical tradition there is a good deal of overlap between legal and ethical expectations. But there are differences in the approaches taken to this overlap by Islamic scholars. Some (Mu'tazilites) argue that human beings have an innate ability to know right from wrong and can thus be held accountable by God for their actions (Sachedina, 2005, p. 255). Their focus as representatives of the rationalist camp of Islamic philosophers was on "justice" (Ibid., p. 6). But other groups (Ash'arites) reject this inherent ability and say that knowing right from wrong is a simple matter of following the commands of Allah in the scripture (Ibid.). Some of the reason for such differences can be understood by the nature of the Qu'rān itself. It is composed "entirely of exceptionally powerful lyric poetry" (Matthewes, 2010, p. 67), and is thus open to interpretation as a polysemic text. "Of the 6,346 verses in the Qur'an, around 500 'have the form of law,' directly commanding or forbidding believers to do something. Indeed, in the entire Qur'an there are only about 200 verses directly commanding believers to pray, and three times that number commanding believers to reflect, to ponder, and to analyze God's magnificence in nature, plants, stars, and the solar system" (Ibid.).

Unlike Aristotelian ethics, Islamic ethics is based not in empiricism, but in metaphysics. In that sense it is more like the starting position of Kant (Mujtabavī, 2004, p. 3). And it does not focus on "happiness" as the end of the ethical life (Ibid.). The Mu'tazilites' focus on ethics was similar to both Plato's and Aristotle's approach. Justice "is complete virtue in its fullest sense because it is the actual exercise of complete virtue. It is complete because he who possesses it can exercise his virtue not only in himself but towards the neighbor also; for many men can exercise virtue in their own affairs, but not in their relations to their neighbors. . . . Justice in this sense, then, is not part of virtue but virtue entire, nor is the contrary injustice a part of vice but vice entire" (Aristotle, quoted by Ibid., p. 7).

Kenya, among many other countries in Africa, has multiple religious perspectives, including Christianity, Islam, and traditional religion. There have been attacks on the country, including the attack on a Nairobi shopping mall, by Islamists from Somalia in retaliation for the Kenyan armed forces' participation in peacekeeping operations in their country. In Kenya the indigenous peoples with commitments to different traditions also sometimes find themselves in conflict.

Case 3.2: Hate Speech in Kenya

In 2008 the Kenyan government established the National Cohesion and Integration Commission to facilitate and promote "equality of opportunity, good relations and peaceful coexistence between people of different ethnic and racial backgrounds" (Warungu, 2014). This was in response to the deaths of over 1,000 Kenyans in clashes that occurred following the 2007 election. But in 2014 Kenyan police began investigating "hate leaflets circulating in Lamu," and other communities had experienced similar leaflet distribution in which certain "others" were warned to leave the area or else. Although there had been some arrests in the past – including of musicians – such actions had netted "hardly anyone of substance to make an example of. It didn't help that at some point comedians and artists found themselves severely restricted, as their staple of jokes based on ethnic stereotypes seemed to verge on hate speech. This led to an ongoing debate – where does freedom of expression end and hate speech start" (Ibid.). Moses Kuria, "an aspiring MP [Member of Parliament] from the governing Jubilee Coalition, was charged with hate speech for a message he posted on Facebook . . . while . . . former Prime Minister Raila Odinga . . . found himself at the centre of a private prosecution by a man who is accusing him of hate speech over allegedly inflammatory words he uttered at a rally earlier in the year" (Ibid.). Code words, such as "removing of weeds" and references to "foreskins," are used in hate-filled posts. Research conducted by iHub in Kenya found that in 2013 "more than 90% of online 'dangerous speech,' with potential to catalyze violence, was found on Facebook" (Ibid.).

Commentary on Case 3.2

The year 2014 was the twentieth anniversary of the Rwandan genocide, in that case largely fomented by partisan radio stations in Kigali. Most of the world knew of the atrocities there only after the fact, since the stations broadcasting the call for filling graves with Tutsis were local. Facebook, however, is international, appealing not only to Kenyans at home and those in the Kenyan diaspora, but to the world at large. Since the internet (including Facebook's more than one billion users) has been promoted as a "democratic medium," should there be restrictions on what can be posted there to assure its ethical use? At about the same time as Warungu's comments, this question was raised in reference to the activities of British-born jihadists in Iraq fighting with the Islamic State of Iraq and Syria (ISIS). Their sophisticated use of social media, uploading videos and photos of their exploits, included specific references to martyrdom for those who joined the cause, especially young people in the West to whom English-language materials were addressed (see Figure 3.1). ISIS followed a radical interpretation of Islam to justify their activities (including beheadings) in both Iraq and Syria. The group had even been disowned by Al-Qaeda. Many Muslims condemned their cause and claimed their

Figure 3.1 Examples of materials posted on social media by British-born jihadists fighting with ISIS in Iraq, targeting young people in the West.

interpretation of the Koran was unorthodox, even in violation of its basic tenets. They especially rejected justifications for killing fellow Muslims. Yet there were no real efforts made by Facebook or other social media sites to prevent such postings, or to remove them rapidly after posting. "Jihad," the group claimed, "is a purification no matter who you are or what sins you have, no good deeds are needed to come before it. Don't let nothing hold you back" (Roussinos, 2014). Does a medium that allows people to share their perspectives, photos, and comments online have any responsibility for what is posted there, or would it be irresponsible for such media (Facebook, blogger, WordPress, Twitter, Instagram, Flickr, etc.) to censor such postings?[4]

Case 3.3: The Media in the Chilcot Report

In July 2016 an inquiry into the United Kingdom's involvement in the second Iraq war was released. The inquiry, led by Sir John Chilcot, had harsh criticism for Britain's government under Prime Minister Tony Blair that had made the decision to join the United States in the invasion and subsequent occupation of Iraq (see http://www.iraqinquiry.org.uk/the-report/). Al-Jazeera reported on the release of the report, beginning its story "John Chilcot's massive report on the calamitous invasion and occupation of Iraq is now out" (Stone, 2016). Al-Jazeera's report acknowledged the effort of the Blair administration to shape British public opinion to favor intervention, but criticized the British press for giving readers wrong or fabricated material that assisted the pro-war case and for taking editorial positions that strongly supported the government's position (Ibid.). It also provided specific instances of the British press's culpability in distributing false reports as well as those of American newspapers that had promoted the war based on the George W. Bush administration's advocacy of that strategy. "In all fairness," the Al-Jazeera report said, "there was probably more critical coverage in the UK media than in US outlets. Indeed, some papers, such as The Guardian, the Daily Mirror and The Independent, opposed the war. But, once the invasion had started in March 2003, British reporting became more propagandistic" (Ibid.). Al-Jazeera also reported, on July 8, 2016, that the release of the Chilcot report would provide little consolation to average Iraqis. One Baghdad resident, Mohammad Jawad, interviewed by Al-Jazeera, said that Blair and former U.S. president George W. Bush were "responsible for every life lost in Iraq, from 2003 until now. The invasion has left our country in chaos, and in ruins . . . now all we have are dead bodies everywhere" ("Iraq report brings little solace to war-torn country," 2016).

Commentary on Case 3.3

The reports from Al-Jazeera on the Iraq investigation in the United Kingdom would certainly be applauded within the individualist ethical tradition, especially among libertarians who expect the press to serve a watchdog function over government activities. Utilitarians, social contract theorists, deontologists, and virtue theorists would all endorse both the report and its reporting, although for different reasons. But such ethical theorists would also question the failure of the report to address the original positions taken by the press during the run-up to, and invasion of, Iraq. They would certainly condemn the role of the press in misleading the British public, passing along lies or questionable conclusions based on faulty intelligence or too closely following the lead of the U.S. administration. Although Al-Jazeera did a service in reporting the results of the investigation, it might also be judged too little too late: the damage had been done, both to the democratic process and to the people of Iraq.

But what of the collectivist tradition? Would it reach the same conclusions? If Al-Jazeera was to provide an antidote to the domination of international news by Western news organizations, and to represent different publics' concerns in world affairs, do these reports also accomplish that? Would such reports help mend the fractured publics of the Middle East or somehow represent their interests? Or are these two reports merely the same reportage as would emerge from Western news organizations, but simply from a different direction? From a Muslim, Hindu, or Buddhist perspective, is there truly some new type of report here that should be celebrated? Or are such reports disappointments to the collectivist ethicist?

Conclusion

The moral/ethical context that affects expectations of the media – its entertainment and information – is significantly different from one country to the next. Some countries have a dominant religious context, sometimes with minority components, while others have multiple contending ethical systems at work. The influence of Western news and entertainment values has gradually worked its way around the world, influencing how television programs are made (or re-created from Western models), the styles of music that are popular, and the expectations of the information media. The widespread adoption of the internet has also allowed many voices to be heard in countries where before there was only the majority voice. These developments have often put a strain on dominant moral/ethical contexts, turning what at one time might have been consensus expectations into a fractious and contentious milieu. When the moral/ethical context is considered alongside the issues introduced in Chapter 1, the exercise of social responsibility can become a very difficult effort indeed.

Discussion Questions

1   Is it desirable, ethically speaking, that people's actions are in accord with their roles in communities, or that the community is superior to the individual? Why or why not?

2   Some of these traditions find ethics and politics intertwined at least to a degree. Does this strengthen or weaken ethics? Why or why not?

3   Should individual rights be the focus of ethics, as some Western philosophical theories suggest, or is it better to divorce the issue of individual rights from the dignity of persons?

4   Should the place where you stand as a professional media practitioner affect your ethical choices?

5   Some of the African ethical commitments seem to draw from the more individualistic perspective of the West, while others seem closer to the Asian collectivist perspectives. What reasons might there be for this difference?

6   Excommunication at one time was a common practice within the Western church, but it has fallen out of favor (although was used in 2014 by the Pope against corrupt politicians in Italy). Does the practice of excommunication (also integral to the idea of communication itself in

Africa) add ethical authority to these traditions, authority lost as its use declined? Should it be reinstituted?

7 Is ethics more likely to be effective in the modern world if it concentrates on the "I-ness" of individualism or the "we-ness" of collectivism?

8 What are the crucial differences among the ethics of the three monotheistic traditions? Would it be possible, based on a person's actions, to know him as Christian, Muslim, or Jew?

9 What are the similarities among the ethics of the three monotheistic traditions? Are the similarities enough to allow adherents of them to live together in peace and still maintain their crucial ethical positions?

Notes

1 Some authors say this is a Xhosa maxim, but the languages are similar, so it could be either.
2 "A related concept which confers social status on a person based on living up to the principles of *cieng*, is *dheeng*, appropriately translateable [*sic*] as dignity. When a young man is initiated and moves from being a boy to being a man, he is said to have become *adheng*, a 'gentleman,' with the attributes of *dheeng*. But *dheeng* is a word with multiple meanings – all positive. *Dheeng* is equally applicable to women. As a noun, it means nobility, beauty, handsomeness, elegance, charm, grace, gentleness, hospitality, generosity, good manners, discretion, and kindness. The social background of a person, his physical appearance, the way he walks, carries himself, talks, eats, or dresses, and the way he behaves toward fellow human beings, are all factors in determining his *dheeng*. *Ting adheng*, or *nyan adheng* mean, respectively, a woman or girl who lives up to the principles of *dheeng*" (Francis M. Deng quoted in Twining, 2007).
3 Robert worked with the Dinka on a research project in 2007. The young men who were the interviewers trained to do the research said I needed a name and they decided it was "Deng," which means "blessing" in their language. They were also adamant that I needed more than a single wife, to produce both more girl children – as I could then become wealthier through cattlewealth – and more boy children – to protect the wealth I would accumulate. This was their effort to engage me with their value system. However, I had to decline their invitations to help find additional wives.
4 These screen captures are from Roussinos (2014). They are taken from ISIS posts on Facebook.

4

Ethics and Political Economy

Introduction

The effort to control access to information is as old as the development of the modern means of information creation and distribution – the printing press. Both the Christian Church and secular authorities in the West tried to guarantee that neither heresy nor sedition would develop from the ability to print and distribute large numbers of tracts, broadsheets, books, and leaflets even at a time when the number of literate people in Western societies was a minority. Every means of communication developed since the mid-fifteenth century has faced efforts to restrict what could be published and distributed, either for moral reasons (pornography, explicit sexual portrayals, nudity, all of which might corrupt youth, or advertising for intruding on the sanctity of the home), or for politico-economic reasons (claims of national security, prevention of aid to the enemy, control of propaganda, protection of copyrights and trademarks, false advertising that would give unfair advantage in the marketplace, etc.). As the means of creation and distribution of information have developed, the dispute over who would control their use has intensified. This is where political-economic analysis finds its purchase.

The significance of information and communication is laid out by Robert McChesney (2004a, p. 3): "It is axiomatic in nearly all variants of social and political theory that media and communication systems are cornerstones of modern societies. . . . [M]edia is central to the emerging global economy as well as to any notion of political democracy." McChesney calls the notion of a free press a myth that has fogged "our ability to see the actual power relations at hand, and therefore inhibit[ed] our capacity to move toward establishing a more democratic and humane media system, and a more democratic and humane society" (Ibid.). This is due, he argues, to the rise of neoliberalism and a global media system that increasingly produces and distributes international products. This system is controlled by "the power of the dominant media corporations to defend their interests and propagate a mythology to protect their very privileged role in society" (Ibid.).

Defining Political Economy

Political economy is rooted in ideas from moral philosophy (Balaam and Veseth, n.d., n.p.). The first full articulation of political economy is found in Adam Smith's *An Inquiry into the Nature and Causes of the Wealth of Nations* published in 1776, with many philosophers further refining its ideas since then. As Balaam and Veseth (Ibid.) explain:

> Many works by political economists in the 18th century emphasized the role of individuals over that of the state and generally attacked mercantilism. This is perhaps best illustrated by Smith's

World Media Ethics: Cases and Commentary, First Edition. Robert S. Fortner and P. Mark Fackler.
© 2018 John Wiley & Sons, Inc. Published 2018 by John Wiley & Sons, Inc.

famous notion of the "invisible hand," in which he argued that state policies often were less effective in advancing social welfare than were the self-interested acts of individuals. Individuals intend to advance only their own welfare, Smith asserted, but in so doing they also advance the interests of society as if they were guided by an invisible hand. Arguments such as these gave credence to individual-centred analysis and policies to counter the state-centred theories of the mercantilists.

In the modern era, "The field of political economy today encompasses several areas of study, including the politics of economic relations, domestic political and economic issues, the comparative study of political and economic systems, and international political economy. The emergence of international political economy, first within international relations and later as a distinct field of inquiry, marked the return of political economy to its roots as a holistic study of individuals, states, markets, and society" (Ibid.).

Colonialism, Political Economy, and Ethics

Most countries across the globe have experienced colonialism in one form or another. The legacy of colonialism is most apparent, however, in the global south. One explanation of this legacy is provided by Immanuel Wallerstein (2006, pp. 32–33):

> Notwithstanding European social ignorance of the world of the so-called Oriental high civilizations, the expansion of the capitalist world economy proved to be inexorable. The Europe-dominated world-system spread from its Euro-American base to encompass more and more parts of the world in order to incorporate them into its division of labor. Domination, as opposed to mere contact, brooks no sense of cultural parity. The dominant need to feel that they are morally and historically justified in being the dominant group and the main recipient of the economic surplus produced within the system. Curiosity and a vague sense of the possibility of learning something in European contact with the so-called high civilizations thus gave way to the need to explain why these zones should be politically and economically subordinate to Europe, despite the fact that they were deemed "high" civilizations.

Assumptions about the superiority of developing European-defined modernity to the civilizations of "other" cultures preceded the rapid expansion of colonial domination as well as rationalizing its aftermath (see Said, 1978, p. 39).

Wallerstein, continuing to reference Said, argued that "words matter, . . . concepts and conceptualizations matter, . . . knowledge frameworks are a causal factor in the construction of unequal social and political institutions – a causal factor but not at all *the only* causal factor" (Wallerstein, 2006, pp. 38–39). The words and concepts of colonial authority claimed a moral and cultural superiority to that practiced in their conquered territory. They established the order of things, the modernity that eventually free states should aspire to, and the means by which authority should be exercised – in many cases with brutality. This was all the inheritance of conquered peoples.

Such order and inheritance was dehumanizing – even to the conqueror, the colonialist (Césaire, 2000, p. 41). It masked the immorality of the civilizations that claimed superiority over subjected peoples, and thus confused their traditional ethics that were now deemed barbarous. Likewise, it provided the mask that conquering nations could lay over their own callousness, a mask that claimed the only history is white, the only ethnography is white, the only ethics is white (see Ibid., p. 71). As

Edward W. Said (1993, p. 37) has argued concerning claims about the exclusivity of the Western literary canon, "[this] is an indication not only of a highly inflated sense of Western inclusivity in cultural accomplishment, but also of a tremendously limited, almost hysterically antagonistic view of the rest of the world." Frantz Fanon (1963/2004, pp. 5–6) puts this in even starker terms: "The colonialist is not content with physically limiting the space of the colonized, i.e., with the help of his agents of law and order. As if to illustrate the totalitarian nature of colonial exploitation, the colonist turns the colonized into a kind of quintessence of evil. Colonized society is not merely portrayed as a society without values. The colonist is not content with stating that the colonized world has lost its values or worse never possessed any. The 'native' is declared impervious to ethics, representing not only the absence of values but also the negation of values. He is, dare we say it, the enemy of values. In other words, absolute evil."

The ethical and cultural imperialism of colonial expansion were justified by their connection to the imperial powers' economic and military superiority. Albert Memmi (2006) concludes, "It has always been this way between oppressor and oppressed; the culture of the oppressor goes hand in hand with its economic and political power" (location 1305). Frantz Fanon (1967, pp. 1–2) goes so far as to suggest that colonized people are those in whom an inferiority complex has taken hold – goaded by the assumption of colonialism that non-whites are less human than they; the colonized person must assimilate the cultural values of the colonial metropolis, including its language, if he is to escape the bush and become a true human being.

These crippling set of assumptions, that eventually became part of the "being" of subjugated peoples, were part and parcel of the imperial enterprise, an enterprise undertaken for both economic and cultural reasons. On the economic side was the assumption that raw materials and new markets would result from settling and ruling distant lands. On the cultural side was the assumption that "civilization" and the Christian faith as known and practiced by colonial powers could be exported to these lands. From the political-economic perspective, however, both rationales were false. "The central nationalist/Marxist assumption is, of course, that imperialism was economically exploitative; every facet of colonial rule, including even the apparently sincere efforts of Europeans to study and understand indigenous cultures, was a root designed to maximize the 'surplus value' that could be extracted from subject peoples. The central liberal assumption is more paradoxical. It is that precisely because imperialism distorted market forces – using everything from military force to preferential tariffs to rig business in the favour of the metropolis – it was not in the long-term interests of the metropolitan economy either" (Ferguson, n.d., locations 152 and 161). Imperialism was coercive and thus a distortion of economic and market realities – unsustainable in the long run. Considering the resultant political economy of colonialism thus suggests both an economic and cultural/moral failure that mortally wounded the moral sensibilities of colonizer and colonized alike.

International Political Economy of Media

In the 1960s and 1970s political economists warned of "cultural imperialism" at a time when Western countries were swamping developing countries with cheap television and film exports that reduced the incentive to spend money on indigenous productions to such an extent that television screens were filled with U.S.-made police dramas and westerns and Hollywood- and London-based films, radio stations with Western pop music, newspapers with Western-based wire copy, and libraries with Western novels and academic works. The concern over cultural imperialism died down when these countries began slowly to develop their own production capacity, and local artists (especially musical) began recording their own material, although many of the formats and styles of these productions were copying or adapting Western models. Despite the reduction in concern, "Given that only a handful of industrialized nations have the ability to produce and circulate culture globally, those who create cultural commodities and how culture shapes national identities are important considerations" (Riordan, 2004, pp. 419–420). In the 1990s the international push for free trade among various blocs of countries, the creation of the North American Free Trade Agreement (NAFTA) and World Trade Organization (WTO), and the reduction in tariffs on intellectual property replaced these concerns (also incidentally designed to protect Western-based intellectual property by reducing the incentives for piracy).

Poorer countries, however, have had difficulty keeping up with the technological changes in production and distribution systems, although the arrival of the mobile smartphone has begun to provide reception service that was long denied to the majority of the world due to the cost of wired telecommunications infrastructure and expansion of electrical grids. There are still significant gaps though, now known as the "digital divide" (see Digital Divide Institute, n.d. and "The Digital Divide, ICT and the 50x15 Initiative," n.d.). What political economists see in such changes are the social, political, and economic pressures and interests that influence them. It is here that the question of ownership and control of information again arises, along with issues of fair access to information resources and the various factors that play into investments and expansion of broadband access. As Seán Ó Siochrú wrote:

> We stand at [a] crossroads in media and communications. At stake is the type of media environment we seek to inhabit, from [the] local to global level, for ourselves and future generations. Formidable forces propel us down one route, the commercialization of activities and outputs, subsuming media and communication "products" under general market rules. The alternative route, currently much less prominent, is a road in which media are focused on fulfilling human needs and reinforcing human rights and aspirations, under a revised and invigorated structure of global governance.
>
> *(Siochrú, 2004, p. 23)*

Putting it somewhat differently, Siochrú's statement suggests a movement away from negative liberty, where the freedom of media organizations is paramount, and toward positive liberty, where interests of people are superior and human possibilities are enshrined in expectations of media services.

Media trade unions have also warned of the results of increasing concentration of ownership, not only in traditional analog media sectors but in the more recently developed digital media as well: "Digital technology has made available a host of new media services, including digital TV, digital radio and digital film and also including such things as webcasting, interactive television, MP3 music, and video-on-demand. Unlike analogue technologies, digital media are not limited by bandwidth considerations. Despite the apparent opportunities for greater choice, however, existing media groups have moved rapidly to dominate the new digital arena" (Bibby, 2003, p. 6).

Although it is to be expected that trade unions would object to developments that might threaten the employment status of their members, their concerns are not unique. The European Audiovisual Observatory, for instance, published a paper in 2001 that related media concentration to that in other industries: "While the harmful effects of commercial concentrations in other sectors are mainly economic, journalistic aspects are also involved where media concentrations are concerned. Unlike other companies, media undertakings . . . also serve to support one of the most fundamental human rights – freedom of opinion, information, the press and broadcasting, an indispensable part of any democracy . . . . The control of media concentrations is therefore a special case, reaching beyond pure competition law" (Palzer and Hilger, 2001, p. 6). The concern of political economy, then, is that freedom of information and the right to communicate (including the right to receive information) can be severely compromised by media concentration, especially when such concentration is undertaken for the purpose of increasing profits that can have the effect of disenfranchising people – especially poorer people not defined as relevant to the profit incentive. The division between the information "haves" and "have-nots" is thus continued and increasingly foundational to media operations, allowing profit to define the reality of citizenship and human rights.[1]

Positive liberty from a political-economy perspective is one that would alter the economic relations in society such that social justice and individual fairness could be achieved. But the economic incentives for achieving worldwide distribution of cultural materials as protected by international copyright conventions has driven consolidation of systems, and massive personal and private investment in bypassing limited technological infrastructure in many countries has made considerations of fairness and justice problematic (see McChesney, 2004b, p. 69). When these developments are considered alongside the increasing commodification of personal information by data mining operations in the hands of such entities as Google, Facebook, Microsoft, and Apple that are required to play in their sandboxes, considering non-economic/non-commodity concerns has largely evaporated outside academic circles (see Mosco, 2004, p. 273).

But this is not all. State players, including intelligence services, the military, and major corporate suppliers of advanced technologies to these entities, have all increasingly engaged in surveillance activities, diplomacy and counter-terrorism operations, and the spreading of disinformation through wired and wireless internet services to assure competitive advantages in negotiations, military operations, and intercepting terror plots. At the same time those who would spread their anti-statist or ideological propaganda have become increasingly adept at exploiting the possibilities for direct access to potential recruits, funders, and the general public to pursue their objectives. Both of these activities are occurring in an increasingly interconnected global environment (see Miége, 2004, p. 124). Governments have also sought to stop leaks to the outside, prosecute those who leak or accept leaked information, and clamp down on vulnerable systems to protect strategies in the world arena or to deny their own citizens access to information (see Washington Post, 2013; Greenwald, 2014; Gurnow, 2014). Involvement of normal citizens in democratic exercises, or even the intent to remain abreast of significant but publicly unacknowledged activities, have become increasingly difficult, essentially disenfranchising involvement in what would at one time have been seen as necessary for engagement in the public sphere and maintaining the legitimacy of national states. So Colin Sparks (2000, p. 289) has argued that the impact of the developing World Wide Web, rather than opening up the public sphere or expanding democratic access, would more likely be to exacerbate "existing tendencies to separate politics and ordinary life, and to concentrate public debate and information in just a few hands." And Brian Winston (1998, p. 2) has written that "historical consciousness reveals the 'Information Revolution' to be largely an illusion, a rhetorical gambit and an expression of technological ignorance."

The Right to Communicate

Beyond these issues of fair access and surveillance is another moral concern of political economists – the "right to communicate." One way to understand this right is to recognize that "communication represents an essential and very important human need as well as a basic human right. Without having the possibility to communicate and talk to other people, no individual, community, group or any other institution would be able to exist, or prosper" ("Communication – an essential human need," n.d., n.p.). This need is met by recognizing four specific pillars that constitute the right to communicate: (1) communicating in the public sphere, (2) communicating knowledge, (3) using communication to exercise civil rights, and (4) communicating cultural rights (Ibid.).

This right is not yet enshrined in international law, but has been under debate for more than a decade. Article 19, an international advocacy group for the right to communicate, argues that freedom of opinion and expression, along with the right to receive information from both state and private sources, are necessary for this right to be realized. The organization claims that key elements of the right include "the right to a diverse, pluralistic media; equitable access to the means of communication, as well as to the media; the right to practise and express one's culture, including the right to use the language of one's choice; the right to participate in public decision-making processes; the right to access information, including from public bodies; the right to be free of undue restrictions on content; and privacy rights, including the right to communicate anonymously" (Article 19, 2002, n.p.). This right is endangered by several factors, including homogenization of the media and exclusion of minority voices, globalization and commercialization of media, governmental rules and regulation aimed at exerting political control over media and telecommunications, and the increasing dominance of large media corporations around the world (Ibid.).

One difficulty of arguing for such a right is that the notion of individual rights, or basic human rights that would include this dimension, is a Western concept based in a post-Enlightenment sensibility. As such this right to communicate has less legitimacy in more collectivist cultures where rights are themselves created and maintained in community, rather than on an individual basis. The question of whether such a right should have less purchase in collectivist societies as opposed to individualistic ones has not been adequately addressed. For instance, Salik Shah from Nepal, dealing with the issue of piracy on the internet, writes:

> The internet has played a crucial role in my life and countless others of my generation all over the world. In their attempt to prevent piracy these acts will dismantle the very medium that enables communication and the free exchange of ideas. The proponents of these acts want us to believe that piracy is an evil thing. The younger generation of the world knows very well that piracy is a necessary evil that enables revolutionary online publications like Wikileaks to perform their crucial role for democracy. They know that we can no longer trust politicians who want to control information, who want to control our lives, and worse, dictate the future of mankind.
>
> *(Shah, 2012)*

Michelle J. Foster's introduction to her 2012 report to the Center for International Media Assistance argued:

> Around the globe, traditional news media – newspapers, magazines, and broadcast networks – are operating in more concentrated environments with fewer owners and less diverse voices. Growth in the number of news media outlets and channels has not resulted in a parallel expansion of viewpoints in traditional news media, especially within local communities. This failure to expand viewpoints has adverse consequences for the ability of citizens and communities to hold their governments accountable. If media cannot be free and competitive, they can be neither plural nor diverse. Who owns the media and its infrastructure and who controls its sources of capital and revenue are crucial for any media system.
>
> *(Foster, 2012, p. 4)*

Patricia Lancia (2009) agrees:

> If only some people are given the opportunity to express themselves in society, if some people are denied access to tools for self-expression and, therefore, denied the ability to actually exercise their rights as citizens and as human beings, then the groups that allow that to happen are acting unethically. It is the intention of this paper to show that the current media monopoly environment interferes with the right to free expression of the vast majority of people in society – by eliminating viable alternative sites of communication, by limiting direct access to media outlets as tools of communication, and by preventing the creation of independent media outlets – and is, therefore, unethical.

These are, of course, political-economic arguments, demanding that the media, however owned or operated, have a positive requirement to act for the public, to enable the public to engage in meaningful communication, and to provide an environment where robust argument can occur, which includes not only the owners of the media but also minority voices, the poor, and otherwise disenfranchised public.[2] And so we arrive at our first set of cases.

How much authority, if any, should governments have to determine who can practice journalism? Should journalists be licensed? Should they be required to sign secrecy agreements? Should they be required to print stories that governments would find useful for their own purposes?

Case 4.1a: Licensing Journalists

The head of South Africa's public broadcaster, Hlaudi Motsoeneng, stated in July 2014 that all journalists should be licensed to practice. He claimed this was necessary because some journalists were lazy, made up facts, and failed to provide objective reports. He also complained that journalists often failed to report on the good news of the government's efforts to improve people's lives. Although he faced scathing criticism from various groups in South Africa, he said he intended to stand firm in making a recommendation to the country's communications minister.

The National Editors' Forum criticized Motsoeneng for his "ignorance of journalistic practice." Sue Valentine, the Africa Program Coordinator for the International Committee to Protect Journalists, said the proposal took South African press freedom, hard won since the end of apartheid, backwards. She also responded to Motsoeneng's argument that journalists should be licensed just as doctors and lawyers were: "The difference is that a doctor or a lawyer is a profession, whereas journalists deal with the issue of fundamental human rights, of freedom of expression and the right of access to information. So the right of freedom of expression and access to information is at the heart of what journalists do, and for that reason journalists should not be licensed."[3]

Commentary on Case 4.1a

This case highlights a long-standing issue in journalism: licensing. Are journalists professionals, such as doctors and lawyers, who should be licensed to assure basic competencies that will protect the public? Or is their role more vital than that of healthcare providers and legal representatives, as Ms. Valentine obliquely suggested? The case also provides some insight into the political-economy arguments about the moral and human right to communicate. If there is a right to communicate, then there should not be any restrictions on it by any means. Licensing is a way of putting authority in the hands of government officials to determine who can, and cannot, be a journalist. But is there a body of knowledge agreed on by all professionals in the field, that must be known prior to entering the field? Or is it a set of techniques of writing, asking questions, probing newsmakers, and so on, that would be difficult to test in the absence of real-world experience? And if journalists were licensed, would this mean that others whose activities might be construed as journalistic (such as citizens photographing the result of bombings or massacres on social media sites, or bloggers expressing opinions on a political issue) could find their efforts legitimately banned?

What is the socially responsible position to take in such cases? On the one hand, would licensing requirements not result in a "chilling effect" on reporting, for fear that reporting on events, scandals, or corruption by members of the government in power might result in de-licensure and loss of income? Would it not make the press timid? On the other hand, is it socially responsible to allow journalists to be completely unaccountable for their reports or the damage they may cause to others by inaccuracies, distortions, half-truths, or bias?

We can ask ourselves such questions using some of the philosophical perspectives explained in Chapters 2 and 3. The collectivist perspective tells us that the most ethical position on this dispute would be the one that has as its consequence the flourishing of community and its communal values. Here values are in conflict. Journalists argue that they must be free to pursue the truth regardless of the damage that may be inflicted on authority. The community needs a trustworthy and uncontrolled source of information. Authority counters that journalists cannot be trusted as they sometimes lie or miss the truth as a consequence of bias, haste, or incompetence. The community thus suffers from their behavior.

The utilitarian would ask who would benefit or suffer, and to what degree, by licensing journalists. Certainly authority would benefit and journalists, they say, suffer. But what of the larger community's stake in the question? Would those without vested interests be more likely to benefit from licensed or unlicensed journalists? Some among them would object to licensure because they want the opportunity to report events, or express opinions, in forums that are journalistic in nature. News agencies are now soliciting such reports from conflict zones, or distant locales, through social media. These quasi-journalists would object to their activities being constrained by such a law and would argue that the result would be the continued silencing of unorthodox or minority views. There would be no way to respond effectively to oppression, no Arab Spring, no dissent from a rigged electoral count, no recourse in cases of fraud.

Rawls would ask all these parties – as well as those unrepresented outsiders – to stand behind a veil of ignorance to determine what the best outcome should be. He would give preference to those less represented. Will licensing journalists further consolidate opinion and alienate those outside the circles of power? Is there any way to protect unsanctioned perspective in a licensing regime? Would such protection allow licensing to proceed without concern in the interests of truth-telling?

Kant would intervene and tell us that truth-telling is an imperative – an inviolate one. Christians would agree here, demanding that the universal proto-norm of truth-telling be protected however the decision is made. Is there a reasonable answer to be found?

Case 4.1b: Secrecy Agreements in China

China has a tightly controlled press. In July 2014 the government decreed that all mainland journalists had to sign a secrecy agreement with their employers before they would be able to obtain a press pass. This press pass would give them the legitimacy to obtain a press certificate from the government itself in order that they could have access to significant state events and official interviews. The confidentiality agreement between employers and journalists was to require that, before releasing any information from interviews, press conferences, or other events on personal blogs, microblogs (such as Twitter) or the messaging app WeChat, the journalist must obtain the employer's consent. The government also banned "referencing this information in public events, such as forums, and passing on tips to the foreign media or writing columns for them" ("China to grant 'more' press passes," 2014). Any breach of the secrecy agreement would result in disciplinary action or civil punishment. An estimated 250,000 press passes were expected to be issued.

The *South China Morning Post* (2014) claimed that this new law took censorship to a new level and would prevent information of public interest from finding its way into the public domain: "This is an attempt to ensure information is reported only after a tight censorship process. It does lay down rules for handling state secrets, but the definition of these remains so broad that the law has obvious potential for abuse by officials wanting to hide information from the public. That is precisely why the information gag is to be condemned. It remains the duty of journalists to report matters of public interest."

Commentary on Case 4.1b

The Chinese requirement takes the issue of licensing one step further by demanding that confidentiality be a part of any news coverage, and that employers evaluate all information to be included in releases before its distribution (a form of self-censorship). Chinese authorities hold all media organizations responsible for information shared with them, especially information originating from official state sources. The new requirement may or may not inhibit information-gathering or distribution by individuals (that remains to be seen), but it does certainly put organizations on notice that failure to control the release of information gathered by their employees could result in serious negative consequences. This is, of course, another effort to reduce the widespread distribution of embarrassing information about the Communist Party, the Politburo, state agencies, and members of the party via social media, with the assumption being that all such information must originate from media organizations themselves.

If media workers are working independently, how should they act in response to such demands? They could acquiesce, or sign the agreement (and then leak information), or they could refuse to do so. What would be accomplished by each approach, and what ethical consideration would justify that choice?

Case 4.1c: Supporting Government Activities

A third aspect of the relationship between media workers (especially journalists) and governments is demonstrated by the situation that developed in Singapore in July 2014. Robin Chan, writing in the *Straits Times* on July 14, said that a senior civil servant had asked him, "What can the media do to strengthen the public's trust in the Government?" After questioning whether that should be a role for the press, Chan wrote that "the Government has long defended its stand on what the media should be: It should not be an adversary to the Government, as [it] is in more liberal media models, but one that is a partner with the Government in nation building." Chan then reflected on Singapore's media history, from the period of heavy-handed control to a "kinder, gentler" effort to "shape media coverage through persuasion or even cajoling of journalists and editors," to the present when the changing media landscape had suffered from fragmentation where some online sites had gained credibility because of their contrarian views. "While this is not in and of itself a bad thing, society is not well served when messages are distorted, untruths are spread, and soundbites and images create misperception and more confusion, in a vicious circle." Chan agreed with other commentators who objected that this situation had "given rise to a Wild West of journalism where news, opinion and entertainment are becoming merged and harder to distinguish." What was needed, he concluded, was for the government to "help strengthen public trust in the media," and this required the government to provide "timely and broader access to government information and data," and "respect and trust mainstream media journalists to act in the interests of the nation, and give them wider space to operate in."[4]

Commentary on Case 4.1c

These three cases are variations on a theme: the proper relationship between governments and media. Although each case differs in degree from the others, they all share this foundation: media and government operate in a symbiotic relationship, each dependent on the other. Governments wish to have their policies understood by the public, and to achieve legitimacy with the public. Governments are dependent on the media for that link. At the same time, media depend on governments for much of what they report: government data (census, trade statistics, inflation, value of currency, housing costs, infrastructure improvements, and so on), press conferences, various studies and reports, legislation and legislative debates, election results, and so on. If a government did not provide such information, or provide access to it, not only would the media suffer for news, but government would find it more difficult to achieve legitimacy. Only authoritarian regimes operating state-controlled media do not worry about such matters.

This tenuous relationship between government and media is not restricted to a mere handful of instances. Several Western-trained journalists resigned from their positions with Russia Today (an international television service in English) as a result of the ongoing conflict in Ukraine. As one of those resigning put it, she had been "'taking a paycheck' to spread Russian propaganda. 'We do work for Putin,' she admitted on Twitter. 'We are asked on a daily basis if not to totally ignore then to obscure the truth'" ("Another RT anchor resigns: 'I'm for the truth,'" 2014). Another journalist, Pavel Sheremet from Belarus, left Russia's public television service (ORT) protesting the country's policies on Ukraine as well ("TV journalist quits in protest at Kremlin's policies on Ukraine," 2014).

In Nigeria, Deputy Senate President Ike Ekweremadu "has appealed to Nigerian journalists to play down . . . the activities of [Boko Haram]. He hinged his appeal on the premise that the media reports have created fear in the minds of most Nigerians. . . . According to him, terrorism is a mind game which primary purpose is to instill fear in the minds of the people by carrying out acts of destruction of human lives and property to give the impression that they are in charge" ("Ekweremadu to media: Reject Boko Haram propaganda," 2014).

Finally, in Sudan, the Minister of State for Information excused the admitted censorship imposed on the press in his country by "saying the political situation does not allow to fully respect press freedom. 'The situation in Sudan is explosive and would be uncontrollable, so it is difficult to allow full press freedom,' said state minister Yasir Youssef in a speech at Ramadan organized by the Organization of Press Freedoms" (Sudan Tribune Editorial Team, 2014).

International Media Domination

Fewer than 10 international media conglomerates effectively control the production and distribution of entertainment and news products around the world. All these conglomerates operate out of wealthy Western countries, although many of them deny their identification with a particular country, referring to themselves instead as international companies. Which 10 are the largest depends on how their ranking is calculated.

Ranked by revenues derived from advertising support, the 10 largest media companies are Google, DirecTV, Walt Disney Company, 21st Century Fox, Comcast, Time Warner, Cox Enterprises, BSkyB, Bertelsmann, and CBS Corporation ("Top 10 global media owners," 2014). Ranked by sales, profits, assets, and market value, Comcast is number 1, followed by Disney, 20th Century Fox, Time Warner, Time Warner Cable, DirecTV, WPP (a UK-based holding company), CBS, Viacom, and DISH Network (a U.S.-based holding company) (Le, 2014). Another ranking has the five largest global media companies as Comcast, DirecTV, Walt Disney, News Corporation, and Time Warner ("Top five global broadcast media companies," 2014). Whichever way the rankings are done the conclusion is identical: Western-based media companies – and especially U.S.-based ones – continue to dominate the world's media stage.[5] In 1997 McChesney reported that nine corporations dominate the "first tier" of the global media system: "The five largest are Time Warner (1997 sales: $24 billion), Disney ($22 billion), Bertelsmann ($15 billion), Viacom ($13 billion), and Rupert Murdoch's News Corporation ($11 billion)" (McChesney, 1997; see also Le, 2014).

Although the size of these media giants is disproportionately a function of their engagement in the American media market, where both media properties and the market dwarf that of most other countries, these companies are also "often in a position to effectively compete with – and even dominate – the local media in other countries.[6] [They] can draw on their enormous capital resources to produce expensive media products, such as Hollywood blockbuster movies, which are beyond the capability of local media" (Croteau and Hoynes, 2006, p. 102). They can also adapt media products for new markets much less expensively than new ones can be created, and use both existing and adapted media products to "tap a lucrative source of revenue at virtually no additional cost" (Croteau and Hoynes, 2007, p. 35). So, as the United States Department of Commerce (2014) reports about American media, they "often attain shares in international markets in excess of 90 percent due to high global interest in U. S. filmed entertainment." In recorded music, too, "The U. S. has the world's largest performance rights market and earns half of global sync revenues" (Ibid.). By 2017 global spending for media and entertainment is projected to reach $2.2 trillion, with the United States continuing as the largest single market (James, 2013).

And the efforts at further consolidation continue, with 21st Century Fox making a failed bid of $80 billion to purchase the Time Warner media conglomerate ("The truth about Rupert Murdoch's new plot for world domination," 2014). "It's always worth taking seriously when one of the biggest and most culturally influential media conglomerates in the English-speaking world threatens to buy another of the biggest and most culturally influential media conglomerates" (Ibid.). If this sale had gone through, it was possible that the company that owned and operated Fox News would also own and operate CNN. It would also have further consolidated Hollywood film production. Susan Crawford "Makes a compelling case that both Rupert Murdoch [21st Century Fox] and Jeff Bewkes [Comcast] are well aware that their future health and prosperity requires getting bigger" (Ibid.).

Implications of Global Media Consolidation

As Chan-Olmsted and Chang (2003, pp. 213–214) put it, the implications of this consolidation depend on where you stand: those coming from a social/public sphere perspective think of consolidation as leading to content homogenization and threats to democracy, while those coming from an economic/market perspective think of it – as a result of technological change and proliferation of media outlets – as a means to minimize the threat of monopoly power (see also Bennett, 2004, p. 126.) Winseck (2011, p. 12) suggests in his discussion of the social ecology of information that paying attention to the largest media organizations makes eminent sense, since "communication, and the media of communication, provides the 'stuff' from which we build our sense of self-identity, our perceptions of the world, and the social ties of others; it is a source of pleasure and conviviality and the basis upon which societies are organized." Of course, this is an understandable reason for governments and commercially driven entities to attempt to control communication as it provides them the means to direct people's attention toward those sources of pleasure and self-construction that directly benefit the directors.

But is it the case that as consolidation of media production and distribution continues, it necessarily alters the "stuff" in ways that are detrimental to individuals and communities? After all, the media landscape has changed significantly with the arrival of the internet, creating new means of channeling information, new sources of that information, and opportunities for amateurs (what some people call "prosumers," since they both produce and consume) to express themselves and address grievances that in the older one-way system were difficult to impossible. This is one reason among many others that countries take steps to control information. The result, even in a country with free media such as the United States, is that the important role that media are expected to play has been crippled by corporatization. As Croteau and Hoynes (2006, p. 258) put it, "the corporate commercialism so rampant in today's media has dramatically undermined the potential contribution of the media to our public life."

Three results emerge from the increasing commercial orientation of the international media system. The first is a continuing and accelerating commodification of media materials. "The WTO agreement reduced barriers to trade and encouraged countries to adopt an export-driven corporate-based economic system and targeted local media content rules for elimination" (Jin, 2011, location 4286). Corporate ownership implies the necessity of meeting shareholder expectations – and thus an increasing level of profit. The reduction in local content rules would allow the multimedia corporations to make further inroads into markets with their commercially driven programs and advertising campaigns. Christopherson (2011, locations 3333–3342) writes: "films made outside the United States do not fit into the conglomerate strategy – synergies across their multiple distribution gateways of theatrical exhibition, broadcast, cable, DVD, and ancillary markets – and so do not get distributed on key platforms, even if they are excellent films that win international awards." This logic also applies to television programs and music production: one distribution gateway is to beget another with streamlining and predictable flows paramount in order to increase profits. There is no place for independence and insertion of alternative voices in the corporate flow – one reason that people have taken to producing their own music and video to release via the internet.

Two points are worth noting here. The first is that this same process is developing within the internet itself, only instead of the corporate interests mentioned above having control, the principal corporate agents are search engines (Google, Yahoo, Bing), social networks such as Facebook and Twitter, and retailers such as Amazon and eBay (Van Couvering, 2011, location 4581). The second is that this phenomenon is not restricted to obviously capitalist countries such as the United States, Japan, South Korea, Australia, New Zealand, and Western European countries, but even to China:

"The fusion of party state and market power has created a media system that serves the interests of the country's political and economic elite, while suppressing and marginalizing opposing and alternative voices" (Zhao, 2004, p. 179).

In addition to commodification is the shift from professionally crafted to user-controlled content. While this shift has been heralded as indicative of the democracy available via the internet – and a new plethora of voices – it also has a dark side when wedded to corporatization and commercialization. It follows in the wake of the shift in restaurant practices that began in the United States in the mid-1950s and then was exported to the world via corporations such as McDonald's, KFC (formerly Kentucky Fried Chicken), and Pizza Hut. The change was the replacement of restaurant staff with self-service. People wanted inexpensive restaurant food. These chains, and many more like them, supplied that by getting their patrons to do the work formerly done by employees: delivering food to the table, providing condiments, and removing waste. The chains could cut costs and increase profits by using their clientele as unpaid staff. Similarly, the growth of user-generated content has provided the billions of photographs, videos, graphic images, music, and prose that search engines identify and catalog for other users to find – along with the obligatory delivered advertising messages. Google and its competitors do not create the content (or pay for its creation), but essentially sell the user-generated content to others at a profit. The efforts that some corporate owners (particularly Facebook) have made to attempt to formalize their ownership of this content – albeit unsuccessfully so far – are indicative of this development.

Finally, the user-generated content also provides the basis for the third result: rapidly developing 24/7 surveillance societies. What users post and tag on Facebook, for instance, provides the raw material for facial recognition systems that can then be employed by either governments or corporations to identify individuals. While this may assist law enforcement, it also allows continual tracking of people engaged in everyday life. Most of the focus on this issue so far has been on calls for greater privacy protection, but such activity is not merely an invasion of privacy. It is in effect an invasion of personhood. This brings us to our second set of cases.

As the global media have grown in both breadth and depth, and engaged in increasing levels of convergence and synthesis to maximize profits, they have also become ever hungrier for means to connect with users. This has meant expansion of technological capability such as the move from analog to digital video distribution and the push for ever-increasing data transfer capacity to populate large screens with acceptable image quality; the push for realism in popular first-person shooter games (which puts the user in the center of "missions" and is played from the user's perspective); and efforts to port content from one delivery system to another to maximize return on investment. We will consider video games in our first case study.

Case 4.2a: Video Games and History

In 1989 the United States, in a controversial move, invaded the country of Panama, ostensibly to protect democracy. Manuel Noriega, the president of Panama, was arrested and brought to the United States to stand trial for drug-trafficking. He was convicted and imprisoned. In 2012 Activision released its first-person shooter video game, *Call of Duty: Black Ops II*, depicting Manuel Noriega's "duplicitous actions" prior to the invasion.

> Crucially, the game portrays Noriega as betraying the CIA and aiding the escape of the game's main antagonist, Nicaraguan terrorist Raul Menendez. This re-scripting of Noriega's relationships with the CIA is politically significant given that he was legally prevented from speaking

about it during his original defence in the US following his capture in 1989. In the game, the escaped Menendez re-emerges as a populist figure in 2025 to ferment [*sic*] a cold war between China and the USA. The past has been re-imagined to make Noriega the cause of a fictitious future war.

(Robinson, 2014)

Similar first-person shooter games, including the original *Black Ops*, *Medal of Honor*, and *Army of Two*, have depicted U.S. military engagements in Vietnam, Iraq, Afghanistan, and even the Bay of Pigs invasion of Cuba by CIA-funded Cuban dissidents. Noriega, who had been released from prison after serving his sentence, was threatening a legal challenge against the game because he was not compensated for his "appearance," as is routinely done in sports-based games according to legally sanctioned intellectual property rights.

Commentary on Case 4.2a

At least two issues emerge from this case. The first is the obvious question of why Manuel Noriega, who never gave permission for his portrayal, should not be compensated for his "role" in the game. His portrayal may have helped increase the sales of the game, and thus contribute to Activision's profit, but he is without compensation. The second is the rewriting of history to create an action line for the game itself. This new action line, according to Robinson (2014), misrepresents history and justifies the questionable American action in invading Panama. The other games mentioned do so as well. These games are exported around the world – *Black Ops 2* made total global sales of $500 million on the day of its release.

The question of historical accuracy is a continuing issue within the media entertainment world. Television programs and films have been criticized for dramatizing events for which there is no written record – and even in cases where a record exists, such as with the 2012 film *Lincoln*, which was based on American historian Doris Kearns Goodwin's book *Team of Rivals*, there are complaints of historical inaccuracies (Wickman, 2012). When the portrayal occurs in a video game, with its clearly animated characters and involvement of players external to the game itself (although they enter into it via controllers), it should be obvious that it cannot be perfectly accurate. There are unknowns: strategies, re-plays. Is it then reasonable or ethical to expect historical accuracy in such games?

The accompanying issue relates to the apparent justification provided by such games for particular military incursions. Such justifications may have significant propaganda value for the nation whose actions are legitimized by such games. In the absence of a true history taught (and learned) in schools, such portrayals can easily constitute a layer of interpretation that contributes to what Jean Baudrillard (1998) has called "hyperreality," a situation in which the simulation of the real becomes the lens through which the real is understood, but in a perverted way, and which may eventually become a simulacrum having no relation to any reality whatsoever. Again, is it reasonable to think a game can potentially have such an impact? And if so, is it ethical to write game scenarios in such a way that this might occur?

Case 4.2b: Photoshop and Benetton

The advertising business around the globe is growing exponentially. In 2014 advertisers spent more than $540 billion, doubling the growth rate from only one year before (Global ad spending growth to

Figure 4.1 Benetton's "*UNHATE*" campaign. *Left:* German chancellor Angela Merkel and French president Nicolas Sarkozy. *Right:* President of China Hu Jintao and U.S. president Barack Obama.

double this year," 2014"). While advertising messages are often the most creative aspects of media production, just what is allowed in the interests of profit?

The Benetton clothing manufacturing company has been known for controversial advertising campaigns since at least 1991. Luciano Benetton, however, has said that the company "did not create our advertisements in order to provoke, but to make people talk, to develop citizen consciousness" ("Top 10 controversial United Colors of Benetton ads," 2012). In 2011 the company launched its "*UNHATE*" campaign to benefit the Benetton *UNHATE* Foundation. This campaign featured large posters placed in cities around Europe showing world leaders presumed to be in conflict kissing one another, including Pope Benedict XVI kissing Egyptian imam Ahmed el-Tayeb; Hugo Chavez, president of Venezuela, kissing U.S. president Barack Obama; North Korea's leader Kim Jong-Il kissing South Korean president Lee Myung-bak; German chancellor Angela Merkel kissing French president Sarkozy; and Obama kissing president of China Hu Jintao. People were invited to send similar pictures of themselves kissing others to the *UNHATE* website where they were then displayed on their kiss wall (kisswall.benetton.com) as part of the larger website (unhate.benetton. com) (see Figure 4.1 and Figure 6.6). The Vatican threatened legal action over the use of Pope Benedict's image and it was subsequently removed from the campaign. The White House complained about appropriation of President Obama's image but the two photos of him were retained by the company.

Commentary on Case 4.2b

In American law the use (or appropriation) of a person's name or image for commercial purposes without explicit permission is considered by the courts to be an invasion of privacy and can sometimes cost the violator tens of thousands of dollars in civil damages. The case law and precedents used in such disputes, however, are based on situations occurring before the global explosion of the internet. Given the thousands of photos posted, morphed, tagged, commented on with overlays, shared, and re-purposed must give us pause to wonder whether this older idea is still relevant.

The images shown in Figure 4.1 were Photoshopped, using other photos and altering and combining them to create the illusion of people kissing one another. None of the events depicted actually occurred. Again, Alessandro Benetton responded to questions about the point of the campaign, saying:

> It means not hating. In a moment of darkness, with the financial crisis, what's going on in North African countries [the Arab Spring], in Athens, this is an attitude we can all embrace that can have positive energy. What does UNHATE mean? UN-hate. Stop hating, if you were hating. Unhate is a message that invites us to consider that hate and love are not as far away from each other as we think. Actually the two opposing sentiments are often in a delicate and unstable balance. Our campaign promotes a shift in the balance: don't hate, Unhate.
>
> *(Radovic, 2011)*

Is it ethical to create images illustrating events that never occurred, to use images for which you do not have permission, and that clearly suggest an intimate relationship between people who are known to be in conflict? Is it ethical or reasonable to suggest that such images can be removed from a campaign when it is nearly impossible to do so once they have reached the internet (and the image of the Pope is still widely available)? Have such images commodified world leaders inappropriately, or are they commodities as a function of being in their positions and thus appropriatable for commercial purposes without fear? If so, is such treatment of the Pope more reprehensible than that of political leaders?

Stephanie Blake (2011) wrote about the campaign that "In a number of ways, the campaign is brilliant. It encourages engagement by asking people to post kissing photos on its online kisswall; it aligns with the decades-long slogan 'United Colors of Benetton,' building on prior campaigns simultaneously juxtaposing and uniting people of different races and ethnicities; it pushes the boundaries of sexuality; and it creates attention and discourse by making some people uncomfortable and others maybe a bit more aware of world politics."

So it is good marketing – but maybe poor public relations: "It is the PR folks who must now respond to the backlash of the campaign. And, my guess is the backlash was highly anticipated. As PR people, we work hard to anticipate and avoid controversies and crises, rather than ignite them. However, we also strive to know our audiences and create messaging for those audiences. What happens when our messaging to one audience directly conflicts with messaging to another? If we are striving to create real, lasting social change, conflict is part of the process. And, how do ethics play into this? Is it ethical to Photoshop photos, even if we agree a 'reasonable person' will view the photos as fake? Is it ethical communications to place an advertisement we know will be pulled less than 48 hours later?" (Ibid.). But she also applauds Benetton for "igniting conversation and pushing the envelope of acceptable communication" (Ibid.).

Other comments about the public relations value of the campaign were more positive. Sam Oxley, managing partner at House PR, claimed that "Sex, humour, fame, controversy – the latest campaign from Benetton has all the makings of that golden goal in the PR world: talkability. It's been 25 years since the last 'United Colors of Benetton' campaign and since the brand's earlier heyday the baton has been passed on to other high street brands like French Connection with the FCUK campaign. It is a risky strategy that Benetton have taken but this is a great example of a brand creating something that is a global discussion point – which is no mean feat. Whether or not it will sell more clothes remains to be seen. But will it drive brand awareness? You bet" (quoted by Rundle, 2011).

Others have suggested that the manipulated photos were "quasi-erotic" ("Art, ethics and social responsibility," 2011) and others, when posting them on Tumblr, referred to them as "offensive and disrespectful towards religious people" (Alfonso, 2011). One Tumblr comment came from

Katie on Conservative Perspective: "First of all, I just don't think clothing companies should produce ads like this. They're a clothing company, not like Amnesty international. Ads like that don't sell clothes. It's totally random and they do it just to make statements for the sake of making statements" (Ibid.).

These photos were used, as suggested above, to make a social statement, and to draw attention to a non-profit foundation run by Benetton to assist in peacemaking – a laudable goal: the end justifying the means. Is this an appropriate ethical perspective to take or is the campaign forever tainted by its commercially driven sponsor? What does this suggest about the social responsibility of corporations?

(We return to this case in a different context in Chapter 6 – see Case 6.3.)

Case 4.2c: Misrepresenting People for a Good Cause

This next case may seem a little out of place when speaking of political economy since it does not involve any government action or the exploitation of government figures for political gain. But this is too narrow a focus for political economy. In this case the inability of the Nigerian government to protect its citizens, and to rescue several hundred young girls who were kidnapped from their school (as we touched on in a different context in Case 3.1), led to a worldwide Twitter campaign to raise awareness and to put pressure on governments to act on behalf of vulnerable people, thus fulfilling one aspect of social responsibility and ethics – to protect the innocent.

In early 2014 the Nigerian rebel group and militant Islamist sect Boko Haram took several hundred young girls captive after raiding their school in the northern part of the country. This followed several years of raiding villages and killing civilians (with some estimates as high as 12,000) in a campaign to impose strict Islamic law there and to prevent girls from receiving an education. CNN reported (Karimi and Carter, 2014) that "the militant group has bombed schools, churches and mosques; kidnapped women and children; and assassinated politicians and religious leaders alike. It made headlines again recently with the abduction of 230 schoolgirls in the town of Chibok in northeastern Nigeria. After a fierce gunbattle with soldiers, the militants herded the girls out of bed and onto buses, and sped off. Only a few dozen of the girls have escaped." Boko Haram does not consider all Muslims its allies and sometimes has attacked mosques where members had spoken out against it. "Its attacks are aimed at striking fear at the heart of the local population to prevent cooperation with the government, analysts say. Although the northern populace mostly abhors the violence, there is considerable sympathy and support for Sharia law, seen by many as the only way to end what is widely regarded as a corrupt and inept government" (Ibid.).

After the mass abduction of the girls on April 14–15, 2014, a campaign began for their return. A Nigerian creative director, Emmanuel Hephzibah, "found photos on the website of The Alexia Foundation, a charitable organization that supports photographers as agents of social change" (Vitale, 2014). When parents and other Nigerians began using social media to complain about the government's slow response, mass protests were held in major Nigerian and Western cities, and Hephzibah created the hashtag #BringBackOurGirls using a black and white version of the photos and credited the foundation site. The hashtag trended globally on Twitter. By mid-May it had attracted more than 2.3 million tweets. U.S. First Lady Michelle Obama became involved and a video of her holding up her hashtag sign appeared on YouTube. The White House website began a petition drive, along with Change.org and Facebook (see Kristof, 2014). In July the Pakistani activist for educating young women, Malala Yousafzai, became involved in the effort to free the girls (see Oyekanmi and Adigun, 2014).

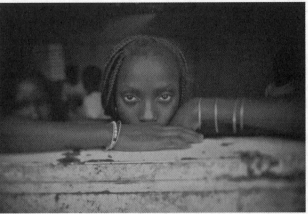

Figure 4.2 *Left:* One of the photos as it appeared on the #BringBackOurGirls campaign. *Right:* The original photo of Jenabu Balde by Ami Vitale. Both photos reproduced with kind permission of Ami Vitale.

The photos used in the campaign were actually of young girls in Guinea-Bissau. They were taken by photographer Ami Vitale, who explains they "were meant to portray a beautiful side of Africa, one separate from the stories of famine and abduction" (Shalby, 2014). Figure 4.2 shows one of the photos as used in the campaign, and Ms. Vitale's original version. In May 2014 James Estrin spoke with Ms. Vitale about the photos, and she told him:

> There were three photos that were taken from either my website or the Alexia Foundation website, and someone made these images the face of the campaign. But these photos had nothing to do with the girls who were kidnapped and sexually trafficked.

> There are many times when I get upset when people take my photos without permission, but this isn't about that. I support the campaign completely and I would do anything to bring attention to the situation. It's a beautiful campaign that shows the power of social media. This is a separate issue.

> This is about misrepresentation.

> These photos have nothing to do with those girls who were kidnapped. These girls are from Guinea-Bissau, and the story I did was about something completely different. They have nothing to do with the terrible kidnappings. Can you imagine having your daughter's image spread throughout the world as the face of sexual trafficking? These girls have never been abducted, never been sexually trafficked.

> This is misrepresentation.

> I know these girls. I know these families, and they would be really upset to see their daughters' faces spread across the world and made the face of a terrible situation.

> The photos were taken from two separate stories. I was there in 1993, in 2000 and then in 2011 for the Alexia Foundation. I lived there for six months, learned the language, learned about their lives and became very close to all the people in these pictures.

> *(Estrin, 2014)*

Commentary on Case 4.2c

Even if you can justify Benetton's actions in attempting to show corporate responsibility by using public figures in manipulated postures, this case raises the question of whether you can also ethically defend a situation where photos used to illustrate a social campaign are not of public figures but of private persons taken for an entirely different reason. There is no commercial interest here, so does that make the campaign more, or less, ethical than Benetton's?

Is there an implied superiority or callousness in appropriating images from the powerless? It is unlikely that the young women from Guinea-Bissau will ever see the use made of their photos and there is the implication that all black Africans are alike, so what is the harm? If people decide to join the campaign to return the Nigerian girls wouldn't that be a positive result? Doesn't that justify the use of their photos even if they are out of context? Is the misrepresentation that Ms. Vitale objects to actually worse than she suggests, or not as bad as she proclaims – since it was all for a good cause and there were no corporate interests involved?

Ms. Vitale also says that the photos were lifted from the Foundation website where they were originally posted. They were probably discovered by searching for photos of African girls, and, since they were taken by a professional photographer, likely were more powerful than most available photos. Using them would enhance the campaign. This then raises the ethical question of what is "fair use" once photos are posted anywhere on the internet. Ms. Vitale has spent months working to get these images off the internet, but to no avail. Once something is on the internet it is difficult to remove it. Google's search engine, for instance, will search for photos using keywords of a user's choosing. Pages of photos may turn up, absent all context unless the user takes the time to click on each one and request to be taken to the original site. It is likely that many online campaigns are put together in the heat of the moment with little regard for truth – or are they? Is truth only connected to an original intent (in this case illustrating the dignity and resilience of people who lived between two great truths: war, famine, abduction, sex trafficking and beautiful safaris and exotic animals) (see Estrin, 2014). Or can a new truth be illustrated through the use of photos taken for other purposes? Ms. Vitale asked this question in her *New York Times* interview: "Can you imagine having your daughter's image spread throughout the world as the face of sexual trafficking? These girls have never been abducted, never been sexually trafficked" (Ibid.). Likewise we might ask whether we could imagine a daughter's image who had been sexually trafficked spread throughout the world. Which is the greater horror? What does truth demand of those who use the media for good causes?

One step that Ms. Vitale took in the aftermath of this issue was to create a survival guide for those who might face the same problem in the future. As she put it: "When a photo is published on the web, it falls into nimble, anonymous hands that upload and share millions of images each day. Context becomes a casualty. Its loss threatens photographers' reputations, may endanger their subjects, and chips away at journalistic credibility. If a photojournalist's responsibility is authenticity, her challenge is control" (Vitale, 2014). She continued: "But [my] colleagues understood 'that it's not just me. It's their reputation, too. We are all connected. All we have is truth. Every time a story like this happens it just erodes that fundamental truth that we try to impress upon people.' The attention amplified her outrage. Ami was furious that her subjects had been misused in a way that Westerners would not tolerate. It was not about race, but about changing the rules where the developing world was concerned. 'It's not a black or white issue,' she insisted. 'It's about applying the same standards across the planet'" (Ibid.).

This case raises the issue of human dignity. Were the girls whose photos were used afforded the dignity that all humans deserve – as universal ethical commitments suggest – or, as Ms. Vitale says, is a double standard at work here? Are those who live in the global south due less respect than those who live in the developed world merely because they do not have the access to communication systems that are readily available in other places – and thus wouldn't know the difference? And does it matter that the use of these photos was initiated by a member of the global south as well, rather than by someone from a former colonial power? Is it just that those in the global south exploit one another, even if for a good cause?

Conclusion

Political economy warns us about the subtexts of media practice. Media can exploit anything for commercial purposes, engage in propaganda for political authority, commodify people's lives, even provide the foundation for surveillance by clandestine agencies. One does not have to be a conspiracy theorist to recognize that the quest for profit may result in situations that do not serve the public, or that even good causes can sometimes lead to results that are both negative and unanticipated.

We must also recognize that good causes do not necessarily justify all means, even if they are in the non-profit sector and the harm might be reduced as a function of the poor access that victims may have to the communication systems that otherwise might tip them off. Given the power asymmetry between governments and elites versus the common citizen, might we excuse the appropriation of their images for a good cause or to respond to an atrocity? Recognizing the situation as uncovered by political economists may assist in traversing this difficult terrain.

Discussion Questions

1   As the world's political economy moves toward greater international engagement on economic issues and an ever-increasing commercial/marketing orientation, will protection of intellectual property be enhanced or eroded? Does it matter ethically which of these outcomes becomes reality?

2   Is there a significant difference, ethically speaking, between use of intellectual property for commercial or non-commercial purposes? Should intellectual property have equal protection in both types of use?

3   Do corporations that operate across different cultures have ethical responsibilities to know each culture and to operate differently according to the "rules" of each one? Or should "one size fits all" be the operational principle for business activities?

4   Should there be an ethical imperative for countries that have benefited from colonialism to raise the living standards of people in formerly colonized societies by major investments in such things as medical care, education, and provision of adequate food and water supplies? On what basis would such investments be justified or avoided?

Notes

1   Eli Noam (2013, p. 5), examining the net number of voices (controlling for cross-ownership of media properties) across 30 countries, reports that the United States – where concentration of ownership questions have been most sustained – actually has the most voices (71) compared to others. Noam

looked at all companies within each country that had more than 1% of market share. Three countries had fewer than 30 voices (Poland, Finland, Chile), while eight had less than 40 (Brazil, Ireland, Italy, Portugal, South Africa, Australia, South Korea, and Belgium). China had approximately 58 voices, India 56. The world average, based on these 30 countries, was approximately 46 sources, but this overstates the actual world average, since it included almost no countries from sub-Saharan Africa, Latin America, or Southeast Asia. When the number of net voices is compared to population, providing a net per capita voice total, the eight lowest countries are Egypt, Japan, Russia, Mexico, the United States, Brazil, India and China, all with less than 0.5 voices per million population – not particularly comforting for the right to receive information (Ibid., p. 7).

2 Information on concentration of ownership in the media can be found on the *Columbia Journalism Review* website: http://www.cjr.org/resources/. Accessed July 16, 2014. Discovery Communications, which claims (2014) to be the world's number 1 pay-TV programmer, has 2.5 billion cumulative subscribers in more than 220 countries and territories, including more than 200 different television networks. Report available from the Discovery Channel: *Discovery Communications*.

3 This case is based on a report from the Voice of America on July 15, 2014, and available at voanews.com. Accessed July 16, 2014.

4 This part of the case is taken from a reprint of Chan's original opinion, "Role of the media in need of rethink," in news.asiaone.com. Accessed July 17, 2014.

5 20th Century Fox and 21st Century Fox are the same media organization.

6 The media and entertainment industry in the United States represents one-third of the global industry, with a 2014 market of $546 billion, according to the United States Department of Commerce.

5

Boundaries on Civil Discourse

Introduction

Traditional roles of the media are to assist the public in understanding public events, to link citizens and their representatives, and to facilitate civil and political discussion. The media accomplish these tasks by, as the Hutchins Commission put it, "explaining the day's events in a context which gives them meaning," providing dramatic and comedic looks at the foibles and actions of constituent members of society and the political establishment, and providing fora for representation, discussion, and interpretation of society's complexities. The media assist different groups in a society to know and understand one another better, to understand the common humanity that connects us all, and to show the consequences of actions – both good and ill – practiced by people in their professional, personal, family, and community lives. Media in these respects provide crucial public and social services.

The Hutchins Commission (1947, p. 21) was of the opinion that the media, as a first requirement, "should not lie." This was a basic and difficult requirement to meet, especially in the political arena. The Commission wrote:

> [T]he moral right of free public expression is not unconditional. Since the claim of the right is based on the duty of a man to the common good and to his thought, the ground of the claim disappears when this duty is ignored or rejected. In the absence of accepted moral duties there are no moral rights. Hence, when the man who claims the moral right of free expression is a liar, a prostitute whose political judgments can be bought, a dishonest inflamer of hatred and suspicion, his claim is unwarranted and groundless. From the moral point of view, at least, freedom of expression does not include the right to lie as a deliberate instrument of policy.
>
> (Hutchins Commission, 1947, p. 10)

These remarks directly tie morality and truth together. To be truthful is to be moral. In the absence of truth, people and communities suffer. Sissela Bok (1978, p. 18) puts this in stark terms: "Deceit and violence – these are the two forms of deliberate assault on human beings. Both can coerce people into acting against their will. Most harm that can befall victims through violence can come to them also through deceit." Although this seems to suggest that lies are principally destructive to individuals, they are equally destructive to society: "A society . . . whose members were unable to distinguish truthful messages from deceptive ones, would collapse" (Ibid., p. 19). The reason: "To the extent that knowledge gives power, to that extent do lies affect the distribution of power; they add to that of the liar, and diminish that of the deceived, altering his choices at different levels. . . . Lies may also

World Media Ethics: Cases and Commentary, First Edition. Robert S. Fortner and P. Mark Fackler.
© 2018 John Wiley & Sons, Inc. Published 2018 by John Wiley & Sons, Inc.

eliminate or obscure relevant *alternatives*, as when a traveler is falsely told that a bridge has collapsed" (Ibid.). "Deception . . . can affect the objectives seen, the alternatives believed possible, the estimates made of risks and benefits. Such a manipulation of the dimension of certainty is one of the main ways to gain power over the choices of those deceived" (Ibid., p. 20).

Deception can take many forms. Lies that are accepted as truth certainly deceive. But the truth can also be cloaked by language and presentation, emphasis, and partial reports. It can be buried in detail, denied by ideology, or simply ignored. The romance of a film can diminish tragedy, as *Titanic* did – assisted by a striking theme song that focused on the lasting quality of love. Clever lyrics in a song, or entry into a forbidden place through music, as country singer Johnny Cash's *Folsom Prison Blues* provided, can often lead the audience to lose sight of true reality. What was the gut-wrenching choice that Sophie was forced to make in *Sophie's Choice*? It was not the choice of sending or not sending her children to a Nazi death camp. It was which child to save – one was surely to die, the other, unknown. But did the film help people understand the true dehumanizing horror of the camps? Which was the more ethical film – *Life is Beautiful* or *Schindler's List*? Both won Academy Awards, but did one or the other more accurately capture the Holocaust, or connect it to the viewers, or assist in the global declaration of "never again"? If Bok is right, then making a film that obscures horror would be, by definition, unethical wouldn't it? And yet a film that did capture such deprivation of humanity would be unlikely to capture an audience of any size – so would be an exercise in futility – leaving us to wonder whether a more upbeat or ancillary story to the true situation might be more ethical after all, since it would at least raise consciousness to a degree not likely with a brutally honest portrayal.

The classical liberal theory of the press takes the position that any speech is valuable. Even speech that is rife with lies, distorts reality, obscures truth, should be protected because eventually the truth will emerge victorious, driving such unethical speech to the sidelines. Unfortunately such expectations seem somewhat naïve today when political mantras, regardless of outrageous falsehoods, continue to be promulgated and fiercely defended in the public marketplace of ideas. Is the quaint notion of a marketplace of ideas still relevant?

Disinformation

Disinformation is false information released in the effort to mislead people about the true state of reality. Disinformation is often practiced by nations at war in the attempt to gain an advantage over the opponent by leading it to believe one reality that is far removed from actuality. The Allied Powers in the Second World War famously engaged in disinformation by creating replicas of military material to convince the Axis Powers of capabilities not actually real. They also used disinformation to draw Axis troops to one site of the expected invasion of France, while planning to land at Normandy. There were many disinformation campaigns run by both the United States and the Soviet Union during the Cold War (Bittman, 1985), and disinformation was used extensively during the Iraq wars beginning in 1991, directed both at the American and the Iraqi publics (see Morano, 2002; Kamiya, 2007; "War Report," n.d.).

In 2007 the film *Taxi to the Dark Side*, the story of an "Afghan taxi driver who was falsely arrested, imprisoned and brutally tortured to death" (Horton, 2008), was shown at the Tribeca Film Festival and received an award for best documentary. But the Motion Picture Association of America (MPAA) "said it had ethical reservations [about the film's poster advertising] showing a prisoner with a hood, that this suggested torture or abuse, and was inappropriate" (Ibid.). Eventually the MPAA relented but the Discovery Channel, which had been scheduled to screen it, decided not to release it because it was "'too controversial' . . . What they meant was that the White House would take offense from it" (Ibid.). Eventually Home Box Office (HBO) carried it, allowing American audiences to "see for the first time, comprehensively, how the Administration consciously introduced torture techniques in American prisons – and how it consciously lied about what it did" (Ibid.). But the word torture was not used officially in Washington until 2014 when President Barack Obama, after seeing a report from the Senate Intelligence Committee, said that the United States had tortured "some folks," thus revealing a decade-plus long disinformation campaign that had avoided using this negatively loaded word.

In another instance the U.S. State Department's official Dipnote blog formally accused Russia Today, a Moscow-based television network financed by the Kremlin, of "an intense campaign of disinformation that tries to paint a dangerous and false picture of Ukraine's legitimate government" (Stengel, 2014). Lawrence Krauss (2009) has lamented: "The rise of a ubiquitous Internet, along with 24-hour news channels, has, in some sense, had the opposite effect from what many might have hoped such free and open access to information would have had. It has instead provided free and open access, without the traditional media filters, to a barrage of disinformation."

Such activities are not only the province of the world's major powers. In early 2014 Susan Thomson, writing for African Arguments ("a multi-blogging site dedicated to informed and vigorous debate on the issues that impact Africa, and hosted by the Royal African Society and World Peace Foundation"), accused Rwanda's RPF (Rwandan Patriotic Front) of "Twitter-gate," the "first crack in the armor of the RPF's longstanding disinformation campaign that has relied on exchange students, public relations firms, commemorative events, and a whole host of other techniques to craft an idealized and often invented version of what Rwanda was like before the onset of colonialism and what it has become since the 1994 genocide" (Thomson, 2014; see also Pottier, 2002). In Pakistan, too, a disinformation campaign run by the Taliban convinced many people that the anti-polio campaign run by the UN World Health Organization was a Western plot to force birth control (or sterilization) on children. This was to prevent the expansion of Islam by reducing population to prevent the continuation of jihad (IRIN, 2007). And in Cambodia, conviction of a journalist for disinformation led to a three-year jail term (Committee to Protect Journalists, 2008).

Some disinformation emerges from non-media groups and organizations, such as governments, terrorist groups, or even benign non-governmental organizations (NGOs). Some of it is intentional, but some is also inadvertent. Regardless of source or intent, the most germane question here is (assuming the media have any choice in the matter), what is the social responsibility of the media? Should the media challenge claims or portrayals that they suspect, or know, are false – or is their job merely to carry the various claims and counter-claims, opinions and counter-opinions: so long as both sides of a controversy are presented, have the media provided the public with socially responsible information?

Case 5.1: *Thrive* and Coverage of Extra-Terrestrial Intelligence

Thrive is a "documentary" film created by Foster Gamble, an heir of the Proctor & Gamble fortune in the United States, which was released in 2011. (The film can be seen here: http://www.youtube.com/watch?v=lEV5AFFcZ-s.) It claims that two fundamental organizing principles govern the universe, from individual atoms through galaxies, that unlimited "clean" power is possible by harnessing the energy created by these organizing principles, and that knowledge of these principles was delivered by extra-terrestrials who have visited the Earth using advanced spacecraft (what are usually called unidentified flying objects, UFOs). The film claims that every fact reported in it has been vetted for accuracy (these claims are available on thrivemovement.com). The film has created a large anti-conspiracy theory backlash, including a website, thrivedebunked.wordpress.com, put together by Muertos. This is part of Muertos' analysis:

> The two hours I spent watching the full Thrive movie for the first time were two of the most hellish hours in my life. It was that bad. It almost made me physically ill. I could feel brain cells dying by the thousands with each excruciating minute of this fulsome, intelligence-insulting geek show. I viewed it as sort of a homework assignment. I collected many pages of notes and then set about breaking down the movie into its constituent parts. The blogs started going up in late November, with the debunking of the "Global Domination Agenda" (Illuminati/NWO by another name) being the most important.
>
> *(Reposted by Clock, 2013)*

A film review by Rob Hopkins (2012) called the film "dangerous tosh which deserves little other than our derision." And Georgia Kelly of the Huffington Post said the film masked "a reactionary, libertarian political agenda that stands in jarring contrast with the soothing tone of the presentation" (Kelly, 2011).

Commentary on Case 5.1

Films that make claims about their adherence to truth are often debunked. Some that may contain truth are also debunked. Now that such films can easily be released (as *Thrive* was) on YouTube, the media does not have the opportunity to make editorial decisions prior to their exhibition. This cannot be the media's social responsibility. But after their release, there is the question of making them known. Should film critics review them? Should the media cover whatever controversy they may create? Should the media become fact-checkers? Or should these activities be left to bloggers and film site reviewers? When such films receive significant traffic (*Thrive* has been accessed on YouTube over 11 million times in addition to its DVD sales), should this trigger media attention, and if so, of what type? Or is the socially responsible action to do nothing at all? On what basis should such decisions be made, and by whom?

Case 5.2: *The Interview*

Most people who watch comedy films recognize that they are fiction. They agree, when entering the theater, to suspend disbelief so that the idiocies, witticisms, or pratfalls that provide the humor in the movie can be enjoyed. However, not everyone evaluates the merits of a film in identical fashion. For instance, in 2014, prior to the scheduled release of the film *The Interview* – which portrayed a television producer and talk-show host landing an interview with North Korean leader Kim Jong-un and then being tasked by the Central Intelligence Agency (CIA) to assassinate him – the country threatened "merciless retaliation" if the film's exhibition was not cancelled. Since North Korea controls all its media outlets, it expects other countries to do likewise (Associated Press, 2014). A North Korean spokesman asserted that "making and releasing a movie on a plot to hurt our top-level leadership is the most blatant act of terrorism and war and will absolutely not be tolerated" (Cooper, 2014). North Korea also filed an official complaint with the United Nations about the film. Its UN ambassador Ja Song Nam wrote to the Secretary General: "To allow the production and distribution of such a film on the assassination of an incumbent head of a sovereign state should be regarded as the most undisguised sponsoring of terrorism as well as an act of war. . . . The United States authorities should take immediate and appropriate actions to ban the production and distribution of the aforementioned film; otherwise, it will be fully responsible for encouraging and sponsoring terrorism" (Newslab, 2014).

Commentary on Case 5.2

There are several ethical questions here. First is the issue of differences in the way the two countries (North Korea and the United States) see their role in regard to the media. When this politico-cultural divide is prominent in such a dispute, which side has the superior claim? The film was produced with private funds for the purpose of profit, not by the U.S. government. But it apparently offended the sensibilities of North Korea's elite and perhaps its population (a collectivist society whose people know little of the outside world beyond what their leader allows them to see). Does the sovereignty of one nation override the principles of another? Second, and closely related, is the question of whether the film should be exhibited in the United States – as demanded – or be scrapped by its producers as a goodwill gesture? Is there an ethical perspective that would suggest that doing the latter would be the more socially conscious decision? And if the film were released on schedule, would it be socially responsible for it to have worldwide distribution, an economic assumption that American film companies generally make? Is this a special case?

On a more fundamental level is the issue of how those in the media (in this case filmmakers, actors, directors) should portray real people, as opposed to fictional characters. Those making the film know little of Kim Jong-un himself. His appearances are scripted and artificial. So they do not know how he would actually react to an American talk-show host or his questions. It is likely that the portrayal would not be true to Un, that his personality would be exaggerated for comedic effect. Although this is standard fare in the American and British media, with comedians regularly portraying or caricaturing politicians and celebrities, it is not the case in most countries. Most protect the image of their leaders, with even the royal family in England having some protection from egregiously negative portrayals. Are films that fictionalize real people socially responsible? Is satire? Can truth prevail when such critical comedic work mocks or ridicules those in authority?

Language and Presentation

Kenneth Burke (1966, p. 366) has called language "symbolic action." He contrasted the use of language with that of motion, which was, he wrote, "the realm of entities that do not respond to words as such." This meant that all human and social sciences called "for treatment in terms of action," while physics and its associated sciences "calls for inquiry in terms of sheer motion" (Ibid.). Language, then, "must be approached primarily in terms of its poetic and rhetorical uses (its functions as expression and as persuasion, or inducement to action)" (Ibid., p. 367). To Burke, action led to passion and passion to revelation (Ibid., p. 368).

Speaking, writing, acting, directing, filming, recording, making media are thus all action. Because acting is meaningful – otherwise it would be mere motion – it leads to belief in the act and what it contains. Belief then results in passion, and passion in revelation – knowledge, understanding. Those who use rhetoric, or the means of persuasion, to relate to others (or to act toward them through what they produce) are altering the world of those whom they address. Seen from this perspective, all language has consequences: meaningless blather is mere motion – the physics of capturing the movement of air via a microphone or the capturing of light and reflection via a camera – but the story that comes from these captures through editing (realigning sound, motion, light, reflection, etc.) is action – it has purpose. Those who encounter this action can make sense of it (although probably not the *exact* sense the creator intended) because "talking is performing acts according to rules" (Searle, 1969, location 469). Indeed it is not only talking that is accomplished by following rules: it is true of any form of expression, from making a television program, to recording music, to writing a news story. They all have rules – often unspoken – as to what would constitute the most effective (rhetorical) composition.

It is because of this complex set of compositions that people face on a daily basis that we can recognize that "cultural practices are not simply speech acts. . . . John Austin introduced ordinary language philosophy to the idea that language could have a performative function . . . . Speaking aims to get things done . . . it is capable of constituting a social reality through its utterance" (Alexander and Mast, 2006, p. 3).

Media provide an increasing amount of the "social reality" to peoples around the world. From satellite television to internet radio and music downloads, to websites devoted to television and film, from news sites to social networking capabilities, more and more people are choosing to supplement their local knowledge garnered from observation, tradition, gossip, and local media with the global views of distant sources. The interpretations that people make of what they experience through these distant sources, while filtered through personal and community lenses, are affected by the presentations they encounter. So the words used, and the type of presentations seen, do matter. They act on people's consciousness, maintaining or replacing worldviews with the unfamiliar.

U.S. president Ronald Reagan once famously quipped that one man's terrorist is another man's freedom fighter. Although this was an effort to deflect criticism at the time, it also indicates one problem with language's connection to social reality: the nature of the words used suggests the social reality it expresses. According to Richard Jackson (2005, p. 1) for instance, "authorities have to make [war] seem reasonable and unquestionable because once public consensus begins to break down and large sectors of society start to doubt the necessity or rightness of the conflict, . . . it becomes extremely difficult to sustain. The process of inducing consent – of normalising the practice of the war – therefore requires more than just propaganda or 'public diplomacy'; it actually requires the construction of a whole new language, or a kind of public narrative, that manufactures approval while simultaneously suppressing individual doubts and wider political protest. It requires the remaking of the world and the creation of a new and unquestioned reality in which the application of state violence appears normal and reasonable." The BBC's editorial guidelines (BBC, n.d.) cautions its journalists not to use the word "terrorist" unless quoting someone else because "there is no agreed consensus on what constitutes a terrorist or terrorist act. The use of the word will frequently involve a value judgment."

The use of language is an issue that affects all writing for the media, regardless of type. A television comedy that uses the word "terrorist" to refer to certain characters, for instance, can ingrain that word and associated concept in the audience's mind as surely as a news report. So we find the people of Kazakhstan objecting to Sacha Baron Cohen's 2006 movie *Borat* for its "disgusting" portrayal of their country and the government banning exhibition of the film. "Tensions were inflamed when the Olympic Committee of Asia accidentally played Borat's spoof Kazakh national anthem during an awards ceremony for shooting medals in Kuwait" (Stewart, 2012). But six years after the release of the film, Kazakh's Foreign Minister Yerzhan Kazykhanov admitted that it had led to a huge tourist boost for the country: "'I salute Borat for helping attract tourists to Kazakhstan,' he said" (Ibid.).

Presentation of material is also closely associated with language. In the *Borat* example, it was not merely the claim by Cohen to be Kazakh that was the problem; it was that the comedy also mocked

Figure 5.1 A still from Sacha Baron Cohen's 2006 movie *Borat*.

the country's morals and practices. Cohen appeared in swimming gear, for instance, that left little to the imagination (see Figure 5.1). The case is made more complicated by the fact that the film was originally condemned, and later embraced, by Kazakhstan. Clearly the Foreign Minister applied the utilitarian perspective: what had been bad for the country had turned into good and thus its effects must be reevaluated. But is this how social responsibility should be judged? Can a media portrayal be both socially responsible and irresponsible depending on its effects for (in this case) tourism?

If we look at portrayals of terrorism further questions arise. As Nachman Ben-Yehuda (2005, pp. 35–36) writes: "Terror's connection with the media has increased in both its intensity and sophistication precisely because the media have created an arena in which terror is not only presented but justified. Thus, in many important respects, the media have become another arena in which terrorists are competing for both exposure and time, preferably – of course – to present themselves in a sympathetic and understanding fashion." For example, in Tunisia the High Independent Board of Audiovisual Communication (a media regulatory authority) forbade the re-broadcast of an episode of *Liman Yajroo Fakat* ("For He Who Dares") hosted by journalist Samir Elwafi in which he had interviewed people close to Kamel Gadhgadhi, a suspect in a political assassination who had subsequently been killed by police. "Elwafi was criticized for presenting 'terrorism' in a positive light and soliciting the audience's empathy for Gadhgadhi and suspected terrorists. 'Justifying terrorism in one way or another is not acceptable,' HAICA president Nouri Lajmi told *Tunisia Live*. . . . The breaches mainly focused on the 'lack of respect for the provisions of the International Covenant on Civil and Political Rights and in particular Chapter 6 thereof, relating to the right to life' and the 'lack of respect for pluralism of ideas and opinions,' according to the HAICA statement" (Smadhi, 2014). The International Covenant on Civil and Political Rights is a 1966 United Nations treaty enshrining basic rights and liberties. It does not mention media coverage of suspects of violent acts. Lajmi explained the ruling by saying the presentation of a terrorist in "the image of a martyr or as oppressed" is "an assault to the right to life of people killed by terrorists" (Ibid.).

In the United States the Fox television program *24* has both been criticized for its excessive use of torture as part of its storyline and pointed to in discussions about interrogation techniques in the

George W. Bush administration as a principal source of ideas (see Green, 2005; Sands, 2008, location 1332–3, 1344; "Over the line, Smokey!," 2009). The result of the fear in the Bush administration that the United States would experience another brutal terrorist attack, the conviction among several important Bush advisors (in particular Vice-President Dick Cheney, Secretary of Defense Donald Rumsfeld, and John Yoo, a legal expert) that torture was effective, and the mythology that developed around the television character Jack Bauer, all troubled William Safire, "the conservative language columnist at the *New York Times*." He wrote of the "bland bureaucratic euphemisms" that could "conceal great crimes. As their meanings become clear, these collocations gain an aura of horror. In the past century, the *final solution* and *ethnic cleansing* were phrases that sent a chill through our lexicon. In this young century, the word in the news . . . is *waterboarding*. If the word *torture* . . . means anything (and it means deliberate infliction of excruciating physical or mental pain to punish or coerce), then *waterboarding* is a means of torture" (Mayer, 2008, location 2957). Jane Mayer referred to the avoidance of this reality through the use of euphemisms as a "corruption of language" (Ibid.).

J.L. Austin (1975, p. 6) puts these two aspects of language – words and their definitions and the performance of these words – into a single concept: performative sentences or performative utterances. These sentences indicate "that the issuing of the utterance is the performing of an action – it is not normally thought of as just saying something" (Ibid., pp. 6–7). Using such performatives is a "rhetic act" (Ibid., p. 95), the truth or falsity of which "depends not merely on the meanings of words but on what act you were performing in what circumstances."

In this case the Bush administration's more hawkish members needed a means to elicit information from irregular combatants, needed to use torture to elicit that information, and needed to violate international understandings ("many of which were hammered out by American lawyers in the wake of harrowing Nazi atrocities of World War II" – Mayer, 2008, location 178) of "humane treatment" such that harsh measures were justified, even if doing so was based on "egregious misunderstanding of the Geneva Conventions" (Ibid., location 1613). Similarly, to apply the new harsh measures – torture without naming it so – the president "determined unilaterally that all prisoners captured in the war on terror were unlawful combatants" and thus not covered by the Geneva Conventions, American legal guarantees, or rules for prisoners of war (Ibid., location 2415). Apparently the only ethical yardstick applied in these cases was utilitarianism – the question of where torture worked or didn't work. The calculation of relative good or harm resulting from it was never in doubt – torturing even a few hundred prisoners potentially to prevent another attack on thousands clearly tipped the balance in favor of such action. The application of the utilitarian standard clearly failed in this case as an appropriate ethical approach.

Such dystopian situations are made possible by the existence of the negative in language. As Burke (1966, p. 9) put it in his definition of man, we are inventors of the negative. "We are here concerned with the fact that there are no negatives in nature, and that this ingenious addition to the universe is solely a product of human symbol systems." What was "torture" and what was "not torture"? It was all a matter of defining what was by what was not, or vice-versa. Language was a tool of necessity. Likewise, the interplay between positive and negative (one of the primary aspects of symbolicity) also provided the basis for catharsis through scapegoating. Since the Bush administration had failed to take seriously threats from Al-Qaeda – although apparently forewarned to do so – it needed identifiable scapegoats on whom to heap this failure (sin), and those imprisoned in Guantanamo – and later Abu Ghraib – provided the means to expunge their guilt and for the American public to direct its hatred – of the evil personified by them (Ibid., p. 18–19).

Conor Friedersdorf criticized *New York Times* executive editor Dean Baquet for his rationalization of the paper's refusal to use the word "torture" in its coverage of President Bush's policies and its belated decision to begin to use the word once President Barack Obama legitimized it by saying "we tortured some folks" in 2014. Friedersdorf wrote:

> The *Times* failed to call torture by its rightful name because it failed as an institution. The exact nature of the failure is only known to people within the organization. Perhaps its relationship to the Washington establishment was such that it could not bring itself to use plain language when U.S. leaders committed war crimes. Maybe its editors mistakenly believed that striving for objectivity required them to back off any claim contested by a powerful ideological or political faction, an act of preserving "The View From Nowhere" at the expense of the truth.
>
> There are other possibilities.
>
> A more forthright explanation of what went wrong might not serve the institutional interests of the *Times*. But I suspect it would help us to think through the other euphemisms and propagandistic jargon that American journalists have employed during the War on Terrorism, often out of sheer familiarity. I've caught myself referring to prisoners as "detainees" and to drone strikes that kill men of unknown identities or innocent women and children as "targeted killings" (though I've seen through attempts to call drone killings "surgical").
>
> I've caught myself using the phrase "The War on Terror," and talking about what's been "redacted" in documents rather than what's censored, hidden, or suppressed.
>
> *(Friedersdorf, 2014)*

Other egregious examples of the misuse of language (even refusals to use some language) include the refusal of the world community – and in particular U.S. president Bill Clinton – to use the word "genocide" when referring to the atrocities in Rwanda in 1994 (which would have triggered the necessity to act), or the use of dehumanizing language ("vermin," "rats," "cockroaches") to refer to groups of people in Nazi Germany, the former Yugoslavia, and Rwanda so as to reduce the guilt that people might otherwise have felt when participating in the slaughter of members of such groups (Jews, the disabled, Jehovah's Witnesses, "gypsies," Bosnian Muslims, Croats, Tutsis, among others). Such terms were the opposite of euphemisms (dysphemisms).

Case 5.3: Graphic Content in the News

It is not just language that can mask or unmask reality. Photographs can also accomplish it – and as the old aphorism goes, a picture is worth a thousand words. In August 2014 a tweet from Australian "terrorist" Khaled Sharrouf, then fighting in Syria, was reproduced by newspapers around the world. "It depicts a boy, thought to be Sharrouf's son, holding aloft a severed head. Though the boy's eyes are blacked out and we cannot see the severed head, the photograph is both shocking and chilling" (Jewell, 2014) (see Figure 5.2).

Commentary on Case 5.3

The photograph was widely condemned, including by U.S. Secretary of State John Kerry and Australian prime minister Tony Abbot (Mazza, 2014; Morgenstern, 2014). After mentioning the amount of footage and number of photographs of atrocity coming in from around the world, Jewell (2014) wrote that "it is

Figure 5.2 The photo that appeared in Khaled Sharrouf's tweet (from *The Australian*).

now widely recognised that journalists who deal with so much graphic content can suffer from post-traumatic stress disorder. It's been argued that the use of more graphic material in mainstream media is at least partly due to the rise of social media." If we are to believe Jewell, then such graphic content in mainstream media is not the result of any "need to know," but rather a brutal necessity in an age of social media where such material, once posted, can appear again and again on timelines that result in a diffusion around the globe. The sensibilities of people – from squeamish to sensationalistic – are made irrelevant even when the mainstream media themselves may warn about graphic depictions prior to revealing them on the web or may pixelate the image in a print publication to reduce its impact.

Ronan Farrow (2014), writing in the *Washington Post*, called social media "radio's modern day equivalent" for the appeal to bloodlust. Pointing out that Sunni Islamic State insurgents "now command a plethora of unofficial channels on Facebook, Twitter, and YouTube," he then notes that "social media companies are leery of adjudicating what should be taken down and what should be left alone." He goes on:

> And so official Islamic State accounts often remain on Twitter for weeks and accumulate tens of thousands of followers before being taken down. A few propaganda videos have been removed from YouTube for "violating YouTube's policy on shocking and disgusting content," but countless others remain, including a last weekend's sermon by Baghdadi, posted by an account claiming to be Islamic State-affiliated and carrying more than 12,000 views. (Rather than direct traffic to those accounts, I decline to link to it here.)

> There are legitimate free-speech questions here: What about reporting on propaganda? What about peaceful lectures by otherwise violent terrorists? But those grey areas don't excuse a lack of enforcement against direct calls for murder, which these companies supposedly ban. "I understand there are freedom of speech concerns, but I don't think that describes what's going on with much of the content on YouTube," says Evan Kohlmann, a counter-terrorism analyst with Flashpoint Partners and NBC News. "No one's suggesting they remove all journalistic clips . . . . This is about extremely explicit content, calling for violence."

> Another objection is practical. There's simply too much content to monitor, and too many openings for it to come back when quashed. An executive at one major social media company described it as the "whack-a-mole" phenomenon – take down one video, it springs up elsewhere.

But flawed enforcement shouldn't excuse inaction any more than it did in Rwanda 20 years ago, when the U.S. government deemed jamming solutions too legally complex, too expensive, too impractical. The perfect, then as now, was the enemy of the good.

(Farrow, 2014)

There are important freedom of expression issues raised by such performative speech, whether in words or pictures. Related to these are issues, as raised by Farrow, about the role of gatekeepers and the question of whether social media sites have the same gatekeeper functions (or obligations) that traditional mainstream media have used to govern their editorial decisions. Farrow argues that it should be no trouble for social media sites to police for such graphic displays as they already do so for a variety of others, including nudity, pornography and the like. The implication is that violence is not in the same category as nudity – thus invoking a criticism that has long been directed in the United States to its media where violence is seen as a legitimate spark for the conflict that drives westerns, police and private detective shows, and more recently forensic-based television. Many countries find the American use of violence to be far more objectionable than nudity, especially in Europe. Since national authorities have limited power of influence over social media compared to that held over the acceptability of television or films for domestic exhibition (what some called paternalistic review), the question now is, whose social mores should prevail in a global social media system, especially when this system is seen as the most democratic medium available? Or are terrorists a special case, and if so, how should they be defined and what messages, if any, should they be allowed to post?

Case 5.4: Tourism Dispute in Hong Kong

On March 9, 2014 protesters rallied in Hong Kong's Mong Kok shopping district to protest against mainland tourists. The rally resulted from a social media-fueled controversy based on video footage of a mainland Chinese toddler urinating in a Hong Kong street. The original incident had quickly attracted an angry crowd that surrounded the family, causing the offending child to cry. The child's mother grabbed a memory card off someone who had filmed the child urinating, and refused to return it. A friend of the videographer telephoned the police. People were shouting at the family in Cantonese (the major language of Hong Kong) and the parents shouted back in Mandarin (the mainland's principal language). The child's parents were then arrested for suspicion of theft and assault (the mother had allegedly slapped one of the protesters). The *South China Morning Post* (Luo, 2014) reported that "Numerous mainland media agencies reposted the news on their official accounts of China's most popular social media platform Weibo, drawing more than a million comments or reposts by Wednesday." The commerce secretary of Hong Kong subsequently urged Hong Kong residents "to calmly teach their mainland brethren better manners" (Tharoor, 2014), but this was interpreted by many of them as condescending. In China itself an online campaign started in response to the anti-mainland fury, calling for more Chinese tourists to take children to Hong Kong to pee in the streets.

In response, some Hong Kong protesters mimicked going to the toilet atop portraits of Chairman Mao. *The Global Times*, a Beijing state-owned newspaper, issued a stern editorial on the matter, condemning Hong Kong's coterie of "hooligans": "This handful of radicals remind us of the rampant skinheads and neo-Nazis in Europe. Xenophobia is the cult of these groups. Their opinions have an effect on public opinion, but their actions will usually make trouble for mainstream society."

(Tharoor, 2014)

The *Shangaiist* (2014) reported that "This incident has gotten far more traction than it deserves on social media, and people are pissed (get it?). Sina ran a poll that was picked up by the *Wall Street Journal*, to test the waters on the issue, and the responses (perhaps predictably) were overwhelmingly favorable to the pint-sized pee-er." It also posted videos from the original incident and reported that "Hong Kongers have called the family's behavior 'uncivilized,' while anyone who has walked down a crowded street in China knows that seeing the occasional toddler gleefully relieving itself on a tree, bush, or curb is just a part of the job" (Ibid.).

Commentary on Case 5.4

Although Hong Kong is ostensibly part of the People's Republic of China, it has a special status which, among other things, requires those from the mainland to obtain permission to travel there. The tourists who travel to Hong Kong live in a very different political environment and public sphere than their counterparts in the city. The availability of public toilets, for one thing, is minimal in many parts of China (particularly rural areas) compared with in Hong Kong, and necessity in one context may not be interpreted as equally necessary in another. In this case we have a clash of cultures that subsequently played itself out on social media (in the mainland's case on the social media site Weibo), and that resulted in little mutual understanding among the contending publics. Community mores, public outrage, retaliatory threats, the engagement of political authority, and probably frustration, misunderstanding, shame, and confusion seemed all to result from one tiny toddler's need to pee in a strange city. A certain amount of voyeurism in videoing the child, the blow-up into group confrontation, arrests, and lack of resolution were all involved in the original incident. But it might have been left there, had it not been for the ease of using social media to express, or embarrass, and then to respond and threaten. Is this what it means to see such systems as "democratic"? Do such incidents imply that expectations for understanding different cultures or political systems and ideologies are poorly placed in these media? How do these systems provide the basis for social responsibility and in this case who acted in a socially responsible manner: the offending toddler, the enraged videographer, the parents, the crowd, the police, the media, the political authorities? Did anyone? Are there ethical systems that provide a foundation for resolving such cultural clashes before they escalate into mutual disgust and retribution?

Case 5.5: Racism in Bollywood

Indians are obsessed with fair skin, the result, says Aditi Jain (2014), of the caste system "where dalits or 'untouchables' often had much darker skin" compared to the higher castes. The assumption or "inherent implication is that if you have fair skin, you are somewhat superior to others around you as if darkness were an illness which one must cure." One cosmetic brand that has been advertised in India since 1975 is "Fair and Lovely," which claims that it can cure dark skin. Another reason for the light skin preference, says Jain (Ibid.), is the "romanticizing of western attributes. The fact is that Katrina Kaif, who is now a successful actress in Bollywood, is of foreign origin and she was welcomed with open arms because of her fair complexion."

Roop Sumal (2014) agrees with Jain's conclusion:

> In a country or even a culture which places (unnecessary) value on skin tone by way of matrimonial ads boasting of fair skin and caste level, it is quite contradictory that people attempt

to wear a badge of liberalism as a sign of modernity, yet default back to ultra-conservatism when faced with the issue of racism. Delayed progress is a given as long as one is encouraged to remain within the confines of ignorance when faced with uncomfortable situations, as is the default cultural norm and tendency. . . .

The advertising industry reaps the benefits of a society obsessed with attaining a "fair and lovely" skin tone and has partnered with B-town to engrain this concept in all aspects of the culture, which in reality is quite damaging to women, forcing judgments based on outward appearance while depleting self-esteem. Bollywood has a tendency to engrain this negativity in many by romanticizing *fair complexion* and western attributes of so-called "beauty." Ironically, most South Asians see racism as a phenomenon which breeds in foreign countries, particularly the west. The fact remains, institutionalized racism is on the rise and India's favored pass time – Bollywood often tends to play into it. Unfortunately B-town dances to its tune by way of song lyrics, dialogues, physical appearance and casting of characters. This begs the question – have we yet to truly unshackle ourselves from the past British rule? Political freedom may have been granted, but socially we remain slaves to our own skewed mentality.

The preference for fair skin shows up not just in the actors cast in Bollywood films, but also in comments made on blogs, in the lyrics of songs, dialogue in film, and the overarching mythology of Indian society. One actress, Bipasha Basu, was even described by Kareena Kapoor as a "kali billi," or black cat, despite her obvious beauty due to her "dusky complexion." Mahesh Bhatt worried that "our minds are coloured by racism that was practised by the British during their rule in India, and it takes years to unshackle oneself from this slave mentality. We may have won political freedom, but socially, we are still slaves to such a backward mindset" (Dubey and Dubey, 2014). Usha Jadhav, an Indian national award-winning actress, also with a darker complexion, said that "many producers refused to cast me because of the colour of my skin. They'd say they want a fair girl to play the heroine." And another Indian actress, Nandita Das, points out that fair skin has been glorified by the film industry for a long time. "This reflects how biased our society is. We keep saying things like, 'Uska rang saaf hai' while referring to fair-skinned people; it's as if dark skin is a dirty thing. This mindset is then propagated in our songs, stories, myths and fables" (Ibid.).

Commentary on Case 5.5

India is a vast country made up of people of many different hues. Just as with African Americans or Caucasians, the color of skin is quite variable. What is the best skin color for a person to have? There is no single answer. Actress Nandita Das decided to combat the preference for fair skin by becoming the poster girl of the "Dark is Beautiful" campaign in India. The campaign was launched in 2009 by activist group Women of Worth to celebrate "beauty beyond color" (*New York Daily News*, 2013). Das backed the campaign and began to hear from Indian women, some of whom had "wanted to commit suicide because they couldn't be fair" (Ibid.).

Das found her own photograph had been lightened by a newspaper even for a feature on the campaign. When looking for a nanny, she was told one candidate was "good, but quite dark." Amid such pressures to be pale, India's whitening cream market swelled from $397 million in 2008 to $638 million over four years, according to market researchers at Euromonitor International. Skin-lightening products accounted for 84 percent of the country's facial moisturizer market last year, their report shows. The bias facing darker-skinned women was raised again in September when an Indian-origin woman, Nina Davuluri, won the "Miss America" contest in the United States. "Had she been in India, far from entering a beauty contest, it is more likely that Ms. Davuluri would have grown up hearing mostly disparaging remarks about the color of her skin," said an editorial in The Hindu newspaper.

(New York Daily News, *2013*)

Beauty, of course, is said to be in the eye of the beholder, but what of the performative aspects of portrayals in the media that prefer one type of person (caste, skin color, race) over another when it comes to casting actors? What of the performative aspects of advertisements that claim to whiten skin – knowing the cultural preference for lighter tones – when many in the culture will never be able to call themselves fair regardless of the amount of bleaching agent used? As for "Fair and Lovely" itself, Das says, "you're telling people they're just not good enough." Such whitening cream advertisements are "regressive and derogatory" (Ibid.).

What then is the social responsibility in a society that can be divided into different communities according to color (or even caste – although officially banned)? Should there be a quota system to assure that actors of different shades have an equal opportunity to be cast as princes or heroines? Would it be socially responsible in a post-colonial society where values of "whiteness" were promoted by white overlords to ban advertisements or products that suggest that a continuation of inferior status is preferable, perhaps even inevitable? Is harmony among people possible if such actions are not taken – and if they were, would it make any difference?

Conclusion

There is no perfect society, one free of prejudice or preference. Media organizations often say they reflect their society by holding a mirror up to it, but such claims minimize their role in directing people's assumptions and promulgating their myths. The reality is that through the choices media make in their use of language and presentation, they perpetuate lingering biases or create new ones. Sometimes these biases are positive – the bias toward peace over conflict, or community over selfish aggrandizement. But, as in the examples above, they can also be negative, sowing division among people who differ through no fault of their own, exacerbating cultural conflict, allowing destructive speech to have the same prominence as that aimed at ameliorating hatred, promoting conspiracy theories, or creating comedy that is more interested in laughs (and gate receipts) than in the realities of the world. What are the appropriate boundaries of civil discourse? Or does anything go in the world where gatekeeping no longer controls the flow of information?

Discussion Questions

1   Would people in societies where collectivist ethics are central be more justified in judging a person by skin tone or color than those in more individualistic ethical cultures?

2   Are there good ethical reasons to engage in disinformation, for instance to protect national secrets or to conceal war plans? If so, where should the line be drawn to separate legitimate from illegitimate disinformation?

3   Is it more ethical for journalists to use euphemisms when the subject of a story would likely disgust readers, or to use dysphemisms when the impact of an important story might be missed by readers and the journalist wants to make sure the audience sees the true horror of a reported situation?

4   Do those who produce documentaries have more responsibility to truth-telling than those who produce fictional films? Or are these distinctions so artificial as to have no real value when judging the potential impact on viewers?

6

Advertising, Public Relations, and Materialism

Introduction

Thomas Malthus predicted in 1798 that the planet would be incapable of supporting its geometrically expanding population in less than 200 years, at which time his population projections suggested that the anticipated population of 256 billion would be living on a food supply capable of feeding only nine billion. His projections were incorrect. Currently there are somewhat more than seven billion humans on the planet and still enough food – if distributed effectively – for everyone to have adequate nutrition. However, there are warnings: the dependence on fossil fuels and the creation of greenhouse gases are heating the planet and melting the ice caps. Coastal cities are at risk. Water supplies may be more critical than food supplies as the climate changes. The United States, with a population of only 310 million (about 3% of the global total) uses disproportionately more resources by a large margin than most other countries on the planet. Only China approaches the U.S. consumption rate, and these two countries (providing less than 20% of total population) create 40% of the planet's "global footprint" ("Reckless consumption depleting earth's natural resources," 2008). The World Wildlife Fund (WWF) has said that there would need to be two planets to sustain the world's current lifestyles within a generation (Ibid.).

Agricultural technology has enabled the world to continue to produce enough food to match population growth since Malthus' prediction, although it is unevenly distributed. But water shortages threaten continued yield rates and the ability to use increased arable acreage. In a context of limited resources, what is the ethical approach to media that exist to promote increased consumption?

Advertising as a Post-Enlightenment Enterprise

Modernity developed from the Enlightenment. As David Harvey (1989, p. 13), depending on the thought of Ernst Cassirer, explains: "Enlightenment thought . . . embraced the idea of progress, and actively sought that break with history and tradition which modernity espouses. It was, above all, a secular movement that sought the demystification and desacralization of knowledge, and social knowledge and social organization in order to liberate human beings from their chains." To do so humanity's essence was defined as "creatively destructive," a singular path to "affirmation of self" (Ibid., p. 16). This creative destruction involved "religious myths, traditional values and customary ways of life" (Ibid.). Capitalism fit into this model of creative destruction, especially the entrepreneur who pushed "the consequences of technical and social innovation to vital extremes" (Ibid., p. 17).

World Media Ethics: Cases and Commentary, First Edition. Robert S. Fortner and P. Mark Fackler.
© 2018 John Wiley & Sons, Inc. Published 2018 by John Wiley & Sons, Inc.

Capitalism, too, benefited from the romantic movement that sought the aesthetic experience and that "generated that wave of 'radical subjectivism,' of 'untrammelled individualism,' and of [a] 'search for individual self-realization'" (Ibid., p. 19). It was the task of the individual to pluck meaning from the maelstrom of ephemerality that characterized the modern age. It was the individual who, in his search for self-actualization, made himself the target of those who would "solve" his dilemmas, his self-doubts, and his imperfections through ideological panaceas, patent medicines, scientific break-throughs, and advances in efficient production (Fordism). It was to this insecure or ambitious individual that advertising would be directed. Written artistically and with proper attention to people's insecurities, the products advertised could freeze time by providing eternal youth, or halting the natural aging process, or solving the infirmities to which human beings are prone. It could demonstrate to people how the well-dressed person could transcend his class, how the purchase of the right automobile could raise others' estimation of his place in society, and how – with the right credit score – he might live beyond his means in perpetuity (see Boorstin, 1973, especially Parts 3, 7, and 9).

Georg Simmel (1903/1950), writing about the effects on mentality of living in rapidly developing metropolitan centers, said that "ultimately the only means of saving for themselves some modicum of self-esteem and the sense of filling a position is indirect, through the awareness of others." He goes on to explain that "in the nineteenth century, through Goethe and Romanticism, on the one hand, and through the economic division of labor, on the other hand, another ideal arose: individuals liberated from historical bonds now wished to distinguish themselves from one another. The carrier of man's values is no longer the 'general human being' in every individual, but rather man's qualitative uniqueness and irreplaceability" (Ibid.). This desire to distinguish oneself from others, to find a handhold for individuality in a teeming city marked by conformity, to escape from what were seen as oppressive definitions of self located in religion, class, or trade, provided the psychic foundation to which those with remedies could appeal. "Our only outlet, he seems to say, is to cultivate a sham individualism through pursuit of signs of status, fashion, or marks of individual eccentricity" (Harvey, 1989, p. 26).

One explanation of transition is provided by T.J. Jackson Lears (1983):

> "On or about December 1910," Virginia Woolf once said, "human character changed." This hyperbole contains a kernel of truth. Around the turn of the century a fundamental cultural transformation occurred within the educated strata of Western capitalist nations. In the United States as elsewhere, the bourgeois ethos had enjoined perpetual work, compulsive saving, civic responsibility, and a rigid morality of self-denial. By the early twentieth century that outlook had begun to give way to a new set of values sanctioning periodic leisure, compulsive spending, apolitical passivity, and an apparently permissive (but subtly coercive) morality of individual fulfillment. The older culture was suited to a production-oriented society of small entrepreneurs; the newer culture epitomized a consumption-oriented society dominated by bureaucratic corporations.

Advertising was also rooted in the sensibilities that emerged from these developments. Advertising was a means to define the way out of conformity (despite the conformity that it promoted). It was a method of distinguishing oneself from peers and redefining the individual self in a post-Enlighten-ment reality that redefined personal significance apart from the herd (see Benhabib and Bisin, 2000). In the early days of mass media advertising (the 1920s) it broke away from the older forms of intelligence that had supported the commercial focus of newspapers. It began to appeal outside the limited orbit of businessmen to that of ordinary people – often promising them opportunity to solve chronic aspects of the human condition occasioned by its fragility. But it was every man or woman for him/herself. Individual investments were required to acquire the requisite solution.

> Advertising offered itself as a means of efficiently creating consumers and as a way of homogeneously "controlling the consumption of a product." . . . To create consumers efficiently the advertising industry had to develop universal notions of what makes people respond, going beyond the "horse sense" psychology that had characterized the earlier industry. . . . The vanguard of the business community found the social psychology of such men as Floyd Henry Allport extremely useful in giving an ideological cohesion to much of what one sees in the advertising of the twenties. Explicating the notion of the way in which man develops a sense of himself from infancy, Allport asserted that "our consciousness which others have of us . . . [m]y idea of myself is rather my own idea of my neighbor's view of me." This notion of the individual as the object of continual and harsh social scrutiny underscored the argument of much of the ad texts of the decade.
>
> *(Ewen, 2001, pp. 33–34)*

After the end of the Second World War in the United States (and later in Europe once it had recovered from the devastation and disposable income had begun to rise in the post-war boom), expenditures on advertising began a rapid ascent. In 1946, some 3.34 billion dollars was spent on advertising in the United States. By 1950 this had more than doubled and a decade later it had doubled again, to nearly 12 billion dollars. By 1975 the total spent on advertising had reached nearly 28 billion dollars, in 1985 nearly 95 billion, in 1995 162.93 billion, in 2000 247.472 billion, and in 2007 almost 280 billion dollars (Coen, n.d.). A similar increase in advertising expenditures, but at a lower level, occurred in Great Britain despite the lack of consumer goods available for several years after the war (see Clayton, 2010). Throughout the period from 1946 to 2000 the United States was targeted by roughly half of all the advertising expenditures worldwide. This percentage began to fall somewhat after 1988, but in 2005 the United States still accounted for 48% of worldwide expenditures (Assadourian, 2007).

The global dominance of advertising expenditures in the United States is explainable by the fact that it had the largest economy in the world over this period and was the largest single consumer market. According to the United Nations, the U.S. consumer market was 29% of the world's consumer market, compared to the European Union's 27%. The world's two most populous nations, China and India, provided 5.3% and 2.1% of the global consumer market respectively in 2009 (see "World's 25 largest consumer markets!," 2011). But the situation began to change in 2010. China surpassed Japan as the second largest consumer market that year, and by 2011 China was either the first or second consumer market for shoes, consumer electronics, and jewelry (Stalk, 2011). Chinese Minister of Commerce Chen Deming claimed in 2012 that China would be the world's largest consumer market by 2015 (Rapoza, 2012). Although the figures are inconsistent, it appeared that China had become the second largest consumer market in 2015, and would be the top consumer market in 2016 – meaning that Minister Deming was only one year off in his prediction.

Manufacturers of consumer goods responded to this Western economic reality by creating advertisements in tune with the cultural tropes of a rapidly changing economic, psychological, and artistic landscape. Ads appealed to different mentalities with content aimed at market segments (children, youth, women, sport addicts, the upwardly-mobile, the insecure, etc.) responded to their various interests and desires. And this was all done within the West's post-Enlightenment individualistically oriented mindsets.

> Popular culture is used as a resource [by advertising practitioners] . . . [A]dvertising is reactive and relies on siphoning off ideas from culture – practitioners strategically raid new cultural

trends they see appearing across a range of sites (fashion, art, popular music, design, television) and put selected elements of them to work in their campaigns.

(Cronin, 2004)

The Growth of Global Advertising

One study published in 2008 indicated that economic growth in a national economy was closely related to rising advertising expenditures, which were a measure for aggregate advertising demand (van der Wurff, Bakker, and Picard, 2008, p. 28). As the effort to expand businesses has become increasingly global, so has the development of advertising. With the development of an increasingly commercially-subsidized international media regime, it has been necessary for the advertising used to pay for the production and distribution of "free" content to develop apace. This has meant, too, that the cultural values of acquisition, material comfort, and the solution to personal and community problems by purchasing products and services have been introduced to new cultures.

> Advertising lies at the juncture where culture and the economy interact: its primary purpose is to sell products and services by stimulating purchasing power and it does this by using strategies that rework culture, creating aspirations and new desires for products. . . . Advertising is itself a cultural product which increasingly affects social attitudes, defines social roles, and influences cultural values. . . . In recent decades advertisers from the industrialised nations have increasingly targeted international markets, expanding the consumption of foreign products and bringing about widespread cultural change.
>
> *(Ciochetto, 2004, p. 1)*

One question we should ask about the export of advertising as a medium from those countries that are part of the post-Enlightenment tradition to those that are not (especially Asia) is whether this export is, on its face, ethical. As discussed in Chapters 2 and 3, the philosophical traditions undergirding ethics in the post-Enlightenment world are largely individualistic in orientation, matching the cultural shifts that were occasioned by the Enlightenment itself. But Asia is far more collectivist in its philosophical traditions. Can advertising that is premised on the role of the individualist self, personal choice, and the acquisition of consumer goods to support ideas of success, self-worth, and status appropriately be ported into collectivist-oriented cultures without doing serious ethical damage to their foundations?[1] Kelly, Lawlor, and O'Donohoe (2005, p. 645), remarking on the pivotal role of advertising in ascribing symbolic meaning to consumer goods, suggest that "The discourse of advertising has a dialogic and reciprocal relationship to other cultural institutions and social systems such as family, religion, arts, literature and music, and through this interactive and fluid relationship advertising has developed into a potent 'cultural system' which shapes and reflects consumers' sense of social reality."

Of course, this is already happening and Asia is expected to outpace the European Union in advertising growth within a few years as household incomes and levels of urbanization increase. Is this the triumph of post-Enlightenment philosophy over collectivist traditions, or do these traditions have the resources to adjust or accommodate a shift toward consumption-based economies? To return to Ewen (2001, p. 35), in the early days of advertising in the United States, "advertisers were concerned with effecting a self-conscious change in the psychic economy" (see also Burroughs and Rindfleisch, 2002, p. 348). Since, as we have seen, the "psychic economy" of collectivist cultures significantly differs from that of individualist cultures, we may expect that different approaches would have to be taken in the two systems. If the same strategies or assumptions about people's relationships with one another are identical in the two cases, we may expect psychic damage in at least one of them. In India and Sri Lanka one study indicated that advertising and television programming had "transformed public culture and resulted in mass consumerism," a result conforming to earlier research in the Middle East and China (Speck and Roy, 2008, p. 1211). In Romania and Turkey a study indicated that those investigated believed "that materialism is the way of the modern Western world [and] legitimates an entire culture's escalating materialism" (Ger and Belk, 1999, p. 196).

The change in psychology, whether "damaging" or not, can be seen in several studies of the developing consumer cultures of Asia. In India, two studies were carried out – one of older middle-class informants in Baroda and the other of younger informants in Bangalore. Although the two groups differed in their degree of moralizing about a materialist ethos, in both cases consumption was "an embodied marker of status – whether in the addition or the lack of a mobile phone, Nike trainers, a sari and gold jewelry, or a twinset and pearls. The established middle classes are always more likely to moralize against the materialist urges of the newly moneyed – and there is certainly a lot of new money circulating amongst the liberalization-era Indian middle classes" (Nisbett, 2007, pp. 943–944).

A tearing of the social fabric in Asia as a result of the headlong rush into urbanization and the rapid creation of a consumption class has been noted by several commentators (see Richardson, 1994, on Malaysia; Doctoroff, 2012, on China; see also Wirekoh-Boateng, 2010, on Africa; and Bales, 2012, on the relationship between wealth and modern slavery). There has even been a backlash in China against the pell-mell rush to embrace Western consumption values, as Chinese consumers began to "re-instill Chinese culture in the consumption process" (Wang and Lin, 2009, p. 400). These cultural values include frugality and social status (related to face) that inspires conspicuous consumption: "When conspicuous consumption is coupled with low disposable income and frugal habits, it influences the use of counterfeit products" (Ibid., p. 402). Chinese consumers also respond more favorably to advertising emphasizing relational ties with significant others and relational interdependence rather than the individualism, independence, uniqueness, and autonomy that are more typical of Western ads (Ibid.).

Of related interest is the anticipated boom in economic growth and internet access in Africa. Although internet penetration in Africa was only 16% in 2013 – mainly due to the large number of rural citizens, the vast expanse of Africa, the lack of electrical-grid and landline infrastructure, and poverty – the McKinsey Global Institute has predicted that Africa "is poised to make a digital leap" on par with the rapid rise of mobile devices already experienced (Al-Jazeera America, 2013). While this appears to be a positive development for a continent that has lagged behind all others in economic development and communication, if the prediction is correct then the one billion Africans expected to encounter this change by 2025 will also face unprecedented advertising for consumer goods on both social media and information platforms that were designed for and are supported by advertising aimed largely at more developed consumer societies. Africa, like many countries in Southeast Asia that have already crossed the threshold into mass use of the internet, will find its citizens eager to use a system that they will not understand due to the low levels of education generally, and media literacy specifically. Advertising will blend with the sites visited, not as a separate stream of ignorable content, but as an integral feature. In other words, the new consumers who will encounter these sites will do so as naïve netizens who have only recently been able to access the cornucopia of the internet and not the more jaded consumers of developed countries who had gradually been engulfed in advertising years before and had developed cynical skins to ward off the continual chant of "buy, buy, buy."

In Africa as in Asia the communal orientation of society will face severe challenges. Modern advertising assumes an atomistic society comprised of individuals each deciding how to respond to individual consumption messages. People may see the intrusion of advertising as annoying as it finds ever more nooks and crannies in the media system to insert its pitches, but a long history of encountering such messages – at least among those with secondary educations or above – instills a knowledge that the buyer should beware – not only of the shoddy, overpriced product but also of the pitches that encourage consumption beyond one's means. Even then, however, the debt load of millions of people in these societies increases virtually every year. In cash societies the first requirement will not be education about the systems encountered but the acquisition of a debt mentality. In countries where people care for one another, share one another's burdens, often eschew personal fulfillment to care for their family or clan, there is the distinct possibility that the debt of one will become the debt of many, with the potential to wrench tight-knit communities asunder.

There is little doubt that consumer societies will continue to spread around the globe – indeed, this appears to be one of the underlying premises of globalization itself. Globalization is not merely about free trade, or the movement of labor and capital, but about the spread of capitalism that is dependent on the development and growth of markets for consumer goods. This is why the question of ethics in the rapidly growing consumerist world is so crucial.

Tobacco Advertising

The year 2014 was the fiftieth anniversary of the release of the U.S. Surgeon General's report on the health effects of smoking. In 2003 the Framework Convention on Tobacco Control was adopted and ratified by 177 countries in a global effort to reduce smoking and its associated health risks. Although globally the prevalence of smoking has decreased for both genders, since 2006 there have been increases in the number of smokers in several large countries, including Bangladesh, China, Indonesia, and Russia (Ng et al., 2014).

Despite these efforts to reduce smoking, the tobacco industry advertises its products at a rate that is 50% higher than the average industry. The World Bank reports that comprehensive bans on cigarette advertising reduce cigarette consumption, but that those who are poorer or less educated (especially men) are more likely to smoke than those who are wealthier or better educated. This translates into the fact that 80% of the world's smokers now live in low- and middle-income countries (where the largest populations themselves are located), and that these smokers are less likely to quit than those in wealthier countries. The result: "About 1 billion people will die from smoking in the 21st century – ten times as many as the 100 million lives claimed by tobacco throughout the previous century" (World Bank Group, n.d.).

Despite the evidence linking smoking to a variety of health problems and premature death, tobacco companies have continued their campaign against new anti-smoking legislation in many countries. They sued the Australian government over its plain packaging law prohibiting the display of logos, brand imagery, symbols, or other images, colors, or promotional text on tobacco product packaging, and the mandate "that packaging be a standard drab dark brown colour and that graphic health warnings occupy 75% of the front and 90% of the back of packaging" (Liberman, 2013). Japan Tobacco, Philip Morris, and British American Tobacco have followed similar tactics in other countries, too, including Thailand, Indonesia, Brazil, and Uruguay. Indonesians have sued their own government over lax anti-smoking laws, angered by the prevalence of children smoking in that country. The government responds "by saying the country depends on the jobs created by the tobacco industry" ("Cigarette giants in a global fight against tighter rules," 2010). It even gave tax incentives for the manufacture of hand-rolled cigarettes due to the employment of workers by local firms in east Java. According to the Indonesian statistics bureau, smoking is such a pervasive habit "that tobacco products are the number two item in household expenditure after rice" (Rondonuwu and Bigg, 2012).

It is easy to condemn the ethics of governments, manufacturers, sales kiosks, and parents for allowing children to smoke, or of media outlets for carrying the advertising that promotes greater levels of smoking. It is perhaps an even more egregious breach when this happens in countries where incomes do not easily support the purchase of such products, or people are not as aware of the risks associated with smoking. But what of other products whose harm is not so well publicized? Do advertisers have any responsibility to limit their pitches to only certain outlets, or to use only adverts that are either not very persuasive or have no appeal, at least, to the youngest potential users? And what of products that might be considered vanity-products only, with little to no real value to human life?

Case 6.1: Skin Whitening Products in Asia

Skin whitening products are a $13 billion industry in Asia. Global sales are expected to reach $19.8 billion by 2018 "driven by the growing desire for light-coloured skin among both men and women primarily from the Asian, African and Middle East regions" (McDougall, 2013). In India these products account for 45% of the total skin care market. "According to a 2004 study by global marketing firm Synovate, nearly 40 percent of women in Taiwan, Hong Kong, South Korea, Malaysia and the Philippines used skin whitening and lightening products that year" (Martin, 2009). The Chinese expression often heard to justify use of such products is "one white can cover up three kinds of ugliness."

Several reasons are given for this desire for lighter skin. A prevalent one – and the one expressed to Robert Fortner when he was conducting fieldwork in Indonesia in 2010 – is that dark skin indicated a person was a peasant who worked in the fields. Fieldworkers were at the bottom of the status ladder and no one wanted to be mistaken for one if they could avoid it. Another reason, according to Gerald Horne at the University of Houston, is that the winners of the Second World War were white and should be imitated (Martin, 2009). Still a third reason given is self-hatred – Chao-uan Tsen of the Taipei women's rights organization Awakening Foundation made this claim, saying that Taiwanese women desire to be as white as Japanese women, "as beautiful as a cherry blossom" (Ibid.). The multinational company Unilever uses social media to sell Pond's skin-lightening products called "White Beauty." In some countries skin lightening products are sold even for genital areas, with the argument that tight clothes cause darkening of that area and call for the use of "Sanofi's whitening feminine wash" (see Tan, 2012; Dolan, 2014; Glory Surgery, n.d.).

Still another reason given is that pale-skin beauty is deeply embedded within East Asian culture: "Nithiwadi Phuchareuyot, a doctor at a skin clinic in Bangkok who dispenses products and treatments to lighten skin, said: 'Every Thai girl thinks that if she has white skin the money will come and the men will come. The movie stars are all white-skinned, and everyone wants to look like a superstar'" (Fuller, 2006). China in particular has several old sayings which associate fair skin with desirability. For example, the saying: "'white, fortuitous, beautiful!' That is the standard for female beauty" (Diaz, Cheung, and Lee, n.d.; see also Li et al., 2008). As Pan (2013, p. 6) puts it, "Nearly all facial and body lotions sold in China and Taiwan contain chemicals that lighten the skin. These skin-whitening creams, known as *mei bai*, are popular cosmetic products used by 'Culturally Chinese' women to achieve the socially constructed notion of beauty." In other words, there seem to be several cultural and aesthetic biases that contribute to the notion that people – especially women – should do all that is possible to change their appearance by lightening their skin. This will make them more beautiful and increase the odds that they will find true love or, at least, a suitable mate.

At the same time, however, various objections – both rational and emotional – have been raised about these practices. In addition to the self-hatred argument referenced above, the BBC (2013) has asked whether this activity, and the cosmetics industry that creates the products for it, is "pandering" to a negative cultural reality, while Kate Hodal (2013), writing in *The Guardian*, has reported that a Unilever advertisement "that appeared to offer university scholarships to students with fairer skin has stoked a debate over racism in Thailand," forcing the company to apologize for any "misunderstandings." Thomas Fuller (2006) in the *New York Times* reported that "some of the most effective agents are also risky – and are often the least expensive, like mercury-based ingredients or hydroquinone," which has been banned in cosmetics in the European Union since 2001 and causes leukemia in lab animals.[2] It is not uncommon for people who use such products to ruin their complexions completely or to end up in hospital emergency rooms. And there are accusations of racism, even among those within relatively homogeneous racial categories (Dravidians in India, for instance),[3] merely because people are born with differing amounts of skin pigmentation that is seen to give advantages to some over others simply on the basis of skin color. The result is often that women who cannot afford the expensive treatments to change skin color resort to "illegal bleaches and creams containing mercuric chloride that have left them disfigured" (Martin, 2009).

The multinational cosmetics companies excuse their creation and promotion of these products with a simple claim – they're giving people what they want. There is merit to such claims, since it's clear that there are multiple reasons – historical, cultural, aesthetic, mythological – for people to use such products. More recently the products, which have traditionally been pitched to women, have begun to be produced and aggressively advertised to men. The creams cost about one dollar (U.S.), or half a day's wage for many Indians. Given this economic reality, some companies are now selling the creams in tiny packages so that poorer people, who cannot afford an entire tube of the product, can still strive toward the cultural "norm" (see Wax, 2010).

Commentary on Case 6.1

Although we have concentrated on Asia in this case, the phenomenon of skin whitening is global. There is a YouTube channel devoted solely to skin whitening, with multiple videos claiming that the promoted product is the "best" (skin whitening guru), with no indication of the affiliation or expertise of the young woman whose photo graces her home page. In many countries radio and television are used to promote these products, as also are billboards, so that anyone passing by can be reminded of an available product. The billboard in Figure 6.1 advertising "Khess Petch," or "all white," in Dakar, shows a young Senegalese woman whose skin has been lightened by the product ("Whiter skin in 15 days," 2012). It advertises a cream that is available for 2 Euros, or more than two dollars (U.S.). But according to dermatologists, its main ingredient, clobetasol propionate, should only be used in cases of serious skin diseases. Other products available use corticosteroids and hydroquinone, "which are harmful and carcinogenic when applied in significant doses on the skin" (Ibid.).

There is also a Tumblr site on skin whitening, with one young woman, "nhuyae," (Nhuyae, n.d.) writing about one cleansing foam product that it "burns your eyes like a bitch" but does "brighten" her skin "somewhat," about another that "irritates her skin like crazy," and about a third that "dries up the skin even worse than the rice bran or likas soap" and that is "too harsh for my skin." She observes however: "75% of lotions in Asia have the words 'whitening,' 'brightening,' etc on the label. It's a craze that I myself cannot disown. This lotion [Nivea Body Whitening Lotion] hasn't shown me any results yet, although I know it'll take a lot more than one bottle of .02% whitening ingredient in it. I think it's

Figure 6.1 A billboard advertising "Khess Petch," or "all white," in Dakar.

the psychological effect it has on me; knowing I'm using some sort of whitening product no matter how little it actually pales me up, makes me feel like I'm doing something for myself."

Advertising does often appeal to people's insecurities, no matter what the product. People have wanted to emulate the "Marlboro Man," drive a Mercedes-Benz, or wear the latest trendy clothes because they want to feel better about themselves. In one respect these skin whitening products are no different – they promise a psychological boost, a chance to land the spouse of your dreams, the opportunity to rise more quickly in your profession, or at least to feel better about yourself. But how far is too far in meeting a cultural desire?

Is it ethical, for instance, for one Korean company selling skin lighteners to use what the company declares is the most popular character in the country ("Molang") as the name of its own product? (see Figure 6.2). The brand is Chica 7 Chico, and the product is Molang Whitening Cream. It contains colostrums from New Zealand cattle as one ingredient, reputedly to make it suitable for sensitive skin. Its proof: testimonials from users.

Or what should we make of the website www.healthlozenge.com which recommends "DR.JAMES GLUTATHIONE Skin Whitening Pills" (see Figure 6.3)? The presentation perhaps provides extra "expertise" for the product as it comes from what appears to be a doctor with the same name as the product. Did he invent it? Who can tell? Although he notes the possibility of "severe side-effects such as hair fading and skin damage," and says "it is better to refer a doctor before captivating one for you," he does promise that the product "Almost, it creates the skin tone smooth and whitens by retrogressive the absorption of melanin pigment revolving black pigment into bright ones."[4]

P. Ravi Shankar and P. Subish of the Department of Pharmacology in the Manipal College of Medical Sciences in Pokhara, Nepal, reviewing the skin whitening phenomenon, write that "the natural preference for a fair skin has been fanned by the manufacturers of fairness creams. Advertisements in the media aim to produce a hierarchy of values based on the notion that a fair skin is a necessary prerequisite for success in both the professional and the personal sphere. The natural anxiety of men and women regarding skin colour has been heightened" (Shankar and Subish, 2007, p. 102). After listing the various skin-bleaching agents that are prevalent in fairness creams, and the

Figure 6.2 "Molang" the cartoon character, and the skin-lightening cream named after it.

DR.JAMES GLUTATHIONE Skin Whitening Pills   **Figure 6.3** One of the products available on the website www. healthlozenge.com.

serious side effects that can result from their use, they report "that up to 60% of those who practice skin lightening may suffer from at least one complication" (Ibid., p. 103). They conclude that such products are a form of "disease mongering," creating a problem and then providing a product to solve it (Ibid.).

In another study Evelyn Nakano Glenn (2008, p. 283) writes:

> The Internet has become a major tool/highway/engine for the globalized, segmented, lightening market. It is the site where all of the players in the global lightening market meet. Large multinationals, small local firms, individual entrepreneurs, skin doctors, direct sales merchants, and even eBay sellers use the Internet to disseminate the ideal of light skin and to advertise and sell their products. Consumers go on the Internet to do research on products and shop. Some also participate in Internet message boards and forums to seek advice and to discuss, debate, and rate skin lighteners. There are many such forums, often as part of transnational ethnic Web sites. For example, IndiaParenting.com and sukh-dukh.com, designed for South Asians in India and

other parts of the world, have chat rooms on skin care and lightening, and Rexinteractive.com, a Filipino site, and Candymag.com, a site sponsored by a magazine for Filipina teens, have extensive forums on skin lightening.

Glenn reports that the Indian mass media shape notions of feminine beauty in South Asia, including popular viewer spectacles such as Miss World – India, where the competitors tend to be lighter than average, and the portrayals of Bollywood actresses such as Isha Koopikari and Aiswarya Rai (Ibid., pp. 289–290). She also credits the marketing of three multinational corporations, L'Oreal (Lancome), Shiseido (White Lucent), and Unilever (Ponds and Fair & Lovely), that actively promote their products to lighten skin. Their advertisements, she says, "can be seen as not simply responding to a preexisting need but actually creating a need by depicting having dark skin as a painful and depressing experience. Before 'unveiling' their fairness, dark-skinned women are shown as unhappy, suffering from low self-esteem, ignored by young men, and denigrated by their parents. By using Fair & Lovely or Ponds, a woman undergoes a transformation of not only her complexion but also her personality and her fate. In short, dark skin becomes a burden and handicap that can be overcome only by using the product being advertised" (Ibid., p. 298). What once might have been merely a wish, or preference, within societies where many people have darker skins, and where such products were a marginal, underground activity, "has now become a major growth market for giant multinational corporations with their sophisticated means of creating and manipulating needs" (Ibid.).

When a product is legal and largely unrestricted, and cultural traditions or prejudices provide the basis for desiring it, is it necessarily ethical to create and advertise it in the quest for profit? Do corporations that develop and market such products to exploit people's fears or to respond to their demands have a social responsibility to avoid creating them? Especially in societies with a collectivist ethics, when products appeal to individualistic desires and thus contribute to what may be destructive cultural biases, or may even result in disfiguration or serious health problems because of the willingness to take the risk, can we conclude that corporations are acting within the boundaries of ethical behavior? These products – in these societies and others like them – raise serious ethical questions.

Case 6.2: Pharmaceuticals and Natural Remedies in Africa

In 2001 John Le Carré published the book *The Constant Gardener*, subsequently made into a film released in 2005. The novel and film explored the underside of the international pharmaceutical industry. In the film a multinational pharmaceutical company was using the slums of Nairobi as a testing ground for a tuberculosis drug with severe side effects, under the cover of AIDS tests and treatments. Medical experiments were being conducted on the naïve and ill-educated slum dwellers, who suffered and died as a result. Although the story was fiction, it exposed the exploitation of vulnerable people for testing drugs destined for those in richer countries. Conducting such experiments on an unsuspecting and uninformed population is an activity that most people would condemn as unethical.

Unfortunately, the novel and film were not really fiction. In Nigeria in 1996 the American pharmaceutical company Pfizer tested an experimental antibiotic called Trovan in the Infectious Diseases Hospital in the northern town of Kano during an outbreak of meningitis. More than 50 children died and many others developed mental and physical deformities (although Pfizer claims that "only" 11 of the 200 children in the trial died). A Nigerian expert medical panel set up to review the drug concluded that the test was a "clear case of exploitation of the ignorant" (Murray, 2007). In the mid-1980s, too, the German Bayer unit, Cutter Biological, having discovered that a blood-clotting medicine for hemophiliacs was infecting them with HIV, introduced a safer medicine in the West but continued to sell the old medicine in Asia and Latin America: "By continuing to sell the old version of the life-saving medicine, the records show, Cutter officials were trying to avoid being stuck with large stores of a product that was proving increasingly unmarketable in the United States and Europe. Yet even after it began selling the new product, the company kept making the old medicine for several months more. A telex from Cutter to a distributor suggests one reason behind that decision, too: the company had several fixed-price contracts and believed that the old product would be cheaper to produce" ("Bayer's unethical behavior in addition to Cipro poisoning," 2009).

These examples demonstrate the exploitation of innocents in the quest for profits. But such products were not advertised – they were "merely" tested. What of products that are marketed for other maladies? Are the claims made for pharmaceutical products reliable?

One study suggests they are not. It was conducted in Germany and concentrated on advertising material and marketing brochures sent to general practitioners. The study showed that about 94% of the information in these materials had "no basis in scientific evidence. . . . About 15% of the brochures did not contain any citations, while the citations listed in another 22% could not be found. In the remaining 63% the information was mostly correctly connected with the relevant research articles but did not reflect their results. Only 6% of the brochures contained statements that were scientifically supported by identifiable literature" (Tuffs, 2004). The author concluded that the drugs featured were presented with distorted profiles (including misrepresented, mis-quoted, or changed medical guidelines from scientific societies), minimized side effects, contained incorrect definitions of patient groups, repressed study results, exaggerated treatment effects, manipulated risks, and included claims of effects drawn from animal studies, not human ones (Ibid.).

In Africa, as a result of economic crises beginning in the mid-1980s, the medical infrastructure in many countries began to deteriorate. Many hospitals and clinics suffered from severe budgetary cutbacks and the deterioration of remuneration for medical personnel, leading to a "mass exodus of qualified personnel" (Council for the Development of Social Science Research in Africa (CODESRIA), 2008). Structural adjustments demanded by the International Monetary Fund and the World Bank also "contributed to the demise of local medical laboratories and factories. . . . The full depth of the crises of public health provisioning experience in Africa has been brought out in sharp relief by the activities and interventions of the global pharmaceutical companies that seat atop the international production and supply chain for medicines and related health services. . . . In the face of the power projected by the pharmaceutical majors and the influence which they are able to mobilise, most African health systems are, perhaps unsurprisingly given their crises, easily vulnerable to the pressures which they exert in order to secure their interests" (Ibid.).

CODESRIA (2008) also drew attention to the pharmaceutical companies' practice of dumping products on African markets, thus depressing local pharmaceutical industries, and the use of "pilot experiments" for "diseases such as tuberculosis, HIV/AIDS, and malaria" which raised serious ethical issues. They also highlighted campaigns by multinational firms to discredit less expensive local generic drugs that claimed such "fakes [were] both ineffective and damaging," and which had pushed many people to look for alternative methods for "meeting their health needs, including faith healing and the revival of indigenous medicine. It has also opened a window for a flourishing market in fake medical products that take a daily toll in lives lost" (Ibid.). Finally, CODESRIA pointed out that these major pharmaceutical firms had "pillaged" Africa's indigenous medicines and taken out patents on "local herbal remedies used in the treatment of common diseases," and "taken a frontline role in the 'invention' of diseases and treatments for them . . . . [T]he consequences of their activities for the health and well-being of the peoples of the continent are numerous" (Ibid.).

Commentary on Case 6.2

The use of traditional remedies in many parts of the world is a complicated issue.[5] China, of course, has the most highly developed set of practices. In Africa, however, the fragmentation of the continent by artificial colonially-created boundaries, by linguistic, tribal, and clan differences, has meant a much more localized set of practices. The situation is further complicated by the close association that traditional medicine has with animist religion. Both the practices of healing and the "evil arts of witchcraft" are seen as parts of African science (Ashforth, 2005, p. 215). As Ashforth explains, "'African science' in everyday talk occupies a place alongside the miracles of Scripture and the magic of what is usually referred to as Western or White science in its ability to transform the world in mysterious ways" (Ibid., p. 216). To doubt that these two aspects of African science are as powerful as White science is "tantamount to betraying a lack of faith in Africa and Africans" (Ibid., p. 217).[6]

We are not in a position here to evaluate the relative efficacy of traditional versus Western approaches to medical care. Other than the close connection that traditional medical practices have with the belief systems of many Africans, the other major difference between these two approaches is the means by which remedies are discovered and adopted into practice. In the Western tradition this occurs through drug testing regimens that are regulated by external expert review before any new compound is approved for sale to the public – and, theoretically, only for certain declared maladies.[7] But there is no such system in place for traditional medicines and remedies. This is due partly to the connection between traditional practices and spirituality (by definition, untestable), and partly the development of such practices within a system that is outside the science-based system of the West.

Several ethical issues are raised by the use of two types of healing practice in the same environment. First, how are people to evaluate the relative value of the two approaches when their bases are so different as to make them non-comparable? Second, what are the appropriate (i.e., ethical) sorts of information that would allow someone – either an individual needing health care for himself or another in his care, or a government regulatory body – to make a reasonable choice of therapy? Third, what should the source of this information be – the individuals or organizations that provide these therapies, regulatory bodies, consumer protection groups, or others – and do independent agencies exist to provide such information?

We would suggest that the primary issue raised by all these questions is that of advertising. Should the advertising directed to the public for each of these forms of therapy be held to the same standards? Should advertising be permitted at all? What claims could advertisements legitimately make – that is, what claims would be non-deceptive, truthful, and morally correct given the very different origins of the therapies and testing regimens that apply?

These are not merely academic questions, with one form of therapy having an obvious advantage over the other and thus having a more legitimate basis for advertising. For instance, in the case of Western pharmaceutical products, one study of the advertisements in medical journals – examining more than 6,700 ads over a 12-month period in 18 different countries – found a variety of problems, including lack of information about negative effects, warnings and precautions, side effects, and contraindications. Although 96% of the ads included one or more pictures, 58% of them were irrelevant. And pricing information was only included in ads placed in journals in countries where a social security system paid for the medication, thus omitting important information that doctors should reasonably use in prescribing drugs for their patients (Herxheimer, Lundborg, and West-erholm, 1993). Another study – of reproductive health advertisements from 2001 to 2005 in South Africa – found that, like ads for many other products aimed at doctors for other maladies and in different countries, the availability of substantiating evidence for claims was extremely low. As the authors conclude: "The quality of advertisements for reproductive health products placed in medical publications appears to fall short of at least some requirements of both existing and draft regulatory instruments. This may potentially have deleterious consequences for prescriber behavior" (Shaw and Gray, 2009, p. 56).

Another report, from Intellectual Property Watch, indicated that "drug companies routinely violate World Health Organization ethical guidelines when advertising and promoting their products in East Africa . . . . The study from Health Action International Africa's Kenya office studied 543 print advertisements examined in five East African countries. Of the brochures distributed at medical facilities, none met six standard criteria as set out by the WHO for ethical advertising of medicines. Only 16 percent of advertisements released to the general public did so" (Wadhams, 2009). Finally, despite the claims of major pharmaceutical companies that the high prices for newly introduced drug therapies are justified by their investment in research and development, one study of American "big pharma" companies concluded that in 2004 these firms were spending 21% more on promoting drugs via advertising than they were on research and development itself ("Big pharma spends more on advertising than research and development, study finds," 2008).

Problems exist, too, in regard to information provided for traditional medicines and methods. For instance, a study of advertising regulations in seven sub-Saharan African countries (Darley, 2002) found that while there were regulations pertaining to pharmaceutical advertising in most countries (the exception being Botswana), such regulations only applied to medications that would be provided by medical doctors, not by traditional healers, shamans, or witch doctors.

Case 6.3: Is it Public Relations or is it Advertising?

As mentioned in Chapter 4 (see Case 4.2b), the Italian clothing company, United Colors of Benetton, has a history of producing provocative ads to get the attention of consumers, as well as to highlight and promote various political causes. It has taken on interracial and possibly homosexual love (1991), AIDS (1993), capital punishment (1996), world hunger (1997), and hate (2011). Although none of the campaigns displayed or asked consumers to purchase its products, all of them included a small Benetton logo (see Figure 6.4, Figure 6.5, and Figure 6.6).

In the UN*HATE* campaign, as we saw, Benetton used Photoshopped images of world leaders embracing and/or kissing one another. The United States White House objected to the commercial use of President Obama's photo in the campaign (see Figure 4.1), with spokesman Eric Schultz saying, "The White House has a longstanding policy of disapproving the use of the president's name and likeness for commercial purposes," but took no action. The Vatican, however, threatened to sue Benetton for appropriating Pope Benedict XVI's photo and suggesting that he would kiss Egyptian imam Sheik Ahmed el-Tayeb, and Benetton withdrew this photo.[8] Later it made a contribution to a Catholic charity to end the dispute.

The photographs were made into posters and displayed in major cities around the globe (Mezzofiore, 2011). Olivero Toscani, who created the campaigns, called advertising "a smiling carrion," and accused traditional ads of "being dull and unimaginative, creating and portraying an ideal world that does not exist" (Ibid.). Benetton created a foundation, the UN*HATE* Foundation, with its own website to accept donations to pursue its goals. In 2012 this campaign continued, this time highlighting unemployed youth and offering prizes for the 100 "unemployees of the year," each of whom would receive 5,000 Euros for their pet projects (Reuters, 2012). By 2015 the UN*HATE* Foundation was working on campaigns against drug use-related deaths, deaths of migrants crossing the Mediterranean from Africa to Europe, and violence against women. It began by soliciting stories

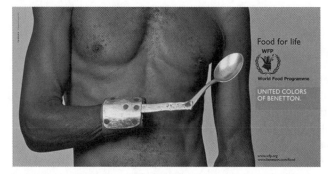

Figure 6.4 Benetton's anti-hunger campaign.

Figure 6.5 Benetton's anti-capital punishment campaign.

Figure 6.6 Benetton's "UN*HATE*" campaign. *Left:* Mahmoud Abbas, president of the Palestinian National Authority, and Benjamin Netanyahu, prime minister of Israel. *Right:* Pope Benedict XVI and Egyptian imam Sheik Ahmed el-Tayeb.

and then looking for projects to make these stories a reality, searching out writers, photographers, and filmmakers who wanted to become UN*HATE* reporters (see the website at unhate.benetton.com).

Commentary on Case 6.3

This case presents a difficult challenge in the discussion of ethics in advertising and public relations. First, although the UN*HATE* campaign created advertising messages, these were not designed to sell products directly, so were actually more public relations in intent. Second, the intent here was ostensibly to spur commitments to reducing conflict between obvious adversaries and to solicit donations for this cause. Although Benetton could keep its brand in the public eye, it could also reasonably claim a noble intent. We could even apply Machiavelli's dictum that the end justifies the means in this case, thus excusing the appropriation of images of world leaders, and the obvious alteration of those images to provide shock value, as a socially responsible means to reduce global conflict. People in countries beset by religious or political conflict, or who suffer under economic sanctions as a result of conflicts between states, might even welcome the campaign for the possibilities it raises that common sense might prevail and people could repair communities, return to tolerance of religious or political differences, and have access to goods that make daily life easier.

However, it is also true that this campaign could be seen as just another cynical attempt by a major clothing brand to continue the "in your face" controversies that have long defined its appeal to buyers. While this campaign may not be as blatantly offensive as some of its earlier campaigns, it still uses images without permission, makes false and trivial claims about reducing conflict, and creates a necessity for world leaders to respond to the campaign when they very well have other more pressing issues to address. Under the common law tradition, there would also be precedent for recognizing the images appropriated to constitute invasions of privacy (assuming the courts would interpret the campaign as having a commercial motivation), a reality only ameliorated by the fact that the people whose images were used were all public figures whose expectations of privacy would be lower than that of private citizens. Even in the absence of efforts to stop the campaign (apart from by the Vatican), it could also be argued that using these images not only trivializes the people in them but also the offices they hold, thus reducing the moral suasion they might use in their own right to reduce conflict. In that respect the campaign would actually work against its own declared intention.

How, then, should the campaign be seen? Is it merely advertising under another name, or a sincere effort to demonstrate the necessity of working out conflicts through personal interaction and respect rather than the use of more violent measures? Should Benetton be applauded for its creativity and message, or dismissed merely as a company attempting to enhance its reputation through exploiting political, religious, and economic realities?

Discussion Questions

1 Are collectivist ethical cultures more, or less, likely to develop materialist/consumerist lifestyles than countries from individualist ethical cultures?

2 Should "science" always be the preferred method of dealing with illness or are there also good reasons to use traditional medical treatments? How should the relative efficacy of these two approaches be evaluated? Would this also apply to what is called Chinese traditional medicine, including acupuncture?

3 Can the world ethically support global lifestyles on the order of what is experienced in the United States or other highly consumerist societies? If not, should these consumerist societies reduce their consumption so that people in other countries can increase theirs, or should squatter's rights prevail?

4 Should media report on the consumerist lifestyle countries in less developed societies? Should the problems of consumerism be emphasized, or criticized, or should consumerism be held up as an ideal? On what set of ethical perspectives could your answer to this question be justified?

Notes

1 One study of the differences in advertising appeals in the United States and Korea did suggest that appeals based on individualistic benefits were not as persuasive in Korea as in the U.S. (Han and Shavitt, 1994).

2 The problem is not restricted to Asia. In Mexico, for instance, "skin creams containing mercury are widely available in pharmacies and beauty aid stores. . . . The label on some of these products does not specify their ingredients, so the consumer does not have any choice for selecting suitable products. . . . A study of 119 Latino women from California, Arizona, New Mexico and Texas that were using bleaching creams to lighten skin tone, showed that 87% of them had elevated mercury levels in urine" (Peregrino et al., 2011, p. 2516).

3 India does not classify its population by race, having eliminated that category from its census data in 1951. Indians appear to be a complicated mixture of various racial groups, including Mongols, Caucasians, and Australoids. They are sometimes referred to as Dravidians.

4 Healthlozenge.com/skinwhiteningpills.php: "DR.JAMES GLUTATHIONE Skin Whitening Pills." Accessed March 1, 2015.

5 The World Health Organization defines traditional medicine as "diverse health practices, approaches, knowledge and beliefs incorporating plant, animal and/or mineral based medicines, spiritual therapies,

manual techniques and exercises applied singularly or in combination to maintain well-being, as well as to treat, diagnose or prevent illness" (quoted by Munyaradzi, 2011).

6 Since 2002 the World Health Organization has recognized traditional healing as a legitimate form of medical practice. It has been estimated that between 60% and 80% of Africans rely on traditional medicine practitioners as their first contact when seeking advice on or treatment of health issues (Munyaradzi, 2011).

7 This is problematic, however, as the widespread use of some medications far outside their approved sphere, especially for the elderly and in mental health facilities, has resulted in efforts to crack down on such practices in the Western world.

8 These photos all from http://top10buzz.com/top-ten-controversial-united-colors-of-benetton-ads/. Accessed May 4, 2015.

7

Global Entertainment

Introduction

Worldwide, people like to play, and that liking starts at a very young age. Educators have recently verified what child care-givers have long known: play encourages confidence, self-esteem, social skills, vocabulary growth, self-control, memory, and cognitive flexibility (Bartlett, 2001). Is that reason enough to think well of play? There may be one other important factor: play is fun, and fun is hard to find in most places where people gather to work out their common life.

Using media for play is increasingly popular. The vast majority of television and radio programming is all play, called entertainment. Compare the number of people attending feature films to those watching documentaries, and the entertainment function wins over the information function everywhere, every age. The argument can be made (and eventually will be verified) that the internet is mostly play: Facebook, Twitter, iTunes, video-gaming. Relief from the stressful realities of work, home, and community obligations drives people to play.

Some forms of recreation are so complex that expertise requires years of experience, not to mention an initial endowment of intelligence and memory. Take chess, for instance, a game played by millions since AD 300. Very good play at chess is the result of years of watchful gaming or the unique giftedness of a child prodigy. Playing golf is an exercise of learning and re-learning fine motor skills that very few players ever master to their satisfaction.

Dutch social philosopher Johan Huizinga concluded that play was the first order of human business. He titled his 1938 classic *Homo Ludens* – not *Homo faber*, Marx's well-known "man the maker," but *ludens*, humankind the player. Before inventing city councils or workers' unions, or even alphabets, humans invented games to entertain themselves in a sphere that permitted the standard rules of civility to be temporarily lifted. From play came ritual, poetry, music and dancing, political campaigning, and battle protocol, wrote Huizinga (1938/1950, p. 173). The rules of play became the framework of international law. Games and treaties each changed in response to human wants, until games more than treaties settled into universal form. Imagine the chaos should the size of a goalkeeper's net ever change, or the number of strikes required to declare a baseball batter out. Redrawing national boundaries would be the easier task.

Playful media is called popular culture, produced for the most part without government oversight and addressed to a market which will return benefits to producers, from expressed gratitude to wealth in the form of sales and royalties. Popular culture is imaginative, and law cannot keep up with it. Rules barring this-or-that playful media are notoriously ambiguous, full of legal loopholes and escape valves. Because of this imaginative freedom, popular arts often "incorporates elements of subversive narrative, and does so in a playful manner" (Okome, 2001).

World Media Ethics: Cases and Commentary, First Edition. Robert S. Fortner and P. Mark Fackler.
© 2018 John Wiley & Sons, Inc. Published 2018 by John Wiley & Sons, Inc.

Ethics and entertainment at first seem like an odd pair. Playfulness necessarily bends normal rules; it allows imagination and suggestion to take priority over tradition and hierarchy. Enjoying entertainment means suspending the rules that govern the normal day. Imagine how difficult it would be to propose normative global "rules" to govern mediated entertainment. Even formulating local rules seems intractable; global rules have no chance at all. But that is exactly what this chapter proposes to do: global rules guiding ethical entertainment are needed now more than ever, since media knows few boundaries and entertainment may be the world's most popular shared experience. Everyone loves football (soccer); FIFA has fallen into corruption. A global ethic may save the game and its entertainment from ruin, or if not, fallen football will be a worldwide loss.

How will a global ethic for entertainment be articulated and communicated, accepted and practiced? Will such an ethic emerge from debate over categorical imperatives, the result of rational discussion about essential rules of play? Such a debate could go on for centuries. One culture will argue for its imperative, one for another, and finally hands will go in the air (a common sign of fatigue and surrender) and debaters will plead: Give us a rule governing the choice of one imperative over another.

Will a global ethic of entertainment emerge from a worldwide prioritizing of virtues – courage and truth-telling on top, patience and humility down the list, perhaps tidiness and courtesy appearing as low-level virtues not all that important for global play? Cultures as diverse as the Castilians of the Canary Islands and Mongols of the Asian plateau are unlikely partners in a global virtue setting, but no more unlikely than other pairings separated by climate, language, and tradition. No matter that such a conversation seems quite impossible, since "courage" or "generosity" or "honesty" are names of quite different social expectations from place to place and time to time. A world culture of virtue is a world away. The world's experience at virtue clarification is as difficult to assemble as its experience at recreation, entertainment, and play.

Pure play, fortunately, keeps a short memory and requires little to no capital investment. Mediated play carries costs, and the business of mediated play is organized by billion-dollar corporations. Disney and Miramax are empires of play, offering succor to millions of subjects and wealth to networks of international media tetrarchs. Perhaps the nation state, the world's organizing institution for some few recent centuries, will one day give way to play stations and avatars. But science fiction is not our purpose here. Understanding the ethics of mediated entertainment draws us back to Nollywood – Nigerian film-making – for a glimpse of what is in store for the millions who find relief from stress in the fictional world of odd and ancient stressors just beyond the reach of reason and rational rule-making.

Case 7.1: The Nollywood Film

Living in Bondage (1992, 1993, hereafter LIB) now has the place of honor in Nollywood that Victor Fleming's *Gone With the Wind* (1939) has in Hollywood. LIB is a classic in the world's third largest film industry, and of the three, the most recent to develop. In the first big Igbo hit, LIB's main character, Andy, becomes jealous over the business success of his friend Paul, who drives into the film in a Mercedes-Benz, a worldwide symbol of success (Green-Simms, 2010, p. 218). Of course, Lagos is not an easy city in which to forge business success, when you start at the bottom. (In Nigeria there is little of the Western myth of rags-to-riches by sweat and hard work.) Paul has the answer to Andy's anxiety, however. He guarantees that Andy can make and spend money, but as a warning of the moral compromises to come, Paul advises: "To become rich, you must be ready for very strong things" (Haynes and Okome, 2000, p. 65).

His meeting with Paul appears to be Andy's lucky break, until he is confronted with the ultimate demand: Andy must present his wife Mercy, whom he loves, for ritual sacrifice before the group of Igbo elites Paul represents.

Andy tries a tricky dodge. He picks up prostitute Tina and presents her as his wife. But Tina knows enough to get away, shouting "Jesus Christ" as she makes her escape from the sinister clan. Alas, Mercy herself must die in a bizarre ritual scene, after which Andy begins nearly at once to attain the wealth he craves. He becomes a chief and acquires a fabulous mansion. He has money for posh hotel getaways, womanizing in high-end bars, and for crude yet conspicuous consumption of wasteful kinds. Andy's dreams have come true, until he arranges for a second marriage.

Now the warning whistles blow. News of his impending marriage reaches his village, and a family delegation demands explanations. Andy rejects the interrogators, but he cannot reject Mercy's apparition, which haunts him as his conscience comes to terms with his cultic excesses. Unable to control Mercy's ghostly appearance, Andy goes mad.

Who should appear as Andy's savior? It is Tina, of all people. She has left the sex trade to become a Pentecostal believer, and convinces Andy, though he does not deserve her intervention, that confession and redemption through prayer is his only hope. Tina leads the small church in singing as Andy, exhausted and nearly comatose, slumps into conversion and rescue.

Commentary on Case 7.1

Opening an ethical critique of Nollywood and LIB is fraught with intellectual danger. Film scholar Onookome Okome lashes out at would-be moral critics whose ideas are "the vestiges of a colonial education" (Okome, 2010, p. 28). Okome cites Ademola James as a "good representative" of Nollywood critics who "perceive their task as one of correcting the erroneous and banal way that Nollywood films represent Nigeria to its own public, to Africa, and to the rest of the world" (Ibid.). Indeed James, former head of Nigeria's National Film and Video Censors Board (NFVCB), was a vocal opponent of Nollywood's "occultism, fetishism, witchcraft, devilish spiritualism, uncontrolled tendency for sexual display, bloodiness, incest, violence, and poisoning." James called for a "sense of social responsibility and relevance" among video producers, and urged that film and video "be used as a tool to promote positive social transformation" (Ibid.).

One can hardly imagine rhetoric more morally tuned than James's, yet that is precisely the trouble, and not only with him. James is not alone as the voice of traditionalist criticism. Rosaline Odeh, also a past leader of the NFVCB, sought to ban from television broadcast films containing "violence, rituals, voodooism, and the like" (NFVCB, 2002, p. 59). Her "narrow Catholic dogmas," according to her critics, were as oppressive of free expression as the parallel Islamic censorship in Nigeria's northern Kano state (McCain, 2013, p. 226), and we should add, as the Legion of Decency's campaign against the same types of content in the Hollywood industry (Fackler, 1984, p. 181). Since Nollywood video producers "are concerned about the everyday and with those things that matter to the men and women in the street," would-be critics should be cautious (Okome, 2010, p. 36). The patrons of Nollywood find "answers . . . to the many questions of everyday existence in a brutal post-colonial city such as Lagos" (Ibid., p. 39). Collateral concerns about the possible effects of fetishism and occultism on youth must answer first to the social utility adults find in LIB and its kin. In Nollywood viewers of all kinds discover "the popular consciousness of the African continent and its diasporas" more fully articulated than in any other world medium (Ibid., p. 27). By implication, considering LIB as a moral text is equivalent to denying its legitimacy as a cultural gateway and disallowing a playful moment for viewers who find entertainment in it. Let Nollywood find its audiences, and let audiences take their delights, seems to be the libertarian defense against moral judgment on a young, immensely popular art. Nollywood "gives the ordinary people the occasion and the pleasure to create a symbolic world of their own in which they are temporarily and symbolically in control of the situation" (Dipio, 2007, p. 66).

Moral questions concerning entertainment programming have always run the gamut of social scientists and anthropologists who prefer to let culture express the will of the people without imposing rubrics drawn from guesswork about good and bad. Restricting entertainment themes based on culturally sensitive criteria, or worse, theologically grounded criteria, would take civilization back to the medieval era, an impossible retreat. The only fair evaluation of popular art is the market, for there a creative product either satisfies or disappoints as people make discrete choices on the use of their time and money. Anything else imposes a rubric and quashes novelty. In one famous U.S. Supreme Court case involving a young man prosecuted for wearing a jacket containing an obscene word, the court declared that government cannot act as a moral censor over messages delightful or repugnant, for "one man's vulgarity is another's lyric" (Harlan, 1971).

LIB is a Mephistophelian tale in which greed and envy lead a man to sell his future (his soul in *Faust*, that is, his entire future) to the devil in exchange for the riches (Green-Simms, 2010, p. 218). Andy's greed leads to the loss of control over his life, which no person can rightly will to do. To lose control over life is to become a slave, in this case to wealth within the cult. There is no moral argument favoring Andy's choice. It is wrong in every circumstance and culture. Slavery is not an option for a morally robust human life.

Short of slavery, wealth has its practical pleasures. Andy wants them, as much as he can get, but once on the road he loses his way. Wealth accumulation is not morally wrong on its face, but for its dehumanizing consequences. The road to wealth has debilitating detours: the most heinous is that wealth becomes an end in itself.

This is precisely the danger that producers of LIB and others in its genre face as part of their enormous worldwide success. Nollywood had its origins in the "people's art," popular travelling theater groups among the Yoruba in the 1970s. Elements of the genre developed to meet the needs and satisfy an audience of ordinary people for whom the price of a traditional theater ticket was out of reach (Dipio, 2007, p. 66). Availability of cheaper cameras permitted an informal production industry to draw on Yoruba success; by the 1990s, Nollywood had discovered its unique identity (Ibid.). Endless varieties on themes of sexual gratification, excessive wealth, moral trade-offs, ritual sacrifice, and the occult have led to a thriving Nollywood trade. People do get rich and famous at helping other people dream about it.

Moral guardians cannot deny Nollywood's popularity. An East African advocate argues that Nollywood's themes have satisfied such an entertainment hunger that "it is no longer appropriate to denigrate [Nollywood films] as simply escapist and unserious art" (Dipio, 2007, p. 67). This utilitarian defense has at least the weight of market prowess behind it. Successful film producers have capacities to make more art than do unsuccessful ones, opening the possibility for more nuanced themes in future Nigerian films. Audiences also become accustomed to what they want. As life seems generally happier when wants are satisfied, we might expect any moral argument favoring a change in Nollywood themes, or a tempering or discontinuance of their exploration of evil per se, would bring distress to the many who like LIB and its progeny just as they are.

The utilitarian-market defense of popular art is both explained and challenged by Sissela Bok who raises questions about antiquity's entertainment choices. In the five centuries from 200 BC to AD 300, Bok claims, "no people before or since have so reveled in displays of moral combat as did the Romans." The reveling included close-quarter gladiatorial combat as entertainment at dinner parties, which, according to sources, may have been all the more intriguing for its proximity and immediacy:

> Hosts would invite their friends to dinner . . . when sated with dining and drink, they called in the gladiators. No sooner did one have his throat cut than the masters applauded with delight at this feat.

(Bok, 1998, p. 15)

We grimace at such choices today, mindful of the corruption a steady diet of death-as-entertainment could cause to the average human conscience. For such reasons as merely protecting conscience, vast bureaucracies have invented warning labels for films, television programming, music, and perhaps eventually the most democratic of all media, the internet. Bok summarizes four reasons for such warnings, each reason appealing to most grown-ups even before the verification of causality required from social scientists: fear, desensitization, the appetite for more violence, and aggressive acts played out in the real world (Ibid., pp. 61–90). Fear is most liable to prey upon child viewers, while the other three effects show up regularly among adolescents and adults. In tragic cases the last effect takes the lives of multiple innocents, though no direct link to entertainment viewing has ever been proven beyond a reasonable doubt, nor ever will be, given the complexity of human decision-making (Christians *et al.*, 2012, p. 257). Thus the history of media reform movements and media vetting boards is checkered with claims of over-sensitivity for children and under-concern for adult viewers both vulnerable and free. The invention of the microchip revolutionized communications technology, but no one has invented a dependable system of filtering media entertainment to generate human character that is good, true, and beautiful. That task we leave largely to individual media users and to care-givers for children deemed under the age of mature decision-making.

Where freedom to make personal choice is stronger than the opportunity taken by bureaucracies to constrain choice, media makers stretch boundaries of morally acceptable content with an eye to market and a blind-eye to censors. Japanese *manga* have been such an opportunity for talented artists and writers. Korean *manhwa* have also enriched producers and generated worldwide audiences with tales of greed, blood, horror, and ritual murder.

Case 7.2: Korean Comics and Films

Priest is one of the most successful of Korean *manhwa* comics, achieving the distinction of becoming an American-produced motion picture in 2011. It features an orphan, Ivan Isaacs, who becomes a Catholic priest when his young love, Gena, is rescued from a relationship with him. Ivan's bitterness feeds his distorted appetite for power and revenge, the perfect fit for a plot by the morally compromised Order of St. Vinetz to free the souls of "fallen angels" who were made into rock statues by the command of God. Belial and Temozarela, the two angel leaders, have captured the body of Holy Knight Vascar De Gullion, who himself lost his love and seeks revenge against God. The convoluted plotline involves mysterious discovery, allegiances with cosmic evil, vampires, razor-sharp knives, terror, and witchcraft, all against the backdrop of the Bible's mysterious battle of good and evil in which angels (both loyal and fallen) play their ambiguous part. It is the type of story that can go on forever, one killing or vampire confrontation leading to another, one grossly played ritual sacrifice leading to new levels of mayhem and oppression. Love means blood must flow; heroism leads to cynical compromise; ghosts of the dead reappear to bedevil the so-called living; the "good guys" (Vatican secret warriors) wear white hoods and kill opponents at will; heaven, earth, and hell are barely distinguishable.

Priest has its spinoffs (just as it was a spinoff of the video game *Blood*) – in addition to the 2011 film and a video game of its own, popular music, and the *manhwa* series *Weird West*. One very popular story deserves another, and another, and another.

Commentary on Case 7.2

Readers may complain about *Priest* on several levels. For one, the most sacred symbol of Christian faith worldwide is the cross. In *Priest*, the cross appears often: as the gateway to evil, on the cover of a Bible touted as the recriminatory "law of God" (Hyung, 1999, n.p.), as markings on foreheads of devilish agents. In each case, the symbol is ambiguously presented as co-opted by evil or powerless against it.

On another level, the future of the world (in Christian theological language, eschatology) is clearly in the hands of dominating evil, and the outlook for humanity and the environment is ruinous and painful. This is decidedly not the eschatology taught for centuries by the Christian church. But parts of the Christian tradition, magnified as the whole, have entertained *Priest* followers worldwide.

Characters identified as Christians in *Priest* are wholly pathetic creatures void of sensitivity and careless to the pain they inflict. A witch-like woman with a Bible in hand and hangman's noose as backdrop urges a crowd to "drag that witch [Lizzie] out and implement God's law!" (Ibid.). Granted the historical reality that many who claimed Christian virtues have acted the contrary, *Priest*'s woman-witch no doubt has real-life precursors. But the point here is the ubiquitous stereotype.

Others may find nothing in the content of *Priest* objectionable, except that ardent readers come away with nothing by which to act with more intellectual or moral insight in the real world. In terms of political or social payoff, *Priest* is a waste of precious time, pure escapism. As providing tools for human growth or paradigms for justice, no and no. The classic texts of any culture will feature the same raucous violence from time to time. Preserving "the classics" but marginalizing *manhwa* only makes sense if the classics create reflection on the tragedies of the human condition, and sometimes provoke courageous action leading to relief of human suffering. "Low culture" appeals to raw survival through violence and greed. Reading *manhwa* shrivels the soul. A steady diet clogs the arteries of the human spirit. If the political leader of your country were to take a week's vacation on the Black Sea reading *Priest* and discussing its relevance to the future of your people, you would have cause to worry, and on his or her second such holiday, to emigrate.

Despite these issues, *manhwa* and *manga* prosper. Comics scholar John Lent, in his review of Asian comics, credits the success of *manga* and *manhwa* to rampant illegal piracy and the persistence of a profitable marketplace. In conservative South Korea, government censors would attempt their clean-ups, with rules governing the depiction of kissing but not deep kissing, prohibitions against nudity, profanity, stabbing, shootings, and amputations. For a time, children's *manhwa* could show a weapon as long as the weapon was not used. With such micro-managing of comics, censors won occasional battles but lost the war decisively. By 1990, over a fifth of all *manga* were being published in South Korea (Lent, 2010, pp. 297–303). The more censors attempted to curtail *manhwa* content, the less such content adhered to guidelines and mandates. Faced with unrelenting competition from Japan and the start of the industry in China, South Korea began to encourage its own industry with festivals, libraries, museums, grants, and subsidies. Producer and historian Lee Won Bok observed that South Korea was forced to "open the moral door" or be swept aside by an international market hungry for more (Ibid., pp. 303–308).

Defenders of *manga* speak as if it were history's first art form. From cave paintings to medieval tapestries, wrenching tales of suffering, violent death, and evil have been the stuff of human storytelling. Who can hold back that fearsome tide? In 1950, the graphic novel *It Rhymes with Lust* featured a scheming female red-head named Rust, pictured with ample bosom and a small pistol just right for protection and revenge. In the 1960s, *His Name is . . . Savage* set new standards for visual violence in its 40-page story of Simon Mace, who saved kidnapped presidents, quashed threats of world wars, and knew how to use his teeth-shattering .357 Magnum, definitely a more formidable weapon than Rust's. In the Western hemisphere and Eastern, graphic tales were feeding a market starved by storylines of sweetness, hungry for grit and ghoul.

Moral questions raised by *manga/manhwa* echo those raised by other entertainment media. Are viewers negatively affected by plotlines involving bloodshed, revenge, overpowering evil, collegiality between humans and the undead – all the elements that make stories bizarre, scary, and playful? Will some viewers/readers slip into fantasyland while making real-world choices and actions? Can the human appetite for stories be trusted to lead the species toward moral development, or is chaos the coming finale?

Social science approaches answers but finally must resist pronouncing the final word. Studies are inconclusive, because human behavior is not predictable; human reporting of one's own mental processing is not a 1:1 transfer. The answers social science provides to the causal questions are generalizations over large audiences, but the consequences of bad choices in real-world behavior are matters of individual decision-making, or group pressure, and escalated by one's immediate circumstances or breakdowns in judgment brought on by personal crises. Social science cannot track those developments, thankfully. If science had access at that level, personal privacy would already be smoldering on the ash heap of history. Science must be content with generalizations that predict the behavior and development of no one in particular.

Moral Reasoning and Play

Moral science is another creature altogether. Not a science so much as a tradition, moral reasoning is the cumulative wisdom of a region, religion, or association that informs people of the proper approach to wrongdoing, of bad behavior that cannot be callously enacted, of moral strictures that cannot be held in contempt. Moral reasoning over time, when done well, informs one's conscience of attitudes and actions that contribute to life's flourishing and put brakes on life's diminishment.

Does life suffer diminishment during periods of play? Ants do not play; they work selflessly to build a colony. Even the term "selfless" is odd when applied to ant behavior. Ants are wired for work and colony (Hölldobler and Wilson, 2009, p. 10). Work is the only life an ant knows, as far as we non-ant observers can tell. Lions and bears play, more so when young than during years of birthing and parenting. Animals play with their kin, touching, wrestling, sniffing, rolling – forming bonds that will see them through the hard years of food-gathering for offspring. Ants permit ant-energy no wasted moment; no relaxation at the end of a stressful day for them. What inspires lions and bears to play we can only surmise, but we note that play across species is rare; boundaries of play are set by long experience of opening the play-circle too wide – long experience leading to instinct and survival. Play is not on the insect agenda. Too much play in the mammalian world is forbidden. Gazelles do not share game-time with lions.

To the human dimension of play, moral reasoning universally asserts a trajectory from one play-form to another, from play as priority to play as restive and recreational, on a timeline from youth to adulthood. What then constitutes morally wrong behavior? We might say, wrong moral behavior would be a life of uninterrupted play, a wasted life; yet a life without play would be hopelessly dull, morally and humanly wrong, a life in the gulag, to borrow Solzhenitsyn's term for hell on earth. We might also assert a moral claim concerning the type of play one enjoys along the same timeline. Forcing a child who cannot comprehend the chessboard to play nonetheless would be foolish; an adult who plays endless rounds of "ring-around-the-rosy" would be considered odd at best, wasteful or sick, at worse. How we play, when and where, engages moral concerns.

Traditionally, play has supported and upheld the moral life. Children who play at being adults are discouraged from adopting criminal or psychopathic roles. To be "good moms" or "caring bosses" or "generous business owners" in their role-play games is normal. When guns are used in play, as often they still are, it is not the use of guns typical of Joseph Kony, the brigand of Uganda, that children are encouraged to emulate. It is the use made by a hero of some sort, a "David" who saves his people from Goliath with a sling, a Lone Ranger doing violence with silver bullets aimed only toward the criminally violent, with which children are prompted to identify. But not all of old King David's exploits are play-worthy (see 2 Samuel 11). Sex in children's play is universally forbidden. Play is not disguised moral lesson-learning, but play engages moral development and traditionally underscores and illustrates the virtues formally taught in homes and schools.

Much more latitude is granted to adult game-playing, where moral condemnation may be articulated but play continues nonetheless. Gambling is play; reckless gambling is morally wrong but done frequently under the umbrella of adult privilege. As you make your own bed, so you must lie in it, goes the moral escape clause. Ruin yourself if you will, but own up to your personal foolishness. Compensate victims of your moral flirtations and excesses. When an adult cannot limit the damage of questionable behavior, gambling for instance, it is morally proper to save innocents at risk by stopping play. Often, adult play must be prevented from excess by penalties applied through state police power or culture. Casinos, which never lose in the long term, place limits on losses any person may ring up, a rare case of limiting corporate profit to protect game-wild customers.

Entertainment choices which place users in roles considered anti-social, violent, greedy, or sexually criminal are increasingly beyond the reach of state or culture. The internet has created an immense new marketplace where persons may hide their identity and enjoy such entertainment as they would not admit publicly. Among the entertainment options of most concern to traditional moral precepts are sites offering child pornography. States have made various rulings in an effort to control the distribution of child pornography, but only recently has the possession of such material been considered a criminal act. Japan, a major source of child pornography for international markets, outlawed (in July 2014) possession of such material, with the imposition of stiff fines and imprisonment penalties delayed for one year to permit possessors to rid themselves of the contraband. Japanese leaders did not explain why 52 weeks was required to cleanse newly criminalized hard-drives, but such compromises with large-scale business interests are sometimes the only political solution to intractable appetites. *Manga* publishers, however, are spared this inconvenience, along with anime video producers (and possessors) and all child pornography depicted by computer-generated graphics (Deutsche Welle, 2014). Will such restrictions and exceptions explode the *manga* industry?

A BBC report (BBC News, 2014) claims that "tens of thousands of pedophiles are using the so-called dark net to trade images of sexual abuse." One dark porn site boasted 500 page views per second and 12 gigabytes of visual material, all encrypted and presently untraceable. Its founder boasted to the BBC in a statement that sounds more like a dare: "I don't want to go into details about my security set-up but it is designed with many layers to keep me safe from even the most capable adversaries in the world." The Virtual Global Taskforce, a coalition of international police agencies, is working on untangling those details and finding the purveyors, in a process resembling one of the world's oldest games, hide and seek. In the meantime, a worldwide "force" of video-game players are ready for a good fight.

Case 7.3: Video Games

The *Grand Theft Auto* series epitomizes a popular perception of video games: they are popular, profitable, and controversial. *Grand Theft Auto V*, released in September 2013, rapidly became the biggest single entertainment title in history, pulling in $1 billion in three days (by comparison, James Cameron's film *Avatar* took a lengthy 16 days to reach the same amount). And just like the other releases in the series, critics decried *Grand Theft Auto V*'s extreme violence and misogynistic representations of women (Schut, 2013, p. 54).

Video games can present players with significant ethical challenges. This is true even of the many non-violent titles released every year. It's the violent games, however, which grab ethical headlines.

Take *Fallout: New Vegas*, set in alternate-reality Nevada long after a nuclear war. The game has an elaborate political back-story about the struggle for regional dominance between a bloody and tyrannical empire called Caesar's Legion, a corrupt democracy called the New California Republic, and a hyper-rational homegrown dictator called Mr. House. The player controls a character who must choose which faction to support.

It would be easy to leave the description of the game at that. Fighting for Caesar would mean the player supports totalitarian terror. Except, of course, that there is, in reality, no post-apocalypse Mojave Wasteland to terrorize. Mowing down a tribe of innocent civilians in *Fallout* kills precisely zero physical, breathing people.

Not all interaction in a video game is solely between a player and a pre-programmed world. Many of the most popular video games focus on player-to-player interaction, and this can lead to tricky ethical situations. The *World of Warcraft* (*WoW*) is a massively-multiplayer online game that allows hundreds or thousands of players to be interacting simultaneously in the same imaginary world. Many players join groups called "guilds" that generally work together on completing quests or fighting other guilds.

In 2006, a member of a guild died (in real life). To commemorate her passing, her *WoW* guild arranged a funeral gathering. The event, however, took place in a version of the game that allowed player characters to attack and kill each other. So a rival guild decided to take the opportunity to ambush their enemies and attacked during the funeral. The attackers recorded the event. The video was posted on YouTube and widely circulated ("Serenity Now").

Commentary on Case 7.3

Video gamers have to consider how to be wise about playing: it's easy for a play session to swallow up productivity, sleep, and money. And many games explicitly challenge video gamers to make ethical choices: the popular *Fallout* series, for example, allows players to either be murderous psychopaths or noble heroes.

We have already raised the issue of applying Western ethical traditions to matters of entertainment and play. Is it possible to apply virtue ethics to imaginary characters in the adventure game *The Wolf Among Us*? Is it reasonable to use Kant's categorical imperative when deciding whether to be a peaceful or a warlike empire-builder in *Sid Meier's Civilization V*? Can Bentham's utilitarianism provide guidance on whether to hurt innocent bystanders in *Grand Theft Auto V*?

Back to *WoW* . . . Attacking a real funeral would, of course, violate a wide range of social taboos, and would be hard to justify using any ethical system. But video games provide a considerably different context for social interaction than real-life conditions. One of the core purposes of games is competition, and most players realize that actions in a game have a different reality than actions outside a game – otherwise, chess would be a competition of bloodthirsty tyrants.

The funeral raid in *WoW* started a vigorous online discussion. On one side, many argued that the attackers were deeply insensitive and violated the Golden Rule. Other gamers, however, pointed out that the ambushing guild violated no rules and was, in fact, staying true to the spirit of the game. Because there are versions of *WoW* that don't allow players to kill other players, if the grieving guild wanted to avoid combat, it should have set the event in a place where an ambush would not have been possible.

Our questions remain: Does the context of a video game change the moral obligations of players? Is it even possible to apply normal ethical guidelines to game-playing, which to gamers is a kind of alternate social space with different rules? If the traditional, time-tested moral systems of world civilizations also oversee all the alternate worlds in 100 million game rooms, why play at all . . . *where's the freedom?*

That is precisely the objection raised by Miguel Valenti in *More Than a Movie: Ethics in Entertainment* (Valenti, 2000). Fully aware that talk of ethics in a circle of entertainment producers is likely to be as popular as tax hikes, Valenti opens his book with a made-up dialogue between a Skeptic and a moral Inquirer. "Why ethics?" the Skeptic intones. Creativity is key to art, not the stifling, rule-keeping, autocratic pronouncements of critics who know nothing of art and care nothing for good stories. Moralists never "push the envelope," that is, stretch a story past morally acceptable behavior. Moralists fail to reckon that artistic growth happens when creativity is freed from moralism and given a chance to fly.

Nay brother, responds the Inquirer. "The unexamined life is not worth living" said Socrates for the ages. Socrates believed that meaningful human life was characterized by personal and spiritual growth. We grow toward greater understanding of who we are when we examine and reflect on life, which is the point and purpose of telling stories, the heart of entertainment. If Socrates' insight is true (and do you really want to argue with Socrates?), then it is also true that "the unexamined creation is not worth creating" (Ibid., p. xxv). Again, a truism that rings true to the total truth of human experience, to put it redundantly for emphasis. What storyteller would not want his/her audience to process, evaluate, interpret, talk about, and find wonder in his/her art? We are *Homo interpretans* as fully as we are *Homo ludens.* We cannot not interpret our experience. The frameworks by which such interpretation is done are shaped by teaching and experience concerning the good and the bad, the healthy and the unhealthy, the desirable and the futile. To hope for a "just watch it" audience is to hope for an audience of squirrels. People will not "just watch" anything, but sort and sift, laugh and weep, ponder and criticize nearly everything they encounter.

Eventually the Skeptic in Valenti's introductory drama wants to discuss violence in storytelling. He is asked, with each moment of violence in drama, is there not a need to "up the stakes" with more violence, more graphic and frightening material, the next time? Finally, violence cannot easily be contained within any moral traditions which value life and truth-telling. When its multiplier goes past acceptability and shadows into disrespect of valued norms, audience tolerance and critical interpretation becomes disgust, revulsion, abrupt condemnation. All cultures have seen this response.

The Skeptic answers: yes, true, violence must become more violent, otherwise "people get bored" (Ibid., p. xxvi). So violence breeds its own foul path, spiraling toward obscenity and sadism. What can hold the spiral in check? Valenti suggests meekly that artists, whose point is to make a point, might be wise to recognize "the responsibility to make sure that we do not inadvertently send out statements or moral messages that we don't really advocate" (Ibid., p. xxxi). Unintentional advocacy appears to be morally bad behavior. But inadvertence is a thin thread on which to hang a culture's moral balance. It requires making moral judgments based on uncertain reports of intention and perception. Cross culturally, such judgments become thickened with suspicion and acrimony (an example is *The Interview* studied in Case 5.2). In the world today, divided by many tribes, faiths, and political premises, trying not to offend may be the best an entertainment can do. Yet inoffensiveness strikes artists as the apex of boredom.

Forbidden Knowledge?

Another strike just as offensive to the modern artist comes from literary scholar Roger Shattuck in his brilliant study *Forbidden Knowledge* (1996), identified by the cover blurb as "a landmark exploration of the dark side of human ingenuity and imagination." Shattuck begins with three engaging questions for all producers of knowledge and culture: "Are there things we should not know? Can anyone or any institution, in this culture of unfettered enterprise and growth, seriously propose limits on knowledge? Have we lost the capacity to perceive and honor the moral dimensions of such questions?" (Shattuck, 1996, p. 1).

Shattuck ranges over a broad swath of literature, finally focusing on the life and writings of Donatien Alphonse François de Sade, better known as the Marquis de Sade, whose name following his death in 1814 was taken as synonymous with foul acts beyond the pale of human acceptability. Has there been a soul since Sade more forsaken of human sympathy? Likely so, in many places, but Sade was French, survived the Revolution, and left a literary legacy of desperate perversion. Anything in there that readers today should *not* know, Shattuck ventures to ask?

His inquiry leads to conclusions that some readers should not know Sade's work, namely children as a group and adults of weak discernment. To overexpose oneself to stories which elevate the destruction of self and society is an entertainment choice motivated less by play than by morbid curiosity. The nightmares of childhood are awesome enough without such stimulation. But finally, Shattuck maintains, to burn Sade's work would be to lose a fable. Something of John Milton's proscription against book burning prevents even the Sade's demolition. (Milton famously wrote in the *Areopagitica* (1644/n.d., p. 681): "who kills a Man kills a reasonable creature, Gods Image; but hee who destroyes a good Booke, kills reason it selfe, kills the Image of God, as it were in the eye.") Shattuck refuses to hand to censors the future of literary or artistic choice, but concludes that proper labeling is morally required to spare vulnerable readers/viewers the potential harm of an imagination painted with fundamental evil (Shattuck, 1996, p. 299). Freedom must be preserved, as it alone carries the future into progressive change; responsibility must be accepted for the collateral damages positive freedom may inflict. Mitigated damages join maximum opportunity in a social order of tempered exploration, positive amusements, and moral reflection.

Concluding Remarks

Making moral decisions concerning the production and use of entertainment carries us beyond traditional ethical principles into the heart and soul of our very identity. We do not select this or that entertainment by conversing with ourselves (or anyone else normally) on the rightness of our selection in the light of the teachings of the Buddha or the European greats. We just ask, do I want to see this? Will viewing this video or playing this game refresh me? Will it please me? Will I have fun? And that conversation, short as it is, based on the responses of many prior decisions of using and rating similar pleasures, depends entirely on who "I" am.

If "I" am despondent of love, short on opportunity and prior success, willing at any cost to dabble in love's pleasures, my choices will be wide and daring. If "I" am careful about the approach to sharing life and love with another, careful about the construction of the "me" – for "me" is what I present to the Other in any relationship – then my choices may be restricted and I may even forswear the exploration of morally questionable material for the sake of its possible toll on the integrity I desire to build in the only life I possess, the only "me" that walks the real, non-virtual world. I may say of certain forms of RAP: Yes, that music expresses my outrage and listening to it creates an avatar of who I would be if real consequences were not so severe and such freedom as the artist conveys were less likely to lead me to hardship. Or I may say NO, it's trashy and tasteless and I want no fuel from it. These are decisions not made in reference to moral norms or centuries of moral reflection. They are made in reference to the "me" I intend to become: better at meeting people, better at facing conflict, better at standing up for my and others' rights and welfare; better at finding the road ahead, clouded as it always is, but still visible if my eyes are clear.

Huizinga believed that play fostered poetry, dance, battle protocol, and international law – basically all the rudiments of sorting out our identities and relationships. Perhaps Huizinga's claim goes too far, covers too much of the territory claimed by other motivators. Today, it would be difficult to argue that play holds the germ of solutions to the structure of nations in the Middle East or the construction of nuclear warheads in contested regions of the Levant. No legal system recognizes play as a legitimate excuse for moral hurt or mayhem. The American teenager Ronnie Zamora tried that once in court, claiming that the playful watching of television violence was to blame, and not himself the person, for the killing of an old neighbor lady and the stealing of her purse money (Christians, 2012, p. 257). It was such an unlikely criminal defense that no lawyer has tried it since. Play cannot cover that much human action.

But play can make the "me" who begins to think in Zamorean terms, opening the door to a self who is free of moral anchorage and finally unable to be let alone to live in the world of people. Or, play can make a "me" of ambition, imagination, generous heart, cheerful energy, sturdy defense of rights hard-won over centuries of conflict – a person liked and respected. Play has its consequences for a morally mature life. The trajectory leading to that life needs disciplined decisions over time – not boring sameness or closeted isolation from cultural change – but right, conscientious, significant decisions on how to play well. Thus the "me" becomes a person to be trusted, depended on, respected, even loved.

These choices are yours in large measure; the aggregated results are you in public measure. Play in Huizinga's analysis generates international treaties; more commonly play generates the interior you who shows up in healthy relationships and fulfilled human personhood.

Discussion Questions

1   Some people reason that entertainment should be personal choice alone, no interference from authorities. And you say . . . ?

2 If media entertainment were more free, that is, unrestricted, would your family be better served? Your workplace?

3 If media entertainment must have boundaries, who do you trust to set them wisely?

4 "Freedom" is a commonly held virtue among entertainment producers and users. "Responsibility" is less popular as a moral goal or standard. True or false? Reasons according to you, to favor one over the other?

5 Over the past 5–10 years, have you grown more free, or more responsible, with media entertainment choices?

8

Media and the Political Process

Introduction

In the Western democratic tradition with its roots in the philosophy of democracy developed in the Greek city state of Athens, public discourse is a necessity. Once the printing press, and then newspapers, developed, communication became a necessary, but dangerous, aspect of this discourse. Those in power feared the power of the press, often limiting the number of printers by licensure, taxing their output, and censoring their content. Over time freedom of the press became a reality and was defined as a bedrock necessity for democracy. As the European empires developed, especially the British Empire, this commitment to a free press was exported around the globe, although the indigenous peoples in that empire were usually not allowed to develop a free press until the imperial authority withdrew. Even then, however, the nascent states controlled the press through licensure, limitation, and censorship. In other non-Western political traditions, even this limited commitment to a free press was often eschewed, or in the case of the Soviet empire (1917–1991), denied altogether.

After the end of the Second World War in 1945, however, the nations of the world began the slow process of creating a global commitment to a free press. This commitment gradually encompassed not only the print media, but other media as well. Article 19 of the Universal Declaration of Human Rights, adopted by the United Nations General Assembly on December 10, 1948, states that "Everyone has the right to freedom of opinion and expression; this right includes freedom to hold opinions without interference and to seek, receive and impart information and ideas through any media and regardless of frontiers."[1]

This is a human right, not a right of the press or media. It is, therefore, unlike the United States constitutional guarantee of a "free press." However, the Article also incorporates – to a degree – the right of individuals to use the media, both to provide and to receive information from others, and both within their own country and across borders with other countries. This would apply not only to individual citizens but also to media practitioners, who enjoy the same universal rights as others, even though they would have easier access to traditional media, such as newspapers, magazines, radio, and television. All would have under this provision equal access to the internet and its various services.

These guarantees were the result of heavy lobbying by U.S. delegates in the early days of the United Nations, especially by Eleanor Roosevelt, the former First Lady. They represent an expansion of the principles enshrined in the American Constitution and reflect the Enlightenment philosophy that informed the creation of the Constitution and the expectations of the French Revolution of 1789. They are Western, rational, and individualistic to their core. They do not take account of different social structures or community organization. They do not privilege one class, ethnic or age group, gender or

World Media Ethics: Cases and Commentary, First Edition. Robert S. Fortner and P. Mark Fackler.
© 2018 John Wiley & Sons, Inc. Published 2018 by John Wiley & Sons, Inc.

race over another. Yet their interpretation and application must occur within societies where profound differences in values and expectations exist, often making them problematic, neither universal nor absolute.

Media and Public Discourse

Democratic theory expects that the media will provide a significant platform for public discourse on important issues. But there are two traditions within this theory that take quite different perspectives on the significance of media. The first is what James W. Carey (1996, p. 27) called the liberal-utilitarian tradition that emphasizes individual desire and the role of media as a useful means to expand liberty. By Carey's reckoning this tradition reached an apex in the thinking of Walter Lippmann, whose work for the Woodrow Wilson administration and claims about public opinion were to justify a shift from concern about the media as means for the achieving and maintaining morality, political engagement, and freedom to one emphasizing psychology and epistemology (Ibid., p. 30). "He established the tradition of propaganda analysis and simultaneously, by framing the problem not as one of normative political theory but as one of human psychology, opened up the tradition of effects analysis that was to dominate the literature less than two decades after the publication of *Public Opinion*" (Ibid.).

The second tradition – and one to which Carey was far more committed – was grounded in the work of scholars at the University of Chicago, especially John Dewey, George Herbert Mead, and Robert Park. It applied more to the United States' situation than that of other countries (except perhaps Australia, and to a lesser extent Canada). In such cases, where a shared and inherited culture was lacking, the social integration that would ordinarily occur through such a way depended on the means of communication: "In the absence of a shared sentiment, the only means by which. . . communities could be organized and held together was through discussion, debate, negotiation, and communication" (Ibid., p. 32). Here Carey was capturing the essentiality of communication to the democratic process which, we would argue, applies not only to the creation of a democratic state *ex nihilo* but to any state transitioning from a non-democratic to a democratic one. Societies where autocracies are replaced by more democratic institutions face the same necessities; so do those that transition from Soviet-style, monarchical, or tribal societies to democracies. Any time that citizens who have been ruled by elites are called upon to engage in discourse and influence policies, legislation, or the exercise of police power – or in new forms of economic activity newly legitimized by nascent democracies – the necessity to engage in dialogue, debate, negotiation, and compromise will quickly develop if democracy is to take root.

A similar perspective animates Jürgen Habermas' notion of "deliberative democracy" that assumes that citizens are intimately involved in the decision-making process that results in the rules under which they live and the allocation of resources to which they have access (see Habermas, 2001). Habermas' claims fit into the model of liberal democracy, an idea that itself emerged in the Enlightenment from the pens of Jean-Jacques Rousseau, John Locke, and, before them, Immanuel Kant. This idea inspired both the American and French Revolutions in the late 1700s. Chantal Mouffe (2000, p. 1) claimed that "liberal democracy seems to be recognized as the only legitimate form of government," and that the paradigm of deliberative democracy "is currently becoming the fastest growing trend in the field." The main idea of deliberative democracy: "political decisions should be reached through a process of deliberation among free and equal citizens," a perspective that "has accompanied democracy since its birth in fifth century Athens" (Ibid.).

Although examining the relationship between media and democratic politics might lead to obvious ethical issues, this is complicated by the fact that democracy is rarely fully installed – certain classes, or groups of people, are often excluded from participation in even the most basic activity: voting. Such exclusions can result from conscious policies by governments or can be the result of inadvertent realities such as minority languages unused in political activity (but central to a group's identity), or environments inhospitable to ease of movement (see Kaplan, 2015, for examples from around the world). Intentional policies of exclusion can then result in revolt, demonstration, or even violence as people feel their rights are purposefully being restricted compared to others in the society.

An even more relevant and poignant issue for democracy, and the role of media within it, is how people define democracy itself and what they expect from it. As Arundhati Roy (2009, p. 22) puts it: "This is the wonderful thing about democracy. It can mean anything you want it to mean." Direct democracies – such as the Athenian model – are quite different from representative democracies. Representative democracies themselves differ. In addition, the relationship between economic and political systems alters the nature and expectations of democratic systems. Finally, we must also recognize that over half of the population on this planet does not live in countries that can, "under well-respected definitions," be described as democracies at all (Beller, 2013, p. 7). The social responsibility as defined by non-democratic states, or by differing types of democratic systems, can vary quite profoundly.

For instance, in two mature democracies – the United Kingdom and the United States – a fundamental shift in the nature of democracy as defined by political elites occurred in the late 1970s and early 1980s with little to no discussion. This shift was the result of commitment to a new economic model adopted to fight stagflation and to reinforce the political philosophies of Margaret Thatcher (first elected prime minister in the UK in 1979) and Ronald Reagan (elected U.S. president in 1980). This politico-economic shift made many of the assumptions about democratic life – those promoted by the Chicago School, James W. Carey, and Jürgen Habermas – essentially obsolete. Democracy, rather than being a consensus-building process grounded in participation and dialogue – was redefined as merely having the right to vote for parliamentary or congressional representatives (and in the U.S. case, the president). Even this restrictive definition has recently been further eroded by the introduction in the United States of stricter identification rules for voting, ostensibly to combat a virtually nonexistent "voter fraud," that has disenfranchised many minority and poor citizens who cannot produce acceptable documents.

Stephen J. Rosow and Jim George (2015) explain that this shift was the result of a change from liberal democracy to neoliberal democracy in which economic inequalities came to play an increasingly important role, both to define the nature of democracy and to privilege some forms of power (economic) over others (participation). They write:

> [A] neoliberal democracy is both intellectually and structurally designed to serve the interests of the capitalist market and of a systematic status quo that dominates global society in the early twenty-first century, a status quo that does not seek to privilege genuine political participation and social justice but profit maximization and corporate elitism. In this regard, democracy in a neoliberal context is, at best, a severely limited form of "market democracy" and is riven with antidemocratic tendencies and motivations.
>
> *(Rosow and George, 2015, p. 40)*

The philosophy of this new form of democracy is "that those living in market-based societies should not expect the kind of social justice or equity in the marketplace that socialists and liberal progressives demand. The argument instead is that this should not be expected of market-based societies. Instead, the capitalist marketplace – as the preeminent rationalized articulation of the modern human condition – is designed to allow the entrepreneurially astute individuals to successfully achieve security, prosperity, and profit, while those less capable in this context fall behind and must take responsibility on themselves to improve their condition" (Ibid., p. 44). The result for people in the United States: "substantial levels of social exclusion, including high levels of income inequality, high relative and absolute poverty rates, poor and unequal outcomes, poor health outcomes, and high rates of crime and incarceration" (Schmitt and Ben Zipperer, 2006, quoted by Rosow and George, 2015, p. 50).

The United States, as the country currently with the largest gross domestic product on the planet, exports this philosophy to other countries, including nascent democracies that often restrict participation in non-economic ways for the political purposes of their own prevailing elites. This occurs through the demands made by the World Bank, the InterAmerican and other development banks, the International Monetary Fund, and in Europe, the European Union and the Eurozone (promoted primarily by Germany as the continent's largest economy). So, when countries' economies falter and they seek assistance from such transnational organizations, it is their demands that determine levels of public spending, investments in infrastructure, education, health and welfare services – not the will of the people themselves whose active participation in democratic fora might otherwise be solicited by their political representatives. This not only strains the resources of civil society, but makes its objections on behalf of social justice or moral commitment largely irrelevant. This is then what Robert Dahl calls managed democracy, or polyarchy:

> Put simply, polyarchy refers to a system in which a small group actually rules, and mass participation in decision making is confined to leadership choice in elections managed by competing elites. It is, in this sense, rule by an elite with "democratic" characteristics, in which democratic participation is limited to the electoral process and the simple act of choosing between elites every few years. More significantly, the polyarchic notion of democracy does not acknowledge the significance of economic equality as integral to democracy.
> *(Rosow and George, 2015, p. 53)*

Such a system thus defines democracy is such a way that it "deemphasizes the questions of social and economic inequality intrinsic to democracy's classical and early-modern articulations and suggests, instead, that the minority monopolization of wealth and power is in fact consistent with democracy – as long as there are 'free and fair elections' at regular intervals" (Ibid.). And Arundhati Roy (2009, p. 7) asks this question: "What happens now that democracy and the free market have fused into a single predatory organism with a thin, constricted imagination that revolves almost entirely around the idea of maximizing profit?" His answer provided in the title of his first chapter: "Democracy's Failing Light" (Ibid.).

It is worth noting here that efforts to assure fair and free elections, defined as removing obstacles to voting, abstaining from ballot box "stuffing," and fair vote counting methodologies pursued by international monitors (including former U.S. president Jimmy Carter), are defined by the same limited expectations. Democracy is thus "promoted" and "demeaned" in one fell swoop by this new orthodoxy. But democracy, as Neera Chandhoke (2015, p. 13) puts it, "is a project that has to be realized through sustained engagement with holders of power. Citizen activism, public vigilance, informed public opinion, a free media and a multiplicity of social associations are necessary preconditions for this task."

It is not just these two older democracies that have taken this path. Roy (2009, p. 24) laments that "the hoary institutions of Indian democracy – the judiciary, the police, the 'free' press, and, of course, elections – far from working as a system of checks and balances, quite often do the opposite. They provide each other with cover to promote the larger interests of Union and Progress." And these two words are codes for neoliberal, or market democracy. So, he asks (Ibid., p. 25), "How does a government that claims to be a democracy justify a military occupation [of Kashmir]? By holding regular elections of course."[2]

The question of social responsibility for the media in participatory democracies versus that for media in polyarchical democracies is quite different. In the case of participatory democracies, the role of the media is to facilitate dialogue – providing the intelligence necessary for robust public debate to occur and for civil society organizations to actively participate as representatives of the disenfranchised or otherwise marginalized groups in society. As James W. Carey (1995, p. 382) explained the role of the press in participatory democracy:

> [T]he critical factor was that the press, journalism – its freedom and its utility – was not an end in itself, but was justified in terms of its ability to serve and bring into existence an actual social arrangement, a form of discourse and a sphere of independent, rational, and political influence, its ability to provide one mode in which public opinion might form and express itself. . . . [It] reflected and animated public conversation and argument. It furnished material to be discussed, clarified, and interpreted, which constituted information in the narrow sense; but the value of the press was predicated on the existence of the public and not the reverse.

Likewise, Neera Chandhoke (2015, p. 26) writes: "Above all, there is nothing, but nothing, like dialogue to depress pretensions that we know everything there is to know. Dialogue instils modesty in our own capacities to understand, analyse, predict and resolve."

The dialogue envisioned by Chandhoke is not possible in all contexts, however. In countries where the media are controlled with a heavy hand, or where intimidation makes certain facts or opinions "off limits," the possibility of dialogue is severely restricted. Many of the countries that emerged as newly independent states with the collapse of the Soviet empire, including those in Eastern and central Europe, and those hived off of the Soviet Union itself, such as Belarus, Moldova, Georgia, Ukraine, and the so-called "stans" in central Asia, have all made efforts to control the media. In other areas, such as Zimbabwe, control of the public media has meant that constructions of identity and belonging by different ethnic groups, such as Shona and Ndebele, have largely occurred within social media – much of it hosted outside the country (Mpofu, 2013).

In Malaysia the public (or mainstream) media are tightly controlled, too. The internet had been left largely free, but following the loss of Barisan Nasional's two-thirds parliamentary majority for the first time since independence – which the then prime minister Abdullah Ahmad Badawi characterized as a defeat in the internet war, the cyberwar – new strategies were adopted (Hopkins, 2014, p. 10). These included increasing government influence on online content by transforming the Malaysian Bloggers Association, organizing "cybertroopers," and establishing a presence in the blogosphere, Facebook, and Twitter by the prime minister, Najib Razak (Ibid.). Cybertroopers, who were drawn from a youth organization affiliated with the ruling party, would respond to posts considered critical of, or embarrassing for, the government, ostensibly to make sure people using the internet would be able to make a fully informed decision (Ibid., p. 13). The result: although dissent possibilities increased through internet use, "the architecture of the Internet can be adapted to suit the powerful" so as to "neutralise threats to the hegemonic consensus" promoted by the ruling party (Ibid., p. 17).

Beyond these examples are many others. Turkey shut down Twitter for a period after criticism of Erdogan began appearing on the platform. Iran denies its citizens access to social media sites and has even set up its own internal "mirror" sites. France, Germany, the United Kingdom, and the United States are all engaged in widespread data-gathering from mobile telephones and internet traffic, and the U.S. has prosecuted those who have released military data and state department cables to sites such as Wikipedia, and forced Edward Snowden, who revealed the extent of the government's surveillance activities, to take refuge in Russia. Russia itself has declared certain types of information as taboo (especially what it calls "gay propaganda"). China has famously installed its so-called "Great Firewall" to limit its citizens' access to information outside the country and has pursued civic groups of various kinds; it has recently added the "Great Cannon" to prevent internet users accessing blocked websites (see Perlroth, 2015; In China, civic groups' freedom, and followers, are vanishing," 2015"). The country has also adopted a variety of internal controls, including demanding that all social media users be clearly identifiable (no more screen names), ostensibly to protect public morality.

The rationales and excuses used by the nations to attempt to control information access and exchange are seemingly without end. Monroe E. Price (2015, location 709) writes that "the rapid diffusion capacity of social media clearly transforms the information ecology. The rise of social networks leads to a rethinking of the power of the individual in receiving information, deliberating and mobilizing. Social networks change the balance between open and closed terrains of speech. They threaten existing intermediaries and create new ones. They are a challenge for governments, democratic or not." Hence the efforts to contain these systems in a variety of ways.

But in the polyarchical democracy, although people might like the press to continue to play such a role, it would be insignificant. What would be called for is the watchdog function, investigating and rooting out corporate and political corruption, propaganda, obfuscations, secret dealings, prevarications, and hidden agendas. It is empowerment of a different order, at once more intrusive and belligerent. Without such a role for media, civil society organizations, groups representing particular social or cultural interests, are inert. They flounder, unsure of who the "enemy" is or what strategies to adopt to overcome the overwhelming advantages of the ruling polycrats. In the first case the role is both informational and catalytic – public engagement is the goal. In the second case the role is archeological and sanitizing – exposing what is hidden, revealing what is anti-democratic and exposing rot to a cleansing light.

Unfortunately, the media in many democracies are in turmoil. Newspapers and magazines are failing. Television audiences for individual stations or cable/satellite channels are shrinking. Radio has become obsolete by and large, except in poorer countries. The ability of mainstream media that at one time had the financial and personnel resources to pursue investigations is becoming increasingly limited as advertising revenue declines and experienced reporters, producers, editors, and program makers are let go to be replaced with amateur citizen reporter freelancers and stringers.

Public Discourse Using the Internet

To some extent the decline of the mainstream media has been offset by the internet. People have been able to publish their own stories, upload information to ireport on CNN (although this is mostly noncontroversial features), tweet news, publish photos of natural or manmade disasters on Instagram, Flickr or Photobucket, contribute to wikis, and create and maintain blogs and vlogs. They can also access information from a variety of websites, some maintained by the mainstream media themselves, others based on aggregation of reports from many different sources, information provided by nongovernmental organizations, think tanks, government agencies, or internet and telephone service providers, still others based on mining data obtained from traffic cameras, satellite photos, people's shopping receipts, loyalty card programs, online purchases, web traffic, Facebook and other social media posts, online surveys, phone logs, criminal and census databases, and so on. Facebook has even begun its own newsfeed, disaggregating content from other news sites, which undoubtedly gives some stories more presence and access than they might otherwise achieve. All of this activity keeps alive the surveillance function of the press even as it indicates the breadth and depth to which people using both wired and wireless digital technologies – or who are unknowingly caught by the growing array of cameras set up to catch thieves, traffic rule scofflaws, terrorist or other violent activities – inadvertently subject themselves to surveillance on a nearly daily basis (at least in urban areas). People can also access information sites from around the world that were not easily available before. They can inquire about events with people in areas of disaster or conflict that they "friend" on Facebook, follow via Twitter, or whose blogs they subscribe to, that would, in an earlier age, have remained unknown. In many respects we have much more information and opinion available than ever. At the same time there is less in-depth investigation, fewer "reports on events in a context that gives them meaning," than ever before.

It is a conundrum. Increasingly reporters are "embedded" with military units engaged in fights around the globe, providing both a richer, but less contextualized, understanding of the conflict itself. People use their mobile phones to photograph or video newsworthy events they happen to witness and post these shots for others to see, giving strangers thousands of miles away the opportunity to see what's happening on the ground in events they might see mentioned in brief news headlines. Sometimes these reports trigger movements, protests, marches across the planet – leaving all of us with the impression that media have been democratized and the flow of information has never been so free (or overwhelming).

At the same time, however, such activities are fragmentary, partial, disconnected. What is lacking is the ability to make sense out of it all: to combine all these partial reports into a comprehensive understanding that can inform reasoned dialogue. People certainly snipe at each other using these tools, providing "gotcha" moments that embarrass, point out inconsistencies or reversals in positions on important issues, or exposing personal failings of character or involvement with condemnable groups (anarchists, racists, promoters of ethnic cleansing, hate groups, etc.). Human beings are continually being exposed as complicated and contradictory, providing fodder for ideological opponents. But with what effect? Little more than defensiveness or outrage – little rational dialogue, little that has any real impact on the democratic experiment. Andrew Keen (2015, p. 8) writes that internet evangelists have promised us a "magically virtuous circle, an infinitely positive loop, an economic and cultural win-win for its billions of users. But today, as the Internet expands to connect almost everyone and everything on the planet, it's becoming self-evident that this is a false promise." Why? It actually plays into the neoliberal trends that have gripped democracies around the world – either by choice or by demand.[3]

> The more we use the contemporary digital network, the less economic value it is bringing to us. Rather than promoting economic fairness, it is a central reason for the growing gulf between rich and poor and the hollowing out of the middle class. Rather than making us wealthier, the distributed capitalism of the new networked economy is making most of us poorer. Rather than generating more jobs, this digital disruption is a principal cause of our structural unemployment crisis. Rather than creating more competition, it has created immensely powerful new monopolists like Google and Amazon. . . . Rather than creating transparency and openness the Internet is creating a panopticon of information-gathering and surveillance services in which, we, the users of big data networks like Facebook, have been packaged as their all-too-transparent product. Rather than creating more democracy, it is empowering the rule of the mob. . . . Rather than fostering a renaissance, it has created a selfie-centered culture of voyeurism and narcissism. Rather than establishing more diversity, it is massively enriching a tiny group of young white men in black limousines. Rather than making us happy, it's compounding our rage.
>
> *(Keen, 2015)*

It is undeniable that access to social media (Facebook, Twitter, Instagram, SnapChat, MySpace, Sina Weibo, Sonico, VK, Tumblr, RenRen, Qzone, Orkut, Odnoklassniki, Netlog, and many others) has provided the ability for people in different regions or language groups to connect with one another, or even for global communities to be established. Connectivity globally has never been easier. And there are certainly instances in which this connectivity has facilitated dialogue among dissidents and led to responses, violent and non-violent, to grievances. The first instance of this occurred in 2001 in the Philippines using text messaging (at that time Filipinos were the most prolific text-messengers on the planet). Nearly seven million text messages were sent to organize a protest at a major crossroads in Manila against that country's legislators, who had voted to set aside key evidence in an impeachment trial of President Joseph Estrada. This peaceful protest led to a reversal of the decision by the legislators and the president's removal from office (Shirky, 2011). Sometimes such protests have worked (Spain, 2004; Moldova, 2009; Ukraine, 2012) and sometimes they have not (Belarus, 2006; Iran, 2009; Thailand, 2010; Turkey, 2013). Zeynup Tufekci and Christopher Wilson (2012), examining the role of social media in the Arab Spring – and particularly the Tahrir Square protests in Cairo – argue that it was not merely the use of Facebook and Twitter that was critical, but the existence of a new type of public sphere created by Al-Jazeera, the changed nature of social connectivity via social media, and the expansion of access to sophisticated mobile telephones with photo and video capabilities that fueled the successful and prolonged protests (see also Eltantawy and Wiest, 2011; Joseph, 2012; Lim, 2012; Micó and Casero-Ripollés, 2014).

There is also evidence that the increasing use of social media platforms provides a foundation for non-elites to become opinion leaders as the inchoate public begins to consider political issues – especially those that result in polarized positions. For instance, concerning Turkey:

> In an age of technological infiltration and social media prevalence, the general public is bombarded with information and political opinions in a constant and instantaneous fashion. Looking at popular media, opinion shapers need not necessarily belong to a specific educational or professional stratum. Rather, opinion leaders may simply be those who bring in new information, ideas, and opinions, then disseminate them down to the masses, and thus influence the opinions and decisions of others by a fashion of word of mouth. Opinion leaders may capture the most representative opinions in the social network. They may define the limits and the agenda of popular political arena. They may signal an entire range from uniform to highly polarized positions. Their rhetoric may change quickly or die with the rapid turnover of issues in the media realm.
>
> *(Gökçe et al., 2014, p. 673)*

Clay Shirky (2011) argues that conversation is more important than information when organizing social protest. Certainly social media are resources that allow for conversation to be maximized. But we will argue here that it is not merely conversation, but conversation with particular characteristics, that enables successful social change via public pressure, and that this conversation has to be based in reliable information if it is not to devolve rapidly into character assassination, ideological and sterile propaganda, or merely the expression of outrage. Uninformed conversation is little more than the expression of opinion and emotion – easily dismissed in a neoliberal democracy as "biased" and therefore flawed. But even when conversation is based on accurate information, this information must also be authentic, truthful, and trustworthy. Any of these three qualities can be problematic in a spontaneous, social media-fueled movement.

Authenticity means being true to who you are, expressing your genuine self. There is no pretense, no effort to tell others what you think they want to hear. This idea was central, says Manuel Castells

(2012, p. 177), to the Occupy movement. Since this movement had no leaders, it depended on the entirety of those present to create, maintain, and provide for free communities. This depended on authentic expression of needs, capabilities, ideas, and opinions. This approach was contrasted with inauthentic living in which people take roles, fit into pre-determined categories, and seek to please others to achieve success, fame, income, advancement, or other goals. This inauthenticity also defines much of what people would usually post about themselves or others on social media. People post to be liked, or to be followed. They portray themselves in the best possible light, agree with those who share a particular ideology, or challenge others to post "if they believe," with an implied negative judgment if they don't. This inauthenticity would defeat the challenge posed to authority by Occupy. Inauthenticity meant cloning the despised practices of the oppressive system Occupy was objecting to. Authenticity was thus crucial.[4]

Second is truth. This is closely aligned with authenticity, for one could not be authentic if untruthful. Occupiers had to be truthful with themselves, about who they really were, about what their true motives for participation were, about what actions they were willing to engage in – no pretense, no omissions, no avoiding the reality. They had to be ready to endure possible police action, violence by authority – several Occupy locations did find themselves under siege and encountered eviction strategies. If the participants were not truthful about the reality of what they were doing and facing, they would not be fully legitimate. Acknowledging the truth and acting on the truth were crucial.

Third is trust. In an egalitarian movement the ability to trust the one who marches next to you is crucial. It is the same logic as that relied on by soldiers – you have to trust the man who shares your foxhole. Confronting authority in a phalanx only works when the one next to you doesn't cut and run. People depend on their solidarity and their solidity in the face of danger to enable them to face it with some semblance of equanimity. People's involvement in the Occupy movement was triggered by anger, but the normal human reaction to armed force is fear. Castells (2012, p. 219) explains: "Anger increases with the perception of an unjust action [charging police, for instance] and with the identification of the agent responsible for the action [the mayor or university president]. Fear triggers anxiety, which is associated with avoidance of danger. Fear is overcome by sharing and identifying with others in a process of communicative action. Then anger takes over: it leads to risk-taking behavior. When the process of communicative action induces collective action and change is enacted, the most potent positive emotion prevails: enthusiasm, which powers purposive social mobilization." This enthusiasm would not be merely the result of solidarity on the front line, either, but would be reinforced by the unseen collective: those behind you in the phalanx, those posting on the Occupy websites, those whose photos and videos from earlier confrontations in other places would be available for inspiration before confronting authority. Trust, like truth and authenticity, was crucial.

These three qualities were crucial, as an interconnected unit, to avoid the one result that has proved fatal: violence.

> Violence provides spectacular, selective footage for the media, and plays into the hands of those politicians and opinion leaders whose aim is to suppress as quickly as possible the criticism embodied in the movement. The thorny question of violence is not just a matter of tactics. It is the defining question in the life and death of the movements, since they only stand a chance of enacting social change if their practice and discourse generates consensus in society at large.
>
> *(Castells, 2012, pp. 226–227)*[5]

The social responsibility of media in the political process, then, can be varied. In some situations the media need to play their traditional role of providing background intelligence and context that allow citizens to participate in the political process itself. In others, if they are to be of use in a political process dominated by elites (a polyarchy), the media should take on a more robust investigative role to bring to light political activities that otherwise might not be uncovered. Third, the media – and especially social media – need to provide the connection capacity to facilitate citizen mobilization. Fourth, the media need to find the means to avoid attempts to prevent information flow, and provide information to dilute propaganda and enable people to act in their own best interests in a highly controlled media environment. Fifth, the media should, in all cases, be engaged in creating and maintaining a comprehensive media ecology that empowers people in a democracy and provides hope for solving widespread social, environmental, and physiological problems – and overcoming geographical, linguistic, and cultural issues – in situations where more highly centralized political authority has choked off opportunities. Although there may be times where the status quo could legitimately be supported, these are far outnumbered by those where change of one type or another would be appropriate. In other words, the media should be agents of change, with the exact nature of such agency varying from one situation to another.

Case 8.1: *Charlie Hebdo*

"Ever since a Danish newspaper drew death threats and incited protests by publishing cartoons satirizing the prophet Muhammad in 2005, American news organizations have wrestled with a question: to publish or not to publish the offending, if clearly newsworthy, cartoons?" (Farhi, 2015). But this is not merely an American issue: what is the ethical choice to make when opportunities to caricature or otherwise portray others arise? In most countries it is not unusual for political figures or celebrities to be the subject of editorial cartoonists, and often these portrayals are not flattering. They show the peccadillos, illicit sexual liaisons, political inconsistencies or results of failed policies, or other aspects of people and actions that are easily satirizable and eminently recognizable. Late night talk-show hosts and satirical comedy news programs in some countries also bring such information to light. So what is so different about portraying the Muslim prophet Muhammad?

Many within Muslim communities see the portrayal of Allah or Muhammad as blasphemous. Some take it upon themselves to "defend" these religious figures using violence. At *Charlie Hebdo*, a Paris-based satirical newspaper, 12 people lost their lives in 2015, apparently defying "violent threats from Muslim extremists." In the United States later that year two Muslim extremists were killed by police when they tried to attack a venue where "a provocative contest" to portray the prophet Muhammad in cartoon form was being held (Parker, 2015). *Washington Post* columnist Kathleen Parker wrote that Pamela Geller, who had organized the event, had abused the idea of free speech with the event. What happened in Texas, she said, "gives pause to even the most passionate defenders of the First Amendment. Not since Westboro Baptist Church's 'God Hates Fags' message and Florida pastor Terry Jones burning the Koran has the principle of free speech been so sullied and abused" (Ibid.).

This was not an unusual response to Geller's activities in the American media. The *Washington Post* also carried a report by Gregory Castillo (2015) (originally published in the *Dallas Morning News* and carried by the Associated Press with the headline: "The week that cable news failed free expression") quoting a variety of news anchors, commentators, and comedy-show performers condemning the exhibit. Castillo accused the American media of "cowardice and rationalization" for refusing to carry the pictures. He concluded: "A judgment has emerged that preaches compliance with the notion that this particular form of expression means you're *asking for it*. That viewpoint has trickled down from the bosses of these news organizations into the coverage, as Geller has discovered. Once the media draws a line, it's tough to undraw" (Ibid.).

There are a variety of religions in the world that people adhere to. While this situation refers to Islam – and while that is certainly the one whose most extreme adherents have had the attention of the world's peoples for the past two decades – the problem of portraying religious figures is not limited to this religion. Neither is the idea of blasphemy. Is blasphemy a special case? Should those that adhere to a particular religion or ideology have the right to determine what is an acceptable portrayal of their leaders, saints, gods, or prophets? (Certainly Marxists and Nazis have had their share of unflattering portrayals, along with many genocidaires and ethnic cleansers, warring parties, and other opponents of prevailing elites.) Is it ethical for the media to carry portrayals that they know, or suspect, will evoke violence? Do cartoons or satirical portrayals constitute hate speech? Should hate speech be avoided by the media, even if it means that news will go unreported?

Commentary on Case 8.1

John Durham Peters (2005, p. 10) begins his book on free speech with this remark: "Ever since the beginnings of democratic theory and practice in ancient Athens, communication – understood as the general art of concerted living and acting in the polis through the gift of logos (speech or reason) – has been considered the lifeblood of civic life."

Many free speech advocates take the absolutist position that, regardless of the content of speech (including even hate speech), it must be allowed as it is a basic human right. It is one of the fundamental underpinnings of democracy and since, as John Stuart Mill argued, any effort to prevent speech necessarily assumes that the censor is infallible, censorship must be condemned. Different ethical traditions, however, approach this problem with more nuance. As Loren E. Lomasky (1987, p. 10) puts it, "the tendency to couch all moral disagreements in terms of rights is disruptive and obfuscatory." One reason for this is that when rights – such as the right to communicate – are invoked, we are also invoking assumptions about the sovereignty of the individual (Ibid., pp. 11, 12): the individual's rights cannot be abridged by preference for the rights, or needs, of community. But, as Ronald C. Arnett and Pat Arneson (1999, p. 14) write, "we must work together to create a democratic community by encouraging independent voices to work together as interdependent voices united in a given historical moment."

Peters (2005, pp. 31–32) argues that this tradition of unfettered speech, however, does not have global acceptance and that its allure may, in fact, be waning, although "its tropes remain indispensable for anyone caught in a pinch" – a convenient and comfortable retreat when under siege. And, while absolutists claim that all speech should be protected in the interests of the democratic experiment, Peters questions such an unyielding position:

> Defenders of absolute openness might ponder the price we pay for the scope of our minds. How hard must our hearts become [having witnessed so much mayhem and blood in our media]? Liberals have no time for tenderness, no regard for faith or folly. If life and death are at stake, who can blame people firm enough to close their eyes? Sometimes simple rage is a more humane response than rational consideration. The condescending term fundamentalist does not do justice to the impulse to say no to the madness of the world. Must we watch the video of Daniel Pearl being beheaded? Is *Hustler* publisher Larry Flynt a great hero, as Milos Forman's film suggests? Please.

(Peters, 2005)

Some countries, notably China, have taken steps to protect public morality within their borders. China has added regulations that will "scrub social media of the 25 most popular dirty words in China" (Tani, 2015). As mentioned, Russia has also taken a similar step by banning what it terms "gay propaganda" (Titova, 2015). Iran also attempts to limit the exposure of its citizens to Western culture, but most restrictions on internet use around the globe are aimed at protecting those in power from criticism, with the most egregious example being Turkey (as of this writing) (see Kruse, 2014; *Today's Zaman*, 2015).

Different ethical systems do have varying responses to the issue of free speech generally, and to objectionable (immoral, racist, or other hate-filled) speech more specifically. In the Western tradition the sovereignty of the individual suggests that anything less than total immunity for speech (with certain tightly proscribed exceptions such as aiding an enemy by publication of troop movements, ship sailings, military strategies, etc., or speech that incites violence or panic) would demean certain individuals, thus denying equal dignity to all. Such commitment to individuality, however, lacks the universal commitment that would make it acceptable within more collectivist cultures – at least without serious reservations. Loren E. Lomasky (1987, p. 19) captures the essence of this reality when he writes: "Rights ascriptions, it may be said, are a generally reliable rule of thumb – at least when they are purged of rhetorical excrescences – but to rule out of court otherwise salutary actions merely because they involve rights violations is to transform a useful instrument into a fetish."

The essential problem, of course, is that when proscriptions on speech emanate from elite authority (whether corporate or state-based), there is the risk that what might otherwise be legitimate challenges to that authority would never see the light of day. And, as Lomasky (Ibid., p. 18) puts it, "human beings are notoriously susceptible to temptations to pursue their narrow self-interest at the expense of others." How, then, ethically speaking, is speech that might provoke violence or insult others to be treated? What is the ethical value to society of uncontrolled expression – or of expression confined within moral or political parameters? Is it possible to say that only speech with obvious political meaning – or social, economic, religious, or cultural meaning – is to be protected – unless, of course, the result of protection would be the slaughter of innocents? If not, does that mean that individualism as defined within the Western canon must be the standard for protecting speech? Is social responsibility possible in the free for all that sometimes passes as rational debate? Or are the interests of community peace, tolerance of difference, protection of the right to life, or social flourishing more crucial than allowing freedom of expression – or cataloging it as a basic human right?

Social responsibility implies that such a universal right is unsustainable. Societies differ in respect to values, commitments to other members, and the tolerance of dissent. Who, then, would adjudicate claims made by dissenters within a given society that has no interest in the claims made? Islamic societies often protect the name of Allah and Muhammad from criticism. But they also disallow conversation about conversion from Islam to another religious tradition. Should these restrictions have equal protection, and can we expect others – outside these societies that wish to change such commitments – also to obey them? If not, what is to prevent violent response? The same question can be asked of the *Charlie Hebdo* situation in Paris. France is part of the Western tradition, protecting free expression. All can be criticized. But it also accepts (sometimes grudgingly) Muslim immigrants from North Africa, many of whom come from countries that France oversaw as a colonial master. The attraction for immigrants is their knowledge of the French language, making their transition somewhat less frightening. Should such immigrants be required or expected to jettison their former ways of thinking (constrained by their religious faith) by the very fact of crossing an international boundary? If not, what is the socially responsible behavior to be exhibited – both by the majority and by the Muslim minority, who see the world in fundamentally different ways? Is it more socially responsible to curtail majority speech in the interests of minority sensibilities, or to demand of the minority that they "fit in" and – even if they have violent objection – accept the fact that they must develop a thicker skin to weather the storms of criticism or blasphemy that they will undoubtedly witness in their new home? Is accommodation possible between two vastly different community value systems? Is a single moral community worth striving for, and is it possible in a global environment?[6]

Case 8.2: *In the First Circle*

Alexandr Solzhenitsyn was a Russian novelist who had served time in the Soviet Union's gulag. He found his writing subject to a hostile censorship that prevented him from publishing his novel, *In the First Circle*, despite him "lightening" it into an "ersatz, truncated" version (reducing its 96 chapters to 87 and changing the focus from nuclear technology to a medical device) in an unsuccessful effort to get past the Soviet censors. In 1968 he agreed to publish the reduced version in the West. Although the novel was received with praise in Western circles, Solzhenitsyn – who was subsequently exiled to the West by Soviet authorities – was not satisfied, being anxious to see publication of the original manuscript. It finally appeared in its original form in 2009, a year following Solzhenitsyn's death. He dedicated the book "to my friends from the *sharashka*," and included an author's note indicating that the novel had been written between 1955 and 1958, distorted in 1964, and restored in 1968 (although not published in its restored form for another 40 years).

The title of Solzhenitsyn's novel came from Dante. The *sharashka* was a prison camp for intellectuals – professors, engineers, scientists. It was so much better than the usual prison camp that one newcomer was told "my dear sir, you are still in hell, only you've ascended to its highest and best circle – the first" (Solzhenitsyn, 2009, p. 37). The novel was made into a 1992 Canadian television film and into a 2006 Russian television miniseries.

The novel is replete with moral questions. When one of the main characters, Volodin, discovers that a stunning secret has fallen into his lap – one concerning the Soviet nuclear program – "Volodin asks himself, 'If we live in a state of constant fear, can we remain human?' He exchanges the potentially self-indulgent principle that 'we are given only one life' for the consequential principle that 'we are given only one conscience.' His action establishes the ideal of 'humanity,' and thus sets the bar by which all the novel's characters are judged. . . . Readers are left to ponder, along with him, the ethics of betraying the worst sort of regime – a variation on the age-old theme of the legitimacy of tyrannicide" (Ericson, 2009).

Commentary on Case 8.2

Solzhenitsyn's attempt to publish a novel that would highlight the treatment of political dissidents (initially found in *One Day in the Life of Ivan Denisovich*, published during a brief "thaw" in superpower relations, eventually fully revealed in *The Gulag Archipelago*) was a sensitive issue for the Soviet Union during the Cold War that pitted two superpowers against one another militarily, each attempting to recruit other nations to its cause. *In the First Circle* was a major embarrassment, an indictment of a totalitarian political system with no tolerance for criticism. Soviet society, like all societies – democratic or not – was a conundrum. People were certainly not free as they were in the West. Dissidence was not tolerated. Underground literature (*samizdat*) circulated, typewriters were licensed, and radio and television signals from the West jammed. The Soviet bloc (including several countries in Eastern and central Europe and along the Baltic Sea, along with now independent central Asian countries) made every effort to block their citizens from accessing information from the West. They also attempted to dampen any internal dissent that would call into question their domestic and foreign policies, the availability of basic goods, or the superiority of the quasi-Marxist ideology that undergirded the totalitarian state.

When Solzhenitsyn was awarded the Nobel Prize in Literature in 1970 he was unable to leave the Soviet Union to travel to Stockholm because he feared that, once he left, he would not be allowed to return. He sent a speech, part of which told of his vision for literature: "The task of the artist is to sense more keenly than others the harmony of the world, the beauty and the outrage of what man has done to it, and poignantly to let people know . . . By means of art we are sometimes sent – dimly, briefly – revelations unattainable by reason. Like that little mirror in the fairy tales – look into it, and you will see not yourself but, for a moment, that which passeth understanding, a realm to which no man can ride or fly. And for which the soul begins to ache . . ." (quoted in "A bright flame," n.d.). Irving Howe (n.d., p. 645) writing a review of Georg Lukacs' book on Solzhenitsyn, says that Solzhenitsyn "had apparently reached the 'instinctive' conclusion that in an authoritarian society the role of the writer is to recover fundamental supports of moral existence, direct intuitions of human fraternity, encompassing moments of truth. . . . The first task of such a writer [with religious vision], as he takes upon himself the heavy and uncomfortable mantle of moral spokesman, is to remember, to record, to insist upon the sanctity of simple fact and uncontaminated memory."

There have been many examples of artists and writers using fiction or creative activity to reveal truths about societies, truths that those societies did not wish to have acknowledged. Jonathan Swift famously criticized British society with *Gulliver's Travels*, and many other efforts have followed. Most of these have been released in "free," or non-totalitarian societies. Artists and authors have put themselves at risk with such elliptical comments, telling the truth as they saw it through the medium of fiction. Despite the literary or artistic value of such work, however, along with its ostensibly non-factual nature, governments have sought means to suppress it.

Are such works worthy of protection as part of the public sphere, or does their fictional or "made-up" quality disqualify them from serious non-literary or artistic debate? Such works are disruptive when they are released within the societies on which they are focused. We could argue that it is counter-productive, even dangerous, to raise the consciousness of oppressed people, aiming to free them from the shackles of enforced orthodoxy, or shaming them for what is revealed by fictive stories. Or we could say that it is essential that such works find the light of day, even if they have to be smuggled out of suppressive countries and then smuggled back in again for public review (in secret, of course). This might even result in arrest, imprisonment or worse when they are found in the hands of readers by various forms of secret police. In the West authors such as Solzhenitsyn are seen as heroes, but to those with whom treaties must be signed, who stare across the abyss of nuclear confrontation, or step lightly in highly contested hotspots such as Kashmir, such works are condemned as potential incitements to further violence. Should the danger of mayhem that such fictive works might unleash be enough reason to consider their publication socially irresponsible?

Case 8.3: Death of a Social Media Celebrity in Pakistan

In July 2016 a Pakistani woman and model, Qandeel Baloch, was murdered in her sleep by her younger brother. Ms. Baloch had appeared on "Pakistani Idol" and had become a social media sensation. Some referred to her as the Pakistani Kim Kardashian. She had posted many provocative selfies, pursued fame, and made controversial statements on Facebook questioning the patriarchy of Pakistan and defending the rights of women to order their own lives. The UK's *Independent* (2016) said that she had "established herself as a household name in Pakistan for posting bold, sometimes risqué photographs and videos and challenging social norms in a conservative Muslim country." Throughout her rise to celebrity status in the Pakistani social media community she had used a pseudonym: Qandeel Baloch. But several weeks before her murder media outlets had disclosed her original name of Fauzia Azeem. This was, according to Pakistan's *Express Tribune* (2016), what put her life at risk. So long as she was not using her real name her brother and other family members could disavow any connection to her. But once her name, marital status, hometown, and other personal details were revealed, her two brothers were scandalized and one decided to take her life. Even family photos had been posted without her permission. Her request to the Interior Ministry for security had been ignored.

Commentary on Case 8.3

Pakistan is a country where collectivist ethics are paramount. Somewhere between 500 and 1,000 young women are killed in the country each year because they have dishonored their family. As the carriers of the family honor, they are in a uniquely fragile situation. The law also allows the family to forgive any murderer so very few of them are ever prosecuted, especially when they are members of the victims' families. Although Islam itself does not condone such violence, interpretations of its strictures in many Muslim countries, especially where Sharia law is practiced, allow such deaths to go unpunished. The honor of families is deemed more important than the lives of individuals who are accused of dishonoring them.

In this case the dishonor visited on Qandeel's family by behavior that was on the edge of respectability, perhaps even beyond it, did not become an issue until her true identity was revealed by media organizations. They were, of course, on the hunt to discover that identity due to her notoriety. She had hundreds of thousands of Facebook friends and Twitter followers, and was often on Pakistani television programs expressing her views. But always as her alter ego.

This raises the issue of the social responsibility of media in such a society. If the society accepts the legitimacy of honor killings, and young victims of such killings are buried without fanfare and their killers escape condemnation, is the socially responsible action what occurred here? The media exposed the true identity of one seen by some elements of the society as dishonorable. Or is the media culpable in her death? Western ethicists routinely condemn such killings: they value the individual life. But is that relevant in this case? If a society does not choose to protect free expression when it is directed at deep-seated social values, when criticism of the treatment of women is not accepted as legitimate, and those who express what are considered "anti-social" views attempt to protect themselves with false names, is that falsity unethical, or should human rights prevail when it might disrupt elements of the basic social structure itself?

Conclusion

In some restricted societies the possession of alternative scripture (Bible, Koran, etc.) is forbidden: imprisonment or exile is surely to follow if discovered. Even in democratic societies, however, certain taboos are the subject of vigorous condemnation and defense. In the United States, for instance, the artistic photographs produced by Andres Serrano resulted in a congressional debate about the public funding of the arts. Though Serrano himself is Christian, his "Piss Christ," a photograph showing a crucifix plunged into a vat of his own urine, deeply offended many Christians. Bill Donohue, president of the Catholic League, argued that "ethics should dictate that you don't go around gratuitously and intentionally insulting people of faith. I don't care whether you're a Muslim or Jewish or Catholic or whatever you might be" (Holpuch, 2012). French Catholic fundamentalists in Avignon attacked this same photo with hammers on Palm Sunday in 2011 (another copy was used in New York the following year). Of course, conservative Christians in the United States did not follow the same logic as that expressed by Bill Donohue when the Muhammad cartoon exhibition was mounted in Texas in 2015. Neither did the French fundamentalists, Australians who vandalized it, or neo-Nazis who ransacked a Serrano show in Sweden in 2007.

> Serrano defended his photograph as a criticism of the "billion-dollar Christ-for-profit industry" and a "condemnation of those who abuse the teachings of Christ for their own ignoble ends." . . . The [Avignon] gallery director, Eric Mézil, said it would reopen with the destroyed works on show "so people can see what barbarians can do." He said there had been a kind of "inquisition" against the art work. In a statement, he said the movement against Piss Christ had started at the time of President Nicolas Sarkozy's ruling UMP party's controversial debate on religion and secularism in France. At a record low in the polls before next year's presidential election, Sarkozy has been accused of using anti-Muslim and extreme-right rhetoric to appeal to voters and counter the rise of the Front National.
>
> *(Chrisafis, 2011)*

Clearly double standards abound when it comes to the nature of speech within the public sphere. It is this speech that raises the specter of discord, insult and violence, and requires attention to civic social responsibility. The question thus becomes one of priorities. What is more important: peace, respect for the other, taboos, or iconoclasm? All of these, and much more besides, can result in civil unrest, demonstration, riot, imprisonment, even death in some cases. Does social responsibility and civil participation in the life of society require that all points of view be honored or that some may be excluded for the social good? And who can legitimately police the public sphere: artistic elites, government authorities exercising police power, moral police, internet censors, or religious authorities? What is, in fact, the socially responsible action on issues of significance?

Discussion Questions

1 Different countries define the value of political conversation using different criteria. What is seen as necessary in one context may be defined as revolutionary in another due to differences in cultural and moral values. Does this mean the value of free expression should also be defined within the prevailing cultural/moral context?

2 If free expression is defined differently in different contexts, does this imply its value is also variable? The various human rights documents that ostensibly guarantee free speech don't make that distinction. Which foundation should prevail, human rights or moral/cultural values?

3 Do the media owe different social responsibilities to different countries? Are such responsibilities different for indigenous media and multinational ones?

Notes

1 See http://www.un.org/en/documents/udhr/index.shtml/index.shtml#a19. Accessed February 13, 2017.

2 Roy (2009, p. 52) also complains that Indian democracy "is on its way to being owned by a few corporations and major multinationals. The CEOs of these companies will control this country, its infrastructure and its resources, its media and its journalists, but will owe nothing to the people. They are completely unaccountable – legally, socially, morally, politically."

3 There are some differences in use of the blogosphere according to the political values that people identify with, at least in the United States. Shaw and Benkler (2012) indicate that those who identify with progressive (or left-wing) politics are more likely to use the blogosphere for mobilization and discursive participation and are more inclusive of wider publics than those on the conservative (or right-wing) side of the political spectrum, which are far more dependent on elites to exclusively set its agenda.

4 There were those who objected to the authenticity of the Occupy movement, however. One anti-Occupy site was "We are the 53%," where people who were ostensibly represented by Occupy objected that they were taxpayers (hence the 53%) who didn't believe that anyone should rely on others and not themselves (Recuber, 2015).

5 Neera Chandhoke (2015, p. 33) writes that "violence negates, subverts and defies the fundamental presuppositions of democracy. . . . How can then democracy and violence live together in the same political or conceptual space, ever?" But she also argues that "revolution is justified when people have been denied what is their due according to the creed of democratic justice – an equal share in the burdens and benefits of society" (Ibid., p. 134). Finally, however, she writes that, even when violent protest – or revolution – can be understood, even sympathized with in the absence of good faith efforts to respond to just and long-standing complaints and discrimination, "when violence holds individuals and groups in thrall, moral disintegration follows. For we cannot control violence, violence controls us" (Ibid., p. 136).

6 This question was even raised in the United States at the University of Minnesota when several professors put together a panel to discuss the *Charlie Hebdo* murders and advertised it using a poster with an image of Muhammad carried by the magazine's first post-murder issue. After complaints from the university community the Office of Equal Opportunity and Affirmative Action (EOAA) ordered staff to take down the flyers and to expunge the image from any university websites. The Dean of the College of Liberal Arts reversed this order and refused the EOAA's request that he condemn the use of the Muhammad image. The *Minneapolis Star-Tribune* weighed in, quoting EOAA's director as saying "there are limits on free speech, and that would be where you have harassment of an individual based on their identity." Eugene Volokh (2015) then wrote in the *Washington Post* about this controversy: "the flyer contained an image that some individuals find offensive because of their religion. If *that* is enough to trigger an investigation – on the theory that any speech offensive to individuals of certain religious groups may be 'harassment of an individual based on their identity' – then something is very badly wrong in the EOAA."

9

The Rule of Law

Introduction

In June 2014, the same month 100 years earlier that Archduke Franz Ferdinand and his wife Sophie, Duchess of Hohenberg, were shot and killed in Sarajevo, Libyan attorney Salwa Bugaighis was assassinated in her Benghazi apartment by unidentified political enemies dressed in military fatigues. Ms. Bugaighis was not royalty, not a member of government, and not an international celebrity, though she had the respect and admiration of all who hoped for a peaceful, democratic government in the wake of Muammar Qaddafi's ouster. Bugaighis played an advocate's role in that chapter of the Arab Spring, and served for a time on the National Transitional Council, before threats to her life caused her to flee. She and her husband Issam, who was abducted by the gunmen and never seen again, had returned to dangerous Benghazi to vote in Libya's general election. They cast their ballots, went home, and were cut down and kidnapped. She was 50.

The Archduke, who should have been more cautious after a bomb injured his police escort earlier on his last day, was also a 50-year-old casualty of terrorism. His death led to the First World War, which changed the history of the world. He would have inherited the Austro-Hungarian empire, which disappeared in the post-war partition of Europe. His last words were the memorable appeal to his wife to live, for their children. Ms. Bugaighis, shot several times and unable to offer last words, was remembered in one published obituary as a martyr for the rule of law in a country too weak to control its patchwork militias or to conduct safe, secure elections (Anderson, 2014).

Considering the level of greed and savagery apparent in many places around the globe, a cynic might conclude that law – written, codified ordinance – is the script used by tyrants to effect what they would otherwise get without it. Law is a sham, a gloss. It creates the means of extracting wealth and power from people who cannot afford the protections law provides, favoring people who can buy courts for their own ends. "Anything I say is law, literally law," declared Hastings Banda, first president of Malawi (Drogin, 1995). "It is legal because I wish it," said Louis XIV, king of France (Rule, 1969, p. 371). "The more laws, the less justice," observed Rome's great orator, Cicero, who was legally murdered by Rome's Second Triumvirate in 43 BC.

But law as organizing framework for nations must not be dismissed as cheap chaff. Since the Magna Carta in AD 1215, subjects have demanded negotiated restraint by those who rule. King John's acceptance of the Great Charter may have been short-lived, and the ensuing baron's war another testimony to the weakness of words over swords, but an idea was unleashed on the world at Runnymede that eventually took hold in constitutions, juries of peers, independent judiciaries, and appeals processes. A phrase coined in 1885 captured this concept of mutual and redundant accountability, the "Rule of Law." It has been the banner for responsible freedom ever since.

World Media Ethics: Cases and Commentary, First Edition. Robert S. Fortner and P. Mark Fackler.
© 2018 John Wiley & Sons, Inc. Published 2018 by John Wiley & Sons, Inc.

When "Rule of Law" appeared, its meaning was expressed in four formulae (Bingham, 2010, p. 3–4):

1. *The state can take neither goods nor life from any person except by breach of law established in an ordinary manner and arbitrated in an ordinary proceeding. Stated positively, your property and body are securely your own, apart from behavior publically proscribed and adjudicated. You have rights the state cannot arbitrarily suspend.*

Thus President for Life Banda must have been duly surprised when his three decades in power ended to discover that the murder of four political opponents in 1983 was to be adjudicated in a court of law, and he was the defendant. And King Louis XIV (1638–1715), the Sun King, longest-reigning monarch in European history, would have been incensed and dismayed at the French court's decision, five generations later, finding King Louis XVI guilty of high treason. The latter Louis was executed by guillotine in January 1793, under the simple name, "Citizen Louis Capet." The former Louis' *Ancien Regime* was gone for good. (We note sadly for Louis XIV that his young love, Marie Mancini, could not be made queen no matter the force of Louis' passion. There were limits to *L'Etat, c'est moi*; Lossky, 1994, p. 78.)

The Rule of Law protects personal property from arbitrary taking, but can it protect personal opinion, expressed and publicized, from backfire and violence? That will be one of the key questions in this chapter.

2. *All persons are subject to the same law in the common courts. If ministers steal, they must appear in the same court as everyone else. No special treatment for the high and mighty. The judges and juries hearing complaints concerning the rich and powerful are to be the same "citizens" who render justice to folks of the common life.*

The goal is impartiality and the reduction of corruption in a nation's justice system. At the center of this mandate is the Golden Rule. Juries "of the people" will want to be treated with the fairness they render to all before them. Wealth will not be able to buy reprieve from the law, since few can afford to bribe in this manner. Common folks sentenced to prison or fined for crimes against the people will more likely be "rehabilitated" into the common life if their treatment under the law is not tainted by preferences for defendants with great social and political capital. Are journalists people with social capital, or common folks? Do journalists require a shield from some aspects of the law, or preferential treatment under the law in order to foster an open communicative environment, which is the only kind of social ecology in which the rule of law thrives? These questions will occupy the discussion in this chapter as well.

3. *The rules to which all are responsible emerge from the decisions of courts, not from the philosophizing of the powerful. The Rule of Law travels a bottom-up trajectory, not top-down.*

Doing philosophy is the privilege of the educated class. Rendering justice under the law is the responsibility of all citizens to each other and to the wider collection called nation or republic. The notion that better rules originate in circles of higher education, circles of philosophers, was once a popular idea; many world leaders put their trust in it. In the United States, Woodrow Wilson (28th U.S. president, 1913–1921) was a proponent; his admiration for German planning and public policy under Otto von Bismarck, the Iron Chancellor (1815–1898), is well documented (Murray, 2014). Alas, following Bismarck's reign and during Wilson's presidency came the horrors and bloodbath of the First World War. Scholars are still trying to sort out how it started, why the European peace was broken, and why the millions of war dead inspired the sacrifice by European leaders (and eventually

Wilson) of still more lives to such a pointless war. Philosophers let it happen, stoked its fires, and fumbled its conclusion. The Rule of Law can neither afford nor survive such leadership. Journalists and other media producers are the voices that inform the people, and media are the kiosks that publicize the people's wisdom, bottom-up, open forum. Protecting this marketplace of ideas and its league of professional contributors may require special recognition under the law. Media professionals cannot be considered above the law or a law unto themselves, but certain legal privileges may need to be extended to keep the public forum open and vital. This issue and its surrounding questions will be considered in this chapter.

> 4. *The rule of law cannot be made capricious by ordnances which draw scorn and ridicule from the people. Good law must be inherently advantageous, as well as serious, just, and enforceable.*

When Vladimir Putin signed a law restricting the use of profanity in the arts in Russia, critics scoffed. "Well, now they ban swearing, and tomorrow maybe they'll allow it again," mocked Sergei Shnurov, front-man for Russia's most popular punk band. The new law covered literature, theater, film, and music. And another Russian law passed at the same time subjects popular bloggers to stiff fines for swearing online. A reporter covering this development modestly understated the Russian government's capacity to enforce such laws, particularly since the law does not define what specific language triggers enforcement (Razumovskaya, 2014).

Kilometers west of Moscow, around the same time, a British court sentenced the former editor of the tabloid *News of the World* (*NOTW*) to 18 months in prison for one count of conspiring to intercept telephone voice calls. The case involved phone messages from a missing teenager who was later found dead. In the aftermath of the scandal, *NOTW* ceased publication and media magnate Rupert Murdoch, its executive chairman, made profuse public apology. No mocking that blunder, no chortling about government over-reach, no parodies about law forcing virtue from the profane (Flynn, 2014). What law requires, a nation's people must recognize as important to its common life, not superfluous or cranky. Mr. Bumble in *Oliver Twist* offered wisdom on silly law: "If the law supposes that . . . the law is an ass" (Dickens, 1837/1970).

Eventually, anyone concerned for the Rule of Law must ask, how are its ambiguities and concessions to be reconciled? If the Rule of Law is to be more than a formal social negotiating tool – common sense and fair play applied with an even hand – from where does it derive legitimacy? Is law rendered by the Divine as part of creational order? Invented by republicans as the most practical of social compromises? Derived from intrinsic human nature? These issues must be addressed, because eventually, the Rule of Law requires public certification; law works only as a public is willing to certify that it offers the best chance for mutual flourishing. A century before Bismarck and the genius of German planning, Immanuel Kant observed in *Critique of Practical Reason* (1788): "Two things awe me most, the starry sky above me and the moral law within me." The cosmos humbled him while the moral law ennobled him, adding wisdom and nuance to our search for origins and applications of the Rule of Law.

The First Amendment to the U.S. Constitution guarantees freedom of speech and press in words that enshrine an ideal of democratic theory: the state may not "abridge" the communicative freedom of its people, nor may the state threaten, intimidate, or suppress minority opinion, lest positive social change be silenced before it wins majority support. Those words, written by James Madison, later the country's fourth president, comprised the first of 10 amendments to the U.S. Constitution, presented to Congress and the States to alleviate fear that central authority, so recently overturned by the war of rebellion (or War of Independence, as it is known in the United States), would show its treacherous face again in the new federal system designed by the Philadelphia Convention of 1787. The amendment reads, in relevant part: "Congress shall make no law . . . abridging the freedom of speech, or of the press; or the right of the people peaceably to assemble, and to petition the Government for a redress of grievances." Each phrase has had its parsing in the opinions of the Supreme Court and lesser courts, and no part stands today as word-for-word absolute. But the concept stands: government restriction on freedom of speech much be the least restrictive means of achieving carefully defined state interests, without over-reach into opinion or suppression of minority dissent. Thus it is lawful in the United States to protest military action by wearing obscene messages on one's jacket (Harlan, 1971), or to publish humor that will excite the passions of 1.6 billion worldwide (Christians, 2012, p. 56). But the courts in other lands have not been so generous in their interpretation of law relating to publication of news and opinion.

Case 9:1: Aiding Terrorism

As we write, three journalists on assignment with Al-Jazeera are serving jail sentences of seven to ten years for "aiding a terrorist group" (the Muslim Brotherhood) and in one case, "possessing ammunition" – a spent shell casing picked up during a protest in Cairo. Is this the rule of law, Egyptian style, or something that nations respecting the Rule of Law rightly condemn?

If they serve full terms, their names will go down in journalism history: Peter Greste, 48, Australian, for 20 years a correspondent for the BBC and Reuters, in Kabul during its trouble, in Somalia, an Al-Jazeera bureau chief stationed in Nairobi at the time of the Arab Spring; Mohamed Fahmy, 40, experienced in the Middle East and North Africa, worked for the *New York Times* and CNN; and Baher Mohamed, 30, a recent university graduate who had hired on with Al-Jazeera only a month prior to his arrival in Cairo, but who had worked for Japan's *Asahi Shimbun* and CNN (BBC News, June 23, 2014).

These three journalists were tried in a Cairo court, duly sentenced and confined, despite worldwide protests and vigorous denunciations by world news organizations and the United Nations, and tepid responses from governments who are uncertain about the legitimacy of the Brotherhood's overthrow but want the new al-Sisi government to line up as friend. The U.S. Secretary of State issued a statement on the "chilling and draconian" verdict (Al-Jazeera, June 26, 2014). "Chilling" presumably carried the sense that news coverage inside Egypt will now lean toward the interests of the al-Sisi government, and "draconian" refers to the severe punishments doled out by Athenian magistrate Draco circa 620 BC, not to the death/doom metal band from Sweden. No further comments from the secretary were forthcoming.

Several other Al-Jazeera journalists were also tried, though not present in court, and sentenced to prison. Al-Jazeera's English-language managing director said that the Egyptian court's decision "defies logic, sense, and any semblance of justice," and promised to continue trying for his colleagues' release. Note that Al-Jazeera is not trying for diplomatic relations or foreign trade with Egypt, which explains the director's vehemence in contrast to more official sources (Al-Jazeera, June 23, 2014).

The parents of Peter Greste and the Australian foreign minister also vowed to continue legal appeals. When the rule of law fails, we sometimes appeal to the Rule of Law as if it were a banner in the sky. Hope seeks resolution, no matter the obstacles.

Greste himself is not bashful about describing his state of mind as "devastated and outraged" at the prospect of his best career years wasted in an Egyptian prison (Al-Jazeera, June 26, 2014).

Supporters of Egypt's decision are not particularly bashful either. A leading Egyptian academic, defending the court, said that "the anger from Britain, the U.S., and Australia is not important to us because we are applying Egyptian law that governs Egypt. We don't comment on judicial matters in the U.K. or America, so why should they comment on ours?" And President Abdel Fattah al-Sisi insisted that "Egypt's judiciary is independent and glorious. We must respect the judicial rulings and not criticize them" (BBC News, June 24, 2014).

Commentary on Case 9.1

"In contemporary Egyptian society, journalists can be fired, have their printers seized, cause a riot, or find themselves tortured in an Egyptian prison for their coverage. Yet Egyptian journalists have been willing to push the limit of their society, at their own peril" (Perreault, 2014, p. 97). So begins a current study of media in Egypt, which then goes on to describe the pervasive role of Muslim belief and practice, obviating the need for a "religion page" since everything from food to business to fashion, and politics of course, is related to Islam. Indeed, media users outside the so-called First World are amused by the West's near-absolute lack of interest in religion's relevance to food sections, op-ed pages, or sports. There are few "walls of separation," as Thomas Jefferson famously put it, between religious practice and any other form of practice in much of the world, especially North Africa and the Middle East.

The woebegone trio from Al-Jazeera understands that all too well. They are employed by a worldwide news network based in a Sunni-dominated country, Qatar. They were working in a Sunni-dominated country, Egypt, covering a Sunni political and religious movement, the Muslim Brotherhood. With its nearly century-long work, the Brotherhood is believed to be Egypt's most cohesive political movement. Its first success followed the Arab Spring in 2011, when its Freedom and Justice Party won half the seats in Parliament, and its candidate, Mohamed Morsi, won the 2012 presidential election. Not a year passed before Morsi was overthrown in a military takeover and the Brotherhood's leadership imprisoned. By 2013, the Brotherhood was declared a terrorist group, its assets seized, and its agents and members banned. In other words, by every means available, military and legal, the Brotherhood was ended in Egypt. This is a big news story. The three journalists were caught in the vortex of providing much-needed public information about these changes, and legal proscriptions about contact with and publicity about the banned movement. Perhaps they believed too trustingly in the shield from prosecution provided by the press badge, or the immense influence of their employer, or the Sunni connections at every social turn. The lesson they learned, along with the world's media organizations and everyone with an ear to hear: not every ordinance passed by a parliament or signed by a chief executive is exemplary of the Rule of Law.

The reaction around the globe to this court's verdict tells a moral story itself: the court was wrong. Not wrong in its administration of the law perhaps (a question for specialists in Egyptian jurisprudence), but wrong in its moral outcome. Wrong because administrative procedure did not serve the public interest, did not protect public speech in ways it must be free, did not follow the rule of transparency, which is the plain assertion that the story of our times must be told. Human cultures cannot remain silent concerning themselves. We seek understanding across borders. No one admires the jurisprudence of North Korea, for this reason among many others. Egyptian courts took a turn toward North Korea, a step that infringes on the moral sense of humankind.

"The Moral Sense" was the title of sociologist James Q. Wilson's inquiry into why people behave as properly as they do (Wilson, 1993). He was curious about why more people were not following a life of crime (however defined in their own cultures) and why parents worldwide so infrequently abandon their children in favor of economic self-interest. Wilson carried no religious reasoning into his inquiry, made no Kantian claims about rational will, and sorted through no extensive utilitarian calculus. He simply wanted to know why so many people in all cultures display a moral sense and generally follow it (Ibid., pp. 10–15). He concluded that humans have developed a "core self" over time, and that this core human nature can be described, which he then set out to do. The variations will be many, he claimed, but the substance of humanity's moral sense is captured in four uncontested impulses: sympathy, fairness, self-control, and duty. Wherever you find people acting as people say they should, one of these moral impulses or some combination of them will be found. Legal systems based on ethical foundations will reward behaviors that exhibit these impulses; only legal systems that do so are worth the trouble of maintaining them, or living under them, or pledging loyalty to them as all nations require of their citizens. It is no wonder, then, that Egypt's ambassador to Australia, facing angry reaction to Greste's imprisonment, jumped out of his ethical skin when he said that "the word right or wrong is not applicable" to the court's judgment; rather, he "would have loved to see Greste reunited with his family." Then, confounding his moral sense with his presumed pledge to support Egypt's legal system, the ambassador obfuscated: "It's not about my wish, or our wish. It's about when the rule of law is the case" (Willis and Osborne, 2014).

Wilson offers a roadmap toward an ethical assessment of this situation. He insists that the four "senses" common to humankind are not universal givens, as in Kant, or universal rules, as in the world's major religions. They are socially scientific findings that uncover the "cultural origins of our moral habits and our moral sense" (Wilson, 1993, p. 26). The four senses are what humans have come to adopt as our best chance for survival. They could change, but consequences to the species if they did are most uncertain. They could disappear, and in certain historical figures they most certainly did. They belong to no sensory organ and about their application sincere people may disagree. Nonetheless, human persons, Wilson observes, hold these sensitivities as the gift of millennia of generations and their pooled experience. We would do well today to acknowledge them and exploit their benefits.

Of the four, duty and fairness seem most engaged in the present case. The court has a duty to follow the precedent of the law. Most judges in modern civilizations are given latitude in their application of the law, but in the main, precedent is king. (Judges or chiefs in developing cultures enjoy even wider latitude, which often devolves into the troubles noted below.) The doctrine which respects precedent is called *stare decisis* (Latin, "to stand by things decided"). Without *stare decisis*, the judgments of courts would be fickle, unpredictable.

Fairness requires that illegal activity be predictably anticipated. A citizen should be able to know that activity X violates law Y and enforcement of the law would result in penalty Z. If such calculations are impossible because law is secret or penalties are based on a judge's emotions, the law as a guide to civil conduct will fail, and legal process will be scorned as meaningless gesture or fabulous deceit.

Were the three Al-Jazeera journalists aware (the Latin term is *scienter*, usually a prerequisite for a guilty verdict) that their effort to chronicle Egypt's political changes violated law? Reports of their trial (which was really the first go-round in sorting their moral dilemma) suggest strongly that none of the three were knowingly engaged in illegal action. Note that in some crimes, murder for instance, the moral sense of sympathy is so viciously violated that legal systems presume the murderer understands his/her guilt. In other crimes, speech crimes for instance, so much cultural knowledge comes into play that the presumption of *scienter* is not fair; it must be proven. Was the alleged illegal communiqué done in jest, with the intent to produce harm, cloaked in the robe of journalism but enacted by enemies of the state? Only a thorough examination of the facts of the case could ascertain these matters. Such thoroughness is a requirement of fairness to the accused.

Were the three accused granted a thorough review? We cannot know, though the court of worldwide opinion rightly asks Egyptian prosecutors to lay out their evidence. Someday, given the ubiquity of the internet, that may happen.

Not all modern nations agree that journalists have a duty to uncover truth. Such uncovering levels the ground between citizen and leader, firming up leadership's accountability to the governed, and aiding immensely in citizens' general review of leadership's effectiveness. For citizens to intelligently choose their leaders, journalists must be given wide latitude in gathering facts and collecting the stories of people who can provide first-hand, experiential reports on the day's events. If a nation wants to consider itself a member of the modern democratic world, such latitude is a given. It is fair to the duty of journalists, the argument goes, for the state itself to protect and defend a more open, transparent, accountable civil society, even though powerful persons within the state may suffer as a result. Makers of civil law will be held accountable to the rule of law in part by the press. In the United States, the most dramatic episode of the press holding politically powerful persons to the rule of law occurred in the early 1970s when journalists Woodward and Bernstein, working for the *Washington Post*, reported on crimes conducted with the knowledge and approval of then president Richard M. Nixon. So significant was this Watergate scandal and its aftermath, that similar shenanigans worldwide are now regularly given the suffix *-gate* as a way to signal political power run amok.

Should jail terms of seven to ten years be applied to persons dutifully gathering significant public information, even as they are unaware of transgressing certain legal mandates? No, said world citizens expressing their senses of duty and fairness. No, that is too harsh, too much penalty for the infraction (which is questionable anyhow). Would a fairer penalty be expulsion (the trio is no longer able to perform journalistic duties)? Or public denunciation, still useful in some places to deter future behavior? Or, lighter still but more directed to the purpose of the indictments, more reporting on the events at issue – the Brotherhood and its purposes, the al-Sisi administration and its purposes – so that citizens could know more, read and view more, and decide their own future based on a fuller briefcase of information? In that case, the "penalty" laid on the trio would be to produce more news reports, and for others to produce possibly contrary news reports, perhaps showing the trio's work to be deficient, shallow, or based on false information, discrediting the trio and diminishing their future in the profession. Would this latter penalty be fair to all parties, respectful of the duty of judges to protect civil law precedents, mindful of the duty of news networks to report only what they believe to be true, and congruent with the duty of citizens to make informed decisions about leadership based on wide exposure to information, positive and critical? Positive fairness in a case such as this would be a shock-wave of support for public responsibility.

Case 9.2: Israeli Anti-Arab Politics

Rabbi Meir Kahane (born Martin David Kahane in 1932) emigrated from the United States to Israel in 1971 and organized a political movement he called Kach ("thus" or "this is the way"). Kach advocated the forced though compensated emigration of all Arabs from Israel, the occupation of Gaza and the West Bank, and the change of Israel's government from democratic to theocratic, based on Jewish teaching. The result, he said, would be a Greater Israel, a movement more than a nation.

After several failed attempts at national political leadership, Kach won a seat in the Knesset in 1984, which Kahane occupied. During the middle 1980s, Kach and Kahane were indistinguishable and increasingly militant. Kahane used his membership in the Knesset to put a veil of legitimacy over provocative visits to Arab communities. His purpose was to persuade inhabitants to move away – far away. Kahane wanted a Jewish state in which marriage with gentiles would be forbidden and rights would accrue to Jews alone.

At the Arab town of Umm El Fahm, police, at first tolerant of this extremist group, quickly ascertained that Kach resented a substantial danger to public peace, and prevented Kahane's supporters from entering the town. The police argued that disturbances and bloodshed were thus prevented. But on other occasions when police were not so vigilant, Kach agitators provoked heated responses from Arabs and Jews who opposed them, blocking roads and shouting "Racism won't pass!"

Keenly political, Kahane knew that the police action in Umm El Fahm could set precedents elsewhere and appealed to Israel's courts to overrule the police decisions. In the meantime, the Knesset House Committee voted to restrict Kahane's parliamentary immunity, thus enabling police to arrest Kach members if they posed a threat to public order, which was, after all, Kahane's aim.

This restriction was a rare legal move and required justification. Israel's attorney general, Itzhak Zamir, argued that the Kahanist movement "fundamentally contradicted the values cherished by society" (Cohen-Almagor, 1994, p. 220). Zamir insisted that Judaism was "sensitive to the lives of human beings and respected people qua people, while Kahanism impugned these beliefs." He had misjudged Kahanism as a "sick phenomenon" but peripheral and relatively harmless, and had come to see it as a "danger to society" because it permitted "a member of the Knesset to act in the Knesset against the Knesset." Such acts were contrary to the pillars of the Israeli state, threatened peace at every turn, and should rightfully and legally be suppressed. One Knesset member, Haim Ramon, voting in favor of the restrictions against Kach, recognized the apparent contradiction between declared freedoms and his support of the ad hoc law: "The voting today is the beginning of Kahane's exclusion from this House . . . the Knesset decides today not only on a parliamentary act, but also on an educational act. The entire youth will know that this man symbolizes an illegitimate thing, *an immoral thing*" [emphasis added] (Ibid.).

The rest of the story ended tragically, depending on one's view of such things. Kach was forbidden to run for re-election, its organization banned, and Kahane was ejected from the Knesset. Following a speech to supporters in New York City in November 1990, Kahane was killed by an Arab gunman linked to an early Al-Qaeda cell training in the city. Kach split into two groups, Kach and Kahane Chai, but new names and second-generation leaders did not persuade the Knesset to revisit their ban. Both groups were labeled terrorist organizations by the United States. On December 31, 2000, Benjamin Zeev Kahane, leader of Kahane Chai, and his wife were assassinated by Palestinian gunmen while traveling to their home.

Commentary on Case 9.2

If duty and fairness were engaged in the Greste case (Egypt), sympathy and self-control are engaged here. Sympathy, Wilson (1993, p. 32) said, is the "capacity for and inclination to imagine the feelings of others. It is both an essential skill and an aspect (not a rule or moral law) of human understanding of right and wrong. It may indeed be the source of moral sentiments, as philosopher Adam Smith believed." Self-control is the "habit of controlling or moderating bodily appetites":

> It is a remarkable characteristic of human society that most of the things that are best for us –
> that is, most likely to produce genuine and enduring happiness – require us to forego some
> immediate pleasure. . . . For self-control to be virtuous, it is not enough that the more distant
> pleasure be greater than the more immediate one; it is also necessary that the more distant one
> be more praiseworthy.
>
> *(Wilson, 1993, p. 80)*

These two aspects of moral life, identified by Wilson and others as rising in humankind through centuries of learning and adapting, are found in many sets of moral rules and foundational to every system of ethical thinking. To be other-minded and temperate are key virtues in a life directed toward pleasure and away from pain, as Wilson carefully notes. Sympathy and self-control are embedded in the Golden Rule, in Confucian respect for persons, in the communitarian understanding of mutuality and relationships. Martin Buber stressed both, which in Kahane's context might have proved, had he paid them mind, his keys to success instead of marginalization.

Sympathy would have required Kahane to temper his rhetoric and qualify his policy proposals to account for the interests of those he tried to move out of Israel. Of course, masses of people do not move unless significant incentives are offered. Short of discovering gold in Lebanon, Kahane would likely have failed in his objectives of purifying Israel of foreigners, but if sympathy had been on his agenda as an operating principle, eventually he would have come to see that the people he believed were wrong for Israel were no more right or wrong than he himself was. He would have discovered their humanity as he uncovered the depth of his own. His bias against Arabs would have surrendered to his recognition that all ethnicities share the dignity of humankind, and his considerable persuasive skills might have been re-directed to improving, instead of displacing, Arab communities.

Self-control, or the absence of it, was the missing straw that led to the rejection of Kach and Kahane and his expulsion from the Knesset and from Israeli media. He lost his platform because his views were excessive, laden with race-hate, inciting to violence, and impossible to incorporate into a modern democracy. Kahane tried by political means to create his Jewish utopia. Such projects have occurred worldwide, but the direction of human culture works steadily against them. Kahane of all people should have learned from the destructive immorality of Adolf Hitler, whose effort to purge Europe of kin of Kahane was a fool's errand and one of history's most condemned pogroms.

Self-control rightly practiced is not merely a cover for latent bigotry, as in false kindness to lure one's victim for the kill, the wolf in sheep's clothing effect. Self-control recognizes the passions and appetites that need curbing and discipline. A self-controlled person comes to know, by steady practice, when and where to exert his will or extoll his teachings. From a child's passing of food at family dinner (rather than burying one's head in the potatoes) to an outsider's approach to ethnic enclaves (where Kahane publicly revealed his animus) sympathy and self-control are the virtues which lead to trusting relationships and cooperative flourishing. That his own government adjusted their own free-speech and free-movement laws to compensate for Kahane's bitter message and derelict mission is testimony enough that on these two essential moral aspects, sympathy and self-control, he failed.

The rule of law does not exist apart from the commitments of people to principles and "senses," indeed common senses, of what's right and good. Kahane operated outside those senses, and paid the price in terms of law and social marginalization. He was wrongly murdered. During life, the ban, a rare legal tool in advanced democracies, prevented his words from inciting the murder and displacement of others.

Case 9.3: Opposition Journalism in Uzbekistan

Muhammad Bekjanov and Yusuf Ruzimuradov have been in jail for crimes associated with journalism longer than any other reporters worldwide (Committee to Protect Journalists, 2014). Bekjanov was editor of *Erk*, an opposition newspaper in Uzbekistan; Ruzimuradov was a reporter. The charges against them were publishing and distributing a banned newspaper, participating in a banned political protest, and attempting to overthrow the regime, according to the Committee to Protect Journalists (CPJ), a New York-based non-profit organization that, since 1981, "promotes press freedom worldwide and defends the right of journalists to report the news without fear of reprisal. CPJ ensures the free flow of news and commentary by taking action wherever journalists are attacked, imprisoned, killed, kidnapped, threatened, censored, or harassed" (Committee to Protect Journalists, n.d.). CPJ took the occasion of World Press Freedom Day (annually on May 3) to urge Bekjanov be released, in part due to his deteriorating medical condition.

The two were convicted by an Uzbek court soon after the country became independent of the Soviet Union, in 1990, an odd time in the nation's young history to incarcerate opposition journalists. *Erk*, the newspaper, and Erk the political party opposed the election of Uzbekistan's first and only president, Islam Karimov, who became head of state two days before the end of 1991. Erk was the only opposition party in that first general election. Of course, there were claims of irregular ballot counting and other election tampering, but the top job went to the former Soviet official-in-charge, and Erk was thereafter forbidden to participate in presidential elections. The U.S. Department of State regards Uzbekistan as a republic, but adds that the country's politics is actually "authoritarian presidential rule with little power outside the executive branch" (CIA, n.d.). Little noted in the CPJ's appeal for Bekjanov's release is the guarantee in Uzbekistan's constitution (Article 67): "The mass media shall be free and act in accordance with the law. It shall bear responsibility for trustworthiness of information in a prescribed manner. Censorship is impermissible" (Government Portal of the Republic of Uzbekistan, n.d.). Constitutional interpretation is superintended by seven supreme court judges, all nominated by the president and confirmed by the Supreme Assembly. Apparently the "prescribed manner" of Uzbek law was grossly and permanently offended by *Erk*'s editor, who is paying his debt to the Uzbek people, so to speak, with an adult lifetime of silence and isolation.

Commentary on Case 9.3

Uzbek media leaders are not alone in the jeopardy their important work entails. Notable in American journalism was Elijah Lovejoy, killed by a mob in Alton, Illinois, in 1837 when editor Lovejoy refused to quiet down about slavery. Even though Illinois was a free-soil state (slavery was illegal there), and even though the famous First Amendment to the U.S. Constitution guarantees free speech and press, the tempers of the mob in Alton and throughout the nation at that time were running too hot to retain their human sensibilities. Lovejoy was the first American editor to be killed for his journalism (Simon, 1994).

Uzbekistan is by any measure a rogue republic. It holds elections; it has three branches of government. On paper it appears similar to other democracies. But the same "big man" is elected every time, and his cronies are leading the various ministries. Dissenters are fortunate to be able to buy a dozen eggs. This regime is not leaving town anytime soon.

When a nation's law shows the appearance of the rule of law, but none of the substance, the rule of law is degraded and its subjects turn cynical. Legal freedoms became a farce; using courts to assert legal rights is reckoned a business transaction with decisions going to highest bidders, who are always state officials. In such places, higher law is required for justice to be approached and enacted.

In February 2012, the European Union made such an effort on behalf of prisoner Bekjanov. "The EU is deeply concerned," its public statement began, "by the additional five-year sentence which Muhammad Bekjanov . . . received only days before he was due to be released following his imprisonment in 1999" (European Union, February 9, 2012). The notice goes on to call the new criminal charges "doubtful," to cite "serious concern" over Bekjanov's health, and to "regret" the lack of transparency concerning his physical condition. Such polite language finally comes to its main point when the EU refers to Bekjanov's "right to a fair trial in accord with international legal standards" (Ibid.). The EU does not mention Article 19 of the Universal Declaration of Human Rights, but it might as well have thrown that in. If Article 19 had courts and arms for enforcement of its provisions, or the simple allegiance of Uzbek leadership, Bekjanov would be free. Article 19 (Universal Declaration, n.d.) is a law above the law, reminding rogue republics that a mere show of substance and procedure is a flimsy sign of corrupted democracy. While Uzbekistan may be a billboard republic, world opinion shouts, "Grow up" morally and ethically.

Tom Bingham's final thesis in his survey of the Rule of Law is: *the rule of law requires compliance by the state with its obligations in international law as in national law* (Bingham, 2010, p. 110). No state can rationally claim that its citizens are flourishing when they are afraid to opine publicly, and segregated from the speech of others, essentially fed a diet of information and opinion pleasant to the regime. No nation rationally emulates the suppression that a jailed opinion-leader represents.

The Rule of Law is a noble ideal. It takes shape when morally mature leadership understands its role as servant of the people, open to all suggestions, good ones especially welcome. One of the greatest discoveries of humankind, the Rule of Law awaits its enactment in tinder-boxes around the world. In more stable cultures, treasuring and protecting the core principles of the Rule of Law are a people's best guarantee of a future duly informed and a national leadership duly transparent in motive and power.

Discussion Questions

1   Why respect law? Why comply to a rule you were not consulted about before it was enacted?

2   Are certain people above the law, that is, courts cannot hold them accountable? Do you aspire to such a position?

3   Why do people everywhere need boundaries? Why should media everywhere be regulated by law?

4   If laws related to media content and service were rescinded, what would change in your media usage?

5   Write a law, enforceable in court, concerning media and racial conflict, or media and consumerism, or media and depictions of violence. Argue for your law's public benefits.

10

Treasuring Persons, Protecting Institutions: The Protection of Minority Voices

Introduction

In Chapter 8 we discussed the issue of minority voices as they pertained to participation in the public sphere, and the reality that offensiveness to others is often the result of exercising free speech rights, whether purposefully or inadvertently. We also dealt with the problem of fiction as a component of public discourse, along with its use as an indirect means to raise issues in information-controlled contexts. Finally, we raised the question of what the socially responsible action was when expression might conceivably lead to imprisonment, conflict, or death. These are important questions.

Of equal weight, we think, are the roles of media in protecting people from the police power of the state, and in exposing policies or practices whose effect is to perpetuate institutional racism, ethnicism, and the superiority of one group over another. Such groups would include castes, tribes, clans, professions, bureaucrats, the police themselves, or other identifiable minorities. In a global world with international migration, guest workers, and refugees at an historic high, what is the social responsibility of the media to them? They are usually not part of dominant media institutions' audiences, as they often live in squalid conditions without the benefit of media access, or their language facility in a particular country is limited, or they are living "under the radar" so as not to face prosecution or deportation should they be discovered. Is there a special responsibility owed to such strangers?

There are also those within most societies who wish to expose information, "leak" it if you will, to respond to perceived abuses on behalf of the population or of certain aggrieved parties within the society. In the Western tradition an expected responsibility of the media would be to "give voice to the voiceless," to protect sources who provide information from prosecution, and to investigate wrongdoing by authority or powerful elements of the society. In other traditions the expectations may be to support economic and social development within the society itself, or to ameliorate conflict between long-standing antagonists, or even to provide explanations or justifications for authorities' actions. So we must ask what the social responsibility of media is in these various circumstances.

Media and Society

All societies have expectations of the media. Democracies expect the media to create and maintain the public sphere where issues of public concern are debated and people have the opportunity to exercise their free speech rights. Often there are also expectations that the media should serve as a watchdog to

World Media Ethics: Cases and Commentary, First Edition. Robert S. Fortner and P. Mark Fackler.
© 2018 John Wiley & Sons, Inc. Published 2018 by John Wiley & Sons, Inc.

assure the accountability of public officials. In some states the media are expected to assist the country in human, economic, and social development. In others the media are expected to stay out of the way (at best) or to actively support government policies, both foreign and domestic. In the most controlled circumstances, the media are either owned or tightly controlled (often through censorship) so that there is little to no independent judgment exercised within their newsrooms. Differing expectations lead inevitably to differing definitions of truth: truth as the media define it, as ideology defines it, as government authority defines it, or as the corporate owners of the media define it. Expecting the media to tell the truth (as the 1947 Commission on Freedom of the Press in the United States demanded) doesn't necessarily mean that there is an unequivocal definition of truth used around the globe.

In 1956 the *American Political Science Review* "reported agreement that the psychological attitudes necessary to sustain a democracy – individual liberty, equality, and responsible participation – must be internalized by its citizens for that democracy to survive" (Manwell, 2010, p. 849). But these expectations do not necessarily mean that democratic governments aren't – at least in some cases – as busy attempting to channel debate as is the case in more authoritarian societies. As Manwell puts it: "Preserving democracy requires exposing illusions of external threat that can prevent citizens and leaders from addressing more concrete internal threats to continued self-governance. The use of repression and terror, including threats of censorship, suppression of information, imprisonment, and torture, by leaders to subjugate political opponents and dissidents is not exclusive to authoritarian states – such tactics can also be employed by leaders of democratic states: a fact that can be difficult for people to acknowledge, especially if it is not congruent with their belief system" (Ibid.).

As globalization has increased its grip on both the politics and economics of independent states, the issue of corporate social responsibility has also become more prominent. Corporate enterprises that have interests in several countries are increasingly expected to exercise social responsibility in all places in which they operate. Jian Wang and Vidhi Chaudhri (2009, p. 247) write that China's public expects that its globally integrated corporations deliver both economic benefits and "contribute to building a 'harmonious society,' which includes contributions to community outreach, education, occupational health and safety, and environmental protection." These companies' public relations activities are expected to demonstrate commitments to these activities and goals (see also Liu, Jia, and Li, 2011).

Chinese expectations of foreign companies' social responsibilities have also increased, even while Chinese companies' domestic and foreign practices have drawn criticism outside the country (Tang and Li, 2009, p. 199). Global companies such as Nike, Reebok, Mattel, and Gap have been harshly criticized for using suppliers that maintained sweatshop conditions in China. Famous global brands, such as KFC and Häagen Daas, have been found to fail to meet the food safety regulations in China, and these scandals were subject to widespread publicity. In 2004, Walmart China and its employees entered into a dispute regarding the founding of a labor union in its Chinese branches. After extensive negotiation and state intervention, the retailing giant notorious for its anti-union stance gave in and accepted "officially sanctioned unions" (Ibid., pp. 199–200).

Similarly, American retailers have found themselves heavily criticized for their failures to adequately oversee the working conditions of people manufacturing their products in foreign countries under the auspices of subcontractors. Such companies as Apple, Gap, Walmart, Nike, American Eagle and many others outsource a large number of their product lines to subcontractors abroad, especially to China and Bangladesh (the two largest garment manufacturing countries), as well as to the Dominican Republic, Cambodia, and other places. Bangladesh alone has 5,000 garment factories "handling orders for nearly all of the world's top brands and retailers" (Yardley, 2013).

We should ask whether, in the global environment, companies' social responsibility is universal. Does a foreign company operating in a particular country owe the workers in that country the same responsibility they would owe those in its home country? If so, who would enforce such a vague concept as "social responsibility," especially since the nature of society itself would vary from one place to another?

Public relations practitioners may find themselves attempting to explain why adequate oversight was not exercised when a tragedy strikes one of these outsourced contractors, especially when investigation uncovers widespread abuse by the subcontractor, who may have paid bribes, built facilities that failed to meet minimal code standards, failed to install safety equipment, or locked exit doors to prevent theft on unauthorized breaks from grueling work days for less than local minimum wage. Well-publicized collapses of garment manufacturing buildings in Bangladesh – one of which resulted in more than 1,000 deaths – are well known. But what are the respective social responsibilities of the companies involved in these tragedies? And what should public relations tell the publics – both the affected public where the tragedy occurred, and those in other countries where consumers benefit from lower prices resulting from low wages, bribery of public officials to overlook building code violations, or the refusal to provide adequate safety equipment for employees? And what is the social responsibility of the press in these cases? Must the press oversee the working conditions of every factory operating in a local environment, and uncover bribery that allows unsafe buildings to house hundreds to thousands of unsuspecting workers, or turn a blind eye to the reality because people who might otherwise have no employment have managed to find work that allows them to provide for their families – even if it is inadequate – and by whose standards?

An example is Foxconn in China. This company is the largest private employer in the country with over one million employees, nearly half of whom work in one 20-year-old plant in Shenzen that manufactures motherboards, camera components, MP3 players, and iPhones. The facility is owned by a Taiwanese company. Several employees committed suicide by jumping off the roofs of Foxconn buildings, one of them leaving a note to say he had done so to provide for his family by triggering Foxconn's remuneration policy that provided for them in the event of a death. Shortly afterwards the company cancelled this program. It installed nets 20 feet off the ground around many of its buildings to catch jumpers. Western companies that purchased products from Foxconn were forced by media pressure to defend factory conditions that "some saw . . . as a damning consequence of our global hunger for low-cost electronics" (Johnson, 2011). After visiting the Foxconn Shenzen facility Joel Johnson wrote:

> I seem to be witnessing some of those damage-control efforts on this still-warm fall day as two Foxconn executives – along with a liaison from Burson-Marsteller, a PR firm hired to deal with the post-suicide outcry – lead me through the facility. I have spent much of my career blogging about gadgets on sites like Boing Boing Gadgets and Gizmodo, reviewing and often praising many of the products that were made right here at Foxconn's Shenzhen factory. I ignored the first Foxconn suicides as sad but statistically inevitable. But as the number of jumpers approached double digits, latent self-reproach began to boil over. Out of a million people, 17 suicides isn't much – indeed, American college students kill themselves at four times that rate. Still, after years of writing what is (at best) buyers' guidance and (at worst) marching hymns for an army of consumers, I was burdened by what felt like an outsize provision of guilt – an existential buyer's remorse for civilization itself. I am here because I want to know: Did my iPhone kill 17 people?
>
> *(Johnson, 2011)*

The deaths at Foxconn did trigger a strike at another company that manufactured components for Apple and IBM, motivated by requirements for daily overtime (100 to 200 hours per month) and in criticism of Apple's record mark-ups of its products (at that time an Apple iPhone4S cost $188 to manufacture and sold for $649 retail) (see Soh, 2010; Kunert, 2011; Reisinger, 2011). Foxconn's founder, Terry Gou, led "a rare damage-control media tour to the factory complex in Shenzhen" following the tenth death at the Foxconn facility (Xinhua, 2010).

This was not Foxconn's first encounter with the media or public anger at its practices. In 2006 the company was publicly shamed by the British tabloid, the *Daily Mirror*, for its cramped living conditions, low pay, and long working hours. According to China Labor News Translations:

> Foxconn fanned the flames by launching an absurd defamation case against two Chinese journalists who followed up the story, demanding 30 million RMB (US$3.7 million) in damages. In the end, Foxconn settled for a symbolic one RMB payment from the journalists. Following all that, the All-China Federation of Trade Unions (ACFTU) made a show of requiring that Foxconn set up an enterprise union at the end of 2006, but workers and activists later found that the union was virtually inactive, and the official positions were dominated by management.
>
> . . .
>
> The suicides have ignited debate that reaches beyond Foxconn alone, about China's entire model of economic development, and the systematic exploitation of migrant factory workers. The government has also been criticised by some, for excluding rural migrants from welfare services such as health, housing and education. Both Foxconn and its buyers have gone into damage control, and have unilaterally announced increases in workers [*sic*] wages. Foxconn has announced it will implement an average 20 percent pay rise for all employees (pre-empting a minimum wage increase due in July). And interestingly, rumour has it on English tech blogs that one of Foxconn's major buyers Apple has pledged to direct between 1 and 2 percent of its profits back to Foxconn workers in the form of a direct subsidy (a very unusual corporate social responsibility strategy that defies the normal relationship between buyers, suppliers and labor in a global supply chain).
>
> *(CLNT, 2010)*

There is also the issue of the advertising to consumers of products that are produced in sub-standard conditions. Advertising is designed to increase the sales of products. The more product sold, the greater the demand for additional production. On the one hand, this means increased employment opportunities in producing countries. On the other, it means more incentive to cut corners so that manufacturing costs are competitive, with the ancillary costs to both individuals and communities. Is it ethical to advertise products produced in sweatshops or otherwise unsafe conditions to increase demand in countries where these products are sold? Do the consumers who purchase these products, the retail outlets that provide them, the production and distribution companies that make them available, the advertising agencies that create the campaigns, all bear equal social responsibility for how they are produced and sold? Or are some elements of the production, distribution, and sale chain more culpable for abuse than others? Should public relations obscure negative realities to protect the image of companies involved in this chain so as to avoid negatively affecting profits? Such questions demonstrate the thorny issues that abound in the social responsibility arena.

Double-Standards in Social Responsibility – Not All Are Equal in Media Reports

The United Nations Development Program (UNDP) reports that "gender inequality remains a major barrier to human development. . . . All too often, women and girls are discriminated against in health, education, political representation, labour market, etc. – with negative repercussions for development of their capabilities and their freedom of choice" (UNDP, circa 2015). The UNDP goes on to report (Ibid.) that vulnerable groups around the world include refugees, internally displaced persons, the homeless, orphaned children, prison inmates, long-term unemployed, and people who have inadequate food supplies. Most of these vulnerable groups receive little attention from the media, and their numbers are significant. For instance, 2.1% of the global population was homeless in 2009 (latest statistics) – this amounted to 126 million people, more than the total population of most countries in the world. In 2012 there were nearly 15 million refugees and 4.5 million orphaned children in the world (Ibid.). In 2010 some 77.8% of the global working poor resided in the world's least developed countries, and in 2012 23.5% of children aged 5 to 14 were engaged in labor (Ibid.). On nearly every index calculated by the UNDP women trailed men in human development (except for life expectancy), especially in the least developed countries on the planet.

Britain's *Guardian* newspaper editorialized the stark reality of this situation even in the developed world: "women, unjustly, have become the shock absorbers of austerity. They are paying a far higher price proportionately than men, finding themselves cemented into a lifetime of low earnings and under-utilised qualifications" (*Guardian*, 2014; see also Centre for Social Justice, n.d.). In 2013, *The Economist* carried a blog indicating that education for girls in poor countries was hardly anything to celebrate. Although China, Bangladesh, and Indonesia looked poised to meet the Millennium Development Goal of eliminating gender inequality in education, most of sub-Saharan Africa, while improving girls' access to primary education, was actually regressing in terms of secondary and tertiary education (C. R., 2013).

Occasionally such issues are reported by the media, especially if a sensationalistic crime is committed against a disadvantaged or underreported group, or if a non-profit organization releases a report highlighting the situation in a particular country. As we have seen, the kidnapping of girls by Boko Haram in Nigeria certainly attracted significant media attention, as did the gang rape and subsequent death of a young woman in India (see under Case 10.2). But the media easily tires of the reality that such events are so common as to be routine. Rape and bride-burning in India, sex trafficking around the globe, forced marriages and female circumcision, the plight of refugees and internally displaced persons, the lack of education and employment opportunities, exploitation of workers, widespread hunger or lack of access to clean water, the deaths of women in childbirth for lack of medical intervention or distance from available medical centers – all are reported on only sporadically if at all. An earthquake or volcanic explosion, or deaths on sinking ships, attract attention, largely as the result of reactionary news strategies that can be reported through social media posts or through the availability of stringers or "borrowed" reporters from other organizations which leads to reports that would otherwise go unrecognized in the media. But the disproportionate suffering of women and girls – their hunger, lack of education and job opportunities, their kidnapping and exploitation in sex trafficking rings, their use as housekeepers (often at slave or near-slave wages) by wealthy families often thousands of miles from their homelands – does not seem to be atrocious enough to attract media attention.

Leakers, Hackers, and Whistle-Blowers

In contrast to the lack of interest in systemic inequalities is media preoccupation with those who provide information that could compromise political or economic elites. The names Chelsea Manning (formerly Bradley Manning), Edward J. Snowden, and Julian Assange are well known around the world, either as people who leaked classified information from U.S. military, State Department, or National Security Agency (NSA) documents, or in the case of Assange, the person who facilitated the distribution of such documents through his WikiLeaks service (see Singh and Tanenhaus, 2013). David Sirota (2012), along with James Risen of the *New York Times*, calls them "whistle-blowers," because their actions were undertaken "at great risk to their lives and careers. These were courageous acts of self-sacrifice on behalf of larger ideals." He contrasts their actions with those of some within the Obama administration who "leaked," the difference being that leakers suffer little risk to lives or careers, "craven acts of self-preservation aimed not at protecting ideals, but at burnishing the president's political image." Meredith Clark (2013) adds several other names to the list of whistle-blowers (although she refers to them as leakers) and hackers. They are all, in her estimation, political prisoners.

This is not merely a U.S. problem, either. Snowden leaked his NSA documentation to *The Guardian* newspaper in London. It included details of surveillance on the leaders of several countries, resulting in strained relations between the United States and Brazil, and the United States and Germany. Manning's leaks exposed candid evaluations of leaders in the Middle East that may have undone much of the goodwill that the Obama administration had attempted to engender after the Iraq and Afghanistan incursions that seemed to target Islamic countries. Snowden was granted asylum in Moscow. Assange, an Australian, sought refuge in the Ecuadorian embassy in London to avoid extradition to Sweden and, he suspected, on to the United States for prosecution. In the wake of these events Berlin in Germany has become a haven for hackers and privacy activists fearing prosecution in other countries (Birnbaum, 2013).

Philip Giraldi (2010), a former U.S. intelligence officer, who originally condemned Snowden's leak of a quarter million classified documents detailing the "arrogance" of Bush administration ambassadors and undersecretaries of state in the aftermath of 9/11, changed his mind after reading the leaked documents, and called the prosecution of Manning and the hounding of Assange "despicable." He concluded: "those who favor the narrative that accepts that there is a nefarious government in Washington ruthlessly manipulating a world empire have pretty much gotten it right."

Governments, of course, see the situation differently. They claim that national security has been compromised, intellectual property stolen, terrorism facilitated, identities stolen, privacy invaded. Under the Rule of Law, no one is exempt from prosecution for these activities, especially when the law exposes secret practices undertaken to protect the interests of the state. In 2012 the U.S. Federal Bureau of Investigation (FBI) charged six individuals associated with the group Anonymous with hacking into various private corporations, the Public Broadcasting Service, and a global intelligence firm, Stratfor. The complaint was as follows:

> Since at least 2008, Anonymous has been a loose confederation of computer hackers and others. MONSEGUR and other members of Anonymous took responsibility for a number of cyber-attacks between December 2010 and June 2011, including denial of service ("DoS") attacks against the websites of Visa, MasterCard, and PayPal, as retaliation for the refusal of these companies to process donations to Wikileaks, as well as hacks or DoS attacks on foreign government computer systems. Between December 2010 and May 2011, members of Internet Feds similarly waged a deliberate campaign of online destruction, intimidation, and criminality.

Members of Internet Feds engaged in a series of cyber-attacks that included breaking into computer systems, stealing confidential information, publicly disclosing stolen confidential information, hijacking victims' e-mail and Twitter accounts, and defacing victims' Internet websites.

(FBI, 2012)

Those who whistle-blow, leak, or hack see it differently – they imagine the public service they are providing in exposing corruption, hidden agendas, hypocrisy, opinions not shrouded in double-speak or diplomatic niceties, secret surveillance activities, and so on. And even when they know what they are doing is illegal (and by definition wrong) they can justify it by moral disengagement, a process that blames others for one's actions and perpetuates itself through the adoption of group norms that justify it (Fitch, 2003).

Leakers and whistle-blowers engage in their activities from within organizations, while hackers find security holes to exploit from outside them. Leakers usually attempt to conceal their identity or demand anonymity from those to whom they leak information. Whistle-blowers have to reveal themselves in order to bring information to public attention. Hackers may be known or unknown when the information they reveal is made public, or they may remain in the shadows when they accomplish a hack under the auspices of an organization such as Anonymous. Anonymous has its own Facebook page (https://Facebook.com/OffiziellAnonymousPage) where it declares, "We are Anonymous. We are Legion. We do not forgive. We do not forget. Expect us" (Figure 10.1). They claim to fight for openness, truth, and freedom. Anonymous is a public non-profit organization but its members are anonymous. They hack into businesses, government databases, financial institutions, police records, white supremacy organizations, and terrorist groups. They support Kurds fighting against ISIS and marches against authority (with marchers wearing their trademark masks), and claim to favor revolution. Some of Anonymous' members have been exposed, prosecuted, and imprisoned. In 2014 Twitter suspended an account that wrongly named an innocent man as the killer of Michael Brown in Ferguson, Missouri (Hern, 2014). Nicole Perlroth (2014) wrote:

> They urged the citizens of Ferguson, Mo., to confront the police in the streets. They caused the city's web servers to crash, forcing officials to communicate by text. They posted the names and address of the county police chief's family. And then on Thursday they released what they said was the name of the police officer who killed Michael Brown, an unarmed 18-year-old black man, on Saturday. Members of Anonymous – the shadowy, snide international collective of hackers and online activists – have played a key role in the growing confrontation outside St. Louis over Mr. Brown's death, goading and threatening the authorities, and calling the effort Operation Ferguson.

Were such actions helpful toward resolving the conflict, protecting the innocent, preserving human life – or did they exacerbate tensions, confound others' efforts to respond reasonably to an inflammatory situation, or make a bad situation worse?

Figure 10.1 Image from the Anonymous Facebook page, showing the trademark mask.

In 2014 the group exposed the Russian government's "game plan for a supposedly 'grassroots' demonstration in Moscow in support of its actions in Crimea; details about how the Kremlin prepared Crimea's secessionist referendum; and private emails allegedly belonging to Igor Strelkov, who claims he played a key role in organising the pro-Russian insurgency in Donetsk, Ukraine. [It] also released documents about how Concord, a company owned by Kremlin-connected restaurant owner Evgeny Prigozhin, apparently coordinates an army of pro-Putin internet trolls through an outfit called the Internet Research Agency. Last week the collective released roughly 40,000 text messages apparently taken from the mobile phone of Timur Prokopenko, manager of the Kremlin's Internet policy between 2012–2014" (Turovsky, 2015). The group also hacked the Russian prime minister Dmitry Medvedev's Twitter account and posted messages that appeared to come from him (Ibid.). The Russian government has taken steps to block access to the organization's websites (including WordPress and Twitter sites) after a Russian court convicted it of data theft and the hosting provider did not respond to notifications from Roskomnadzor, the Russian federal agency responsible for media oversight.

In 2015 several Mexican media outlets and civil society organizations jointly set up a digital platform that promised to protect the anonymity of sources using encryption software to encourage leaks that would enable journalists to obtain the information necessary to do accurate reporting on "corruption, criminality and abuse," and to attempt to avoid retribution from either government or economic elites, or drug cartels (Tuckman, 2015). The sites, Mexicoleaks, described its mission "as the construction of a 'Transparent Mexico,' and participants say they hope it will help them document political corruption, human rights abuses and other misuses of institutional and economic power" (Ibid.).

Good intentions. But Deborah Orr (2014) writes:

> [T]here is truth in the contemptuous word "clicktivism." Once it was said that knowledge was power. Now that knowledge is there for anyone's taking, it has become clear that only power is power, and that it is still acquired by humans in the way that humans have always acquired it – through violence. Maybe technology allows human beings to know much, much more about their fellow human beings than is wise. Our vanities, our prejudices, our foibles, our failures of understanding, our anger, our hatreds – the internet seethes with it all. Does all that in itself shake our faith in our idea of humans as developed, refined and civilised? What is civilisation, after all, but the collective and settled expression of our ability to move away from savagery? . . . If you are looking for someone to despise, someone to perceive as different to you in all the wrong ways, then the internet is a good place to look. Only one place beats it for that – the real world, where people hurt, torture and kill other people like they always have, then do one thing that is new – post it proudly on the web.

The Tactic of Trolling

One tactic used by hackers, especially politically motivated ones, is trolling. This involves posting on websites (including blogs and Twitter feeds) that may be operated by potential adversaries and then monitoring the responses. Usually the troll's posts are incendiary or insulting so as to achieve the desired effect. Anonymous members use trolling to identify terrorist-associated targets that they can then take action to shut down.[1] Rick Gladstone (2015a) writes that these "online vigilantes . . . troll Twitter for suspected accounts of Islamic State fighters, recruiters and fund-raisers. Then they pounce. . . . 'Basically our work not only cripples their ability to spread propaganda, but also wastes their time,' said a Twitter vigilante who goes by the screen name The Doctor." Because these trolls (including members of Anonymous, but also many others) view the Islamic State as an "insidious threat," they spend many hours each day hunting using trolling. "'I do this because the atrocities I see from these ISIS scum on a daily basis enrage me,' said a user who identified herself as TouchMyTweets and continued, 'This is my airstrike'" (Ibid.). Some estimates place the number of Twitter feeds used by the Islamic State and its supporters as high as 90,000. Hacking groups, including Anonymous, CntrlSec, and GhostSec, find these sites and report them to Twitter as being in violation of its policies on unlawful use. In March 2015 one cyberactivist reported 9,200 suspect accounts to Twitter (Ibid.). Only a week later the same cyberactivist reported another 26,382 Twitter accounts as suspect, although some of the sites were misidentified as Islamic State accounts (Gladstone, 2015b).

Russia has engaged an army of trolls as well to write pro-Russian and pro-Vladimir Putin propaganda, especially since the absorption of Crimea into the Russian state (Agence France-Presse, 2015). The factory, known as the Internet Research Agency and located in St. Petersburg, also spreads disinformation and hoaxes inside the United States (Brown, 2015; see also Subbotovska, 2015).

Although those with political agendas, those purporting to punish organizations or companies for their activities (such as what Anonymous did when credit card companies and PayPal refused to process donations to WikiLeaks), and those engaging in electronic civil disobedience do make use of trolling, denial of service attacks, and lists of those violating terms of service to pursue their agendas, they are not the only ones using such tools on the internet. Pedophiles also troll social media sites hoping to attract younger users for nefarious purposes. Indian and Pakistani internet users troll one another's cricket fans before matches between the countries' two teams. South Africa has trolls that respond to news articles and opinions with racist remarks (Duncan, 2013). Kathleen Ndongmo (2015) wrote that "while trolling is a common practice on websites around the world, it seems that online trolling in Africa, in particular, is starting to spiral out of control." She says that looking at the comment sections of online blogs will reveal "everything from racial slurs to misogynism to death threats." The website Cracked.com claims that trolls are "driving away business" from legitimate sites, especially social networking and online gaming sites. The reason given is that a very small proportion of people actually write to respond to questions, or posts, on sites that encourage it, and so the comments of trolls – who do nothing but post on sites – take on a disproportionate significance; for instance, the online multiplayer game *World of Warcraft* now finds that 70% of new players try to play the game without interacting with anyone else – essentially defeating the entire purpose of the game itself. Cracked.com then provides five ways to respond to the trolling reality so that the internet can be saved (Wong, 2008).

The problem of trolling has even led some to call the internet a "sadist's playground" (Mooney, 2014). One research study of people who engage in trolling led to characterizing them as Machiavellian, narcissistic, psychopathic, and sadistic (Ibid.). Another claimed that

> to a troll, privacy and freedom are nearly synonymous, making perceived violations of privacy – both at the federal and local/platform level – tantamount to tyranny. That is, something to rail against. In terms of behaviour, trolling ranges from the vaguely distasteful to the borderline illegal: trolls taunt unsuspecting targets with seemingly racist, seemingly sexist and/or seemingly homophobic language; post shocking imagery, including pornography and gore, in order to derail conversation; and flood discussion threads with non sequiturs or grotesque distortions of other users' positions. In short, trolls deliberately court controversial and transgressive humour. They do so to garner what many trolls refer to as "lulz," a particular kind of aggressive, morally ambiguous laughter indicating the infliction of emotional distress.
>
> *(Phillips, 2011, pp. 68–69)*

Two other types of trolls are patent trolls and copyright trolls. Patent trolls purchase patents from bankrupt companies or at auctions, and then attempt to enforce patent rights against those who they claim have infringed on them. They don't actually use the patents themselves to create products, but troll the internet for products they imagine may have infringed on them so that they can sue legitimate companies for infringement. Often, however, the lawsuits claim damages far beyond the patent's actual value or contribution to the product identified. These nuisance lawsuits can result in companies paying damages simply to avoid drawn out and expensive litigation (see Schoenbaum, 2013).

Copyright trolls are similar, purchasing copyrights and then suing secondary users for infringement:

> For many copyright owners, monitoring for and enforcing against infringements is cost prohibitive. This reality, coupled with the ever-expanding universe of copyrighted works, has littered the Internet with "vast swaths of de facto free use" – tolerated or at least overlooked infringements like mash-ups, fan fiction, and remixes that are difficult for copyright owners to identify and thus go unenforced, even though they may not qualify as fair uses. That, in turn, created a vacuum in the copyright system: an unexploited market for copyright-enforcement firms, the so-called copyright trolls. Their emergence threatens to impose heavy costs on society, particularly by chilling speech and discouraging innovation.
>
> *(Greenberg, 2014)*

As David D'Amato (2014) further explains:

> Simply put, "copyright trolls" are law firms, individual attorneys, or other organizations that acquire the copyright of a particular work, usually a movie, and subsequently sue Internet users with the intent of extracting settlements using questionable legal tactics that border on extortion. The tactics typically used by copyright trolls involve copyright infringement allegations against large groups of anonymous "Doe" defendants for the purpose of minimizing court costs, utilizing the incredibly high statutory damages in copyright law to intimidate defendants, and causing them to settle quickly with little or no litigation and without regard to innocence or guilt.

It is apparent that many of the strategies employed by those who use the internet for monetary or political gain exploit either legal or technological "loopholes." In exploiting such loopholes they violate a variety of ethical perspectives. Although the internet provides the opportunity for people to express themselves (thus exercising their right to communicate), it also opens them to abuse by others with differing agendas. To the extent that the internet is an extension of one's humanity – a claim that harkens back to McLuhan's sense of technology as extensions of human capacities – then violation of one person's use and identity as portrayed in the online world by another who twists that use for his own benefit (or that of his agenda or ideology) would seem an egregious exploitation and thus socially irresponsible. Humanity has embraced the possibilities of this technology and poured itself into it with abandon. (That is a chilling tale of its own.) Who, then, should be responsible for policing this new space for human interaction, presentation, and social construction? Is the system one where only *caveat emptor* has purchase? Or is there an implicit social contract triggered by online use, perhaps one that should be concretized by statute?

Case 10.1: Vulnerable People, Suicide, and the Internet

In 2012, according to the World Health Organization (WHO, 2014), 804,000 people committed suicide worldwide, and "Globally, suicides account for 50% of all violent deaths in men and 71% in women." The highest rates are among the elderly (70+) and the young (15–29). Also, for every suicide there are many more people who attempt it (Ibid.). One primary risk factor for suicide is "inappropriate media reporting that sensationalizes suicide and increases the risk of 'copycat' suicides," along with mental health and substance abuse problems, war and disaster, stress among indigenous or displaced populations, discrimination, isolation, abuse, and conflictual relationships (Ibid.). In 2012 only 28 countries were known to have national suicide prevention strategies. This indicates the difficulty of speaking about the issue, especially since suicides are often the result of mental illness, including depression (see Rothkopf, 2014). Over the past 45 years there has been a 60% increase in suicides worldwide (ChartsBin, 2010). Without more effort to prevent them, the number of suicides annually is estimated to double by 2020 (Befrienders Worldwide, n.d.). The countries with the highest suicide rates are Russia, Kazakhstan, Lithuania, Belarus, Hungary, Japan, Guyana, South Korea, Slovenia, and Estonia.

Suicide has no universal understanding around the globe: "suicide, an active termination of life, evokes a variety of emotional reactions from envy to abhorrence and from respect to disgust. In some cultures, a person who commits suicide is a hero or a martyr fulfilling one's duty; in others he/she is disgraced and degraded as a sinful individual. In modern societies, those who commit suicide tend to be seen as maladaptive individuals whose behavior deviates from social orders" (Seko, 2008, p. 182).

There are 12 million websites that can be consulted about ways to commit suicide and 9.2 million devoted to suicide prevention. In many countries even talking about suicide is a taboo, so such websites may be the one place vulnerable people consult when they consider it. In Asia there is a relationship between honor and suicide, such as the practice of hara-kiri in Japan and in other countries that share Japan's collectivist tradition: "where a person's identity is more tied closely [*sic*] to other groups, suicides can be seen as the ultimate way to rebuild or reclean your image" should a person determine that s/he has dishonored family, colleagues, or friends (Erminia Colucci, quoted by Irvine, 2009). Colucci explained: "I think there is something paradoxical in it. On one hand, some see it as a way of maintaining status and restoring honor to you and the people you represent, but the pressure from that group could contribute to you considering suicide" (Ibid.). It is common in Asia to sensationalize suicides, especially those committed by celebrities, including the details of how it was accomplished. This, in turn, affects vulnerable people of a similar age, whether in Taiwan, South Korea, Japan, or China (Paul Yip, quoted by Irvine, 2009).

Japan may have a unique problem when it comes to suicide, hinted at in *Introduction to Suicide Studies* by S. Terayama published in 1975 (quoted by Seko, 2008, p. 182):

> When I think of my suicide, I face a difficulty of separating myself from others. The "self" is no longer an independent being, but has become just a part of others. Killing me means more or less hurting others or even killing others. We are thus living in an era in which we cannot even commit suicide without involving others.

In other words, due to the collectivist nature of Japanese society, the practice of suicide is not merely an individual act, but one that involves others. Japan has several internet sites where people who are otherwise isolated from one another can locate others who are considering suicide and make a pact to carry it out. In 2004 the largest-ever group suicide, involving seven people, occurred in Saitama, while two other women were found dead outside an isolated temple in Yokosuka. A few weeks later six more people died, including three in Fukuoka and three in Sasayama. The Australian Broadcasting Corporation (ABC) reported in 2005 that, "Every night across Japan, hundreds of people meet on-line, looking for strangers to die with" (ABC, 2005). One string of messages located by ABC said, "I want to die." "Can anyone die with me?" "Email if you're serious." "Let's die together."

One prominent site where young people gather online to set up group suicides is called Suicide Club. Kerry O'Brien, opening a report by Andrew Harding for ABC (2005), said: "But try wrapping your head around the concept of a group cyber suicide pact involving people who are strangers to each other. It's become something of a craze in Japan, where the act of ritual suicide, including that of wartime Kamikaze attacks, has always had a cultural significance. Andrew Harding of the BBC 'Newsnight' program examines how the Internet and suicide have come together in Japan with the most tragic consequences, with more than 30 deaths since October." Part of the remaining broadcast was as follows:

Andrew Harding: And there are thousands more apparently sincere messages about pills and despair and death. Japan has always had a quiet fascination with suicide. There's a famous book on the subject which has now sold more than a million copies. The book describes in explicit detail the pros and cons of various methods. . . . You seem to be encouraging people to kill themselves. Why?

Wataru Tsurumi (Author, "The Complete Suicide Manual"): There's nothing bad about suicide. It's an individual's choice. It's not illegal, and we don't have any religion here in Japan telling us otherwise. So we're very broad minded about it. As for group suicides – before the Internet, people would write letters or make phone calls. It's always been part of our culture.

Andrew Harding: In Japan, suicide has always been closely linked to notions of honour: the patriotic sacrifice of Kamikaze pilots in World War II. More recently, Japan's economic slump has driven many struggling businessmen to take the honourable way out, like the three men found in this car. But today, something's changed. Now it's younger, lonelier voices calling up the help lines and driving up the suicide statistics, even as Japan's economy is on the mend. The women answering these phones night after night blame, in part, the Internet.

Yukiko Nishihara ("Tokyo Stop Suicide Manual"): They're almost like a cult, these Internet groups. When people are lonely and suicidal but afraid of death, they find these web sites which egg them on.

In 2002 a Japanese-made film, *Suicide Club*, was released. In it 54 Japanese schoolgirls jump in unison into the path of an oncoming train. Although fictional, it did attempt to present social commentary on this country that has one of the highest suicide rates in the world. The director of the film, Sion Sono, was "allegedly inspired by Japan's rising suicide rate, driven by unemployment, career and academic pressure, and an increasingly dark mood enveloping the country" (Rooney, 2002). The BBC (2004) reported (also Andrew Harding) that, "In Japan, the internet has been blamed for a spate of group suicides which appear to have been arranged in online chat rooms." Harding reported that Japanese message boards were littered with personal ads by those seeking others to die with. One Tokyo-based helpline worker, Yukiko Nishihara, told Harding that, "When people are lonely and suicidal – but afraid of death – they find these websites which egg them on. There's an inhuman element to it." But others, including Ama Terasu (online nickname) who operates a suicide-focused website, denied that such sites were all bad. Terasu said that his site offered the opportunity for people to discuss topics that they couldn't talk about in real life. He did admit, however, that, "There are some vicious sites which really encourage people to die, and when you get in a group there's a momentum which makes it hard to stop – people become irrational."

Commentary on Case 10.1

If the sanctity of life as a universal value is to have any purchase, it requires that not only the problems of violence perpetrated against others, starvation, civil insurrection, and war be addressed, but also domestic abuse and suicide. To do this – especially in developing countries – efforts to prevent suicide must begin with directly addressing this taboo subject (Phillips, 2004, p. 156). Japan, however, is not a developing country, although apparently it is also taboo to discuss suicide openly there. The taboo, along with Japan's cultural celebration of suicide as a way to reclaim honor in the wake of failure, makes this case a particularly difficult one to address.

Japanese young people become depressed when they do poorly on the crucially important examinations that determine their potential for university education, or when they are unable to find acceptable work, or are failing at the work they have dedicated themselves to. They feel they have dishonored their family – an inexpressible loss in this collectivist culture. In the West suicide is typically identified as being the result of mental illness. But in Japan, even if mental illness contributed to the decision to take one's own life, suicide could be seen as an honorable response to failure – failure that is self-defined. Since the suicide chat rooms and websites in Japan do not have opponents to argue against the reasons given for suicide or the efforts to recruit others into a suicide pact, once a person has joined in the conversation s/he is transformed "into a group of lemmings rushing into death" (Seko, 2008, p. 184). Seko concludes:

> [T]he majority of participants including those who completed joint suicides were not committed to social interactions. Rather, they synchronized their predetermined suicidal desires and utilized anonymous others as faceless tools or what I metaphorically call "suicide machines" to put their plans into action. In the case of completed "Net group suicides," therefore, the board was unlikely to offer a therapeutic network and social support but, instead, provided a niche market for "seller" and "buyer" of "suicide machines."
>
> *(Seko, 2008, p. 185)*

In other words, joining in on these planning sessions would net no objections or cautions, but rather result in a type of mechanical efficiency that would result quickly in death. Clearly these participants are vulnerable people.

The media did little to respond responsibly to this spate of suicides. "Due in part to mainstream media's sensationalistic reporting, the phenomenon of the 'Net group suicides' spread quickly. When the first landmark 'Net group suicide' occurred on February 11, 2003, in Iruma-shi, Saitama prefecture, Japanese newspapers and televisions paid enormous attention to this suicide pact and repeatedly reported it with a detailed description of the method used by those who committed suicide" (Ibid., p. 186; see also Matthews, 2008). Later, Seko (2008, p. 187) writes: "In his analysis of Japanese domestic media reports on Internet suicides, Matthews (2008) argues the issue of Internet suicide spawned 'a sensationalistic semantic nexus' in which the detailed and repetitive reporting by mass media not only triggered copy-cat behavior, but also reinforced negative views of the Internet as a murky underworld where undesirable people, like those with suicidal desires, meet and interact." Documented by the mainstream media as harmful "agitators" that stimulate suicidal individuals to put desires into practice, numerous suicide-related websites, chat rooms, and discussion boards have been closed down by service providers and site owners (Shibui, 2005). The Suicide Club website closed down in November 2004. Yet in mid-2015 a Google search of the phrase "how to commit suicide" in Japanese (ジサツの仕方, *jisatsu no shikata*) still resulted in 302,000 hits.

We might glibly dismiss the newspapers that provided the details about how to use sleeping pills and charcoal burners in closed spaces to facilitate suicide – concentrating on the gory details. This hardly seems socially responsible. However, the events assuredly were newsworthy and possibly provided a reality check for those who were considering similar efforts. We might also condemn websites that facilitated suicides among isolated, lonely youth who believed they had nothing to live for. Perhaps they believed that taking their own lives was their last stab at happiness. Even Aristotle might be unable to criticize too much given the high value of suicide as protector of honor in Japanese society.

At the same time, however, Kant's insistence on principle, or Mill's demand that benefits and harms be compared to arrive at the best result would seem to condemn the acts, or even the facilitating internet connections since the principle of life was denied and the level of grief might have resulted in more unhappiness that could not be offset by an individual's "happy" act of suicide.

In the Asian tradition these deaths may have damaged the collective good. The death of one is the death of all – at least figuratively speaking. Does the right to take one's own life supersede the collective? Suicide is an astoundingly individual act, one that seems to ignore the collective good itself in favor of solving one's own problems or sense of self. Being unemployed, or failing to achieve a high mark on an examination, might certainly lead a person into depression, but does it dishonor the collective to the extent that do betrayal, murder, culpability in damning the imperial authority – or the prime minister? Is honor a black and white issue, or is honor on a continuum the majority of which is various shades of grey? Is there a place, even an expectation, that the media would provide a context within which young people could see the relative significance of their acts compared to the time when honor was all? Or are the media merely vehicles for tragedy – reacting only to events and then defining this narrow view of journalism as socially responsible?

This problem in Japan has wider implications, too. If potential suicides are vulnerable, what should we make of homeless, sick, orphaned, widowed, and hungry people, or those who live in fear of natural disasters or violent crime in countries or neighborhoods that they cannot escape? Do media, internet service providers, bloggers, tweeters, owe any of these vulnerable groups more attention and care than others? Should they take steps to assure that their plight is highlighted or that help is readily available to address their problems? Are all equally worthy of compassion and attention or should one group have precedence over another? And by whose reckoning should such decisions be made? All societies have commitments to certain policies or budgets – are these the final arbiter of who is helped and at what level? Or does ethics demand that these priorities shift so that the vulnerable have wider and deeper social nets to support them? Social responsibility would suggest that all those unable to care completely for themselves should be seen as equally worthy of attention – even if adequate resources are not available to solve all their maladies. Is this a reasonable social expectation and within whose ethical tradition?

Case 10.2: The Characterization of Women

It may seem odd to include women – who comprise half or better of the global population – as minority voices, but the overwhelmingly male control of the planet means that females have little comparative voice in most instances. Occasionally women are able to rise to the leadership of nations, but these are merely the exceptions that prove the rule – that men define the terms and determine the place of women in most (if not all) countries. Pierre Bourdieu (1998, p. 5) provides one explanation of why this situation may exist: "Being included, as man or woman, in the object that we are trying to comprehend, we have embodied the historical structures of the masculine order in the form of unconscious schemes of perception and appreciation. When we try to understand masculine domination we are therefore likely to resort to modes of thought that are the product of domination." Later he expands on this claim: "The social order functions as an immense symbolic machine tending to ratify the masculine domination on which it is founded: it is the sexual division of labour, a very strict distribution of activities assigned to each sex, of their place, time and instruments; it is the structure of space, with the opposition between the place of assembly or the market, reserved for men, and the house, reserved for women" (Ibid., pp. 9, 11).

M.Z. Rosaldo (1980, p. 389) wrote the following about anthropology's treatment of women: "The feminist discovery of women has begun to sensitize us to the ways in which gender pervades social life and experience; but the sociological significance of feminist insight is potentially a good deal deeper than anything realized as yet. What we know is constrained by interpretive frameworks which, of course, limit our thinking; what we can know will be determined by the kinds of questions we learn to ask." It is now more than 35 years since Rosaldo made this claim. The interpretive frameworks used to understand gender have certainly shifted since then, at least in academic circles and in countries where feminists have successfully demanded full equality (even if unachieved) in social, political, and economic matters. However, the successes achieved have been uneven and in many cultures have yet to have much impact.[2] For instance, Nancy J. Hafkin and Edna G. Bay (1976, p. 9) write that "numerous African societies possess . . . culturally legitimated ways to ensure the subordination of women. . . . Structural constraints to limit women's potential may have developed as societies moved toward greater male dominance. We can cite examples of such constraints from all over the continent. . . . [R]ites of passage can be seen as culturally legitimated ways of suppressing women."[3]

Assumptions of male dominance, however, also take their toll on men. Again, in the case of Africa, Margrethe Silberschmidt (2001, p. 657) writes, based on her field research in Kenya and Tanzania, that although "stereotyped notions of gender roles and relations abound with men as the dominant gender who have profited more from the development process than women," nevertheless, "socioeconomic change in rural and urban East Africa has increasingly disempowered men," reducing their social value and self-esteem, which, along with unemployment, has resulted in the male identity increasingly linked to sexuality and sexual manifestations and thus "multi-partnered ('extramarital') – often casual sexual relations." This has increased the spread of sexually transmitted diseases, including HIV/AIDS. This, of course, has devastating consequences for family and social structures.

Similar remarks about the secondary status of women can be found from around the globe. Steve Derné (1995, p. ix) writes, for instance, that "women's subordination in Indian society is bolstered by an oppressive gender ideology." Hindu men, Derné says, "continue to *restrict women's activities outside the home.* Anthropologists report that in village India, men sometimes do not allow their wives and mature daughters to go outside the house at all" (Ibid., p. x). This control – along with many other aspects of culture in India – is the result of ideas about honor (Ibid., p. 8).

Fulu et al. (2013, p. 36) report that "the Pacific may have common social norms, environments and practices that normalize or condone men's use of violence against women. Other studies suggest that high rates of violence in this region are related to a widespread normalization of violence against women, tension related to socio-economic transitions across the region, youth culture related to urban crime and violence, and histories of colonization and colonial violence, among other potential factors." They further report that gang rape of women was relatively common in Cambodia, Papua New Guinea-Bougainville, and Indonesia-Papua, and that those who committed rape (individual or as members of gangs) mostly "did not experience any legal consequences, reconfirming that impunity is still a major issue in the region" (Ibid., pp. 48–49). Finally, Mona Eltahawy, a Muslim Egyptian woman who grew up in the United Kingdom and Saudi Arabia, writes:

> I insist on the right to critique both my culture and my faith in ways that I would reject from an outsider. I expose misogyny in my part of the world to connect the feminist struggle in the Middle East and North Africa to the global one. Misogyny has not been completely wiped out anywhere. Rather, it resides on a spectrum, and our best hope for eradicating it globally is for each of us to expose and to fight against local versions of it, in the understanding that by doing so we advance the global struggle.
>
> *(Eltahawy, 2015, p. 29)*

On December 16, 2012, a young woman named Jyoti Singh was brutally gang raped by six young men on what she and her male friend thought was a passenger bus. Her friend was beaten up and both of them were thrown from the vehicle. She died 13 days later. Sonia Faleiro, who grew up in Mumbai and New Delhi, wrote about this assault: "India has laws against rape; seats reserved for women in buses, female officers; special police help lines. But these measures have been ineffective in the face of a patriarchal and misogynistic culture. It is a culture that believes that the worst aspect of rape is the defilement of the victim, who will no longer be able to find a man to marry her – and that the solution is to marry the rapist" (Faleiro, 2013). Otherwise, she is dishonored.

In another similar case in Mumbai (although the victim survived) five young men gang raped a young woman in the same location where they apparently had committed five other rapes. This case "provides an unusual glimpse into a group of bored young men who had committed the same crime often enough to develop a routine. . . . Their casual confidence reinforces the notion that rape has been a largely invisible crime here, where convictions are infrequent and victims silently go away" (Barry and Choksi, 2013). In still another case, this one in Pakistan, the sister of a young man who was accused of having an affair with a woman from a socially higher tribe was gang raped in retaliation on orders of the village elders, after they had rejected a proposal of cross-tribal marriages and determined that the boy had dishonored their tribe. The honor of the tribe could only be regained, the group determined, by dishonoring the boy's family: "In order to balance the twelve-year old boy's alleged affair with the Mastoi woman, the council ordered men of the Mastoi tribe to gang-rape the boy's sister, Mukhtar Mai" (Karkera, 2006, p. 164). Woman as pawn and brutalization of the innocent: the woman had apologized to the council for her brother's alleged behavior, but was otherwise innocent of any involvement.

Commentary on Case 10.2

Beyond the horrific rapes themselves there is also a symbolic issue here: a cultural reality in which the practice of rape is legitimized. One village court in India ordered a woman to be gang raped by 13 men for having an affair with a young Muslim man from an adjacent village (Shears, 2014a). The young woman was raped in full view of the entire village (Shears, 2014b). Another Indian woman "has said she was gang-raped by four officers at a police station" when she refused to pay a bribe to secure the release of her husband (Agence France-Presse in Lucknow, 2014). Two young Indian teens, who had gone into the fields near their village because there was no toilet in their home, were discovered raped and hanged, and protests ensued due to "alleged police inaction" ("Two teenage girls allegedly gang raped and hanged in India," 2014). Nuns and tourists to India have also been gang raped in several separate events in the past few years.

Figure 10.2 One of photographer Raj Shetye's staged images from a photo shoot based on the gang rape of Jyoti Singh on a passenger bus in India.

Following the death of the young woman in India, Mumbai photographer Raj Shetye staged a photo shoot inspired by the events of her death. Shetye defended the project by claiming that it was "an attempt to force people to think about women's safety." He posted his images, entitled "The Wrong Turn," on his website and on the behance.net platform. Public outcry in Indian media and on social networking sites followed: "Among those to criticise the project was Sapna Moti Bhavnani, a Bollywood hairstylist and actress who took part in a recent stage production based on the gang-rape, Nirbhaya. 'There is art and more frequently there is crap in the name of art. This rendition of the Nirbhaya story is . . . ,' she said on social media" (Buncombe, 2014). Figure 10.2 shows one of Shetye's images, posted on *The Independent*'s website to illustrate its story.

Are photo shoots and Bollywood stage productions enough to address what some have called India's "rape culture?" (Deshmukh, 2014). Why a rape culture?

> One of the underlying issues is the attitude toward women. India may be getting wealthier and more literate, but does it respect its women? The superiority of men is so deeply rooted in the Indian culture and psyche that despite some progress allowing women to attain education and be independent, there are still many who believe that a woman's place is only in the home. Sadly, when a woman is sexually assaulted, she is often blamed for luring her attackers.
>
> *(Deshmukh, 2014)*

Jason Overdorf (2012) wrote, too, that, "Every major political party has fielded and continues to field candidates facing criminal charges for rape, harassment and other crimes against women." And Amba Batra Bakshi and Chandrani Banerjee (2013) wrote following the death of this victim that "from the patriarchal content of textbooks to ads portraying women, our society's conditioned to treat women as subservient."

Finally, when filmmaker Leslee Udwin, a rape victim herself, attempted to show her documentary, *India's Daughter*, about the gang rape and murder of Jyoti Singh, authorities in Delhi banned it: "At the scheduled viewing time, television stations broadcast a blank screen instead of the film, and Home Minister Rajnath Singh threatened action against the BBC for ignoring the court-ordered ban. 'This is an international conspiracy to defame India,' Minister of Parliamentary Affairs Venkaiah Naidu told reporters" (Poole, 2015).

This problem is not unique to India. Rape occurs throughout the world and many of the same excuses used here – women invite rape, men are entitled to sex, boredom, and so on – are likewise relied on to justify these brutal attacks. Many rapes result not only in shame or loss of family honor, but in suicide. And the media, from textbook publishers to stage producers, photojournalists, documentary makers, social media sites and reporters, play their part either in excusing such brutality or in attempting to explain, raise awareness, and reduce the incidence of violence against women.

But patriarchy is deeply embedded in culture.[4] Sometimes it is reinforced by religious interpretations or justifications, sometimes merely in history and tradition. What, then, is the ultimate responsibility of media institutions? Should they accept cultural limitations or take them on to protect the innocent and affirm the dignity of women? Should they take on religious authorities knowing, that by doing so, they risk losing audiences or perhaps violence themselves, as the *Charlie Hebdo* attack demonstrated? Did the BBC err in ignoring the Indian court order not to screen *India's Daughter*? When a culture excuses its violence against a downtrodden minority (or even majority), do international media have a social responsibility to address it – even when they will likely be accused of an "international conspiracy," continued colonialism, or cultural imperialism? Should a global problem of violence only be dealt with on a case-by-case basis, or does ethics require that it be dealt with systemically and internationally? Is there a universal Kantian principle here that must be appealed to and applied, or should "community values" prevail? How do we apply community values in a society where an illegal caste system continues to exist and rape is used as a method of oppression and terror by higher-caste men against women in inferior castes? (see Ghosh, 2013). Whose values? Whose community?

Finally, we should ask ourselves if this sort of violence, or the inequality of the sexes, is a solvable problem. As Sabah Carrim (n.d., p. 3) puts it, "the gang rape case shouldn't blame Indian men, but man himself. Some say that men are inclined towards peace and peaceable solutions. Others say that Man is inherently violent and that he will inevitably indulge in some form of horseplay, mixed with chicanery and its various dimensions to really be who he is. Following this line of logic, the Gang rape case can be looked upon as the inevitable consequence of who or what man really is." Inevitability. And, of course, only a minority of sexual assault victims report it so these egregious examples are merely the tip of the iceberg:

> The underreporting of cases of sexual assault is mainly due to social stigma, prejudice with regard to the chances of marriage, being considered promiscuous and responsible for the incident, attendant humiliation and shame, embarrassment caused by appearance and cross examination in court, publicity in press, risk of losing the love and respect of society, friends and that of her husband, if married.
>
> *(Sarkar et al., circa 2003)*

Aihwa Ong (1996) also outlines the differences between collectivist culture's definition of rights and that of Western feminists who often take on the causes of women in the developing world over such issues as land ownership, sexual violence, and inequality. She says that liberal feminism emerging from the West

> requires that the government treat all individuals as equals, in order to ensure conditions for each individual to make moral decisions about their goals in life, as well as to have the right to change them. Liberal feminism, as expressed in international forums, is fundamentally about women's rights as individual rights with men in their society and in the global economy. Although this is a basic twentieth century ideal, North-South conflict erupts when liberal

feminists disregard alternative political moralities that shape the ways women in other societies make moral judgments about their interests and goals in life, and use other cultural criteria about what it means to be female and human.

(Ong, 1996, p. 113)

This means, she says, that moral issues in collectivist societies are always decided by women themselves in terms of the impact of events or decisions, or the application of human rights, for community. While this does not respond directly to the human violation of women by rapists, it does indicate the difficulties of understanding why different societies respond so differently to these atrocities, and why it takes so long for a society to generate enough outrage to step out of its cultural comfort zone to take to the streets in response to them.

Conclusion

As we have seen throughout this book, the differences that exist in moral contexts as defined within various societies create thorny problems for media practitioners. Sometimes these problems are made even worse by the work of eyewitnesses armed with mobile telephone cameras. Reports from the front lines by participants themselves can trigger a perceived necessity in the media to cover events more brutally or comprehensively than they might otherwise do, so as not to see their audiences continue to flock to social media for amateur reports. This situation continues to evolve, and with it the social responsibility question will likewise continue to develop new dimensions.

Discussion Questions

1 Many media institutions claim that they give voice to the voiceless. One such institution is Al-Jazeera. It reports on many underreported parts of the globe and seeks to redress the information flow disparity between North and South. If it does so by concentrating on the intractable problems of the voiceless South, is there an ethical issue raised about victimage? If the voiceless are always victims, how can their dignity be enhanced so as to make coverage of their plight socially responsible?

2 What media institutions should be held most accountable for the reports of egregious and brutal activity? Is it the indigenous media operating within their own country that should take the lead in reporting on such activities, or is it the northern media with vastly more resources that should do so?

3 Should social problems, such as suicide, spousal abuse, child abandonment and the like, become a staple of international news coverage, or should the international media continue to concentrate their efforts on political and economic news?

4 Should victims of violence be named in international media? Does doing so provide them with dignity or does it demean them and their cultures?

Notes

1 For a history of Anonymous and other hacktivist groups see Kushner (2014).

2 Even in the United States, where women have arguably made the most progress over the past 50 years, the fact of massive immigration has raised issues in the legal system. Are immigrants who engage in crimes against women to have their motives understood within an American legal framework or does culture enter into the determination of guilt or the nature of punishment? (See Volpp, 1994.)

3 Writing in a later volume Hafkin (2000, p. 13) said that "new technologies are not gender neutral. Women in Africa will find them difficult to access, and they will not have the time, the tools, or the income to master them. As men become more conscious of the power and global dominance of these tools, they will act more to ensure that men will dominate their use and become dominant in the information economy derived from the use of these tools. The pessimistic view sees ICTs as new tools to enforce and exacerbate social inequality. Left alone, societal forces will prevail, and women will get left behind."

4 In North India women are often left destitute, even resorting to begging, as a result of the patriarchal system that leaves them no recourse when all the land owned by a family is left to the sons or they are married off to distant men who then turn them out (see Agarwal, 1994).

11

Religion and Social Responsibility

Introduction

Religion has been the most important influence on moral decision-making since... forever. When humans first recorded their sensitivities on behaviors good and bad, the God-factor showed up. Winning divine approval, keeping deity on one's side, avoiding the curse – these concerns are as old as time. Strategies to accomplish these mysterious feats and then announce one's mastery have driven people to acts of courage and benevolence – and cruelty – since history began. Long before Genghis Khan contemplated the mystery of the barren plateau, or Kant articulated the Kingdom of Ends, humans have found moral motive and guidance by searching the divine will (Fackler, 2014).

So begins the chapter on values in a major U.S. media textbook, and so begins this chapter on religion and media. Worldwide adherents to a religious worldview are growing faster than newspaper circulation is dropping, we confidently claim. Calls for the disappearance of religion, heard mostly in the West, are regarded by believers in the East and South as part of the nuttiness, the cosmic lostness, of postmodern culture where Self is supreme and values are limited to whatever preserves and pleases King Self. Political scientist John Gray and a choir of academic colleagues may blame first-century Christians for spoiling Western culture with the idea that the future is hopeful – robbing people for centuries of the grim reality that the final moment before death is the final moment (Gray, 2002) – but the people (of the world) are not buying it. Polls are not failsafe barometers of truth, but when you see a wave of human sentiment gathering whitecap strength as it nears the shore, you may swim against it without disrupting its rush one bit. The wave might even say something to you.

In precincts skeptical about religious truth-claims (which includes most newsrooms), it may come as some surprise to learn that the core value of religion is love. "Love," a notoriously ambiguous word, is properly understood for purposes of media ethics as *agape*, a biblical term that speaks to the affection of God and acts of God toward people regardless of their worthiness (Craig and Ferre, 2010, p. 221). *Agape*, a Greek term, is used extensively in the New Testament as a reference to other-centered, self-giving, impartial regard, often entailing personal sacrifice. The term echoes the Hebrew equivalent, *hesedh*, found in the Old Testament and frequently translated as "loving-kindness." Craig and Ferre, in their remarkable study on *agape* as norm for media's mission in the world, draw parallels to other (than Christian) expressions of *agape*, while maintaining that the term finds its central paradigm in the claim that God in Jesus Christ has sacrificed himself for the sake of the unworthy.

Can centrally religious appeals carry a message into newsrooms and entertainment empires? Do newsrooms do justice to the impact of religious belief with an occasional "Religion" column, which usually reads like an oatmeal version of belief anyhow? The answer is affirmative in the first instance, obviously negative in the second. Unless media institutions fix their sight on service to the public beyond profit, fame, and competition, media can make no claim on the human conscience and can maintain no stature as voice of the voiceless or arbiter of justice. No one expects honesty unless honesty is a non-negotiable priority, every time, despite any business consequence.

To readers who are schooled to imagine journalism as a race to publication or as padding to occupy space around advertisements, *agape* will seem exceedingly soft, weak-willed, and emotional – just the traits that are weaned out of rookie newswriters as their careers advance. Craig and Ferre insist that journalists, whatever virtues are expressed in their press codes or newsroom cultures, need *agape* as a regulating principle because it adds two essential dimensions to all communications career fields: steadfastness and fairness (Ibid., pp. 223–224). They illustrate the power of *agape* in these two respects through the success of the Medill Innocence Project at Northwestern University in Illinois. Journalism students at Medill along with lead professor David Protess have re-opened capital crime cases to show that several prisoners on death row are in fact innocent of the crimes that legal process in the United States has determined they committed. Such investigations are exceedingly tedious and controversial. Prosecutors are disinterested in "second looks" that may cause embarrassment or show lack of competence. The entire apparatus of law and imprisonment, in the United States and worldwide, resists such steadfast investment in people the system has determined to be unfit for public life. Craig and Ferre do not find Old or New Testament teaching explicit in the Medill project, but its impulses and discipline are best understood as an expression of *agape*, much as the Good Samaritan parable of Jesus (Luke 10) struck foot-travelers in his day of the need for mutual care beyond superficial or efficient gesture.

World-elite journalists may counter, "We have justice" or "We have liberation" or "We have feminist (or ethnic, or workers') empowerment." Certainly the Bible has no monopoly on concepts of love and fairness. Xavier Yao, comparing Confucian *jen* to Christian *agape*, makes important points and distinctions – for example, their common appeal to treating others as the self would be treated, yet with different starting points and ultimately different end-games (Ibid., p. 221). Each call to moral analytics must answer: does it lead to human flourishing in a manner fair to all, and is it sustainable? *Agape* is not the sole principle able to answer these two crucial requirements, but it has produced results as effective as any other, and it has been a consistent internal corrective to oppressive excesses within faith groups worldwide.

Naturalists and agnostics working in journalism (the majority tribe?) have no reason to trust their moral instincts or coded directives, if indeed such concepts are products of purpose-blind evolution. Knowing truth (a primo journalistic mission) is not necessarily what helps us survive. On purely naturalistic terms, efficient information or outright deception might work better. The theist, however, has good reason to believe that *hesedh* and *agape*, and allied concepts such as *jen* and *tao*, are reliable guides to human flourishing, since they are finally the will of God for human endeavor and energy (Evans, 2015, p. 66). Reinhold Niebuhr, a member of the 1947 Hutchins Commission which articulated the social responsibility theory of the press, taught *agape* as the fundamental, grounding moral principle. Justice derived from it. Love relevant to justice, he insisted, is not an emotional response but a disposition to seek the well-being of persons close-by and far-off. Love draws justice toward inclusions and generosity; it discourages minimalist justice, or disinterested theoretical justice. Absent love, Niebuhr observed, justice deteriorates into "mere calculation of advantage" (Lovin, 1995, p. 199). Of that there is plenty enough in the world and its communications industries, "noisy gongs and clanging symbols" all. But love "hopes all things" (1 Corinthians 13). Niebuhr took love into the political realm, and thus the media realm, as war broke in Europe and as the Hutchins Commission was assembling:

> The kingdom of God and the demands of perfect love are therefore relevant to every political system and impinge upon every social situation in which the self seeks to come to terms with the claims of other life.
>
> *(Niebuhr, 1941, p. 199)*

Indeed, in one of the most daring international investigations done in recent years, the rhetoric of love, care, concern, and justice plays a mighty role – and this investigation is about the life of elephants and the babies of elephants, at first take; international criminals show up as secondary figures, and the people they terrorize as secondary victims (Christy and Stirton, 2015).

This is a chapter on religion and media ethics, not philosophy of religion per se, hence we stop right here to raise the obvious postmodern question: since when does a majority have the right or duty to decide the truth or falsity of religion, any more than a majority of church prelates had the right to temper the revolutionary observations of Galileo? A minority of one may be the sole proprietor of truth. Freedom and responsibility are concepts built on the foundation of universal dignity, without which freedom would be a grab for power and responsibility would accrue only to self and clan, if that. Allow the pronouncements of Israeli philosopher Anat Biletzki (2011): "There is no philosophically robust reason to accept the claim that human dignity originates with God." Religion, she claims, cannot even play in the human rights game since defenders of rights as a religious duty are concerned with "slavish obedience to the arbitrary commands of the deity," and not to human rights per se (Osborn, 2015). The late "New Atheist" Christopher Hitchens called religious education for youth "child abuse" (Evans, 2015, p. 9).

Alas, the relevance of religious claims in debates concerning media freedom and responsibility may be finally in the eye of the beholder. Suffice for now that many beholders, certainly the greater share of humanity, take religious claims seriously, to the chagrin of the intellectual class who find solace in Copernicus' "objectivity" standard of knowing (Polanyi, 1958, p. 5).

Case 11.1: Al-Qaeda in France

Said and Cherif, two brothers trained in war by Al-Qaeda in the Arabian Peninsula (AQAP), must have imagined they were doing the Koran a great honor when, on January 7, 2015, they muscled into an editorial meeting at *Charlie Hebdo* magazine in Paris and executed 11 staff, injured 11, then killed a wounded Paris policeman before making their getaway.

Gheerah, or protective jealousy, is taught in some quarters as the duty to protect the Prophet Muhammad from blasphemy, which is *Hebdo*'s only real plan and purpose for any institution claiming a right to moral leadership. The Catholic Church in France, among many others, has felt their satirical sting until the church became rather immune, as to bee bites: too many, no longer a danger. But Islam was a favorite, given the reluctance of so many other media outlets to risk offending Islam's jihadist fringe. Said *Hebdo* editor Stephane "Charb" Charbonnier, "We have to carry on until Islam has been rendered as banal as Catholicism." Charb died in the January attack.

The *Hebdo* killings sparked mixed and opposite reactions across the world. In Paris on January 11, an estimated two million people and 40 world leaders met in a rally for national unity, many sporting the by-then-famous slogan, "Je suis Charlie" (I am Charlie). When *Hebdo* published its next issue on time, circulation soared from 60,000 to 7.95 million (and from French to six languages). Media outlets expressed renewed commitments to free expression. Even the normally über-respectful BBC reprinted the *Hebdo* cover that sparked the outrage.

Justifying the immense public reaction to the murders, the mayor of Paris told crowds that *Charlie Hebdo* writers and editors "used their pens with a lot of humor to address sometimes awkward subjects and as such performed an essential function." The editor of a German satirical magazine said: "We are beholden to the principle that every human being has the right to be parodied."

Quite opposite reactions received lighter press coverage. In Niger and Pakistan, several churches were burned. In some French schools, students ordered to stand for a minute of silence to honor those killed threatened their teachers and proclaimed their support for *Gheerah*.

The attack bore this result. Eight months later, the editor of *Hebdo*, Laurent Sourisseau, claiming the magazine's mission of satire and free speech accomplished, announced that no further caricatures of Muhammad would appear on *Hebdo*'s pages.

As for Said and Cherif, it can be imagined that their greatest goal was fulfilled. Two days after the shootings and the subsequent nation-wide manhunt, surrounded in a warehouse near Charles de Gaulle Airport by police armed as if for a Final Assault on the Evil Empire, Said and Cherif ran outside shooting and shouting. A torrential hail of bullets, and all was quiet.

The Western press called Said and Cherif terrorists, for they had taken arms against unarmed civilians. Their single shots to the heads of victims were signs of intention and military discipline. Evidence gathered from their belongings showed a history of education in jihadist warfare. They knew what they wanted to do, and did it with executive skill. They had answered for themselves, presumably, the big question facing media which accept the Paris mayor's version of "essential [media] functions": Is violence a legitimate device to make a strong public statement, in this case on religious beliefs and values? The resounding NO from the Enlightenment West, and defiant YES from some parts of the Muslim East, suggest a new division in the world based on secular and sacred, reason and belief, diplomatic oratory and primitive blood feud. It is a fragile peace indeed which keeps these two worlds from clobbering each other, or themselves, as often happens. Readers of *Hebdo* and admirers of satirical dissent may be excused if they weigh-in on the occasional high cost of religious passion. At such times, *agape* as guiding principle appears to be a comic charade, worthy of *Hebdo*'s most outrageous caricature.

Commentary on Case 11.1

In earlier chapters we have raised the problem of prioritizing moral claims. Can the world's diverse peoples and cultures agree on a top-tier morality, and thus overcome the infernal competition of the free marketplace of ideas and get on with rational policy and human flourishing, based on common moral claims? That sounds like a difficult, long, and exhausting conversation. When religions join that conversation, a new level of flash-point emerges. Now the God-factor figures in the sway of sentiments and appeals to sweet reason. Perhaps that is why the media, especially elite Western media, tend toward amusement at religion which takes itself seriously. Alan Wilson, commentator for the BBC and Bishop of Buckingham for the Church of England, believes that journalists would do a service to the profession by stepping out, finding the people around them who say "We believe" and "We practice," as a means of bringing religion and media closer to understanding. The step out would not be so far from the newsroom as most journalists think, Wilson claims:

> As soon as you step outside the cozy conventions of the Home Counties, you encounter a world where the priority and meaning of religion is entirely different. Go to a barrio in Latin America

and try to put across the vibrant potency of its Pentecostalism: there is just no way of describing that experience in a way that conforms to the bourgeois conventions of much English journalism. Almost alone in the world, it just doesn't do God, doesn't know how to, or want to know how to.

(A. Wilson, 2010)

Another notable BBC commentator, the late Malcolm Muggeridge, came to believe that media, television in particular, should be dismissed, avoided, and turned off. Carlos Valle, then general secretary of the World Association for Christian Communication, understands the sentiment but argues for media's benefit. Shunning media is not a realistic option today, for the faithful or the secularist. A better way forward must be found (Valle, 1992).

If media grew more adept at covering the "religion beat" – that is, better at uncovering and interpreting the religious dimensions of public life – much confusion and suspicion could be suspended while people and leaders pursued honest "common ground" absent the worry that such discussion invariably devalues religious distinctives.

Theological pluralism and its problems notwithstanding, the values of media professionals today must take religion into account. For clarity, "religion" in this chapter means the appeal to the divine source for moral footing, and any practice which acknowledges the deity. In the monotheistic faiths, that divine source is called Allah, Yahweh, or the Triune God. Other faith communities prefer to speak of values as inherent; they resist appeals to a creator, divine speaker, or overseer of human affairs. Thus the Dalai Lama, the international advocate for Tibetan Buddhism, uses a rhetoric that is religious only to the extent that his founding Buddha is credited with wisdom at the top of the bell curve.

Some of the fire between secular journalism and religion might be cooled by realizing that religious practice and media practice are bound by common aspirations. As an art form, media, especially imaginative storytelling, is a search for what makes sense and supplies human life with significance. Why wake up? Why get up? Religion and media both tell us why. Media and religion both speak to the flourishing of persons and communities, and to their undoing. At the end of a mediated experience, as a religious one, we may feel the soul's uplift, downfall, or the rocky places between, but media viewing and listening, and religious discourse, are often the places to which we retire when the soul[1] needs repair. We watch and listen to be reminded that the good life matters, that love wins over violence and trauma, and that human relationship, culture in the broadest sense, is in many ways a historical and mystical unity of people bound by language, geography, and belief. That is why we claim that the point and purpose of media storytelling is cultural literacy. Religion is not bounded by culture, but religion is essential to the literacy of culture that media practitioners treasure.[2]

Philosopher C. Stephen Evans suggests two concepts helpful in understanding how religion can maintain its claims to truthfulness but resist the shame of satire and the urge to revenge unbelief. His "wide accessibility" concept recommends that freedom to speak includes the platforms of religious doctrine espoused by advocates, evangelists, and professional clergy. People of all backgrounds and beliefs should have access to the claims of competing faiths, or competing anti-faiths (such as Hitchens and colleagues). The "wide accessibility" principle is the agreement that a relative free marketplace should exist, with religious advocates active players. A working free marketplace of political thought is tempered by prohibitions on fighting words and hate speech (words that incentivize violence), knowing falsehoods, and egregious violations of personal privacy. These restrictions keep the public peace, but do not eliminate all offense, quiet all debate, or diminish all distinctives. Life together for any group of people, to be robust in expression, must also acknowledge boundaries of temperance and mutual respect. Public expression in any free marketplace must include the possibility of saying NO without harm, which leads to Evans' second concept: "easy resistibility" (Evans, 2015, pp. 24–25).

Religious messages, in a free and responsible marketplace, like political messages, must be easily questioned, postponed, or denied; mockery and satire complicate the interpretive process. This does not disqualify the message or threaten its propriety, but it requires the additional step of discernment. Across cultures and languages, that step may acquire harrowing distortions and totally unintended reactions. Surely *Hebdo* editors do not intend to so offend the people whose beliefs they mock that armed assailants will attack them, or anyone. The social contract between satirists and their "victims" includes the proviso that believers, albeit stunned and perhaps chagrined by the "humor," will nonetheless regard the satire as mere opinion, to which all are entitled. Expressions forbidden in certain jurisdictions but free in others are not to be regarded as catalysts for deadly revenge. This contract, of course, is not negotiated but implied. It certainly underlies the vast messaging on networks of social media; most believers are able to shrug off the satire as a trifle. Remedies short of violence are plenteous: cease doing business, urge others to do so, tell advertisers of your group's displeasure, file a lawsuit (if only to use courts to harass), and best of all, publish your own counter-message for all the world to read and consider.

Religion expands one's "line of sight" beyond the boundaries of sight. Belief in a deity entails a meaning and purpose to life that transcends the timeline of birth and death. Even non-theistic Buddhism recommends a posture to human life that will affect life beyond the grave. Secular anti-religionists may scoff at such hope; scoffing is what people do when another's actions or thoughts are judged silly or oppressive. The true believer who kills scoffers must finally reckon that violence is futile; it neither convinces secularists to adopt religious faith, nor makes the religious message more appealing to those open to adopt it. From the media side, satire becomes a vehicle for challenging the fault lines of institutionalized religion, leading perhaps to corrections and at least to more profound humility among those who claim to be doing God's will. Satire has a positive impact when taken as feedback from non-believers. Satire may even be welcomed by communicators hoping to sharpen their religious messages and reach broader audiences. The line of sight generated by religious claims is immensely popular to most people. Satire does not threaten to extinguish this aspiration. Its impact is often quite the opposite.

We have purposely avoided the term "blasphemy" thus far, as blasphemy is notorious as a legally proscribed form of speech, at least in some countries. Are judges qualified to know it when they see it? Are juries able to make the distinction between satire and blasphemy? In the United States, blasphemy as an offense at law disappeared in 1952 in a case involving a motion picture suggesting the Virgin Mary's naïveté. In the United Kingdom, blasphemy survives as a language-based version of keeping the public peace. Hardly ever used to quash speech, blasphemy raises the stakes, inflames vengeful religious motives, and leads invariably to confrontation. To disqualify communication because it is blasphemous is to make theological judgments which secular (and even religious) courts are hardly qualified to perform. Who can know the mind of God, offended or amused?

Religious claims expand one's line of sight, we claimed above. Another way of putting that claim: religion redraws the horizon. Wider horizons are what adventurers seek, novelists imagine, and citizens converse to discover. Horizons can bring shalom or disaster, plenty or hunger, satisfaction or disappointment. Horizons are always beyond, out there in the direction of human work and play, love-making and worship and yearnings. Horizons make the person, claimed philosopher Charles Taylor in his magisterial *Sources of the Self*. Ever the one to provide lengthy introductions to his main point, Taylor begins:

> I want to explore the background picture of our spiritual nature and predicament which lies behind some of the moral and spiritual intuitions of our contemporaries. In the course of doing so, I shall also be trying to make clearer just what a background picture is, and what role it plays in our lives. . . . Perhaps the most urgent and powerful cluster of demands that we

recognize as moral concern the respect for the life, integrity, and well-being, even flourishing, of others. . . . We are dealing here with moral intuitions which are uncommonly deep, powerful, and universal.

(Taylor, 1989, p. 4)

By such language and logic, pointing to transcendence unrecognized in secularist culture, Taylor has helped many in the West recover a sense of the self, and an ability to choose and act morally and responsibly with new vigor and foundational conviction. He insists that persons are spiritual beings, despite modernist reductionism, and, like the communitarians, that human respect for life is universal, part of the moral framework which keeps "the problem of the meaning of life" on the agenda of news journalists, advertising professionals, and entertainment producers (Ibid., p. 18).

Two modern options simply do not work, Taylor insists. The first is the pragmatic reduction of moral conflicts to quantitative measures of greatest happiness, a "wrong model of practical reasoning . . . based on illegitimate extrapolation from . . . natural science" (Ibid., p. 7). The second modern failure was explored by Nietzsche and others – the "dissipation of our sense of the cosmos as a meaningful order" (Ibid., p. 17). Nietzsche's nihilism corresponds to "something very widely felt in our culture," but can never win the day, absent a framework for respecting life or public policy (Ibid.). Adopting as a framework for life the notion that no such framework exists is a pitch for a very small market indeed.

[B]ecause a framework is that in virtue of which we make sense of our lives spiritually. Not to have a framework is to fall into a life which is spiritually senseless. The quest [to find a believable framework] is always a quest for sense.

(Taylor, 1989, p. 18)

What is an adequate, belief-worthy, modern framework? Taylor cites three axes of moral thinking: respect for others, understandings which build a full life, and human dignity. Persons light on these axes operate at margins of public space, or if vicious, at the center briefly. Opponents of these axes have taken themselves out of human commerce. They are recipients of dignity but no longer offer it. Advocates of terror grow popular by selling the opposites of these axes as valid behaviors toward infidels. People flee them. Life diminishes around them. Communication becomes a script spoken but not believed.

Obviously pragmatism and nihilism offer objections which must be addressed, but Taylor wants the conversation to make room for *agape*, the "seeing-good" way of seeing the cosmos, as in Genesis 1: "And God saw that it was good." High standards need "strong resources" (Ibid., p. 516). High standards tend toward "radical hope" (Ibid., p. 521). Persons with high-standard inner commitments can move in and out of institutions without despair or cynicism, and perhaps at times bring recovery and transformation, which was Taylor's own purpose in writing (Ibid., p. 520). Persons are not marionettes of their surrounding culture. High-standard bearers, *agape*-equipped persons, direct the energy of institutions toward human flourishing. Institutions bounded by a vision of justice and fairness in a world never quite on the mark, move us closer and secure the ground thus taken.

Case 11.2: Sharia in Sudan

Ustadh Mahmoud Mohamed Taha climbed up the stairs that day (January 18, 1985) with a peaceful smile, a free man. For Taha, a free person is one who thinks as he or she pleases, speaks as he or she thinks, and acts as he or she says. He himself had lived such a life, not as a violent man intent on imposing will and force, but rather as a man of conviction and expression, calling power to account when power imposed on dignity and natural rights. Taha was a revered teacher as well, a Sudanese imam and leader of the Republican movement, founded in 1945 when the Sudan was still subject to colonial powers, and its educated elites seemed too willing to win independence through the rhetoric of sectarian leaders intent on imposing Sharia law.

A leaflet distributed by the Republicans had called for immediate repeal of the Sharia adopted in September 1983, an end to the civil war in the largely Christian South, and a stop to the distortions of Islam and violations of the freedom of people to choose their faith and their way of life. The "Free Platforms" advocated in the leaflet sought full opportunity of education and employment without respect to compliance with Sharia. Later the leaflet and Taha's teaching on the Koran would be developed into the "Second Message of Islam," a fully developed framework on the relationship of individuals to society, and beyond that, to the universe, with freedom of conscience and expression being the core of his doctrine. Taha was not an Enlightenment thinker home-grown in the heart of Islam, but rather a reflective teacher caught in the net of national independence and Islamic revivalism that was sweeping the northern African continent. His message was extensive freedom within the framework of his faith. Politically, his teaching was a direct challenge to the Sudanese regime.

That smile on the staircase was seen but briefly, when the hood was removed from Taha's head and he took final account of the world and people he had lived to assist. Perhaps he saw the government helicopter nearby, the one which would take his body to an unmarked grave. Perhaps he saw the rope at the top of the gallows' stairs, waiting for him. What the people saw was the visage of a man who was free and at peace, then quickly rehooded, and in a moment, gone.[3]

Commentary on Case 11.2

Horizons were at work in Taha's heart and mind which the regime could not see or, if seen, could not tolerate. In the terms now familiar as moral development theory, the Sudan was clearly a nation at the Pre-conventional stage, while Taha had found something akin to, if not at the very summit of, the Post-Conventional level 6.

Lawrence Kohlberg's moral development step-ladder is well known. He claimed that no one skips a rung, that all move upward often slowly, and that few reach level 6, the level of universal moral reasoning and mutual respect for variances (Cherry, n.d.). In Taha's story, the moral-development distance separating him and his accusers was so great that their small quarter of the world could not endure the survival of one of them, the weaker one militarily, the stronger one constitutionally and developmentally. But reducing religious conflict to numbered stages alone is insufficient. Reducing media coverage of religion to psychological terms is to miss important aspects. Living together is more complex than such reductions, and moving toward successful pluralism requires a more energetic response. The disparities explained by these terms, however, might be more wisely taken into account as journalists reach for the news.

Can media houses conduct normal operations within contested religious environments? By now most people assume such environments to be among the larger risks of the profession.

Case 11.3: The Syrian Civil War

Three Spanish journalists and one Japanese one have disappeared in northern Syria, reports the Committee to Protect Journalists (which organization obviously is less about protection and more about reporting on journalists who need it). They were last seen in the Syrian town of Aleppo, but the Committee spokesperson will not permit the contagion of religious-based factions to cause a jump to conclusions. "The media are at the mercy of all sides in the conflict, which have consistently shown a willingness to use journalists for their own deadly purposes" (Roman, 2015).

In this report, the most defensible claim is that where religious fighters confront each other, all human-rights rules are off. Aleppo is not an environment for free and open debate. It is not where journalists roam with open mic asking for citizen feedback on the conflicts raging throughout their country. Any group of fighters may have kidnapped these reporters. Blame is an open question until one group of partisans claims the hostages. Or until a faction openly touts their violence as good.

In other parts, Tibetan musicians Kalsang Yarphel and Pema Rigzin (freetibet.org) were arrested by Chinese authorities for composing and singing politically themed songs, lyrics which wished long life to the Dalai Lama and freedom for Tibet. Music is at the heart of Tibetan culture and identity. To obstruct musicians from expression is to close avenues of cultural renewal and hope. Of course, the jailed musicians become heroes for the arts and for Tibetan independence, though for 60 years a much stronger neighboring power has occupied the mountainous Buddhist country. Song and melody speak so much more powerfully to the soul than mere words, in many places. Music is not a news bulletin, but it can embody the hopes and aspirations of a people as no print or social media press release can.

Commentary on Case 11.3

Risk is inherent in performance, in art, in news coverage. Without risk, there is no communication. Tempered risk – risk apportioned with cultural savvy and human goodwill – is the beat worth reporting.

Governments which oppress the arts or suppress the news are fighting a foolish war against forces more powerful than jail cells or confiscation of property. In areas of the world such as the Middle East and southern Asia, culture and religion are intermingled and inseparable (unlike the worldviews that bifurcate the West). Such oppression reaches to the core of our humanity, our capacity and will to declare who we are, our nature and substance, with integrity and confidence. Governments may want to redirect loyalty and punish creativity, but finally, authorities discover, sometimes after much brutality, people do not bend that way.

Moreover, the religious aspect of the human quest is not an inflexible force unable to grapple with legitimate demands or accommodate alternative beliefs. The heart of religion is gratitude, not belligerence (Schultze and Badzinski, 2015, p. 2). Gratitude for life, for the world, for existence, for the challenge of good work that helps people flourish, for love between kin and clan and friend from afar, for hope that transcends even death. Religion is not a premise long ago dismissed by science, nor is it the terror of the sword against outsiders (though it can devolve to this). Religion is praise of the Creator, and in certain faiths, the Redeemer, the Truth, the Life. Religion in every case is gladness for revelation, a theological term that speaks to the point of communication between deity and humanity, a relational reality unabated by government intimidation. When people disappear, as happens all too often, religion may be the culprit, in which case a cancer has brought black mould into religion's province. Missing persons are altogether the ancient story of sacrifice and martyrdom for a reality the state cannot touch.

Governments, whether militant, atheist, or secular, would do well to examine what warfare they seek against such a strong force as faith, and whether filling their nation's potholes or building a good hospital might be a better use of resources, if indeed human flourishing is their aim.

Grateful people are peaceful people, generous people, and nurturing people, doing good in the name of God or spiritual leader or ethereal benevolence. To set one's aim against this is to betray the task of the state and the high calling of living as a human person.

Discussion Questions

1 In the West, academic discussion tends to avoid religion, which is regarded as a private matter. In the East, religion is much more a public matter. How does religion work in conversations where you live?

2 In your media experience, where does religion come in? Is it generally a positive factor in problem-solving? In relationship-building?

3 How free do you feel to complete this statement: "I am most likely to watch . . . (medium), and I am a . . . (religious commitment)"?

4 What aspects of religion are best applied to solving issues of problematic media content?

5 Should media and religious institutions work together to create better programming? Should overtly religious programming be permitted, allowed within boundaries, or not permitted?

Notes

1 Use of the word "soul" – a familiar term in religious discourse – conveys the whole person with a focus on consciousness, self-awareness, identity, and one's sense of wellness. The soul is the real you. Psychologists dissect the concept and philosophers note its irreducibility. For this present argument, let *soul* be soul, fully human, all parts included.

2 In a book too suggestive for summary here, Nicholas Wolterstorff (1976) has argued persuasively that "worldviews," including the pervasive religious worldviews of our time, set the parameters of reasonableness, not the other way around.

3 We are indebted to Haydar Badawi Sadig, professor of communications at Qatar University, for this adaptation of his essay on Ustadh Mahmoud Mohamed (Sadig, 2010).

12

War, Violence, and Media

Introduction

The video-recorded decapitations of two American journalists by the Islamic State in August 2014 shocked the world, raised global violence one more notch, galvanized a coalition of nations for a brief and inconsequential response, and sent a harrowing message to anyone standing in the way of the new caliphate. In the grief and pain of those two deaths and several others following, and in the emotional peaks and valleys of the varied responses to these brutal executions, was a lesson on the state of the violent world in which media still attempt to conduct their primary business, a conversation about how peoples of differing opinions and traditions get along, build community, settle disputes, make business work, and find peace. We will explore that media responsibility and its current crisis through the theoretical prisms of Jacques Ellul's propaganda theory, Carey's journalism as cultural ritual, and peace journalism so-called.

Violence and journalism have had a long and profitable partnership. When media compete in the same marketplace, the race to print or blog the most evocative (and usually harrowing) photographs and eyewitness accounts have made desk-jockeys into media SEAL teams. For a long while, print media editors would wring their hands over what photos to display on page one, lest vulnerable audiences might be offended or children's sensitivities violated. Social media has changed all that, with all manner of visual news available. Many print and electronic media have tried to keep-up and catch-up by expanding the moral boundaries, inviting news of atrocities and human mayhem onto their pages and screens. Freedom cries out: the news must be covered in all its grim reality; responsibility echoes back: be careful lest the humanity of victims or the redemption of perpetrators is so violated by news coverage that one or both are lost forever to the community of persons who must forge a future, no matter what.

Why Cover Violence?

Most fair-minded people hear gunfire and run from it. Journalists, however, like police and other first-responders, train to overcome the impulse of flight, and run toward trouble. In times past, the press has called these wrong-way runners "war correspondents." They went to foreign shores to tell stories of young men landing on dangerous beaches. In the present era of gunfire in marketplaces and car bombs in crowded intersections, a journalist need not travel far to face the threat of injury and violent confrontation between opposing warriors. How much danger should a journalist engage? How should victims of violence be given press coverage?

World Media Ethics: Cases and Commentary, First Edition. Robert S. Fortner and P. Mark Fackler.
© 2018 John Wiley & Sons, Inc. Published 2018 by John Wiley & Sons, Inc.

On the first point, the answer has been: no more and slightly less than the combatants themselves. The journalist on site will decide what risks are worth the story. No editor expects human sacrifice for a headline. Journalists have to make their own sense of situations and respond with reasoned risk. On the second, answers are clouded by profit (portrayals of violence sell), perceptions of public taste (viewers may not have the stomach for corpses in the street), and a news company's traditions (some news agencies have branded themselves as not-abetting-violence).

As we begin to consider the morality of press coverage of war and violence, let us settle on this as a pre-condition to the conversation: violence is not the preferred way of settling problems. War is not what the press should want. War signals the breakdown in what the press is supposed to do: facilitate respectful dialogue toward peaceful problem-solving. No member of the press should want or like war. But war and violence happens. Nowadays, it comes to town, often by total surprise.

Case 12.1: Elections in Kenya

If bullets and bloodshed were removed from news coverage, newspapers would be thin indeed, broadcasts short, and blogs boring. What would be left for nightly newscasts but jolly heads bobbling about elite fashions and politicos' foibles? It is remarkable, then, that violence has occasionally been eliminated from coverage to save the companies who would otherwise capitalize on people's fascination with violence. Consider the situation in early 2008, Kenya, following the national elections in late December 2007. The incumbent, Mwai Kibaki, an old Kenyan pol as charismatic as a dull pencil but a survivor and blessed with managerial intelligence, was expected to face a stiff challenge from Raila Odinga, whose father had been part of Kenya's original leadership cabinet until differences with Jomo Kenyatta forced him into the role of ethnic dissenter. The presidential race was also between ethnic groups. Kibaki is Kikuyu; Odinga is Luo. The former "tribe" has occupied State House in Nairobi for longer than any other; the latter has never held the top office. In Kenyan parlance, many felt it was time for others to "eat cake," a short form of saying "enjoy the fruits, righteous or not, of the public treasury and all that the treasury involves."

Kenya's media at the time (and today, largely) was comprised of the national press, the vernacular press, and the alternative press. Of the two national newspapers, the *Daily Nation* (Nation Media Group) began in 1958 and has become a powerhouse of news and comment through the region. The *Standard* was founded in 1902, and was largely a pro-British voice (a White settler paper). Not for a decade after independence (1963) did a native Kenyan take leadership.

Journalism in Kenya has been a dangerous occupation for the most part. Government administrations have long exerted control over media reports with intimidating phone calls, detentions, and imprisonments. When the pressure became too great, journalists sometimes chose life in exile. Internally, corruption (by Western press standards) was common. "Brown envelope" journalism was the common mode of politicians buying positive coverage. At an event, the journalist is handed a gift of Kenyan shillings, intended to cover the cost of transport (since the newspapers typically did not pay for conveyance to the site), and certainly intended to be shared with editors back in the city. The honorable journalist who refused the envelope and had nothing to share found that assignments went to others more cooperative.

Each of Kenya's three administrations (up to 2007) became famous for intrusions into editorial coverage. Kenyatta had near total cooperation; he was, after all, trying to establish a nation and the press came to his aid. Daniel arap Moi, his successor, had agents interview pesky journalists at Nyayo House in Nairobi, not a good place to visit. And then Kibaki, himself a calmer leader, became famous for press interference when his more vocal wife, Lucy, took control of a newsroom in 2005 which had printed a story she did not like. She was forceful, physically abusive, and petulant. But Kenya police typically do not arrest a First Lady, and editors learned a lesson that night.

Leading up to the 2007 national elections, the tenor of political coverage was sensational and divisive. *Nation*, *Standard*, and the third newspaper, *People*, sold a lot of copies with stories of confrontations, expectations of ballot stuffing, allegations of bureaucratic interference, and calls for fairness largely ignored. The news-press took sides, claiming virtue for their party, nefarious evil for the other. Once the violence began, a day following the election, photography played a major role. A published photo of violence perpetrated against one political party would result in a vengeance play by the other. Photography seemed to be escalating actual violence in the streets. Of course, the reporting was dramatic and papers were selling like fine samosas, until the streets and sections of the country became too violent for travel, business, farming, or church-going. In the end, 1,100 people lost their lives, and 350,000 were internally displaced, unwilling or unable to return to their homes when the violence ended. In the words of subsequent documentary portrayals, Kenya burned.

On January 4, 2008, a media breakthrough occurred. All three major newspapers, and some of the lesser ones, published a front-page headline, "Save Our Beloved Country," and editorials calling for a cease-fire in the streets, a return to business, a settling down of the rhetoric and fires and murdering of people by opposing ethnic groups. Indeed, not all media cooperated with the peace effort. Vernacular radio broadcasts were explicit about where and when to meet for violence on the next day; vernacular idioms demonized the "other," as happened also in the Rwanda genocide of 1994. Once violence was unleashed, newspaper editorials alone could not stop it. Media leaders were appalled at the degree of social hatred experienced during the weeks that followed, until international diplomatic intervention settled the scene in April 2008. Nonetheless, newspaper coverage took a decided turn: no more incendiary photography; radio and television coverage avoided screaming politicians and opted for interviews with proponents of calm. Music playlists consciously promoted peace (Fackler and Obonyo, 2011).

Commentary on Case 12.1

In many ways, the coverage of Kenyan election violence engages the problem raised in a prior chapter, the one and the many, the person and his/her rights over or against the people and their security and flourishing. It is a problem that goes back to the beginning of press theory and its interaction with the moral bonds between peoples.

Is the individual the essential unit of reality and history, or is that unit more accurately the group, the community, the tribe and now the nation-state? When we humans think about ethics, are we striving to conform individual beliefs to established standards of the good, or are we speaking to matters of relations between persons? Is moral maturity a private alignment with the good or a network of flourishing relationships?

On matters of media practice and professionalism, the argument has swung both ways. In the West, that swing was keynoted in John Milton's *Areopagitica* (1644), his classic defense of free speech: "Let truth and falsehood grapple; who ever knew truth put to the worse in a free and open encounter?" The rhetorical question posed here begs this further question: who is grappling with whom?

In the history of Western applications of Milton's paean, the media (institutions of public discourse) are grappling with the state, whose army and law-making powers weigh heavily in any power equation. The media, in Milton's classical liberalism, are the bulwark of truth against ruling powers and divine-right kingdoms, and must be protected and nurtured lest the open marketplace of ideas be overruled by arbitrary authority. Is there a more poignant example today than North Korea?

But this storyline begs further questions: Who are the media? Whose voices do media amplify?

Famous for his insistence that individual voices in the "open marketplace" are the foundations of all other freedoms, John Merrill spared no intellectual effort as he laid out the classical liberal theory of the press. At its core, libertarianism holds that educated and alert persons (especially those trained as journalists) should follow the evidence and the truth as each person comes to know it, without the collusion and compromise that team-constructed or, worse, company-constructed news stories would present. "The journalistic *self*," Merrill wrote, "and the journalistic penchant for media self-determinism must be re-enthroned, and the fuzzy social utilitarian thinking that is undermining journalistic integrity and turning journalists into mechanistic robots must be repudiated" (Merrill, 1974, p. 4).

Merrill's polarized options – personal integrity or moral fuzz – were not meant to meld into some theoretical middle ground. Merrill stood for "personal integrity and self-respect and against altruism, toward responsibility *self*-determined and against social responsibility *socially or collectively* determined" (Ibid.). Merrill watched the press in the southern hemisphere slide badly (as he saw it) in the 1960s–1970s, where cooperation between the press and government was considered imperative for national development, and at the same time, a relationship that undercut a central function of the press: watchdog of political power-brokers. Merrill urged media – news and commentary – to be outlets of many voices, without taint of influence from commercial interests or government officials. This was the founding American ideal, he claimed, never fully realized but always the point on the horizon to which media rightly aspired.

As Merrill wrote, Ghanaian journalist and lecturer Paul A.V. Ansah, outspoken leader in West Africa's struggle for freedom, democracy, and national development, was producing essays that mixed a free press (free of imperial control) and fresh national fervor (most African countries were less than 20 years into independence when Ansah wrote). Ansah recognized that news media cannot operate outside a prevailing political environment, hence the very definition of responsible media changes with political moods. This he said was benchmark:

> Responsible journalism . . . is that brand of journalism that provides general information, separates fact from comment, and provides a forum for the sharing of ideas. It studiously separates facts from comments, impartially, fairly, accurately and in a balanced way presents facts as objectively as is humanly possible. . . . Responsible journalism . . . strictly adheres to the professional code of ethics.
>
> *(Ansah, 1996, p. 161)*

Echoes of social responsibility theory ring in Ansah's words, but also a commitment to professional standards negotiated within the profession, arbitrated with the wider culture. Ansah went further, however, widening the gulf between Merrill's autonomous journalist and his own perception of the press's mission.

> A responsible press in a developing country has great responsibilities. . . . It should be an instrument for promoting development and ensuring popular participation in the decision-making process which alone can secure . . . wholehearted co-operation and support. . . . Even poor and hungry people should have the recognized right to say loudly and clearly that they are hungry and the responsible press become the channel through which they articulate their plight.
>
> *(Ansah, 1996, p. 162)*

With national fervor at fever pitch in a state with zero banking credit and little experience at self-government, Ansah struck a necessary deal between freedom and future. Ghana must pull together, and media must amplify the best pullers for the sake of a future in which people pulling and pushing might discover and develop systems to meet basic needs. Food security and free speech both must flourish for the new nation to become plausible. This became Kenya's solution as well. Businesses were closing; churches were burning; planted fields were left untended; newspaper delivery trucks were blocked and destroyed by partisans who believed the newspaper favored the other side. Many wondered if the nation Kenya would survive.

Ansah and his development-journalism cohorts were well aware of the thin line between promoting a national identity and becoming public relations flacks for feckless leaders. The latter Ansah resisted, claiming that the people's welfare was at the heart of a reporter's profession. The people's needs and hopes: a journalist's compass and ambition.

Merrill as well allowed no journalistic ground for totalitarian regimes, which he implied any government would become apart from the vigilance of a watchful media. But for liberalism, watchfulness meant a certain cynical posture toward state power, whether headquartered in Washington or Moscow or Tehran. Merrill's "people" would flourish if left to their own ingenuity and energy. Government had a limited role; media kept government's rapacious hunger at bay. Ansah's vision of the press as instigator of cooperation between small communities and the national assembly was on the far side of Merrill's moon, for whom media were a people's only hope for transparency and truth in the complex economic and diverse political landscape of advanced democracy.

Discontent with the liberal mood, media ethicist Clifford Christians began exploring communitarian ethics, slowly leading much of the academy to relocate the center of moral life to the relation between selves, in the mutuality that defines and cultivates personhood. Christians would preserve and treasure the person as a being of dignity, while re-centering media ethics from personal virtue to communal well-being. Important to this shift was the recovery of an epistemology that recognizes how moral principles are weighted: not by their coherence to external codes of conduct, nor even to external data in the way of scientific verification; and neither by a deductive logic that requires certain outcomes, as in Kant's categorical imperative, through the virtues of rational thought. Moral principles, Christians contends, leaning on Michael Polanyi, arise from "tacit knowledge," that is, deeply interiorized core beliefs held by persons as fundamental interpretations of reality (Christians, 2010a), a strong sense of how the world works, much as a pianist knows music apart from considerations of finger movement.

> Worldviews are the gyroscopes around which thinking and experience revolve, our ultimate commitments at the core of our being. Worldviews give meaning to our consciousness. They represent a set of basic beliefs about human destiny. . . . Presuppositions are *sine qua non* in rethinking moral theory.
>
> *(Christians, 2010a, p. 339)*

What is to be done, then, with presuppositions? Are all equal, worthy of respect or adoption? Of first importance is the recognition of persons as specially gifted knowing agents. People think, plan, articulate, negotiate, and interpret the world. Apart from those incapacitated by illness or disability, all people do this relative to their environments and cultural myths, thus the long search for moral claims with universal application. In the past, scholars have attempted to arrive at moral universals through air-tight logic; this project has been discredited (Alleyne, 2009, p. 386ff.). Moral relativism has been the easy fall-back option, but relativism fails the test of the naturalistic fallacy: "is" statements cannot yield "ought" statements since they engage different phenomena.

> What exists in a natural setting cannot yield normative guidelines. And relativism faces the long-standing contradiction articulated by Karl Mannheim: Those insisting that all cultures are

relative must arise above them and in so doing relativism is nullified. . . . The primary issue is identifying a different kind of universal, one that honors the splendid variety of human life.

(Christians and Cooper, 2009, p. 56)

If the route to universals is paved with neither reason nor materiality, where does one look for an "interactive universal" that can "enable the media to build a civic philosophy and thereby demonstrate a transformative intent" (Ibid.)? Christians and Cooper (2009, pp. 60–61) advance three universals which emerge from life itself, persons doing life with others, in a place, at a time: the sacredness of human life, the necessity of truth-telling, and non-violence.

The imperative of dignity grounded in the sacredness of life moves us beyond an individualistic morality of rights to a social ethics of the common good. It enables us to recognize that an urgent issue on the civic agenda at present is to enable the voices of self-discovery and self-affirmation to flourish among a society's cultural groups. Promoting human dignity does not mean informing a majority audience of racial injustice, for example, but insures those forms of representation from the ground up that generate a critical consciousness for oneself and other.

(Christians and Cooper, 2009, p. 62)

From these universals arise a new focus on human relationships as eminent: how persons interpret the world together become practices of media that honor life and seek its flourishing through many genres and cultural productions. Does *manga* clarify mutuality or dismantle it? Does news reporting set up political polarities as conflict attracts readership, or does reportage address readers' deep beliefs and thus challenge fundamental change? Christians' communitarianism will ask these questions not as overtures of individual investigations but for corporate conscience and interactive dialogue.

Yet the responsibility for creating pro-peace, pro-life reportage is not the media's alone. Technology is not a given to be accepted *fait accompli*. Persons-in-relation bear the load of moral alertness that sustains good media, for that is what media are: persons relating. Christians and Cooper (2009, p. 66) conclude:

Behind this ethic are the spirits of many peoples. From Martin Buber (1965) . . . there is the commitment that when dialog is genuine the speaker will respectfully "behold his partner as the very one he is" (p. 143). Mahatma Gandhi (1947) teaches that "you must be the change you want to see in the world." From Chief Thomas Littleben (1993) is the advice to "listen with all of yourself and only speak what you know." In Mother Teresa's wisdom [1983], "there is no one who does not deserve our caring communication." . . . A global communication ethics must be more than a hollow skeleton of worldwide codes and rhetorical declarations. . . . To be truly effective . . . a communication ethics must . . . be constantly lived and protected by people of every background.

Since the 1990s communitarianism has become one of the moral options by which media professionals engage in discourse concerning their responsibilities to the public, and claims of free speech for the public.

Other discontents with Merrill's classical liberalism arose from the perspective of political economy, with its emphasis on institutions and power. Communications theorists who favor this approach have likely already made several prior commitments to the nature and texture of social life. First among those commitments is the sense that competitive societies, such as those of advanced capitalism, create multiple levels of protection for wealth accumulation, finally starving out the aspirations of the underclass and worker class. Thus the battle is pitched between corporations and persons, corporate managers and line workers, with their radically different goals and needs. In communications industries, where message is everything, hymns to freedom sung by classical liberals sound hollow to those whose economic and intellectual freedom is suppressed by the very culture which claims to afford them access. Freedom is a false message, its inherent truth subverted by corporate greed. "Work, save, and prosper" trumpeted to the working class is equivalent to "be content with your lot," or put more severely, "serve your master well."

When media themselves become entangled in the web of corporate competition, message becomes the servant of consumerism. Entertainment television, in political-economic theory, delivers audience to advertisers, who are the only real point and purpose of media creativity. Political discourse is bounded by the special interests which fund campaigns, the very (corporate) interests that election winners will be expected to defend and protect. Education becomes the delivery of the history and traditions of corporate culture to a next generation of leaders and workers who will sustain the maw of corporate profit and "buy in" to the myths corporatism promulgates about life's meaning and purpose. Education in civic consciousness, one of the aims of a free and responsible media, is subverted by layers of artificial and misdirected bureaucracy. David Coleman, president of the College Board tasked with generating a common-core curriculum for American schools, has said that "career readiness is the goal of K-12 education" in America – students are being prepared to find their role in corporate culture. Critics note that Coleman was once a believer in the power of liberal arts (Neem, 2015, p. 102). Institutional control of news media, entertainment, and advertising provides viewers and readers with what Jacques Ellul called horizontal propaganda: a message so pervasive and unchallenged that, like a blanket of clouds, the sunlight of truth cannot break through.

Jacques Ellul, while not a political economist in theory or inclination, shares with them a lifelong commitment to the underclass and reasoned resistance to the technological paradox. Ellul was not concerned with transnational corporations per se, but with an elusive but pervasive patina to modernity he called *la technique*, for which there is not a good English word but this one has been made to suffice: *technicism*. Modern persons are absolutely staked to the technological grid, Ellul contends, with its ultimate effect of reducing all human interaction to calculations of efficiency. Does a student want a good grade? Then do your homework (your learning) strategically toward that grade. Do media herald "good grades" as pathways to success? The rational modern program for "getting ahead" is the path of least resistance consonant with achieving an A grade. In another era, education would have emphasized learning, review, investigation, and competency. Now institutions of higher education engage issues of teacher relations, pre-test preparation, hiring out papers, or other roundabout means. So thoroughly has efficiency taken over learning that in April 2015, as this chapter is being written, 13 administrators and teachers from public schools in Atlanta, Georgia (United States) are being sentenced to prison for years of test-score cheating, while none of them believed they were at fault: the system required it. *Technicism* has redrawn boundaries and skill-sets for contemporary educators. Imagine its impact on elementary-grade and middle-school students, who have never known another way. Thus imagine public media under the eventual management of these prodigies.

Ellul was a Marxist as a young adult. Political economists find great wisdom in Marx's analysis of corporate hegemony, its impact on other social institutions and on primary human relations. In a recent study on global entertainment, Marx is not cited but everywhere reflected in sweeping claims concerning the delivery of messages through the prisms of consumerism and materiality: "Media are capitalist industries. Capitalist entertainment media have become transnationalized in production and distribution for private profit, generating billions in revenues . . . from the wage labor of production workers, who create value through their production. . . . Media profits are extracted by paying workers less than the value of the products they produce"

(Artz, 2015, p. 85).

The broad strokes of a political-economy approach to media have cast new light on the ethics of wealth accumulation and propaganda. But lost in the generalities about class and status is any workable conception of the person, which is what all who read these words in fact are. Readers and students are not institutions, important as the *communitas* is to our identity and welfare. We are in fact persons with minds, consciences, and wills. Our choices may be bounded by social convention, but the imagination ranges freely. *New York Times* columnist David Brooks (2015) wrote candidly on personhood:

> About once a month I run across a person who radiates an inner light. These people can be in any walk of life. They seem deeply good. They listen well. They make you feel funny and valued. You often catch them looking after other people and as they do so their laugh is musical and their manner is infused with gratitude. They are not thinking about what wonderful work they are doing. They are not thinking about themselves at all. When I meet such a person it brightens my whole day.

Institutions do not "radiate an inner light," nor do many seem "deeply good" as a general rule. You may count on your hand the number of institutions which "listen well" – the International Listening Association and symphony aficionados are the rare examples. Meeting an institution rarely brightens the day. Brooks has recalled something quite important: the meaningfulness of personhood and the intimate delight humans take in meeting persons of quality and spirit. Mr. Brooks himself may be closer to this kind of person than he allows in his column, but the "inner light's" most apparent quality, he does say, is humility, which would mitigate anyone's personal assessment of having arrived at "deeply good." It must also be observed that regiments of public relations professionals, employed by each and every growing institution, are not in their profession to advance the humility of their clients. To find what Brooks has found, you look to persons, not organizations. But the future of persons is certainly linked to the growth of organizations. No hero survives alone for long. The common bond, a culture of transparency, and a strong lean toward truthfulness are survival skills long established and too infrequently exercised.

Norwegian scholar Terje Skjerdal updates the development theory of the press with his work on Ethiopian media. There, media during the Haile Selassie years (1930–1974) were empowered only to support the king's feudal aspirations. The subsequent revolutionary government, called the Dergue ("Committee," 1974–1987), controlled information all the more and every other sector of public life, nationalizing land and industry in its enthusiastic embrace of Leninism. "Land to the Tiller" was the Dergue's slogan for the program to take rural land from tenants and farmers and place it under the control of peasants, which led finally to the great Ethiopian famine of the mid-1980s. In the news business as in every public sphere, career and life itself hung on the fragile sensitivities of the Committee and its street jurists lethally armed. Dissent, or the suspicion of dissent, could lead to a person's disappearance and death.

The Dergue was fast to act and quick to kill. The old sergeant, long since retired from Ethiopia's military, stood guard at Selassie's bedroom exhibit in the museum at Addis Ababa University. He would tell visitors in broken English that one day in August, 1975, a low-level Dergue conscript walked up to the Old Man's bed, where he lay stricken with age and illness, then without words pressed a pillow against his head until his breathing stopped. So ended the life of Haile Selassie, once called the Lion of Judah and King of the Empire, a descendant of Solomon, he claimed: an ignoble suffocation, so characteristic of a movement that defied notions of life as valuable or justice as transparent.

Case 12.2: Casual Talk and Public Discourse

Nega Mezlekia is a novelist, born in Ethiopia in the right year to become a university student when the Dergue was most paranoid about ideas churning inside citizens' heads. Students could not trust each other for fear that a spy of the regime would make of casual residence-hall talk a crime against the state. University instructors would carry cyanide to class, on the possibility of meeting a caravan of shooters or kidnappers on the way (Mezlekia, 2000, p. 296). Nega writes:

> For the young and free-thinking youth of Ethiopia, 1977 was an exceedingly ominous year. Addis Ababa was shaken by political tremor, and threatened to erupt with a ferocity of biblical proportions. The sun shone, but the sky was dark; the wind blew, but nothing moved. Many stayed indoors. When they ventured out, it was with the painful knowledge that they might never again see the light of day. It was a time when many young people simply vanished into thin air. Many were picked up and thrown into the back of a truck. No one asked questions. The jails and prisons were teeming with panic-stricken children whose parents didn't even know their whereabouts. Such information was given out only on a need-to-know basis, and, the junta argued, the family members didn't need to know. The bullet-riddled bodies of children, with notes describing their contrived crimes carelessly pinned to their tattered shirts, greeted us every morning. Their crimes were ill-defined. The tags always read the same: "This was a reactionary! The Red Terror shall Flourish!" What caught me off guard was not the mere sight of bodies of children, but the very arbitrariness of it. I knew those boys and girls were no more guilty of any crime than I, or indeed millions of others. Life-and-death decisions were not being made in the local peasant association. The old judiciary system had been put on the shelf. During the seven months that the "Red Terror" was in full bloom, all crimes serious enough to warrant a jail sentence were punished by the firing squad. An estimated 100,000 political opponents of the regime were dispatched across the bourn by the time the meat-mincer finally stopped whizzing. . . . Two-legged hyenas roamed the neighborhood at will. They walked from door to door at very odd times of the day, searching every possible hideout, looking for their next victim.
>
> *(Mezlekia, 2000, pp. 291–300, passim)*

Commentary on Case 12.2

Nega's experience is not unique to Ethiopia. Novelists around the world can identify with the risks of writing. Salman Rushdie produced a novel and, after threats and fatwa, went underground, or above ground with guards. John Milton expressed his thoughts on the matter of divorce (in seventeenth-century England) and watched his pamphlets burned as if they were public poison. The active imagination subverts well-established interests, and those interests, combined with social power, can put the writer's life on a new plain, neither safe nor significant. Surely the history of communication requires a more complex explanatory theory than mere message transmission, getting a meaning from point A to B. Novelists and journalists, documentary makers and poets, are not simple conduits, carrying the water. Transmission theories – the notion that communication is a transit of meaning to be understood through measurements of time, distance, and medium – fail to account for the impact of the imagination on public discourse. A better theory must also lead to more penetrating commitments on free and responsible communication.

James W. Carey (1934–2006) spent a life in the academy (Illinois, Iowa, and Columbia) building a theory of communication around discourse as ritual, democracy as public debate, and responsible freedom as the essential human obligation. Carey insisted that persons have the means to move the human conversation along; media institutions can build dialogue in public places, maintaining, subverting, and transforming culture. Lawrence Grossberg notes that Carey began his work on communication by seeing culture as "uniquely and essentially human. . . . We live in a symbolic reality of our own making. It is a complex and varied process, not even hardly a process in the common understanding of the term. Carey's concept of culture [engages] polysemy and polyvocality," never singularity or one-voice messaging (Grossberg, 2010, p. 78). Carey himself wrote:

> This particular miracle we perform daily and hourly – the miracle of producing reality and then living within and under the fact of our own productions – rests upon a particular quality of symbols: their ability to be both representations "of" and "for" reality. . . . All human activity is such an exercise. . . . We first produce the world by symbolic work and then take up residence in the world we have produced. Alas, there is magic in our self-deceptions.
>
> *(Carey, 1989, pp. 29–30)*

In Carey's view, palaver, the old village meeting, is now professionalized and largely for-profit, but it can be redeemed. Persons understanding their culture-making role, figuring that words and the meanings they create in persons and culture are ambiguous yet altogether human and necessary, push past set boundaries of reality to create new horizons and new possibilities for subject and citizen, worker and manager, men and women, whatever the pairing or the cultural distance between them. New configurations of culture teem with creativity and political challenge, and cannot be suppressed.

Against the hyenas, in Nega's terms, or above them or in spite of them, communication as ritual for transformation generates new political realities. And so it should, as this is humanity's special giftedness. Carey was closest to the world of the working journalist, yet he understood that role as culture-forming primarily, informational and persuasive and polemical. Nega and Carey are intellectual kin, and with them, all storytellers who resist the script of the technocrats and censors.

Nowhere in the domain of press theory is the question of violence so directly engaged as in peace journalism, clarified, distinguished, and described by its very name. Peace journalism wants peace as an end, and peace as a means. But what can that possibly mean, in a world where peace is far from guaranteed, and frequently dismissed as weakness? Several communications theorists have argued that all media are directed, so why not direct media energies and influence toward non-violence? Why not?

Clifford Christians' communitarianism insists that non-violence must be grounded in a philosophical anthropology that acknowledges the spiritual dimension of human existence (Christians, 2010b). Avoiding attachment to theology or organized religions, Christians argues that spirituality should be defined as

> [h]umans thrusting out beyond their embodiments and the limited social order under which they live. Spirituality is . . . the human attempt to reach unconstrained reality and the ultimate sphere . . . the numinous.
>
> *(Christians, 2010b, p. 21)*

Christians reasons that *Homo sapiens* "is the one living species constituted by language, therefore, humans are fundamentally cultural beings" (Ibid., p. 18). This claim leads to the middle-range conclusion that speech is itself sacred, in that speech (the dialogue of many voices, the palaver as it were), is the act of humans doing their best work to meet the needs of survival, even prosperity. Dialogue is nothing less than humans reaching for a "revolutionary transformation of consciousness" (Ibid., p. 21), something that secular social contract theory cannot provide or project. This transformation, certainly more subtle than dramatic, but nonetheless compelling and deeply human, is "the release of the creative, an upsurge of liberating energy, a freeing of people from suffering and dulling restraints" as "all symbolic creations" reveal and reinforce "the sacramental for the communication process" (Ibid., pp. 21–22). Christians explains this phenomenon in Taoist terms, a "formless mysticism that gives life to all creation and is itself inexhaustible" that "pursues a society that operates without hurting the harmony within its people and the harmony within nature" (Ibid., pp. 24–25). Other expressions of this dynamic philosophical anthropology are captured in terms such as *ubuntu* and *grace*, and the ethical mood emanating from humans-in-dialogue is summed up most adequately in the "normative strategy for living peacefully – the golden rule" (Ibid., p. 25).

Thus Christians brings the issue of war, violence, and media back to an ancient cultural principle of respecting human life and speech as sacred, protecting it through non-violent means, and finding in the ritual of human communication the hope that overcomes its many setbacks reported daily as "breaking news" and headline feeds. One must pause at such a simple, timeless, and universal hope. The pause forces a moment of consideration before secularity, efficiency, and fear remind us that the sword is actually mightier than the pen in most territories where humans have left footprints.

Conclusion

This chapter concludes with another ugly act of inhumanity, the killing of five journalists by the Islamic State in 2014. This time the victims were four Libyans and one Egyptian working for Barqa TV, an eastern Libyan television station. The International Federation of Journalists (IFJ) said the reporters had been kidnapped at an Islamic State checkpoint en route to Benghazi 10 months before their bodies were found, throats slit, on a hillside. "We are deeply shocked by this brutal slaughter," said IFJ president Jim Boumelha. "ISIS [Islamic State] aims to horrify but we can only feel great sorrow and further resolve to see the killers held responsible for their crimes" (Reuters, 2015). Terrible, frightening, and increasingly common events such as this call for responsibility and reckoning.

Perhaps it is simply late in humanity's game to call for media devoted to peace as a means of social change and justice. But that call is never far from the soul of the journalist, who devotes his or her best energies to speaking a word truthfully, for the sake of nourishing something good about our common capacity to seek the welfare of the other, and so secure another day of common life.

Discussion Questions

1   Where are your boundaries when viewing media violence? What will you turn off, walk away from?

2   Some people affirm a commitment to non-violence. Would such a commitment by media programmers be a public benefit?

3   Who should have a role in determining the content of violent programming?

4   What kinds of persons should be specially protected from violence on media? How are protections best enacted and enforced?

5   Some people today worry over micro-aggressions, and thus, micro-violence. Should these concerns receive greater attention by media programmers and regulators?

13

Truth, Conflict, Chronic Problems, and Media Attention

The Problem of the Truth

One of the fundamental precepts of social responsibility in media practice is to tell the truth. Truth-telling is one of the fundamental shared commitments of different cultures around the world, according to Christians and Traber (1997). But is it really that easy to seek the truth, to know the truth, to tell the truth? Aeschylus, the Greek tragic dramatist, reportedly said that, in war, truth is the first casualty. But is that the only place where truth is problematic – in war? We would like to suggest that truth is far more elusive and difficult to define than commitments to it suggest. Even when these commitments seem to be widely accepted, also accepted without much commentary are the "puffery" of advertising, the "spin" of public relations, the "shading" of politics, the fiction of docudrama, and the claims of film and television – even when based on real events and identifiable people – that the events and individuals depicted in their portrayals are fictional and that any similarities to them are entirely coincidental.

Journalists, too, are not immune to the blandishments of falsehoods, denials, and avoidance: they depend on unnamed sources, accuracy of report rather than confrontation (of liars), stories of individuals rather than exposition of history or ideology, the particular over the global – even at the expense of explanation or understanding. The Hutchins Commission of 1947 attempted to address some of these realities in its expectation that journalists, at least, would report the day's events in a context that gave them meaning, but even that can be inadvertently distorted or mistaken in the heat of the 24-hour news cycle that emerged long after its report.

It is not merely in war situations, either, that truth can be compromised. It could be any conflict, hot or cold. The United States and the former Soviet Union both told the truth as they saw it during the Cold War, but they never saw truth the same way. Both used propaganda (public diplomacy), disinformation, and misinformation to influence publics based on their ideological "truth." They fought proxy wars, but never actually fought each other (except for the U.S. incursion during the Russian Revolution in 1917). Likewise, even in democracies, different political parties tell the "truth" differently. They marshal different facts, rely on different experts, shade on-air conversations and use differing talking points in debates to press their case – reminding their followers of the truth as defined by unquestioned orthodoxies. Religious groups likewise interpret history and events differently to press their versions of the truth around the world. If there is one truth, it is not one that the vast majority of people on earth subscribe to. Even scientific proof is questioned or ignored when it is inconvenient to a declared "truth." So Pontius Pilate's famous question to Jesus of Nazareth still stands: "What is truth?"

Michel Foucault (1983–84, First Hour) provided a nuanced and useful perspective on different types of truth. He identified four different types of truth-tellers based on his reading of ancient Greek texts. These were prophets, sages, teachers, and parrhesiasts. Each of them had a different set of

World Media Ethics: Cases and Commentary, First Edition. Robert S. Fortner and P. Mark Fackler.
© 2018 John Wiley & Sons, Inc. Published 2018 by John Wiley & Sons, Inc.

characteristics. All told the truth, but all were focused on a specific concern of the truth. The prophet, for instance, told the truth revealed to him by another (usually God); the sage told the truth that experience had revealed; the teacher told the truth revealed in scholarship and scientific inquiry; and the parrhesiast told the truth about himself in communication about another, taking a risk in revelation that might lead to rejection.

We do not expect our media to act as prophets, although there are prophetic qualities to some of what they present. For instance, science fiction novels or films can reveal potential dystopian or utopian possibilities contained in particular practices or technological developments. Neither are media sages, although their portrayals may present the wisdom of experience in dramas, comedies, documentaries, news conferences, discussion programs, or news reports. Media can teach, but as their primary preoccupation seems to be entertainment rather than instruction, audiences don't usually expect to encounter teachers – although there is always the subtle potential of instruction as people of all ages, backgrounds, and education may be viewing the same program. Finally, we may say that there is little parrhesiast practice in media – if anything there is more cloaking than risk-taking truth-telling: media are conservative rather than radical, seeking to build and maintain audiences rather than push them away.

What, then, is the truth-telling that media should commit to? Is it merely getting the facts right, avoiding rumor in the guise of fact, quoting people accurately, eschewing the attribution of motive to agents who are otherwise unknown? Is the only judgment to be made that which requires double-sourcing for news, emotional truth in drama, or self-effacing comedy rather than laughs at the expense of others? What is the truth we seek from the media?

Fred Vultee addresses this question in one context: the decision of President Barack Obama's administration not to release the photos of the corpse of Osama bin Laden. He outlines an "array of concerns" about this decision and then writes that the questions raised by these concerns were, in many ways, "questions about truth-telling: not just what makes individual facts true or untrue but also how truth is assembled from facts, and most pertinently how news organizations deal with demands to play a role in intervening on the public's behalf when 'the truth' is demanded. That tension between journalism's gaudy storytelling function and its somber mission as the public's schoolmaster is entwined with the history of how it reports public violence" (Vultee, 2013, p. 242). Vultee invokes the teacher here as one expectation of the press, but also journalism's role as sage – although clearly less obviously. In another essay – this one on talk radio – John Shrader (2013, p. 290) writes that "outrage" radio relies on mockery and misrepresentative exaggeration to build its audiences by telling people what they want to hear: truth in the ear of the beholder?

Case 13.1: Sexual Trafficking

In 2005, the Swedish government distributed five hundred copies of *Lilja 4-Ever* (2002), a film on sexual trafficking, to NGOs in the former Soviet Union and southeastern Europe. In addition to establishing educational and cultural relationships with other nations, Swedish politicians and filmmakers intended the mass distribution of *Lilja 4-Ever* to educate vulnerable girls and women about the devious strategies of human traffickers. According to experts, the former Soviet Union and southeastern Europe emerged as hotbeds of potential prostitutes after the fall of Communism in 1989.

(Small, 2012, p. 415)

The film had a profound response from many young women who saw it in southeastern Europe, helping them understand their at-risk status. The film "became factual evidence in human rights education campaigns" (Ibid., p. 416). Anti-trafficking campaigns in Russia and Moldova used it. In addition, "after two decades of virtual silence, filmmakers crafted at least fifty-five films from 1996 to 2008 that addressed sexual trafficking. They range from big-budget Hollywood dramas to independent feminist documentaries; their locations include regions as diverse as Eastern Europe, Southeast Asia, and Southern California; and they are marketed to mainstream Western audiences, 'at-risk' Third World subjects, and women's studies classrooms" (Ibid., pp. 416–417). Clearly such films struck a nerve across the globe as many countries began to understand the underground sex trafficking trade and began to take steps to curtail it.

But there was a catch. *Lilja 4-Ever*, even though it opened the eyes of potential victims of sex trafficking, was fiction. The filmmaker who wrote the screenplay for it "conducted little, if any, research on sexual trafficking" (Ibid., p. 416). He had been inspired by a brief news story in a Swedish newspaper about the topic, but the characters, plot, and details of the film emerged completely from his imagination. Did this film tell the truth as prophet, sage, or teacher?

Commentary on Case 13.1

Certainly the Swedish film did not tell the truth from the perspective of a parrhesiast, but perhaps it was educational, prophetic, or wise. Does its fiction disqualify it as truth, whether seen from the individualistic or collectivist standpoint? It may have erected a barrier to exploitation and the destruction of families or communities. It may have lent dignity to young women who, having seen it, were more vigilant in protecting their personhood. It may have met the universalist standard of Kant or Rawls' test behind the veil of ignorance. But should it be discounted because it was merely the concoction of one man seeking to make a dramatic film based in human misery who couldn't be bothered to do the research necessary to get it factually correct? In many respects the film was not true at all – factually. Its emotional truth would be individual – only relevant to those touched by its fictional portrayal – not authentic, as it was only tangentially related to a particular truth.

Was it ethical for the Swedish government to distribute the film as part of its educational and cultural exchange for the purpose of education rather than entertainment? Should the International Organization for Migration have screened it as part of its anti-trafficking campaigns in Russia and Moldova? Should the film be cited "as evidence of contemporary human slavery" (Small, 2012)? By what standard of truth should such uses of this film be judged? And if its truth cannot be defended, could it still be ethical to use it to educate and warn potential victims?

Case 13.2: Truth and Reconciliation

South Africa pioneered the use of truth and reconciliation commissions as a means to lasting peace by providing a forum in which political activists and ordinary citizens who had suffered under apartheid "could stand before their fellow South Africans and give voice to unimaginable stories of human rights violations" (Holliday-Karre, 2008, p. 78). Public radio, television, local and national newspapers all carried the details of these violations, and the commission that organized and heard stories of abuse "became the subject of international controversy because of its inability to bring apartheid criminals to justice and its failure to represent entire segments of the community" (Ibid.). The atrocities reported, however, by both men and women, largely detailed the suffering of men, with women's countless horrors underrepresented. Holliday-Karre (2008, pp. 78–79) argues that "women and their speech were co-opted by the media in its effort to create a community of awareness about apartheid and post-apartheid 'reality.' I maintain that television, radio, and newspaper coverage did not allow for female torture and abuse narratives. In the case of the TRC [Truth and Reconciliation Commission], where speech is continually adapted for public consumption, silence becomes the primary form of power available against media representation."

Holliday-Karre (2008, p. 79) then argues that a documentary about the TRC that provided viewers with "access to testimony, newspaper reports, journalist interviews, and radio and television coverage . . . including stories told by victims and perpetrators, men and women, and white and black South Africans" provided not truth, but a "simulation of truth." Drawing from the work of Jean Baudrillard, she concludes that the media (including the documentary itself) provided not meaning but staged meaning (Ibid.): "Therefore, the information presented is no longer 'true' or 'real' but hyper-real, given the inability to separate 'truth' from representation. We accept the media message as truth because we see simulation as reality and there is no longer anything standing in opposition to it." The film chronicled the testimony of Nomonde Calata, the widow of a victim murdered by the apartheid special forces who broke down during her testimony sobbing and wailing as language failed her (Ibid.). The event became the defining moment of the TRC, the basis of news reports and memoirs written later by those who were part of the TRC. This single testimony, and Calata's breakdown:

> [T]he cry of a woman in mourning came to stand for the entire TRC process. The literal cry became a metaphor: the woman is country; the country is mourning the loss of her people. . . . Ms. Calata's cry came to represent an entire victimized, feminized nation. The cry became synonymous with women's reality in post-apartheid South Africa and gradually subsumed all other female experiences of the apartheid regime. Although thousands of women came to testify before the commission, few deviated from the message established by the media.
> *(Holliday-Karre, 2008, p. 80)*

Commentary on Case 13.2

Media are always looking for ways to tell stories, framing them into narratives that can easily be understood whether for comedic or dramatic effect, or to place stories into well-known perspectives that will allow for quick understanding. They use stereotypes, memes, and tropes that provide time-worn but easy interpretation, often short-circuiting deep thought and careful analysis of the actual reality they purport to show. In an age of short soundbites, quick video clips (à la Vine), and limited time frames (attention spans are shortening), it is little wonder that the blooming buzzing confusion of reality is often packed into inappropriate containers.

However, Holliday-Karre's analysis does deserve our reflection. She suggests that the attention the media give to one story, however dramatic and heart-wrenching it may be, can distort understanding of reality or authenticity. She also suggests that by making this single story or event represent all similar people and events, the media puts across a simplistic portrayal as reality, thereby dismissing these other stories and people as less significant than the one they choose to tell. In this respect the media may never tell the truth – or, at best, willfully demand that audiences see reality as they choose to portray it – often with little consideration of whether it is typical of the whole, or only a sensationalistic blip ripe for media use regardless of its connection to reality.

Is it fair that what audiences encounter in media are only these often atypical but entertaining and engaging blips of pseudo-reality? Are there really any alternatives to such media practices? Is it ethical to show non-reality as reality, or partial reality, or constrained reality, or invented reality, as truth? Is it reasonable to expect media to portray truth at all, or are people naïve to believe that media are anything other than diversions or entertaining respites from truth itself?

Ethicists and philosophers who demand that we tell or portray the truth may not provide much help to us, then. If the only reliable truth is what each of us personally experiences and interprets as truth, then media has no connection to truth at all. To expect media to tell the truth in that case would seem naïve at best, stupid at worst. But without the media's representation of the day's events, and the attempt to place them in a context that gives them meaning, what would people be left with if they want to understand human suffering, triumph, grace, faith, or pain? Without the media aren't people left deaf to others' realities, blind to their attempts to cope with disadvantages, injustice, or heroism?

Collectivist ethicists/philosophers remind us that it is the community that matters most, not the individual. They would say that what is important in stories of individuals is not the individuals themselves but what their experiences suggest about the human condition more broadly, or at least the reality of a group represented by the single experience. Yet this is what Holliday-Karre objects to – that one woman's experience was used to encapsulate the whole of the female experience in and after apartheid. The larger truth, she suggests, is obscured by the particularity of the individual truth. It was simply too easy, efficient, and cost-effective for the media to pick up the single truth rather than telling the more comprehensive – and thus, to her, more truthful – story. Collectivist ethicists would probably object to her characterization. There is something valuable to be learned here: there is value – and truth. Are they right? And what lessons can be taken away here for media practice? Or is Holliday-Karre right in her objections. Has truth been lost in our acceptance of media portrayals as legitimate representations of truth?

Chronic Truths

We are accustomed to hearing about chronic problems – those that are endemic to a situation and apparently have no easy solution. We have chosen to call the efforts to explain or resolve such problems "chronic truths." These are truths that are trotted out whenever a new crisis occurs that calls for understanding. People go hungry in Africa, for instance, despite the richness of the land and large empty spaces, because of the chronic truths of poor agricultural practices and drought. Or people die by their thousands in monsoons in Bangladesh nearly every year because of its low-lying land areas that present no difficulties for storm surges. More recently we hear that various countries' efforts to respond to climate change are ineffective because there is too much capital investment in fossil fuel power plants, or due to the burgeoning industrialization of China or India, or the intractable positions of politicians who are dependent on donations from energy companies or who are trying to protect jobs in their constituencies. These are all chronic truths.

One chronic truth affecting information flow is that government will do whatever it can to classify information so as to protect "state security." This security may be defined on a national scale, or by smaller units of government. Often failure to disclose information protects nothing except reputations: people err, take bribes or practice corruption, are incompetent or act without explicit legal authority. Failure to disclose such information amounts to a cover-up rather than a legitimate concern for protecting privacy, trade or military secrets, or protecting citizens in harm's way. Sometimes it protects the economic interests of corporations that have violated safety or environmental standards, or failed to correct noted deficiencies in operations, or even have filled the financial coffers of political candidates in return for certain considerations – such as failure to enforce worker protection, building codes, disposal of toxic waste, employment of children in violation of labor laws, and so on.

The media have difficulty with such issues for a variety of reasons. First is the difficulty of obtaining information from sources that are themselves knowledgeable, not part of the problem itself, and can document the extent of the problem. This requires a whistle-blower or "leaker" who will risk his or her own position in the organization or corporation that is guilty of some moral or legal breach. And it requires that the recipient of the information have the ability to report it to the public. Second is the commitment of a media organization to uncover the details of such activities, some of which may take many months of time, and a significant financial investment to comb through information, verify it, determine the impacts of releasing it on other significant concerns (such as national security), and to accept the likely criticism, perhaps the cost of legal defense, when challenged by the exposed organization. Those working under the media umbrella must also be willing to risk their freedom. In some countries this may be prison on a contempt of court citation. In others it may be far more severe.

Third – and perhaps most difficult – is the willingness to avoid the trap of exposing the information or telling the story using the common frames for storytelling. Stuffing new information in such common frames as the horserace, the triumph of the dispossessed, the corruption of politics, the whitewash, the cover-up, and so on, runs the risk of trivializing the reality by making it seem like same old, same old: nothing compelling here, read the headline and move on. Fourth is the fact that one can never be sure that the whole story is told. New events may occur, exposing dimensions of the situation that were unknown at the time. Perhaps these events will even exonerate those who were the focus of the original report. The dangers of rushing to exposure, or reporting with only fragmentary information that may appear complete, or at least constitutes what everyone assumes is the furthest extent of information that can be known, can damage the credibility of a media organization and make commitments to other time-consuming investigations less likely.

As examples of the time investment required to investigate and report on government secrecy, we will cite three cases. First is what is referred to as the Pentagon Papers in the United States. The Papers were a secret 47-volume, two million-word report prepared on the order of Secretary of State Robert S. McNamara (who left office prior to their completion) on the history of American involvement in the Vietnam War. Thirty-eight volumes of this report were provided to the *New York Times* on March 21, 1971. The paper's first installment of the papers was not printed until June 13, 1971 after more than two months of examining and preparing them for publication. This resulted in an attempt by the Nixon White House to suppress further publication, but the U.S. Supreme Court ruled in favor of publication on June 30, 1971 (see http://topsecretplay.org/timeline/). Second is the Watergate revelations, a series of reports prepared by reporters at the *Washington Post* that revealed the extent of the cover-up of a break-in at the Democratic Party's National Committee offices in the Watergate Hotel by a group of "plumbers" on June 17, 1972. The reporting by *Post* reporters Bob Woodward and Carl Bernstein began shortly thereafter and continued for over two years, culminating in the impeachment and subsequent resignation of President Nixon on June 23, 1974. A major source for the stories was W. Mark Felt, reported as "Deep Throat" in the original stories, who leaked information to the reporters (see Watergate.info). The third example is Edward Snowden, a contractor working at the National Security Agency (NSA), who became a whistle-blower by releasing secret documents on American surveillance activities to *The Guardian* newspaper through reporter Glenn Greenwald that resulted in him being granted political asylum in Russia to avoid prosecution in the United States. Snowden, "a former CIA and NSA contractor who had orchestrated the information dump not months but years prior," provided the information that resulted in revelations, not only to the United States, but to several other nations that discovered the NSA had been intercepting their communications activity (Gurnow, 2014, p. 10).

These examples are from the realm of politics, an area that is more event-driven than the chronic issues that take equally long to research and publish. In the latter cases there is not the payoff that political reporters experience in exposing government malfeasance. This makes them even more difficult for news organizations, documentarians, or others to justify the time required to bring such chronic truths to light, or to engage audiences who may have less personal investment in them compared to in politics.

Case 13.3: Chronic Poverty

In 2014 the Chronic Poverty Advisory Network (CPAN) published a nearly 200-page report on poverty worldwide (CPAN, 2014). This report made "the case for a new urgency in eradicating poverty before environmental conditions become much more difficult in many parts of the developing world" (Ibid., p. 1). Although significant progress had been made since the adoption of the Millennium Development Goals, the report argued that "more of the same" would not result in eradicating poverty by 2030, despite discussions that put that goal out to the world (Ibid.). Based on the copious data collected, CPAN wrote: "The road out of poverty is rarely a smooth, one-way street. Many people rise above the poverty line only to tumble back beneath it. Millions of vulnerable people return to extreme poverty, or become poor for the first time, when they are hit by a combination or sequence of shocks, such as a serious drought, a costly illness, and insecurity or conflict in their community" (Ibid., p. 2). In some rural areas the percentage that had risen above, and then fallen back into, poverty was between 20% and 60% (Ibid.); poverty was defined as income levels of less than $1.25 per day per person (Ibid., p. 3).

If extreme poverty was to be eradicated, CPAN argued, three policies would have to be adopted (Ibid., p. 4). First was social assistance that takes "the poorest people closer to a decent standard of living, provides a safety net for them in tough times, and encourages them to make investments and take the risks that could propel them out of poverty, and keep them out of poverty." Second was "massive investment in education," and third was economic growth policies that were pro-poor to ensure "that the benefits of increasing national prosperity reach the very poorest people" (Ibid.). These strategies would assist countries in tackling chronic poverty by providing a firm foundation for national development plans. Countries also needed to "work with civil society to make sure the poorest people are represented politically and are included in the economy, politics and culture of their country on good terms" (Ibid.), in other words ending systemic discrimination against particular groups in society. Other requirements were universal health coverage, addressing major risks such as conflict and environmental disasters, and investing in post-primary education of good quality to provide students with the skills needed for employment (Ibid.). "It is clear, therefore, that getting to zero requires root-and-branch transformative social change that tackles the overlapping and debilitating inequalities faced by the poorest people – in gender, in access to land, in education and in labour markets – and that result in injustices that perpetuate poverty and powerlessness" (Ibid., p. 5).

In 2015 the World Bank released a report on chronic poverty in Latin America and the Caribbean (Vakis, Rigolini, and Lucchetti, 2015). Although this report used a different standard to define chronic poverty ($4.00 per day per person rather than $1.50), and remarked on the "dramatic reduction of poverty" in the region since 2000 (Ibid., p. 1), this report also provided five facts about chronic poverty in the area. These were, first, that one of five Latin Americans lived in extreme poverty in 2012 (Ibid., p. 12), including 50% of the population in Guatemala; second, that chronic poverty tended to be geographically concentrated (Ibid., p. 13); third, that chronic poverty was as much an issue in urban areas as it was in rural ones (Ibid., p. 15); fourth, that economic growth alone was not sufficient to lift the chronically poor out of poverty (Ibid., p. 17); and finally, that the chronically poor had limited income opportunities (Ibid.). While none of these conclusions is itself a great surprise, the report did contradict some prevailing economic mantras, such as a "rising tide lifts all ships" – in other words, that economic growth would solve the issue of poverty. The World Bank issued a press release to highlight this report on March 9, 2015.[1]

What was the response of the media to this information on chronic poverty? The *Times of India*'s sister publication, the *Economic Times*, reported on the World Bank report with the headline, "China, India played central role in global poverty reduction: UN report" (PTI, 2015). Most of the readers' remarks about this report indicated a degree of amazement at the progress, with some crediting Prime Minister Modi's initiatives and others crediting his predecessor since the statistics were for a period prior to his election. The report thus became an occasion for political gamesmanship. The Australian Council for International Development (2014) carried a brief summary of the report on its webpage with a link to the full story. The Wessex Global Health Network carried a similar summary.[2] An Oxfam blog (Oxfam, 2014) carried a more complete summation of the report with a promise of additional information via Twitter. But most other reports were similar to the Australian one, a brief summary only.[3] More complete summations and commentary were, however, carried by *Borgen Magazine* (Ernstes, 2014) and *The Guardian* (Tran, 2014). Otherwise there was little else available on this report, although stories about poverty (especially domestic poverty) were not difficult to find.

Commentary on Case 13.3

We will not suggest here that these various reports were all that the media carried concerning the problem of chronic poverty. Some publications that did not report on the CPAN report did cover the more geographically-specific World Bank one. And some countries, such as Uganda and India, discussed chronic poverty in response to even more specific reports about their own situations. But equally as likely were reports chastising the media for "poverty porn," defined by Ma. Ceres P. Doyo (2013) in the *Philippine Daily Inquirer* as "practices of the media (journalists, photojournalists, documentarists, filmmakers), development aid groups, fund raisers and those who have poverty among their concerns . . . which use and display . . . stark images of persons in extreme poverty that border on the exploitative and intrusive, in order to generate sympathy and donations, to increase newspaper circulation and TV ratings, or even to gain fame. And, it is stressed, noble ends do not justify such 'exploitation.'"

In another venue, reality TV, better than 25,000 people signed a petition to CBS to cancel its show "The Briefcase," in which two families were each provided a briefcase containing $101,000 and asked to decide how to divide it with the other (not knowing they both had to make the same choice). While the executive producer of the show called it "the holy grail" of reality TV, both entertaining viewers and allowing them to learn something about themselves, critics say that such programs "use people's financial struggles for entertainment and reinforce the belief that some deserve to be poor." A similar program planned by the BBC also resulted in a petition, signed by over 26,000, to cancel it (Sagan, 2015). In a similar critique of exploitation, Glendora Meikle (2013) wrote:

> Poverty porn is a well-established trope in media-studies circles. Violent deaths. Bone-chilling rapes. Diseases that leave bodies ravaged and mutilated. Hunger that is evident in the rib cages of small children. These ubiquitous images practically define today's perception of humanitarian work. By comparison, quality-of-life issues elicit little more than a yawn. If no one's dead or dying, there are more compelling causes beckoning.

And as Ali Heller (2013) put it:

> In the world of foreign aid and nonprofit fundraising, organizations are all too often engaged in a race-to-the-bottom of suffering, fighting tooth and nail for a limited pot of money. Good-hearted donors want their money to go the furthest, to make the most difference. So, organizations championing fistula, cleft palette, leprosy, AIDS, domestic abuse, malnutrition (the list goes on) engage in a battle of the superlative pitiable – all making one claim: Our victims are the most deserving; Our victims suffer the most. And anyone with any basic understanding of economics could guess what happens next, organizations compete for donors, reporters compete for readers, and victims become more and more pitiable. A hungry child will no longer do – now the child must be on the verge of death. An abused woman no longer merits attention – now she must be the victim of savage, rifle gang rape.[4]

So we come up against several difficult questions. First, how do we engage in a global conversation (after all, we are told there is a "global public sphere") about the tragedies – manmade and natural – that afflict the people of the world when these problems linger on and on, a bit of progress here, a bit of disaster there, so that people are well-enough informed of their global dimensions without sentimentalizing or sensationalizing them? Second, is sensationalizing them to gain attention more or less unethical than ignoring them altogether or failing to establish them as discussion topics on the world stage? Third, is this one place where the individualistically-oriented ethical perspectives of the West butt up against the collectivist ethical sensitivities of the East? Is it appropriate for a Western reporter to decide whether to report, or how to report, on such realities on his or her own, or should the global collective demand a more holistic and comprehensive stance to allow the planet's seven billion citizens to participate in determining solutions or ameliorations for such issues? When we discuss "social responsibility" here, how large is the social? Meikle (2013) writes:

> I don't believe we've yet found the best way to talk about these complex issues. And that's on us. But two takeaways that strike me most are: the academic criticisms we revel in look different when applied to the realities of aid work; and we need to become better storytellers.

Fourth, if we cannot determine a means to report these stories without resorting to "poverty porn," or if "poverty porn" itself seems a likely outcome of the effort to tell these stories, when does it become unethical to speak out, or ethical to object to the means used to highlight an issue? Can we believe those who say that "poverty porn" provides the means to others for introspection and choices made, or to respond effectively to the source of the porn, or should we merely condemn them for the exploitation of others' situations for the purpose of profit and audience size? Can these two issues even be separated?

This seems a perfect place to use Rawls' "veil of ignorance." If we did so, would it help untangle this knot of self-interest, suffering, exploitation, and profit? Or does Rawls' social contract theory (with its consequentialist bent) disqualify the insights because such grinding poverty and accompanying grief and medical problems are too significant, too foundational, in people's lives to be able to comprehend their significance?

Aid organizations often exploit the poorest of the poor to raise donations to actually respond to them. Is this inevitable given the distribution of wealth around the planet? Should those who hear the pitches from these organizations, which themselves can sometimes seem incessant and impossible to deal with, be excused for not responding with donations in every case? There is income distribution at work here – but at what appropriate level? How much generosity is enough – or is there no limit on it as long as people are suffering?

Finally, should the media merely react to significant events (an earthquake, a report, a UN vote or newly established millennium goal), or should they concentrate on the systemic, intractable, confusing, reality of the world's inequalities and provide forums for a truly global conversation?

Case 13.4: Achieving a Peaceful Planet

One of the most chronic problems of the world is conflict, already discussed in an earlier chapter. The flip side of conflict is peace – or the absence of conflict. There are two aspects to this. The first is the role of the media in reducing potential conflict, The second is the media's role in reporting on conflict in such a way that peace, rather than conflict, may prevail.

There are many institutionalized approaches to talking about conflict around the globe. Obviously various news media outlets talk about conflict as specific news items: these items are tied to particular events in particular places where conflict is occurring. Other institutionalized approaches include the photojournalistic essay, the documentary, the feature-length film, the television drama or comedy, the talk show on radio or television, the first-person essay or blog, the poem or song, the stage production, or even everyday conversation. Each of these forms of discourse have their own dynamic, each has various connections to the conflict and to those who encounter the mediated container within their own context. The conflict itself has varying salience within different societies and each of the containers tell the story of the conflict, or report the specifics of the conflict, using different conventions and frames:

> Conflict discourse systems are ways of thinking, talking, and acting with regard to issues that threaten key interests central to imagined (utopian) or actual ways of life in the news community. Some conflict discourses are highly ephemeral, others deeply rooted and enduring, and they are constantly interacting, reinforcing or diluting one another in everyday conversations about news events and are, to an important extent, observable in the text of mass media news reports.
>
> *(Arno, 2012, location 405)*

In August 2015 the Council on Foreign Relations mapped more than 30 ongoing conflicts occurring in the world outside the United States.[5] Many of these conflicts had been going on for dozens of years, many with periodic flare-ups of violence. Many of these conflicts, too, are outside the interest of news media – with the exception of local media in the area of conflict itself – until a particularly egregious event signals to the media that they should pay enough attention to report on it. While such attention may meet the standards of engagement of media driven by reaction to events, it also violates standards of what is called peace journalism. Peace journalism sees such reactive practices as having impacts on the conflict reported in this way, but in a negative sense: "By reporting in a manner that gives undue attention to violence, journalists' reports may actually spawn a new chain of violent behaviour in a perpetuating feedback loop" (Suchenwirth and Keeble, 2011/2013, p. 169). Others seem to agree: "Conventional coverage of conflicts is constantly and consistently marred by overly dramatic and sensational reporting due to structural, economic and professional traits of journalism" (Mandelzis and Peleg, 2009, p. 79).

If reporters who go to war almost become celebrities as Kunda Dixit claims, and their reports subsequently "cover the war as a series of battles, . . . count[ing] the body bags and chronicl[ing] the carnage" (quoted in C. Wilson, 2010), then it is little wonder that the general perception of conflict itself is that it does, or will eventually, result in widespread destruction and death. And the continuing nature of conflict, as well as the ongoing conflicts themselves, such as the Arab-Israeli disputes, the Eastern Congo flare-ups, the tension along the India–Pakistani border and clashes over Kashmir, the ethnic conflicts in Indonesia and China, provide an unflattering picture of the world as perhaps only one step from chaos. Even the quadrangular conflict among the American Congress, the Obama administration and its partners, the Israeli government, and Iran, even in the absence of actual war (at least in August 2015), is discussed in the same frame as war, using the same language and zero-sum logic. U.S. president Obama's speech on the issue, as reported by Reuters, put issues of congressional approval in stark terms: "Let's not mince words. The choice we face is ultimately between diplomacy and some form of war" (Edwards and Chiacu, 2015).

One response to such war journalism is the peace journalism we have already mentioned, based in the work of Johan Galtung and championed by Jake Lynch. Peace journalism abandons the use of objectivity as a means to seeking truth on the basis that objectivity is not an actual practice but merely a smokescreen for doing business as usual – that is, war journalism. Lynch argues that news is a systematic process, inhabiting and upholding its own set of conventions for representing the world. But this approach, which fails to recognize that such conventions are not inevitable or even the result of a process of elimination in which the "best" approach won out, ignores many of the realities of conflict in favor of certain approaches that are seen as normal (see Lynch, 2008, p. 8).

One glaring deficiency in war journalism, according to Lynch, is its failure to recognize the pervasiveness and perniciousness of propaganda. "Meaningful discussion of media in conflict is impossible without considering propaganda, and to form a useful understanding of propaganda it is essential that these [news] categories be seen as dynamic – the site of constant construction and contestation – rather than as givens" (Ibid.). Peace journalism is a reflective activity, asking not only what the facts are (as any journalist would do), but "how these particular facts, as distinct from a practically infinite number of others 'out there,' come to meet them; and how they, the reporters, come to meet these particular facts. If it's always the same facts, or the same kind of facts, what consequences follow, for the nature of representation produced?" (Ibid., p. 9).

Commentary on Case 13.4

Objectivity as a practice developed in the United States and Western Europe, and has spread around the globe. Although it is more of an ideal than a reality, it is based on individualistic notions of responsibility and the effort to assure that an individual's biases are minimized in the reporting of news. Aristotle might refer to objectivity as a virtue, one to be pursued as a mark of character. Kant might refer to it as a deontological necessity if news is to be trusted as an accurate representation of truth. The utilitarian might ask, "What is the alternative? Isn't seeking objectivity more likely to result in more good than not seeking it?" These may all seem to indicate a level of social responsibility in journalistic practice.

But the collectivist might say, "Wait. If conventional practices in reporting conflict privilege some people's opinions or activities over others, isn't that a violation of the equal dignity of humankind? Why are official views more salient than unofficial ones?" To which the defender of objectivity may say, "Those in authority have the power to act. Make things change. Others may have equally valid opinions, but they aren't able to act on them or sign treaties or agreements to implement them. Some opinions or positions are more equal than others. That's reality."

This may seem an unending debate. How it is resolved (not solved) may be a function of the ethical stance taken: whether holding individuals responsible for their actions as media practitioners is more or less important than maintaining the integrity and inclusiveness of community. Even this is fraught with difficulty, however. People can be members of multiple communities whose requirements are different. In the 1994 Rwanda genocide trials, for instance, several Roman Catholic priests were indicated by the International Criminal Court, or tried in Belgium, or even sentenced to death by traditional Rwandan village courts (see Research Directorate, 2008). At least three nuns were also convicted for their part in the genocide ("Rwanda nun jailed over genocide," 2006), along with the former head of the Seventh-Day Adventist Church in western Rwanda and his son (Simons, 2003).

Members of religious communities who also see themselves as members of an ethnic community (in this case, Hutu) had to choose which dictate to follow. Their religious community clearly demanded "Thou shalt not kill," while the most radical elements of their Hutu community demanded the opposite. They could not respond positively to both expectations: they had to choose which of these communities would take precedence. Those who were convicted of complicity in the genocide were held accountable using individualistic ethics – and law that holds individuals accountable for their actions. But they were also guilty of betraying one of their communities – a collectivist ethical taboo without the legal repercussions.

A further complication in this instance is that many of the victims of the genocide were also members of the same religious (and sometimes ethnic) communities of those who slaughtered them. Some of the religious perpetrators would have been the priests or pastors of those they assisted in murdering.

It seems clear that assisting a genocide that took the lives of more than 800,000 people in 100 days, mostly in face-to-face encounters of unmitigated brutality, was not socially responsible. Death at the hands of incensed mobs, egged on by rhetoric declaring victims to be non-human, is not justified by any ethical system (see Fortner, 2006). At the same time, however, the betrayal of vows, religious tradition, even "God's law," is likewise abhorrent from a collectivist standpoint even without legal consequences. This goes unmentioned in news reports of convictions, thus discounting the significance of betrayal of community. Is this socially responsible?

Conclusion: What Is To Be Done?

Lynch (2008, p. 12) reminds us that "the world we encounter is partly of our own making." We live in symbolic worlds where meanings are learned in community, where what is valued or despised is not internally, but externally, determined and then incorporated into personal systems of belief, valuing, and responsibility. Can an entire community be held responsible for the actions of those within it, especially when they are being egged on by members of that same community? The choice to serve one community over another may be the result of the previous salience of lessons learned within the dominant community. Karl Jaspers (2000) attempted to address this issue in his lectures to German citizens after the atrocities of the Second World War – the question of collective guilt. Adolf Eichmann's defense at his trial in Jerusalem for participation in the Holocaust likewise raised this issue: he was merely a cog in a machine whose workings were defined by others and to whom he reported as a good soldier (Arendt, 1992).

What does it mean, then, to be human? Individualist ethicists talk about human rights: rights that we have merely by existing. We have rights to life, to liberty, to health, to clean water, adequate food . . . the list goes on. Often, however, even where such ethics are paramount there are claims that the continuance of institutions, clans, races, ethnicities, matter more than the rights of individuals. Rights to land propel conflicts that result in human death and expulsion, the destruction of both individuals and communities. What is the maximal value, that which must always prevail in a conflict? Is it life itself or personal responsibility or the survival of the whole?

Clifford G. Christians (2010b, p. 18) argues that there is a different way to look at such issues. Rather than the individualist ethos of Western ethics he suggests that humans be seen as essentially communal entities. Because people are "dialogic agents within a language community," their existence, identity, and value is not individualistic, even when they are individually held accountable for their actions. They are enmeshed in the community-created and maintained symbolic world that makes it possible for them to continue life itself. Judith Butler (2010, p. 44) writes: "if my survivability depends on a relationship with others, to a 'you' or a set of 'yous' without whom I cannot exist, then my existence is not mine alone, but is to be found outside myself, in this set of relations that precede and exceed the boundaries of who I am." Although Christians does not put it quite this way, he does write: "In enhancing rather than suppressing the spiritual dimension [of humanity], a thicker understanding of humans-as-relational emerges, and a normative strategy is made transparent for acting on the ethics of non-violence. Not only is the liberal self reductionistic, but its secular context prevents it from seeing humans in holistic terms" (Christians, 2010b, p. 19). He continues:

> Secular culture . . . lives dangerously by shutting out transcendent meaning. . . . Spirituality opens an imaginative journey into the secrets and mysteries of human meaning. Culture is thus considered an historically transmitted pattern of meanings embodied in symbols, and meaning is the fundamental ingredient in human cultures. For spirituality, communication describes the process of creating meanings. Communication is seen as the human attempt to uncover significance in life.
>
> *(Christians, 2010b, p. 21)*

This is not a call to lift one religious or spiritual tradition above another. Even while the conflict between religions makes for a convenient journalistic focus, it is not relevant here. It is the spiritual dimension of human experience within every religious community that demands that we take account of it. In doing so we are able to discern the significant cultural meanings that such a community creates and celebrates within it. There is a spiritual dimension to the Hutu community as well as the Roman Catholic or Adventist one. This dimension animates the meaning that its inhabitants use in making sense of their world (see Taylor, 1963, p. 45).

So the important ethical issue is not the struggle between one community's definition of responsibility as against another, but how a spiritual community that celebrates its survival and flourishing in difficult circumstances abandons its commitments to humanity under the propagandistic hammering of the most radically anti-human elements within it. Before the first machete is raised in anger the community has already dissolved as the symbolic constructs that undergird it have broken under the force of rhetorical excess. As soon as members of a community begin castigating scapegoats or encouraging the destruction of the "other," they have violated their own spiritual existence. They have surrendered their own humanity in a fabric of atrocity that subsequently collects the blood of the innocent. To the extent that media participate in this process of redefinition and destruction of the "face" of the other, they are culpable (as they were in Rwanda) as agents of evil.

We can extend this claim, we think, to all intractable human problems, from sex trafficking to hunger, ethnic cleansing to genocide, climate change to witchcraft. In every case some subset of the human race are portrayed as unimportant. The hungry can starve. Island residents can simply move onto higher ground. People can be pressed into slavery or tricked into becoming sex slaves by others who refuse to see their true human-ness defined in human terms. Judith Butler argues this in the case of war but it is equally valid in all of the chronic problems of human beings.

> If wars . . . perpetuate a way of dividing lives into those that are worth defending, valuing, and grieving when they are lost, and those that are not quite lives, not quite valuable, recognizable or, indeed, mournable, then the death of ungrievable lives will surely cause enormous outrage on the part of those who understand that their lives are not considered to be lives in any full and meaningful sense.
>
> *(Butler, 2010, p. 42)*

These are the hungry, sick, homeless, trafficked, enslaved, separated from their homeland, raped, left in misery. It is not merely a violation of their rights that is at issue – as individualistic philosophies would have it – but the rights of human beings as a whole. We degrade the most deeply embedded notion of humanity when such practices are allowed, or promoted in any way, by media. So long as we merely report, or document, or tell stories, of the plight of one subset of human beings, we utterly fail to understand what is at stake. It is not "their" problem; it is "our" problem. It is our face that is scarred, our innocence corrupted, our reality distorted by representations that completely miss the reality in favor of short-term sensationalism that can lead to compassion fatigue and, thus, our own diminishing stature as human beings (see Levinas, 1981).

Discussion Questions

1   It is certainly easier to ignore intractable problems than to deal with them in the media. Whether it is through fictive or non-fictive storytelling, the stories are often depressing and can lead to what has been called "compassion fatigue." This may result in lost audiences, a particular problem for commercially driven media. Do such media have a social responsibility to confront the intractable even when solutions seem unachievable?

2   How should the media encourage their audiences to care about people far away and unknown? Or is that a social responsibility that they should be pressed to accept?

3   Regardless of one's own ethical orientation (individualist or collectivist), is there a global social obligation to care for those from other traditions? Should two traditions be thought of as equals in global affairs, or should one of them be considered superior?

Notes

1   See http://www.worldbank.org/en/news/press-release/2015/03/09/breaking-the-cycle-of-chronic-poverty-in-latin-america-and-the-caribbean. Accessed July 24, 2015.
2   See http://www.wessexghnetwork.org.uk/news/news-archive/2014/march/chronic-poverty-report.aspx. Accessed July 25, 2015.
3   See http://wikiprogressafrica.blogspot.com/2014/03/the-chronic-poverty-report-2014-2015.html; http://www.plaas.org.za/bibliography/chronic-poverty-2014; http://devinit.org/#!/post/focusing-chronic-poverty; http://hesp-news.org/2014/03/11/the-chronic-poverty-report-2014-2015-the-road-to-zero-extreme-poverty/; https://cafodpolicy.wordpress.com/2014/03/19/the-chronic-poverty-report-and-post-2015-matching-policy-with-peoples-lives/. Accessed July 25, 2015.

4 CNN carried a piece with the headline "A fate worse than death for scores of African women," to report on the issue of women suffering from fistula. "By sketching profiles of several sufferers, the reporter guided readers who had likely never heard of the condition to understand that fistula's effects are social and psychological, in addition to merely physical. The piece garnered more than half a million page views – a huge win for awareness" (Meikle, 2013). But Ali Heller, a doctoral student in anthropology who was writing a dissertation on fistula patients in Niger, asked in a blog titled "The race to the bottom and the superlative sufferer" (Heller, 2013), "why must we highlight the extreme cases when the norm is bad enough?" Meikle (2013) then said, "The piece was thought-provoking and challenging. And it was probably read by a few dozen people."

5 See http://www.cfr.org/global/global-conflict-tracker/p32137#!/. Accessed August 10, 2015.

14

Conclusion

Introduction

Media worldwide reach for point and purpose, their overall reason for being. This is the quest of all social institutions, though many of them have been functioning so long that they are taken for granted as the way things are. Preceding chapters have presented the idea that social literacy and public dialogue is the point and purpose. Media bring to readers and viewers greater capacity to communicate with others, who, in turn, communicate to rippled circles of others, all engaging in rituals leading to interpretations and meanings. These chapters have insisted that the best media – media which both stabilize and transform social connections – operate within two moral poles: freedom and responsibility.

By now it should be clear that media act responsibly only when people do. When people act ignobly, selfishly, or maliciously, the media they operate do likewise. The flourishing life is both free and responsible, and flourishing requires quality media as monitor and expositor. The flourishing life is free to create, critique, explore, and invest. The good life can neither be slave nor fool, lacking a voice or incoherent. A good life, humanly speaking (our own point and purpose), cannot be programmed to think falsely or deceive others into doing so, apart from our own cooperation. As Pamela Meyer (2015) puts it, "A lie has no power whatsoever by its mere utterance. Its power emerges when someone else agrees to believe the lie." Life, to flourish, must be free to make mistakes and propose corrections. At one time people sincerely believed that the planet was flat. In the modern age people impute no moral blame to them, as long as they made corrections when new evidence emerged that contradicted this belief. If today we met committed members of the International Flat Earth Society, we would rightfully suggest that they rethink their conclusions. Prolonged belief in discredited ideas is the shared fault of isolated minds and irresponsible media. John Milton, the great seventeenth-century British poet, urged tolerance for mistakes and respect for corrections in the "free marketplace of ideas." His trust was in the innate capability of every person to chew an idea until it proved itself to be either nurturing or poisonous. As his own people were in rebellion at the time against the British monarch Charles I, Milton wrote in phrases now immortal: "Let her [truth] and falsehood grapple; Who ever knew Truth put to the worse, in a free and open encounter?"[1]

Many freedom-seekers have echoed those sentiments, longing for a day in their communicative lives when a new idea or new interpretation could be broadcast without suffering intimidation or threats of violence. When Milton wrote, media (institutions of public discourse) were grappling with the state, whose army and law-making powers weighed heavily in any power equation. The media, in Milton's classical liberalism, were the bulwark of truth (the people's common voice) against ruling powers and divine-right kingdoms; free and responsible media needed to be nurtured lest the open marketplace of ideas be overruled by arbitrary authority. But countries continue to defy Milton's expectations for a free media. The internet is controlled by cutting it off or erecting firewalls; journalists are jailed, killed,

World Media Ethics: Cases and Commentary, First Edition. Robert S. Fortner and P. Mark Fackler.
© 2018 John Wiley & Sons, Inc. Published 2018 by John Wiley & Sons, Inc.

or exiled; social media sites are shut down or used to identify activists for punishment. Even in ostensibly free media environments, corporate owners seek to wring every last bit of profit from their investments, giving little thought to altruism or ethical pro-social uses. The media in these countries only provide possibilities for exploitation, sensationalism, or cheap news and entertainment plots, or retelling stories that will over-dramatize or caricature people to gain ratings or circulation. And this, of course, is so they can attract advertisers and increase shareholder value. Human dignity – who needs it? Protection of the innocent – irrelevant. Truth-telling – not if twisting the truth makes for a more colorful and compelling tale.

Case 14.1: Freedom vs. Responsibility

Freedom and responsibility were foremost in the minds of Standard Publishing's managing editors when we arrived at the Nairobi office on Mombasa Road.[2] Our purpose was to conduct a conversation about the role of investigative journalism during the first year of Kenya's fourth president, His Excellency Uhuru Kenyatta, son of the nation's founding president, Mzee Jomo Kenyatta. Our presumption was that investigative journalism in a young democracy such as Kenya, as in any democracy at any age, is essential for political accountability.

We might say that investigative energy in a nation's press corps is a better indicator of democratic maturity than traditional (Western) markers such as balloted elections and power-balanced branches of a federal system. Indeed, those traditional markers have come under criticism in the work of economist Paul Collier, who examines why balloting as a process for choosing leaders has not worked so well for the "bottom billion," including most people in sub-Saharan Africa, where control of armies and banks by long-term incumbents overrules whatever "fair and free" elections may determine to be the people's will (Collier, 2009). In Kenya, the story of "democratic" elections has been single-party rule, open bribery, the chilling effect of the queue system of voting, political parties funding street violence, and the more mundane contortions of stuffing or losing ballot boxes and choosing crony officials as vote counters. Kenya's 2007 national elections became a debacle of corruption and killing, for which the current president had been indicted by the International Criminal Court (see Case 12.1). One irony of that indictment was the United States' (not an ICC signatory) advice to the Kenyan people not to elect Mr. Kenyatta in 2012. Uhuru's campaign urged Kenyans to show the United States it should mind its own business. Kenya responded enthusiastically to that appeal.

Despite these common yet complex political machinations, Kenya as a developing democracy desperately needs improved infrastructure, security, food reserves, reliable power, and citizen-friendly, dependable law enforcement. The press, we thought, would be tracking developments in these tangible areas of national concern, as Hague prosecutors built their case against the newly elected president. Was the press following the foreign aid, the money, the new road projects, and other government initiatives, all of which would require probing avenues into which an earlier generation of media editors feared to tread?

Our research plan that day in Nairobi was not conspiratorial, but rather, optimistic. The new government was not overtly strong-handed. The president carried the demeanor of wealth (which he certainly possessed) and class (yet to be determined). When the research began, Kenyatta had not been portrayed in the press as an enemy of free speech or belligerent toward dissent. Kenyatta had not sent paid thugs to ruin presses or intimidated reporters with interrogations in secretive locations. These tactics of public opinion control were part of the country's past, we believed.

Surprisingly, leaders of Nairobi media reported a different media scene than we expected: very tough, intimidating, corrosive, and clever. So little had been said by government officials about newspaper investigations that we researchers felt the situation to be relatively free and relatively responsible. But the "so little said" part masked a culture of subversion and threat so "real" that reporters had been assigned armed guards. We asked, what are these private guards doing with firearms – intending to shoot government secret police? The mood in that editorial office was remarkable for its denial of the very freedoms we thought the press in Kenya had recovered. Editors were reluctant, suspicious, and cautious. So different from an earlier interview with one of Kenya's leading editorial cartoonists.

Not an investigative journalist, but a celebrity journalist whose readership far exceeds her word-based counterparts, "Celeste," the byline of Celestine Warimu, draws for *People* newspaper. Today *People* struggles to find its voice, a dwarf among the media giants *Nation* and *Standard*. In its heyday, *People* was the voice of radical dissent owned by hotelier and political activist Kenneth Matiba, who was so roughed up by prison guards and police during the regime of Daniel arap Moi (1978–2002) that he became unable to function without assistance.

Hit hard by libel suits and interim owners, *People* is now part of Mediamax, which also owns K24 television and Radio Kameme. Uhuru Kenyatta is associated with Mediamax, making *People* as close to an official state newspaper as one can read in Kenya. Celeste has brought pleasure to dreary pages with her woman's take on Kenyan culture, her drawing talent, and her rags-to-riches popularity.

Celeste was raised in western Kenya by a single mother whose vision for her daughter was far larger than social realities permitted. Mom urged Celeste to study and practice her drawing, despite the appeal of more secure study at universities offering Celeste entry. Those maternal urgings paid off. Celeste satirizes the political and social world of East Africa, as editorial cartoonists do, but with one deeply felt exception: no mocking or satirizing single women, their children, their aspirations, their accomplishments, or their potential for influence in the public sphere. Celeste will not play on the pervasive stereotype of the rural-illiterate "Wanjiku." Nor will she draw the stereotype of women kowtowing to sex-crazed men intent on their lascivious ways. She once stood down her editor, who wanted the next day's cartoon to show the leer of a political Big Man indelicately surveying up the skirt of a soon-to-be-bedded naïve young woman. "I don't draw cartoons I'd be embarrassed to have my daughter see," Celeste said. Her values reflect sympathies for women in a culture where marriage and child-bearing, minimal education and much field toil, are traditional norms. Celeste herself knows that world well, but her talent and wit have led her to a social status very few women enjoy. As for women in the editorial cartoon trade, she stands alone.

Commentary on Case 14.1

Hans Jonas describes persons as inherently valuable, the carriers of life, which itself is inherently valuable. Jonas grounded his high view of persons on an evidential basis open to scrutiny from all perspectives. Typically the champions of "life as supremely valuable" are found among proponents of religious faiths who ground their claims in theology proper. This is important grounding, but not universally reckoned, and in the academy, often closeted. Jonas taught that human responsibility is bounded by the irreducible sanctity of life itself, as a proto-norm, apart from theological or ontological arguments. You are alive, his readers must necessarily admit, and being alive obliges you to respect life above all. This obligation emerges from the "essential sufficiency of human nature, which we must posit as the enabling premise for any creative steering of destiny, and which is nothing other than the sufficiency . . . for truth, valuation, and freedom . . . a thing unique and stupendous to behold in the stream of becoming, out of which it emerged, which in essence it transcends." There is, Jonas argued, an "imperative of existence" which mandates that humankind "ought to be and to be watched over" as primal duty of people currently alive, mindful of generations coming (Jonas, 1984, pp. 33, 43). Nothing is morally permitted which jeopardizes human existence, though threats to life are well within human power. Retreating from the imperative of life and existence is immoral, impossible to justify. Of all human differentiations (race, wealth, education, gender, among others) none disqualifies a person from the dignity which life itself bestows.

Clifford Christians captured Jonas' imperative as a proto-norm, ungirding his appeal to a communitarian ethic with a universal mandate grounded in life itself:

> Natural reality has a moral claim on us for its own sake and in its own right. The philosophical rationale for human action is reverence for life on earth, for the organic whole, for the physical realm in which human civilization is situated. . . . Rather than generating an abstract conception of the good, the primal sacredness of life is a catalyst for binding humans universally into an organic whole. There is at least one primordial reality.
>
> *(Christians and Traber, 1997, pp. 6–7)*

With a "primordial" in place, a foundational claim incontrovertibly true, Christians avoided the Kantian abstraction, a mandate of logic, in favor of a universal claim that is as close to persons as the parenting phenomenon. Jonas observed that parents do not need to be taught the imperative of caring for offspring, anywhere in nature where nature requires care. James Q. Wilson noticed the same phenomenon in his work on ethics: a "most striking fact about human societies," he wrote, is that "children, no matter how burdensome, are not abandoned in large numbers" (Wilson, 1993, p. 15). The moral sense Wilson found to be a universal human attribute was not the product of logic, mind, nurture, or genetics. It is how human societies develop, he observed, and if one's eyes are open, it is plain to see.

"Plain to see?" Is it possible in a world so fragmented by race, ethnicity, and claims to righteous wrath? Are the labors of humanity so "plain to see" that denying certain verities is the denial of humanity itself?

In earlier chapters, we recalled the major positions (and their liabilities) of the great world ideals. We spoke with respect concerning "virtue ethics" whose first systematic thinkers were Aristotle and Confucius. Virtue ethics extolls courage, honesty, trustworthiness, and civility. Hardly a culture can survive (there are notable exceptions today, but tomorrow?) without practicing these common, sometimes rare, moral sentiments. Which virtues take priority will differ from culture to culture, as we have also seen, ranging the globe trying to find commonplaces. Virtue ethics well practiced helps us live with others, and with ourselves.

And we have reviewed deontological ethics, the moral norms that have seemed to many as incontrovertible, above discussion no matter the context, and worth any sacrifice. To avoid the mandate of reality is to deny reality, and that no thinking person can legitimately do. Thus the ethics of duty is a moral law written on every page of history and every façade of humanity's super-structures. We have explored duty ethics with respect, as is our duty in a book such as this.

Narrative ethics has shown up on these pages, the ethics of culture as it weaves its long tale of human flourishing and suffering. This is the ethics of the timeline, begun in ages past and "to be continued" as long as the sun's gases burn. Narratives find moral stepping stones in a community's account of its own search for them, thus they are less set in stone, as it were, and more resilient to the times they are remembered. Oddly but surely, the narratives which weave a culture's moral fabric are so frequently coherent with the duties and virtues told by others that one must often agree on a common human nature, as troublesome as such a concept is to postmodern mentality. Narratives speak to the tragedies of history, the Holocaust and the dividing of India and the wars of religion – and because of this shared memory of suffering, narrative ethics has power over the human heart that deontological proclamations often lack. One must conclude that human duties must be lived and suffered to be made practical and repeated and memorialized. The narrative is the key to the moral principle's survival.

Thus media themselves play their role in the development of public notions of right and wrong. For without media doing much of our public talking, we could not know what people living over the next mountain range cared about, thought about, or planned for. We would be stuck with the range of our own voices, and that is finally too small a range for any modern person.

Yet virtues, principles, and duties called "plain to see" are never quite as plain as the mind and heart wish. We prefer middle-range sentiments: visions of human flourishing that seem as if we, the people, have a common reach for a tangible horizon, a sense that life is meant to hold certain aspects. When absent, we hunt all the more for them. When imposed, we resist. When recommended, we examine. When found reliable, we adopt. When discredited, we expunge. We are adaptable sentient beings seeking "control beliefs" without ourselves being controlled by them, seeking moral ground on which to conduct the journey while sliding, slipping, and fast-stepping our way through the thicket. Describing the journey is the essential role of media.

Case 14.2: Defamation by Corporation

Not every news source is a journalist or professional communications worker. Nitin Mangal of Indore, India, was a financial analyst and thus an investigator in league with financial reports which aim to alert readers/viewers to markets' rising and falling. Mangal produced material for journalists to report. In August of 2012, his advice was SELL, and the company he targeted, Indiabulls Group, was not happy.

Two years went by. Then Mangal was picked up by police and taken on a five-day tour of Indian cities, along with an Indiabulls lawyer. Police told him the purpose of the trip was to gather information for a defamation case against him. Imagine, a potential defendant in litigation compelled by police to hunt for evidence against himself!

Reflecting on this "trip" for the press, Mangal claims the entire purpose was intimidation. One night, chained to his bed, he was threatened by the Indiabulls lawyer with physical harm if he refused to cooperate. Without being accused of a crime or named in a suit, Mangal was then jailed for 12 days in a suburb of New Delhi. "I feared for my life," he told the *Wall Street Journal.* "I didn't know what they would do to me" (Nayak et al., 2015).

Commentary on Case 14.2

Mangal's case is ongoing as we write. A court has threatened him with criminal violations which come with penalties amounting to seven years in prison. No doubt a long period of litigation will follow; long periods work in the interests of those with large lawyering staffs and no need to rush to judgment. It is a high price to pay for analyzing a financial situation and reporting the results of one's investigations, in one of the world's most vibrant economies.

One might conclude that there is no safe zone for truth in any direction, north to south, east to west. Indeed, many news agencies and other reporting companies have concluded that investigations are simply too expensive; the ROI (return on investment) is too weak; the corporate state too strong; the options too messy. If such a culture overruns the world's news bureaus, fear replacing fairness and balance, where will the people turn for perspective and commentary on the complexities they face? It is no time (nor will any time be the time) for the press to shuck its responsibility to public discourse, or neglect its freedom to pursue truth.

Responsibility will come as public institutions are made strong enough to defend open reporting of many voices, a dynamic public journalism granting voice to a culture's constituent groups, eager to present and clarify a culture's goals and values. Freedom to collect and publish news of the world will come as persons recognize their common assets and build for a common future. Motivation to do so needs no explanation: it is a given, "the human yearning for a lever long enough to move the earth."[3]

Concluding Remarks

We, of course, have not solved ethical quandaries in this book. Nor could we. If anything, we have made them more difficult by suggesting that many more factors be taken into account when confronting ethical issues in media practice than might otherwise have been imagined. No society provides perfect freedom for media activities, whatever guarantees might be written into constitutions. Those in society want, too much, to emulate the outside world, to judge their fellow citizens, and to hear their own opinions parroted by the media to accept whatever degree of freedom is actually practiced. And those in the media professions do not always feel they have the freedom to act responsibly, for they are working in an increasingly complex and competitive environment where media of every stripe and flavor are seeking eyeballs and eardrums so that they have sufficient resources to operate another day. And they face the competition of the amateur, the photographer, the citizen journalist, the YouTube channel creator and blogger who often have far more followers than any single media outlet – whatever the nature of the traditional media's content.

Ultimately it may be the amateurs who have the last say, who influence the most, who interact with those who have similar interests to their own, who are the influencers of the twenty-first century. And they, at least at this point, have little fear of ethical finger-pointing; they operate largely without institutional oversight. This is the next great challenge for media ethicists – holding the amateur to the same standards as traditional media have developed, tried, and tested. It will not be an easy task.

Discussion Questions

1   Are freedom and responsibility guiding principles for you in your life with media? Can you add a third? Or a clarification of the first and second terms?

2   Should standards and virtues apply to professional media workers and artists only, or to amateurs as well, even to social media creative artists?

3   Should media "codes of conduct" specify what freedoms and responsibilities media have – and should "codes" be enforced?

4   What keeps media from the extremes? (What is an example of an extreme?) What keeps media centered? (What is a proper "center"?)

5   If you were invited to give a speech at the International Association of Media Professionals, what three major points would you emphasize?

Notes

1 The short quotation is part of a larger classic statement on free speech: "The temple of Janus with his two controversial faces might now not unsignificantly be set open. And though all the winds of doctrine were set loose to play upon the earth, so Truth be in the field, we do injuriously be licensing and prohibiting to misdoubt her strength. Let her and falsehood grapple; Who ever knew Truth put to the worse, in a free and open encounter?" (Milton, 1644/n.d., p. 719).

2 The interviews were conducted in January 2014 by Levi Obonyo and Mark Fackler. Obonyo is a former *Standard* reporter.

3 This quotation, variously worded, is attributed by most sources to Archimedes (280–211 BC), the Greek mathematician and inventor.

Glossary

aporetic Skeptical, doubting, at a loss.

"clicktivism" Using digital media in such a way that social change and on-the-ground activism is encouraged and maintained. The activism promoted may have either positive or negative outcomes, including recruiting activists to participate in demonstrations, sit-ins, occupations or marches for particular causes, such as greater freedom or equality, or, alternatively, for anti-group hate speech or recruitment to terrorist organizations.

Da'ish (also Daesh) A pejorative term based on the name of ISIL, or ISIS, in Arabic: "al-Dawla al-Islamiya fi Iraq wa al-Sham." The "L" in ISIL is the Levant, the "S" is Syria. These acronyms and names are used interchangeably.

dysphemism The opposite of a euphemism. A euphemism is a milder or less direct way of referring to an idea or action that may be offensive. A dysphemism is a harsher or more direct way of referring to something that is otherwise inoffensive.

fetish A cultural term that refers to objects that are believed to have supernatural powers. Fetishes are usually human-made items that have been imbued with claims of power over people.

gulag A system of forced labor camps that were constructed under Joseph Stalin in the Soviet Union to house political prisoners or other "undesirables." They were located in some of the most inaccessible parts of the Soviet Union, especially Siberia.

hacktivism Using computers to enter computer systems without permission, including illegally, to disrupt activities based on those systems. This could include disrupting commercial transactions, government services, and surveillance systems, DoS (denial of service) attacks, redirecting people to other websites, installing viruses or bots on those who visit sites, or taking down a site altogether or replacing its landing page with slogans, pornography, satire, or other content.

hegemony Political or cultural influence, usually dominance, over alternative constructs as the result of more powerful actors or ideologies that claim superior legitimacy.

ICANN The Internet Corporation for Assigned Names and Numbers. This private-sector, non-profit corporation, created in 1986, has responsibility for coordinating the Internet Assigned Numbers Authority (IANA) that is critical to the operation of Domain Name Systems (DNS). It operates under a U.S. government contract. (See www.icann.org.)

intifada An Arabic word that can be translated as tremor, shivering, or shuddering. It is used as a term to describe Arab protests and uprisings against Israeli oppression, usually in the Gaza Strip or the West Bank. It is essentially aggressive non-violent resistance, although in two intifadas there was stone-throwing and building of barriers by Palestinian young people to slow Israeli military movement.

Knesset The single chamber legislative body of the State of Israel.

World Media Ethics: Cases and Commentary, First Edition. Robert S. Fortner and P. Mark Fackler.
© 2018 John Wiley & Sons, Inc. Published 2018 by John Wiley & Sons, Inc.

line of sight Refers to transmitter waves that can only travel from their point of origination to the horizon. VHF/FM radio waves are line of sight, whereas AM/MW/SW radio waves can all travel beyond the horizon.

narcissism An excessive concern for one's own situation or the pursuit of one's own ends (gratifications) at the expense of others' needs, or regardless of their situation.

net neutrality The demand for greater bandwidth to accommodate increasing numbers of Internet connections has led to different practices to control congestion and accommodate traffic paths. Net neutrality is a philosophy that seeks to have all data streams treated equally. Since some streams are more demanding on bandwidth than others (such as video streaming sites vs. static text sites, for instance), some internet service providers (ISPs) have argued that such sites should have preference. Net neutrality denies this argument.

panopticon Refers to a circular prison design by the British utilitarian philosopher Jeremy Bentham that had a central inspection house that allowed a single guard (or watchman) to observe all the prisoners from a single location. Bentham knew that the guard could not watch every prisoner at once, but argued that since no single prisoner would know when he was being observed, this would result in each prisoner assuming he was being watched and then modifying his own behavior on that assumption.

parrhesia A figure of speech in which the rhetor speaks candidly or asks for forgiveness for what he or she is about to say. A parrhesiast is often one who speaks truth to power, calling out corruption, lies or abuse of authority by a ruler.

teledensity Refers to the number of telephone connections for every 100 residents of a given area. It is a means to demonstrate the relative communicative ability of one country vs. another.

teleology Refers to philosophical systems or attempts to describe actions or justifications by the apparent purpose or goal that those who practice or use them had in mind when originally proposed. Since purposes for actions or beliefs are proposed by human beings, whatever those actions or beliefs are, are assumed to be designed to reach a particular goal.

trope Using figurative language – a word, phrase, or image – for impact or artistic effect. In more modern usage a trope is a commonly recurring literary or rhetorical (persuasive) device, motif, or cliché that provides a shorthand means to express an opinion or belief. In social media, tropes are referred to as memes.

YouTube streaming rate 240p/1040p HD YouTube provides different types of compression so that the computer monitors used to access it can show the content most clearly and without the need for buffering, which slows down the video stream. The 240p/1040p HD streaming rate refers to a very high resolution image provided by YouTube to monitors capable of showing it.

xenophobia The fear of the unknown, the strange, the foreign. It is usually applied to people (xenophobes) who fear others who are not like themselves. This applies to those of different races, beliefs, or countries outside of the xenophobe's experience.

References

"A bright flame: In memoriam: Alexander Solzhenitsyn." (n.d.). *Road to Emmaus*. X:2 (#37). 3–21.

ABC. (2005, April 2). "Internet suicide pacts lead to 30 deaths in Japan." TV Program Transcript. http://www.newprophecy.net/japansuicide.htm. Accessed June 26, 2015.

Agarwal, Bina. (1994). *A Field of One's Own: Gender and Land Rights in South Asia*. South Asian Studies 58. Cambridge, UK: Press Syndicate of the University of Cambridge.

Agence France-Presse in Lucknow. (2014, June 12). "Indian police 'gang-rape woman after she fails to pay bribe.'" *The Guardian*. http://www.theguardian.com/world/2014/jun/12/indian-police-gang-rape-uttar-pradesh. Accessed July 9, 2015.

Agence France-Presse. (2015, June 24). "Russian 'troll factory' sued for underpayment and labour violations." *The Guardian*. http://www.theguardian.com/world/2015/jun/24/russian-troll-factory-sued-underpayment-labour-violations-vladimir-putin. Accessed June 24, 2015.

Al-Attar, Mariam. (2010). *Islamic Ethics: Divine Command Theory in Arabo-Islamic Thought*. New York: Routledge.

Alexander, Jeffrey C. and Mast, Jason L. (2006). "Introduction: Symbolic action in theory and practice: the cultural pragmatics of symbolic action." *Social Performance: Symbolic Action, Cultural Pragmatics, and Ritual*. Jeffrey C. Alexander, Bernhard Giesen, and Jason L. Mast, Editors. New York: Cambridge University Press. 1–28.

Alfonso, Fernando, III. (2011, November 17). "Unhate: The unsettling images behind Benetton's latest controversy." *The Daily Dot*. http://www.dailydot.com/news/unhate-bennetton-campaign-controversy/. Accessed July 22, 2014.

Al-Ghoul, Asmaa. (2014, June 19). "Could kidnapping of Israeli boys lead to intifada?" Almonitor. http://www.usnews.com/news/articles/2014/06/19/could-kidnapping-of-israeli-boys-lead-to-intifada. Accessed June 27, 2014.

Al-Jazeera. (2014, June 23). "Egypt court sentences Al Jazeera journalists." http://www.aljazeera.com/news/middleeast/2014/06/egypt-finds-al-jazeera-journalists-guilty-201462373539293797.html. Accessed July 14, 2014.

Al-Jazeera. (2014, June 26). "Peter Greste decries Egypt court ruling." http://www.aljazeera.com/news/middleeast/2014/06/peter-greste-decries-court-ruling-2014625202834194433.html. Accessed July 14, 2014.

Al-Jazeera America. (2013, November 23). "Africa on the verge of Internet boom." *The Daily Ittefaq*. http://www.clickittefaq.com/sci-tech/africa-on-the-verge-of-internet-boom/. Accessed February 21, 2015.

Alleyne, M. (2009). "Global media ecology: Why there is no global media ethics standard." *The Handbook of Mass Media Ethics*. L. Wilkins and C. Christians, Editors. New York: Routledge.

Anderson, J. (2014, June 27). "A death in Benghazi." *The New Yorker*. http://www.newyorker.com/online/blogs/newsdesk/2014/06/salwa-bugaighis-libya-activist-death.html. Accessed June 30, 2014.

"Another RT anchor resigns: 'I'm for the truth.'" (2014). www.mediaite.com. Accessed July 18, 2014.

Ansah, P. (1996). *Going to Town*. Accra: Ghana Universities Press.

Anscombe, G.E.M. (1958). "Modern moral philosophy." *Philosophy*. **33**. 1–19.

Arendt, Hannah. (1992). *Eichmann in Jerusalem: A Report on the Banality of Evil*. Revised and enlarged edition. New York: Penguin Books.

Arnett, Ronald C. and Arneson, Pat. (1999). *Dialogic Civility in a Cynical Age: Community, Hope and Interpersonal Relationships*. Albany, NY: State University of New York Press.

Arno, Andrew. (2012). *Alarming Reports: Communicating Conflict in the Daily News*. New York: Berghahn Books. Kindle e-book edition.

"Art, ethics and social responsibility." (2011, November 17). http://rcad-ethics.blogspot.com/2011/11/benetton-unhate-kissing-ad-pulled-after.html. Accessed July 22, 2014.

Article 19. (n.d.). "Licensing of media workers." http://www.article19.org/pages/en/licensing-of-media-workers.html. Accessed May 18, 2014.

Article 19. (2002, April 27). "Right to communicate." http://www.article19.org/resources.php/resource/3074/en/right-to-communicate. Accessed July 16, 2014.

Artz, L. (2015). *Global Entertainment Media*. Malden, MA: Wiley-Blackwell.

Ashforth, Adam. (2005). "Muthi, medicine and witchcraft: Regulating 'African science' in post-apartheid South Africa?" *Social Dynamics*. **31**. 211–242.

Assadourian, Erik. (2007). "Advertising spending sets another record." *Vital Signs 2006–2007*. http://erikassadourian.com/wp-content/uploads/2013/12/VS06-15-advertising.pdf. Accessed October 6, 2014.

Associated Press. (2014, June 25). "North Korea would consider release of Seth Rogen, James Franco movie 'The Interview' an 'act of war.'" http://www.dailynews.com/general-news/20140625/north-korea-would-consider-release-of-seth-rogen-james-franco-movie-the-interview-an-act-of-war. Accessed August 12, 2014.

Austin, Ben S. (n.d.). "The Nuremberg Trials: Brief overview of defendants & verdicts." https://www.jewishvirtuallibrary.org/jsource/Holocaust/verdicts.html. Accessed September 3, 2014.

Austin, J.L. (1975). *How to Do Things with Words*. Second edition. J.O. Urmson and Marina Sbisá, Editors. Cambridge, MA: Harvard University Press.

Australian Council for International Development. (2014, March 13). "Chronic Poverty Report." http://www.acfid.asn.au/media/sector-news/chronic-poverty-report. Accessed July 25, 2015.

Bakshi, Amba Batra and Banerjee, Chandrani. (2013, January 14). "Rape happens." *Outlook*. http://www.outlookindia.com/article/rape-happens/283458. Accessed July 9, 2015.

Balaam, David N. and Veseth, Michael A. "Political economy." http://www.academicroom.com/topics/what-is-political-economy. Accessed July 15, 2014.

Bales, Kevin. (2012). *Disposable People: New Slavery in the Global Economy*. Updated. Oakland, CA: University of California Press.

Barry, Ellen and Choksi, Mansi. (2013, October 26). "Gang rape in India, routine and invisible." *New York Times*. http://www.nytimes.com/2013/10/27/world/asia/gang-rape-in-india-routine-and-invisible.html?_r=0. Accessed July 9, 2015.

Bartlett, T. (2001, February 20). "The case for play." *The Chronicle Review*. http://chronicle.com/article/The-Care-Fopr-Play/126382. Accessed November 18, 2013.

Baudrillard, Jean. (1998). "Simalacra and simulations." *Jean Baudrillard, Selected Writings*. Mark Poster, Editor. Redwood City, CA: Stanford University Press. 166–184.

Bauman, Zygmunt. (1993). *Postmodern Ethics*. Cambridge, MA: Blackwell.

"Bayer's unethical behavior in addition to Cipro poisoning." (2009, January 8). http://www. levaquinadversesideeffect.com/2009/01/08/bayers-unethical-behaviour/. Accessed March 5, 2015.

BBC. (n.d.). "Language when reporting terrorism: Summary." http://www.bbc.co.uk/guidelines/ editorialguidelines/page/guidance-reporting-terrorism-summary. Accessed August 14, 2014.

BBC. (2004, December 7). "Japan's internet 'suicide clubs.'" http://news.bbc.co.uk/2/hi/programmes/ newsnight/4071805.stm. Accessed June 26, 2015.

BBC. (2013, February 20). "Skin-whitening in Asia: Magic potion or poison?" http://www.bbc.com/news/ world-asia-21525456. Accessed February 26, 2015.

BBC News. (2014, June 19). "Dark net 'used by tends of thousands.'" http://www.bbc.com/news/ technology-27885502. Accessed 19 June 2014.

BBC News. (2014, June 23). "Who are the al-Jazeera journalists on trial in Egypt?" http://www.bbc.com/ news/world-middle-east-27943387. Accessed July 14, 2014.

BBC News. (2014, June 24). "Egyptian view differs on jailing of al-Jazeera journalists." http://www.bbc. com/news/world-middle-east-28004010. Accessed July 14, 2014.

Befrienders Worldwide. (n.d.). "Suicide Statistics." http://www.befrienders.org/suicide-statistics. Accessed June 25, 2015.

Bell, Richard H. (2002). *Understanding African Philosophy: A Cross-Cultural Approach to Classical and Contemporary Issues*. New York: Routledge.

Beller, Steven. (2013). *Democracy: All that Matters*. New York: McGraw-Hill Companies, Inc.

Benhabib, Jess and Bisin, Alberto. (2000). "Advertising, Mass Consumption and Capitalism." http://www. econ.nyu.edu/user/bisina/POMO9.pdf. Accessed October 5, 2014.

Bennett, W. Lance. (2004). "Global media and politics: Transnational communication regimes and civic cultures." *Annual Review of Political Science*. 7. 125–148.

Ben-Yehuda, Nachman. (2005). "Terror, media, and moral boundaries." *International Journal of Comparative Sociology*. **46**. 33–53.

Berlin, Isaiah. (1958 /2002). *Liberty: Four Essays on Liberty*. New York: Oxford University Press.

Bewaji, John Ayotunde Isola. (2006). "Ethics and morality in Yoruba culture." *A Companion to African Philosophy*. Kwasi Wiredu, Editor. Malden, MA: Blackwell Publishing. 396–403.

Bibby, Andrew. (2003). *Media, Entertainment & Arts: Global Concentration in the Media*. Nyon, Switzerland: Union Network International.

"Biden to test US face-saving retreat plan for Ukraine." (2014, April 21). *The Voice of Russia*. http:// voiceofrussia.com/news/2014_04_21/Biden-to-test-US-face-saving-retreat-plan-for-Ukraine-9126/. Accessed September 13, 2014.

"Big pharma spends more on advertising than research and development, study finds." (2008, January 7). *Science Daily*. http://www.sciencedaily.com/releases/2008/01/080105140107.htm. Accessed March 7, 2015.

Bilimoria, Pirusottama. (1993). "Indian ethics." *A Companion to Ethics*. Peter Singer, Editor. Malden, MA: Blackwell Publishing. 43–57.

Biletzki, A. (2011, July 17). "The sacred and the humans." *New York Times*. Quoted in Osborn (2015).

Bingham, T. (2010). *The Rule of Law*. London: Allen Lane.

Birnbaum, Michael. (2013, November 26). "Leakers, privacy activists find new home in Berlin." *Washington Post*. http://www.washingtonpost.com/world/europe/leakers-privacy-activists-find-new-home-in-berlin/2013/11/26/272dc7fc-4e1d-11e3-97f6-ed8e3053083b_story.html. Accessed June 22, 2015.

Bittman, Ladislav. (1985). *The KGB and Soviet Disinformation: An Insider's View*. New York: Pergamon Press.

Blake, Stephanie. (2011, November 18). "PR implications of Benetton's UNHATE campaign." http://www.reasonedpr.com/blog/pr-implications-of-benettons-unhate-campaign/. Accessed July 22, 2014.

Bloom, Paul. (2012). "Religion, morality, evolution." *Annual Review of Psychology*. **63**. 179–189.

Bok, Sissela. (1978). *Lying: Moral Choice in Public and Private Life*. New York: Pantheon Books.

Bok, Sissela. (1998). *Mayhem: Violence as Public Entertainment*. Reading, MA: Addison-Wesley.

Bonhoeffer, Dietrich. (1955). *Ethics*. Eberhard Bethge, Editor. Neville Horton Smith, Translator. New York: Touchstone.

Boorstin, Daniel. (1973). *The Americans: The Democratic Experience*. New York: Vintage Books.

Bourdieu, Pierre. (1998). *Masculine Domination*. Richard Nice, Translator. Stanford, CA: Stanford University Press.

Brooks, D. (2015, April 11). "The moral bucket list." *New York Times*. http://www.nytimes.com/2015/04/12/opinion/sunday/david-brooks-the-moral-bucket-list.html?emc=eta1. Accessed April 16, 2015.

Brown, B. (1977). "Face saving and face restoration in negotiation." *Negotiations: Social-Psychological Perspectives*. D. Druckman, Editor. Beverly Hills, CA: Sage.

Brown, Jeffrey. (2015, June 8). Interview with Adrian Chen on the Public Broadcasting System. http://www.pbs.org/newshour/bb/russian-trolls-spreading-online-hoaxes-u-s/. Accessed June 24, 2015.

Buber, Martin. (1986). *I and Thou*. Ronald Gregor Smith, Translator. New York: Charles Scribner's Sons.

Buncombe, Andrew. (2014, August 6). "'India gang rape' fashion shoot showing model being harassed on board bus sparks outrage." *The Independent*. http://www.independent.co.uk/news/world/asia/india-gang-rape-fashion-shoot-showing-model-being-harassed-on-board-bus-sparks-outrage-9651302.html. Accessed July 9, 2015.

Burke, Kenneth. (1966). *Language as Symbolic Action: Essays on Life, Literature, and Method*. Berkeley, CA: University of California Press.

Burroughs, James E. and Rindfleisch, Aric. (2002). "Materialism and well-being: a conflicting values perspective." *Journal of Consumer Research*. **29**. 348–370.

Butler, Judith. (2010). *Frames of War: When is Life Grievable?* Brooklyn, NY: Verso.

Carey, James W. (1989). *Communication as Culture: Essays on Media and Society*. New York: Routledge.

Carey, James W. (1995). "The press, public opinion, and public discourse." *Public Opinion and the Communication of Consent*. Theodore L. Glasser and Charles T. Salmon, Editors. New York: The Guilford Press. 373–402.

Carey, James W. (1996). "The Chicago School and mass communication research." *American Communication Research: The Remembered History*. Everette E. Dennis and Ellen Wartella, Editors. Mahwah, NJ: Lawrence Erlbaum Associates, Inc., Publishers. 21–38.

Carrim, Sabah. (n.d.). "Gang rape culprit: Indian men or man?" *Brickfields Law Review*. http://www.academia.edu/2347431/Gang_Rape_Culprit_Indian_men_or_Man. Accessed July 9, 2015.

Carville, Matty. (2011, December 1). "An Egyptian woman's nude revolution." Policy.Mic blog. http://mic.com/articles/2667/an-egyptian-woman-s-nude-revolution. Accessed September 7, 2014.

Castells, Manuel. (2012). *Networks of Outrage and Hope: Social Movements in the Internet Age*. Malden, MA: Polity Press.

Castillo, Gregory. (2015, May 7). "The week that cable news failed free expression." *Washington Post*. http://www.washingtonpost.com/blogs/erik-wemple/wp/2015/05/07/the-week-that-cable-news-failed-free-expression/. Accessed May 9, 2015.

Centre for Social Justice. (n.d.). http://www.socialjustice.org/index.php?page=gender-inequality. Accessed June 11, 2015.

Césaire, Aimé. (2000). *Discourse on Colonialism*. John Pinkham, Translator. New York: Monthly Review Press.

Chandhoke, Neera. (2015). *Democracy and Revolutionary Politics*. London: Bloomsbury Academic.

Chan-Olmsted, Sylvia M. and Chang, Byeng-Hee. (2003). "Diversification strategy of global media conglomerates: Examining its patterns and determinants." *Journal of Media Economics*. **16**: 4. 213–233.

Chappell, Timothy. (2012). "Aristotle." *Ethics: The Key Thinkers*. Tom Angier, Editor. New York: Bloomsbury Academic. 48–71.

ChartsBin. (2010). "Current Worldwide Suicide Rate." http://chartsbin.com/view/prm. Accessed June 25, 2015.

Cherry, K. (n.d.). "Kohlberg's theory of moral development." http://psychology.about.com/od/developmentalpsychology/a/kohlberg.htm. Accessed September 8, 2015.

"China to grant 'more' press passes – but journalists must sign secrecy deal first." (2014, July 15). *South China Morning Post*. www.scmp.com. Accessed July 16, 2014.

Chrisafis, Angelique. (2011, April 18). "Attack on 'blasphemous' art works fires debate on role of religion in France." *The Guardian*. http://www.theguardian.com/world/2011/apr/18/andres-serrano-piss-christ-destroyed-christian-protesters. Accessed June 5, 2015.

Christians, Clifford G. (2004). "*Ubuntu* and communitarianism in media ethics." *Ecquid Novi*. **25**: 2. 235–256.

Christians, Clifford G. (2010a). "Theories of morality in three dimensions." *Ethics and Evil in the Public Sphere*. R. Fortner and M. Fackler, Editors. Cresskill, NJ: Hampton Press.

Christians, Clifford G. (2010b). "Non-violence in philosophical and media ethics." *Peace Journalism, War and Conflict Resolution*. Richard Lance Keeble, John Tulloch, and Florian Zollmann, Editors. New York: Peter Lang. 15–30.

Christians, Clifford G. (2012). "Introduction." *Ethics for Public Communication: Defining Moments in Media History*. Clifford G. Christians, Mark Fackler, and John P. Ferré, Authors. New York: Oxford University Press. ix–xxv.

Christians, Clifford G. and Cooper, T. (2009). "The search for universals." *The Handbook of Mass Media Ethics*. L. Wilkins and C. Christians, Editors. New York: Routledge.

Christians, Clifford G. and Traber, Michael, Editors. (1997). *Communication Ethics and Universal Values*. Thousand Oaks, CA: Sage Publications.

Christians, Clifford G., Fackler, Mark, Richardson, K., *et al.* (2012). *Media Ethics: Cases and Moral Reasoning*. Ninth edition. Boston: Allyn & Bacon.

Christopherson, Susan. (2011). "Hard jobs in Hollywood: How concentration in distribution affects the production side of the media entertainment industry." *The Political Economies of Media: The Transformation of the Global Media Industries*. Dwayne Winseck and Dal Yong Jin, Editors. New York: Bloomsbury Academic. E-book. No page numbers.

Christy, B. and Stirton, B. (2015). "Tracking ivory." *National Geographic*. September. 30–59.

Chronic Poverty Advisory Network (CPAN). (2014). *The Chronic Poverty Report 2014–2015: The Road to Zero Extreme Poverty*. London: Overseas Development Institute.

CIA (Central Intelligence Agency). (n.d.). Uzbekistan: Government. https://www.cia.gov/library/publications/the-world-factbook/geos/uz.html. Accessed July 21, 2014.

"Cigarette giants in a global fight against tighter rules." (2010, November 14). *Jakarta Globe*. http://thejakartaglobe.beritasatu.com/archive/cigarette-giants-in-a-global-fight-against-tighter-rules/. Accessed February 22, 2015.

Ciochetto, Lynne. (2004, June 14). "Advertising and Globalisation in India." http://www.sasnet.lu.se/EASASpapers/7LynneCiochetto.pdf. Accessed October 3, 2014.

Clark, Meredith. (2013, March 1). "The new political prisoners: Leakers, hackers and activists." *Rolling Stone*. http://www.rollingstone.com/politics/lists/the-new-political-prisoners-leakers-hackers-and-activists-20130301. Accessed June 22, 2015.

Clayton, David. (2010). "Advertising expenditure in 1950s Britain." *Business History*. **52**. 651–665.

CLNT (Chinese Labor News Translations). (2010, June 3). "Chinese responses to Foxconn suicides." http://www.clntranslations.org/article/55/foxconn. Accessed June 10, 2015.

Clock. (2013, July 3). "Blogs – clock – confessions of a disinformation agent! Chapter 5." http://other. skepticproject.com/blog/79/confessions-of-a-disinformation-agent-chapter-5/. Accessed August 12, 2014.

CODESRIA (2008). "Africa and the global pharmaceutical industry." http://www.codesria.org/spip.php? article68. Accessed March 5, 2015.

Coen, Robert J. (n.d.). "U.S. Advertising Expenditure Data," written by Douglas Galbi from Coen's CS Ad Dataset. http://purplemotes.net/2008/09/14/us-advertising-expenditure-data/. Accessed October 6, 2014. Dataset available at https://docs.google.com/spreadsheet/ccc? key=0AnZb5H7tDMvTcDlMRU5haUtKZW95Qlg0ZVIxRlpFRXc#gid=0. Accessed October 6, 2014.

Cohen-Almagor, R. (1994). *The Boundaries of Liberty and Tolerance*. Gainesville, FL: University Press of Florida.

Collier, P. (2009). *Wars, Guns, and Votes: Democracy in Dangerous Places*. New York: Harper Perennial.

Committee to Protect Journalists (CPJ). (n.d.). "Our mission." http://www.cpj.org/about/video.php. Accessed July 21, 2014.

Committee to Protect Journalists (CPJ). (2008, June 10). "Journalist jailed on defamation, disinformation charges." http://cpj.org/2008/06/journalist-jailed-on-defamation-disinformation-cha.php. Accessed August 12, 2014.

Committee to Protect Journalists (CPJ). (2014, April 29). "Ten journalists to free from prison." http:// www.cpj.org/tags/muhammad-bekjanov. Accessed July 21, 2014.

"Communication – an essential human need." (n.d.). www.crisinfo.org. Accessed July 16, 2014.

Coonan, Clifford. (2014a, June 6). "China releases Tibetan filmmaker from jail after six years." http:// www.hollywoodreporter.com/news/china-releases-tibetan-filmmaker-jail-709815. Accessed February 5, 2017.

Coonan, Clifford. (2014b, April 27). "'Big Bang Theory' axed as China steps up censorship of overseas TV online." http://www.hollywoodreporter.com/news/big-bang-theory-axed-as-699197. Accessed February 11, 2017.

Cooper, Anneliese. (2014). "North Korea calls Seth Rogen's 'The Interview' an 'act of terrorism' but ignores these other parodies." http://www.bustle.com/articles/29351-north-korea-calls-seth-rogens-the-interview-an-act-of-terrorism-but-ignores-these-other-parodies. Accessed August 12, 2014.

C. R. (2013, November 5). "Making room for girls." *The Economist*. http://www.economist.com/blogs/ freeexchange/2013/11/gender-inequality. Accessed June 11, 2015.

Craig, D. and Ferre, J. (2010). "Agape in the service of journalism." *Ethics and Evil in the Public Sphere*. R. Fortner and M. Fackler, Editors. Cresskill, NJ: Hampton.

Cronin, Anne M. (2004). "Regimes of mediation: Advertising practitioners as cultural intermediaries?" *Consumption, Markets and Culture*. 7. 349–369. [Draft text doc: http://www.research.lancs.ac.uk/ portal/en/publications/regimes-of-mediation--advertising-practitioners-as-cultural-intermediaries% 28fdeb89df-6e86-4116-aab1-031ac5590f78%29/export.html. Accessed October 6, 2014.]

Croteau, David and Hoynes, William. (2006). *The Business of Media: Corporate Media and the Public Interest*. Second edition. Thousand Oaks, CA: Pine Forge Press.

Croteau, David and Hoynes, William. (2007). "The media industry: Structure, strategy and debates." *Media Studies: Key Issues and Debates*. Eoin Devereux, Editor. New York: Sage Publications Ltd. 32–54.

Dailey, William O., Hinck, Edward A., and Hinck, Shelly S. (2008). *Politeness in Presidential Debates: Shaping Political Face in Campaign Debates from 1960 to 2004*. Lanham, MD: Rowman & Littlefield Publishers, Inc.

D'Amato, David. (2014). "Bittorrent copyright trolls: A deficiency in the federal rules of civil procedure." *Rutgers Computer and Technology Law Journal*. **40**. No page numbers. http://www.lexisnexis.com. proxy.pba.edu/hottopics/lnacademic/?verb=sr&csi=152490&sr=TITLE%28BITTORRENT+ COPYRIGHT+TROLLS%3A+A+DEFICIENCY+IN+THE+FEDERAL+RULES+OF+CIVIL+ PROCEDURE%3F%29%2BAND%2BDATE%2BIS%2B2014. Accessed June 24, 2015.

Darley, William K. (2002). "Advertising regulations in sub-Saharan Africa." *Journal of African Business*. **3**. 53–67.

Darwall, Stephen L. (2003). "Theories of ethics." *A Companion to Applied Ethics*. R.G. Frey and Christopher Health Wellman, Editors. Malden, MA: Blackwell Publishing. 17–37.

Deng, Francis M. (1998). "The cow and the thing called 'what': Dinka cultural perspectives on wealth and poverty." *Journal of International Affairs*. **52**: 1. 101–129.

Deng, Francis M. (2007). "Southern Sudan and the Cultural Change of Governance." Paper presented at the Conference on the Current Peace and Security Challenges in the Horn of Africa. Organized jointly by the Centre for Policy Research and Dialogue and InterAfrica Group. March 12–13, Addis Ababa. 89–107.

Derné, Steve. (1995). *Culture in Action: Family Life, Emotion, and Male Dominance in Banaras, India*. Albany, NY: State University of New York Press.

Deshmukh, Sahar. (2014, January 17). "India's rape culture." http://www.aquila-style.com/focus-points/ indias-rape-culture/55861/. Accessed July 9, 2015.

De Silva, Padmasari. (1993). "Buddhist ethics." *A Companion to Ethics*. Peter Singer, Editor. Malden, MA: Blackwell Publishing. 58–68.

Deutsche Welle. (2014, June 18). "Japan bans child pornography, excepting manga drawings." http://www. dw.de/japan-bans-child-pornography-excepting-manga-drawings/a-17716818. Accessed June 18, 2014.

Diaz, Roberto Ignacio, Cheung, Dominic, and Lee, Ana Paulina. (n.d.). "How to know Hong Kong and Macau." http://scalar.usc.edu/anvc/travel-and-culture-in-hong-kong-and-macau/asias-skin-whitening-craze. Accessed February 26, 2015.

Dickens, C. (1837 /1970). *Oliver Twist*, quoted in *Respectfully Quoted*. Suzy Platt, Editor. Washington, DC: Library of Congress, 1989.

Digital Divide Institute. (n.d.). www.digitaldivide.org. Accessed July 15, 2014.

Dipio, D. (2007). "Religion in Nigerian home video films." *Westminster Papers in Communication and Culture*. 4: 1. 65–82. London: University of Westminster. http://www.westminster.ac.uk/__data/assets/ pdf_file/0003/20100/005WPCC-Vol4-No1-Dominica_Dipio.pdf. Accessed June 5, 2014.

Doctoroff, Tom. (2012, January 22). "Modern China's spiritual crisis: Does it exist?" http://www. huffingtonpost.com/tom-doctoroff/china-materialism_b_1222589.html. Accessed February 1, 2015.

Dolan, Angela. (2014, September 2). "Forget 'real beauty': Ads for skin-whitening beauty products just won't die." *Advertising Age*. http://adage.com/article/global-news/awful-ads-skin-whitening-products-die/294766/. Accessed February 24, 2015.

Doyo, Ma. Ceres P. (2013, October 17). "Poverty porn." *Philippine Daily Inquirer*. http://opinion.inquirer. net/63489/poverty-porn. Accessed July 25, 2015.

Drogin, B. (1995, May 21). "Malawi tries ex-dictator in murder." *Los Angeles Times*. http://articles. latimes.com/1995-05-21/news/mn-4491_1_tiny-malawi. Accessed June 30, 2014.

Dubey, Gaurav and Dubey, Bharati. (2014, March 25). "Dark side of Bollywood: Racism exists in Hindi film industry." *Mid-day*. http://www.mid-day.com/articles/dark-side-of-bollywood-racism-exists-in-hindi-film-industry/15180078. Accessed August 19, 2014.

Duncan, Jane. (2013, December 11). "South Africa's online trolls: To feed or not to feed?" http:// themediaonline.co.za/2013/12/south-africas-online-trolls-to-feed-or-not-to-feed/. Accessed June 24, 2015.

Dussel, Enrique. (2003). *Beyond Philosophy: Ethics, History, Marxism, and Liberation Theology*. Eduardo Mendieta, Editor. Lanham, MD: Rowman & Littlefield Publishers, Inc.

Edwards, Julia and Chiacu, Doina. (2015, August 5). "Obama defends Iran nuclear deal as U.S. diplomacy over war." Reuters. http://www.reuters.com/article/2015/08/05/us-iran-nuclear-obama-idUSKCN0QA1MG20150805. Accessed August 10, 2015.

Edwords, Frederick. (n.d.). "What is Humanism?" https://americanhumanist.org/what-is-humanism/edwords-what-is-humanism/. Accessed February 7, 2017.

"Ekweremadu to media: Reject Boko Haram propaganda." (2014, July 18). *Leadership Newspapers*. Leadership.ng. Accessed July 18, 2014.

Eltahawy, Mona. (2015). *Headscarves and Hymens: Why the Middle East Needs a Sexual Revolution*. New York: Farrar, Strauss & Giroux.

Eltantawy, Nahed and Wiest, Julie B. (2011). "Social media in the Egyptian revolution: Reconsidering resource mobilization theory." *International Journal of Communication*. **5**. 1207–1224.

Ericson, Edward E., Jr. (2009, October 10). "Re-entering the 'First Circle.'" The Wall Street Journal. http://www.wsj.com/articles/SB10001424052970204488304574431450891084972. Accessed June 5, 2015.

Ernstes, Casey. (2014, March 26). "Global health plays a major role in Third International Chronic Poverty Report." *Borgen Magazine*. http://www.borgenmagazine.com/global-health-plays-major-role-in-third-international-chronic-poverty-report/. Accessed July 25, 2015.

Estrin, James. (2014, May 8). "The real story about the wrong photos in #BringBackOurGirls." http://lens.blogs.nytimes.com/2014/05/08/the-real-story-about-the-wrong-photos-in-bringbackourgirls/?_php=true&_type=blogs&_r=0#/1/. Accessed July 22, 2014.

European Union. (2012, February 9). "EU statement on the sentence of the Uzbek editor Muhammad Bekjanov." http://eeas.europa.eu/delegations/vienna/documents/eu_osce/permanent_council/2012/20120209_901_sentence_of_the_uzbek_en.pdf. Accessed July 22, 2014.

Evans, C.S. (2015). *Why Christian Faith Still Makes Sense*. Grand Rapids, MI: Baker Academic.

Evans-Pritchard, E.E. (1940). *The Nuer: A Description of the Modes of Livelihood and Political Institutions of a Nilotic People*. Oxford: Clarendon Press.

Ewen, Stuart. (2001). *Captains of Consciousness: Advertising and the Social Roots of the Consumer Culture*. New York: Basic Books.

Express Tribune. (2016, July 17). "Revealing Qandeel's real identity put her life at risk." http://tribune.com.pk/story/1143410/sharing-blame-revealing-qandeels-real-identity-put-life-risk/. Accessed July 18, 2016.

Fackler, M. (1984). "Moral guardians of the movies." *Mass Media Between the Wars*. C. Covert and J. Stevens, Editors. Syracuse, NY: Syracuse University Press.

Fackler, M. (2014). "Religious ethics in the world." *Contemporary Media Ethics*. M. Land, K. Fuse, and B. Hornaday, Editors. Second edition. Spokane: Marquette Books. 75–87.

Fackler, M. and Obonyo, L. (2011). "Media and post-election violence in Kenya." *Handbook of Global Communication and Media Ethics*, vol. 2 West Sussex, UK: Wiley.

Faleiro, Sonia. (2013, January 1). "The unspeakable truth about rape in India." *New York Times*. www.njbullying.org. Accessed July 9, 2015.

Fanon, Frantz. (1963 /2004). *The Wretched of the Earth*. Richard Philcox, Translator. New York: Grove Press. Kindle e-book edition.

Fanon, Frantz. (1967). *Black Skin, White Masks*. Richard Philcox, Translator. New York: Grove Press. Kindle e-book edition.

Farhi, Paul. (2015, January 7). "News organizations wrestle with whether to publish Charlie Hebdo cartoons after attack." *Washington Post*. https://www.washingtonpost.com/lifestyle/style/

news-organizations-wrestle-with-whether-to-publish-charlie-hebdo-cartoons-after-attack/2015/01/07/841e9c8c-96bc-11e4-8005-1924ede3e54a_story.html?utm_term=.953dd332a1d0. Accessed January 8, 2015.

Farrow, Ronan. (2014, July 10). "Farrow: Why aren't YouTube, Facebook, and Twitter doing more to stop terrorists from inciting violence?" *Washington Post*. http://www.washingtonpost.com/posteverything/wp/2014/07/10/farrow-why-arent-youtube-facebook-and-twitter-doing-more-to-stop-terrorists-from-inciting-violence/?hpid=z11. Accessed August 19, 2014.

FBI. (2012, March 6). "Six hackers in the United States and abroad charged for crimes affecting over one million victims." https://www.fbi.gov/newyork/press-releases/2012/six-hackers-in-the-united-states-and-abroad-charged-for-crimes-affecting-over-one-million-victims. Accessed June 23, 2015.

Ferguson, Niall. (n.d.). *Empire: How Britain Made the Modern World*. New York: Penguin. Kindle e-book edition.

Fidalgo, Joaquim. (2008). "Journalists: To License or Not to License." Paper submitted to the Journalism Research and Education Section, IAMCR World Congress, July 20–25, Stockholm.

Fitch, Cynthia. (2003). *Crime and Punishment: The Psychology of Hacking in the New Millennium*. GSEC Practical Requirements (v.1.4b). Global Information Assurance Certification Paper. SANS Institute.

Flynn, A. (2014, July 5). "Ex-editor jailed in hacking case." *The Wall Street Journal*. http://online.wsj.com/news/articles/SB30001424052702304359004580008551658018496. Accessed July 9, 2014.

Fortner, Robert S. (2006). "Markers of evil." *International Journal of the Interdisciplinary Social Sciences*. **1**. 149–157.

Fortner, Robert S. (2013). "Truth in 2012 Presidential Campaign Advertising: Results from Content Analysis." Paper presented at the Annual Meeting of the Association for Practical and Professional Ethics, March 1–4, San Antonio, TX.

Foster, Michelle J. (2012). "Calling the Shorts: How Ownership Structures Affect the Independence of News Media." *A Report to the Center for International Media Assistance*. Available on www.academia.edu. Accessed July 16, 2014.

Foucault, Michel. (1983 –84). *The Courage of Truth. (The Government of Self and Others II)*. Lectures at the Collège de France. Frédéric Gross, Editor. Graham Burchell, Translator. London: Palgrave Macmillan.

Friedersdorf, Conor. (2014, August 11). "Counterterrorism and the English language." http://www.theatlantic.com/politics/archive/2014/08/the-war-on-terrorism-and-the-english-language/375834/. Accessed August 19, 2014.

Friend, Celeste. (2004). "Social contract theory." *Internet Encyclopedia of Philosophy*. http://www.iep.utm.edu/soc-cont/. Accessed November 5, 2010.

Fuller, Thomas. (2006, May 14). "A vision of pale beauty carries risks for Asia's women." *New York Times*. http://www.nytimes.com/2006/05/14/world/asia/14thailand.html?_r=0. Accessed February 26, 2015.

Fulu, Emma, Warner, Xian, Miedema, Stephanie, *et al.* (2013). *Why Do Some Men Use Violence Against Women and How Can We Prevent It? Quantitative Findings from the United Nations Multi-Country Study on Men and Violence in Asia and the Pacific*. Bangkok: UNDP, UNFPA, UN Women and UNV.

Geisler, Norman L. (2010). *Christian Ethics: Contemporary Issues & Options*. Second edition. Grand Rapids, MI: Baker Academic.

Ger, G. and Belk, R.W. (1999). "Accounting for materialism in four cultures." *Journal of Material Culture*. **4**: 2. 183–204.

Ghadirian, Abdu'l-Missagh. (2010). *Materialism: Moral and Social Consequences*. Oxford: George Ronald Publisher, Ltd.

Ghosh, Palash R. (2013, January 5). "Delhi gang-rape protests: What about the sex crimes against untouchable women?" *IB Times*. https://scholar.google.com/scholar?start=30&q=gang+rape+India&hl=en&as_sdt=0,23. Accessed July 9, 2015.

Gilligan, Carol. (1982 /1993). *In a Different Voice: Psychological Theory and Women's Development.* Cambridge, MA: Harvard University Press.

Giraldi, Philip. (2010, December 9). "Leaks and leakers." http://original.antiwar.com/giraldi/2010/12/08/leaks-and-leakers/. Accessed June 22, 2015.

Gladstone, Rick. (2015a, March 24). "Behind a veil of anonymity, online vigilantes battle the Islamic State." *New York Times*. http://www.nytimes.com/2015/03/25/world/middleeast/behind-a-veil-of-anonymity-online-vigilantes-battle-the-islamic-state.html?ref=topics. Accessed June 24, 2015.

Gladstone, Rick. (2015b, March 31). "Activist links more than 26,000 Twitter accounts to ISIS." *New York Times*. http://www.nytimes.com/2015/04/01/world/middleeast/activist-links-more-than-26000-twitter-accounts-to-isis.html?ref=topics&_r=0. Accessed June 24, 2015.

Glenn, Evelyn Nakano. (2008). "Yearning for lightness: Transnational circuits in the marketing and consumption of skin lighteners." *Gender & Society*. **22**. 281–302.

"Global ad spending growth to double this year." (2014, July 9). http://www.emarketer.com/Article/Global-Ad-Spending-Growth-Double-This-Year/1010997. Accessed September 26, 2014.

Glory Surgery. (n.d.). "Thailand whitening skin." http://www.glorysurgery.com/beauty/thailand-whitening-skin-14787/. Accessed February 26, 2015.

Gökçe, Osman Zeki, Hatipoğlu, Emre, Göktürk, Gökhan, *et al.* (2014). "Twitter and politics: Identifying Turkish opinion leaders in new social media." *Turkish Studies*. **15**: 4. 671–688.

Goldberg, Carey. (2006, February 8). "Materialism is bad for you, studies say." *New York Times*. http://www.nytimes.com/2006/02/08/health/08iht-snmat.html?_r=0. Accessed May 29, 2014.

Government Portal of the Republic of Uzbekistan. (n.d.). "Constitution." http://www.gov.uz/en/constitution/#a1844. Accessed July 21, 2014.

Gray, J. (2002). *Straw Dogs: Thoughts on Humans and Other Animals.* London: Granta.

Green, Adam. (2005, May 22). "Normalizing torture on '24'". *New York Times*. http://www.nytimes.com/2005/05/22/arts/television/22gree.html?pagewanted=all&_r=0. Accessed August 14, 2014.

Green-Simms, L. (2010). "The return of the Mercedes: From Ousmane Sembene to Kenneth Nnebue." *Viewing African Cinema in the Twenty-First Century*. M. Saul and R. Austen, Editors. Athens: Ohio University Press.

Greenberg, Brad A. (2014). "Copyright trolls and presumptively fair uses." *University of Colorado Law Review*. 85. No page numbers. http://www.lexisnexis.com.proxy.pba.edu/hottopics/lnacademic/?verb=sr&csi=139179&sr=TITLE%28COPYRIGHT+TROLLS+AND+PRESUMPTIVELY+FAIR+USES%29%2BAND%2BDATE%2BIS%2B2014. Accessed June 24, 2015.

Greenwald, Glenn. (2014). *No Place to Hide: Edward Snowden, The NSA, and the U. S. Surveillance State.* New York: Henry Holt & Company, Inc.

Grossberg, L. (2010). "James W. Carey and the conversation of culture." *Key Concepts in Critical Cultural Studies*. L. Steiner and C. Christians, Editors. Urbana: University of Illinois Press.

Guardian, The. (2014, January 18). "Gender inequality: For society to thrive, women must thrive." http://www.theguardian.com/commentisfree/2014/jan/19/observer-editorial-gender-equality-women. Accessed June 11, 2015.

Gurnow, Michael. (2014). *The Edward Snowden Affair: Exposing the Politics and Media behind the NSA Scandal.* Indianapolis, IN: Blue River Press.

Habermas, Jürgen. (2001). "Constitutional democracy: A paradoxical union of contradictory principles?" *Political Theory*. **29**: 6. 766–781.

Hafkin, Nancy J. (2000). "Convergence of concepts: Gender and ICTs in Africa." *Gender and the Information Revolution in Africa*. Eva M. Rathgeber and Edith Ofwoma Adera, Editors. Ottawa, Canada: International Development Research Centre. 1–15.

Hafkin, Nancy J. and Bay, Edna G. (1976). "Introduction." *Women in Africa: Studies in Social and Economic Change*. Nancy J. Hafkin and Edna G. Bay, Editors. Stanford, CA: Stanford University Press. 1–18.

Hallen, Barry. (2004). "Yoruba moral epistemology." *A Companion to African Philosophy*. Kwasi Wiredu, Editor. Malden, MA: Blackwell Publishing. 296–303.

Han, Sang-pil and Shavitt, Sharon. (1994). "Persuasion and culture: Advertising appeals in individualistic and collectivistic societies." *Journal of Experimental Social Psychology*. **30**. 326–350.

Hansen, Chad. (1983). *Language and Logic in Ancient China*. Ann Arbor, MI: University of Michigan Press.

Harlan, J. (1971). *Cohen v California*, 403 U.S. 15.

Harvey, David. (1989). *The Condition of Postmodernity: An Enquiry into the Origins of Cultural Change*. Cambridge, MA: Blackwell.

Hayden, Patrick. (2001). *The Philosophy of Human Rights*. Paragon Issues in Philosophy. St. Paul, MN: Paragon House.

Haynes, J. and Okome, O. (2000). "Evolving popular media: Nigerian video films." *Nigerian Video Films*. Revised and expanded edition. Athens: Ohio University Center for International Studies.

Held, Virginia. (2006). *The Ethics of Care: Personal, Political, and Global*. New York: Oxford University Press.

Heller, Ali. (2013, May 28). "The race to the bottom and the superlative sufferer." *Sai Hankuri: Fieldnotes from Niger*. http://anywherethewindblows.com/~niger/?p=822. Accessed July 25, 2015.

Hern, Alex. (2014, August 15). "Twitter suspends account which wrongly named Ferguson policeman." *The Guardian*. http://www.theguardian.com/technology/2014/aug/15/twitter-suspends-account-ferguson-policeman-michael-brown. Accessed June 23, 2015.

Herxheimer, Andrew, Lundborg, Cecilia S., and Westerholm, Barbra. (1993). "Advertisements for medicines in leading medical journals in 18 countries: A 12-month survey of information content and standards." *International Journal of Health Services*. **23**. 161–172.

Hindery, Roderick. (1996). *Comparative Ethics in Hindu and Buddhist Traditions*. New Delhi: Motilal Banarsidass Publishers Private Limited.

Hodal, Kate. (2013, October 27). "Thailand racism row now reignited by Unilever ad for skin-whitening cream." *The Guardian*. http://www.theguardian.com/world/2013/oct/27/thailand-racism-unilever-skin-whitening-cream-citra. Accessed February 26, 2015.

Hölldobler, B. and Wilson, E.O. (2009). *The Superorganism*. New York: Norton.

Holliday-Karre, E. (2008). "A simulation of truth: Reconciling gender in the media and the truth and reconciliation commission in South Africa." *The Journal of the Midwest Modern Language Association*. **41**. 1. 78–87.

Holpuch, Amanda. (2012, September 28). "Andres Serrano's controversial Piss Christ goes on view in New York." *The Guardian*. http://www.theguardian.com/artanddesign/2012/sep/28/andres-serrano-piss-christ-new-york. Accessed June 5, 2015.

Hopkins, Julian. (2014). "Cybertroopers and tea parties: Government use of the internet in Malaysia." *Asian Journal of Communication*. **24**: 1. 5–24.

Hopkins, Rob. (2012, January 10). "Film review: Why 'Thrive' is best avoided." http://www.resilience.org/stories/2012-01-10/film-review-why-%E2%80%98thrive%E2%80%99-best-avoided. Accessed August 12, 2014.

Horton, Scott. (2008, March 1). "How Hollywood learned to stop worrying and love the (ticking) bomb." *Harper's Blog*. http://harpers.org/blog/2008/03/how-hollywood-learned-to-stop-worrying-and-love-the-ticking-bomb/. Accessed August 12, 2014.

Hourani, George F. (1985). *Reason and Tradition in Islamic Ethics*. New York: Cambridge University Press.

Howe, Irving. (n.d.). "Lukacs and Solzhenitsyn." *Dissent*. http://www.dissentmagazine.org/files/Irving%20Howe%20on%20Lukacs%20and%20Solzhenitsyn.pdf. Accessed June 5, 2015.

Hsieh, Ying-chun and Hsieh, Ching-chun. (2010). "Chinese ethics, mass media, and the global development." *Ethics and Evil in the Public Sphere: Media, Universal Values and Global Development*. Robert S. Fortner and Mark Fackler, Editors. Cresskill, NJ: Hampton Press, Inc. 249–260.

Huizinga, J. (1938 /1950). *Homo Ludens*. Boston, MA: Beacon Press.

Hurthouse, Rosalind. (2009, Spring edition). "Virtue ethics." *Stanford Encyclopedia of Philosophy*. Edward N. Zalta, Editor. http://plato.stanford.edu/entries/aristotle-ethics/. Accessed November 5, 2010.

Hutchins Commission [Commission on Freedom of the Press]. (1947). *A Free and Responsible Press*. Chicago: University of Chicago Press.

Hyung, M. (1999). *Priest*, vol. 3 Los Angeles: Tokyopop.

Ignatieff, Michael. (1984). *The Needs of Strangers*. New York: Picador USA.

Ihara, Craig K. (2004). "Are individual rights necessary? A Confucian perspective." *Confucian Ethics: A Comparative Study of Self, Autonomy, and Community*. Kwong-loi Shun and David B. Wong, Editors. Cambridge, UK: Cambridge University Press. 11–30.

"In China, civic groups' freedom, and followers, are vanishing." (2015). *New York Times*. http://www.nytimes.com/2015/02/27/world/asia/in-china-civic-groups-freedom-and-followers-are-vanishing.html?emc=edit_th_20150227&nl=todaysheadlines&nlid=48963716&_r=5. Accessed May 23, 2015.

Independent, The. (2016, July 18). "Qandeel Baloch death: Brother of social media star in Pakistan suspected 'honour killing.'" http://www.independent.co.uk/news/people/qandeel-baloch-death-brother-of-social-media-star-arrested-in-pakistan-over-suspected-honour-killing-a7141141.html. Accessed July 18, 2016.

"Iraq report brings little solace to war-torn country." (2016, July 8). Al-Jazeera. www.aljazeera.com. Accessed July 15, 2016.

IRIN. (2007, February 7). "Pakistan: Fighting disinformation in polio campaign." http://www.irinnews.org/report/69975/pakistan-fighting-disinformation-in-polio-campaign. Accessed August 12, 2014.

Irvine, Dean. (2009, May 27). "The cultural contributors to suicide in Asia." CNN. http://edition.cnn.com/2009/HEALTH/05/26/asia.suicide/. Accessed June 25, 2015.

ITU (International Telecommunication Union). (2014). "ICT Facts and Figures. The World in 2014." Geneva, Switzerland.

Jackson, Richard. (2005). *Writing the War on Terrorism: Language, Politics and Counter-Terrorism*. New York: Manchester University Press.

Jain, Aditi. (2014, January 7). "Racism in 21st century India: The obsession with fair skin." *The Times of India*. http://timesofindia.indiatimes.com/nri/contributors/contributions/aditi-jain/Racism-in-the-21st-century-India-The-obsession-with-fair-skin/articleshow/28508975.cms. Accessed August 19, 2014.

James, Meg. (2013, June 5). "Global spending for media and entertainment to rise steadily." *Los Angeles Times*. http://www.latimes.com/entertainment/envelope/cotown/la-fi-ct-media-pwc-20130605-story.html. Accessed September 26, 2014.

Jaspers, Karl. (2000). *The Question of German Guilt*. E.B. Ashton, Translator. New York: Fordham University Press.

Jewell, John. (2014, August 13). "Dealing with graphic content is a moral minefield for journalists." http://theconversation.com/dealing-with-graphic-content-is-a-moral-minefield-for-journalists-30383. Accessed August 19, 2014.

Jin, Dal Yong. (2011). "Deconvergence and deconsolidation in the global media industries: The rise and fall of (some) media conglomerates." *The Political Economies of Media: The Transformation of the Global Media Industries*. Dwayne Winseck and Dal Yong Jin, Editors. New York: Bloomsbury Academic. E-book. No page numbers.

Johnson, Joel. (2011, February 28). "1 million workers. 90 million iphones. 17 suicides. Who's to blame?" *Wired*. http://www.wired.com/2011/02/ff_joelinchina/. Accessed June 10, 2015.

Jonas, H. (1984). *The Imperative of Responsibility*. Chicago: University of Chicago Press.

Joseph, Sarah. (2012). "Social media, political change, and human rights." *Boston College International and Comparative Law Review*. **35**: 1. 145–188.

Kamiya, Gary. (2007, April 10). "Iraq: Why the media failed." *Salon*. http://www.salon.com/2007/04/10/media_failure/. Accessed August 12, 2014.

Kaplan, Robert. (1996). *The Ends of the Earth: A Journey to the Frontiers of Anarchy*. New York: Vintage Books.

Kaplan, Temma. (2015). *Democracy: A World History*. New York: Oxford University Press.

Karenga, Maulana. (2004). *Maat: The Moral Ideal in Ancient Egypt*. New York: Routledge.

Karimi, Faith and Carter, Chelsea J. (2014, April 22). "Boko Haram: A bloody insurgency, a growing challenge." CNN. http://www.cnn.com/2014/04/17/world/africa/boko-haram-explainer/index.html. Accessed July 22, 2014.

Karkera, Tina. (2006). "The gang-rape of Mukhtar Mai and Pakistan's opportunity to regain its lost honor." *American University Journal of Gender, Social Policy & the Law*. **14**: 1. 163–176.

Keen, Andrew. (2015). *The Internet is Not the Answer*. New York: Atlantic Monthly Press.

Kellner, Menachem. (1993). "Jewish ethics." *A Companion to Ethics*. Peter Singer, Editor. Malden, MA: Blackwell Publishing. 82–90.

Kelly, Aidan, Lawlor, Katrina, and O'Donohoe, Stephanie. (2005). "Advertising ideology and the encoding of advertising meaning: An ethnographic and discursive approach." *Advances in Consumer Research*. **32**. 645–646.

Kelly, Georgia. (2011, December 28). "*Thrive*: Deconstructing the film." *Huffington Post*. http://www.huffingtonpost.com/georgia-kelly/thrive-film_b_1168930.html. Accessed August 12, 2014.

Kierkegaard, Søren. (1987). *Either/Or. (Part II)*. Howard V. Hong and Edna H. Hong, Translators and Editors. Princeton, NJ: Princeton University Press.

Kirkland, Alice. (2014, May 27). "EU project to explore media freedom and pluralism." https://www.indexoncensorship.org/2014/05/eu-project-media-freedom-pluralism/. Accessed February 5, 2017.

Kirtley, Jane. (2010). *Media Law Handbook*. Published by the Bureau of International Information Programs. http://iipdigital.usembassy.gov/st/english/publication/2011/04/20110428143515su0.4137776.html#axzz32ASjJeiH. Accessed May 18, 2014.

Kiss, Jemima. (2012, October 17). "Who controls the internet?" https://www.theguardian.com/technology/2012/oct/17/who-rules-internet. Accessed February 11, 2017.

Kitiyadisai, Krisana. (2005). "Privacy rights and protection: Foreign values in modern Thai context." *Ethics and Information Technology*. **7**. 17–26.

Koterski, Joseph W. (2001). "Introduction to the 2000 Edition." *The Question of German Guilt*, by Karl Jaspers. E.B. Ashton, Translator. New York: Fordham University Press. vii–xxii.

Krauss, Lawrence M. (2009). "War is peace: Can science fight media disinformation?" *Scientific American*. http://www.scientificamerican.com/article/war-is-peace/. Accessed August 12, 2014.

Kristof, Nicholas. (2014, May 3). "'Bring Back Our Girls.'" *New York Times*. http://www.nytimes.com/2014/05/04/opinion/sunday/kristof-bring-back-our-girls.html?_r=0. Accessed July 22, 2014.

Kruse, Shermin. (2014, July 24). "Iranians consumption of Western media, and the government's concessions." *Huffington Post*. http://www.huffingtonpost.com/shermin-kruse/iranians-consumption-of-w_b_5615714.html. Accessed June 5, 2015.

Kumar, Sanjay. (2010, July 29). "India's paid news problem." http://thediplomat.com/2010/07/indias-paid-news-problem/. Accessed May 28, 2014.

Kunert, Paul. (2011, November 24). "1,000 Chinese workers strike at Apple and IBM supplier." *The Channel*. http://www.channelregister.co.uk/2011/11/24/chinese_workers_strike/. Accessed June 10, 2015.

Kurtz, Paul. (1980). "Does humanism have an ethic of responsibility?" *Humanist Ethics: Dialogue on Basics*. Morris B. Storer, Editor. Buffalo, NY: Prometheus Books. 11–25.

Kushner, David. (2014, September 28). "The masked avengers." *The New Yorker*. http://www.newyorker.com/magazine/2014/09/08/masked-avengers. Accessed June 24, 2015.

Lago, Cláudio and Fernandez, Andrea Ferraz. (2011). "Journalism as a profession in Brazil." *Estudos em Comunicação*. **10**. 255–271.

Lai, Whalen. (2002). "Buddhist ethics in the absence of a civil religion – deconstructing civil society." *Chinese Ethics in a Global Context: Moral Bases of Contemporary Societies*. Karl-Heinz Pohl and Anselm W. Muller, Editors. Boston, MA: Brill. 137–166.

Lamont, Corliss. (1949). *Humanism as a Philosophy*. New York: Philosophical Library.

Lancia, Patricia. (2009). "The Ethical Implications of Monopoly Media Ownership." The Institute for Applied and Professional Ethics, Ohio University. http://www.ohio.edu/ethics/2001-conferences/the-ethical-implications-of-monopoly-media-ownership/. Accessed July 16, 2014.

Le, Vanna. (2014, May 7). "Global 2000: The world's largest media companies of 2014." *Forbes*. http://www.forbes.com/sites/vannale/2014/05/07/global-2000-the-worlds-largest-media-companies-of-2014/. Accessed September 26, 2014.

Le, Vanna. (2015, May 22). "The world's largest media companies of 2015." *Forbes*. http://www.forbes.com/sites/vannale/2015/05/22/the-worlds-largest-media-companies-of-2015/#fe7fa5b2b64e. Accessed June 30, 2016.

Lears, T.J. Jackson. (1983). "From salvation to self-realization: Advertising and the therapeutic roots of the consumer culture, 1880–1930." *The Culture of Consumption: Critical Essays in American History, 1880–1980*. Richard Wightman Fox and T.J. Jackson Lears, Editors. New York: Pantheon Books. 1–38. Reprinted in *Advertising & Society Review*. 2000. Muse.jhu.edu. Accessed October 6, 2014.

Lendman, Stephen. (2014, January 16). "Net neutrality: RIP?" http://www.veteranstoday.com/2014/01/16/net-neutrality-rip/. Accessed February 11, 2017.

Lent, J. (2010). "Manga in East Asia." *Manga: An Anthology of Global and Cultural Perspectives*. T. Johnson-Woods, Editor. New York: Continuum.

Levinas, Emmanuel. (1981). *Ethics and Infinity*. R.A. Cohen, Translator. Pittsburgh, PA: Duquesne University Press.

Li, Chenyang. (2002). "Revisiting Confucian jen ethics and feminist care ethics: A reply to Daniel Star and Lijun Yuan." *Hypatia*. **17**: 1. 130–140.

Li, Eric P.H., Min, Hyun Jeong, Belk, Russell W., *et al.* (2008). "Skin lightening and beauty in four Asian cultures." *Advances in Consumer Research*. **35**. 444–449.

Li, Xiaorong. (2001). "'Asian values' and the universality of human rights." *The Philosophy of Human Rights*. Patrick Hayden, Editor. Paragon Issues in Philosophy. St. Paul, MN: Paragon House. 397–408.

Liberman, Jonathan. (2013, September 27). "From Australia to Thailand – defending tobacco packaging laws against multinational tobacco industry lawsuits." McCabe Centre for Law and Cancer. http://www.mccabecentre.org/blog-main-page/from-australia-to-thailand.html. Accessed February 23, 2015.

Lim, Merlyna. (2012). "Clicks, cabs, and coffee houses: Social media and oppositional movements in Egypt, 2004–2011." *Journal of Communication*. **62**. 231–248.

Liu, Xi, Jia, Sixue, and Li, Fei. (2011). "Corporate social responsibility as a legitimate concern for Chinese enterprises: An analysis of media depictions." *Public Relations Review*. **37**. 207–216.

Lomasky, Loren E. (1987). *Persons, Rights, and the Moral Community*. New York: Oxford University Press.

Lossky, A. (1994). *Louis XIV and the French Monarchy*. New Brunswick, NJ: Rutgers University Press.

Louw, Dirk J. (1998). "Ubuntu: An African Assessment of the Religious Other." Paper delivered at the 20th World Congress of Philosophy, 10–16 August, Boston, MA. Ngkerk.org.za. Accessed February 22, 2011.

Lovin, R. (1995). *Reinhold Niebuhr and Christian Realism*. Cambridge, UK: Cambridge University Press.

Lu, Xing. (2000). "The influence of classical Chinese rhetoric on contemporary Chinese political communication and social relations." *Chinese Perspectives in Rhetoric and Communication*. D. Ray Heisey, Editor. Stamford, CT: Ablex Publishing Corporation. 3–24.

Luo, Chris. (2014, April 23). "Hongkongers clash with mainland parents after toddler urinates in Mong Kok Street." *South China Morning Post*. http://www.scmp.com/news/china-insider/article/1494356/hongkongers-clash-mainland-parents-after-allow-two-year-old. Accessed August 19, 2014.

Lynch, Jake. (2008). *Debates in Peace Journalism*. Sydney: University of Sydney Press.

MacIntyre, Alasdair. (2008). *After Virtue: A Study in Moral Theory*. Third edition. Notre Dame, IN: University of Notre Dame Press.

Mahbubani, Kishore. (2012). "The global village has arrived." *Finance and Development*. **49**: 3. 1–2.

Mandelzis, Lea and Peleg, Samuel. (2009). "War journalism as media manipulation: Seesawing between the second Lebanon war and the Iranian nuclear threat." *Peace Journalism in Times of War*. Peace and Policy, vol. 13. Susan Dente Ross and Majid Tehranian, Editors. New Brunswick, NJ: Transaction Publishers. 79–92.

Manwell, Laurie A. (2010). "In denial of democracy: Social psychological implications for public discourse on state crimes against democracy post-9/11." *American Behavioral Scientist*. **53**: 6. 848–884.

Marsh, James L. (2000). "The material principle and the formal principle in Dussel's ethics." *Thinking from the Underside of History: Enrique Dussel's Philosophy of Liberation*. Linda Martín Alcoff and Eduardo Mendieta, Editors. Lanham, MD: Rowman & Littlefield Publishers, Inc. 51–68.

Martin, Phillip. (2009, November 25). "Why white skin is all the rage in Asia." *Globalpost*. http://www.globalpost.com/dispatch/china-and-its-neighbors/091123/asia-white-skin-treatments-risks. Accessed February 24, 2015.

Matthewes, Charles. (2010). *Understanding Religious Ethics*. Malden, MA: Blackwell Publishing.

Matthews, J. (2008). "Suicide and the Japanese Media: On the Hunt for Blame." *Electronic Journal of Contemporary Japanese Studies*. Discussion Paper 7 in 2008. http://www.japanesestudies.org.uk/discussionpapers/2008/Matthews.html. Accessed June 26, 2015.

Mayer, Jane. (2008). *The Dark Side: The Inside Story of How the War on Terror Turned into a War on American Ideals*. Kindle e-book edition.

Mazza, Ed. (2014, August 12). "Australian boy, 7, poses for photo with severed head in Syria." *Huffington Post*. http://www.huffingtonpost.com/2014/08/12/australian-boy-severed-head_n_5670673.html. Accessed August 19, 2014.

McCain, C. (2013). "Nollywood, Kannywood, and a decade of Hausa film censorship in Nigeria." *Silencing Cinema: Film Censorship Around the World*. D. Biltereyst and R. Vande Winkel, Editors. New York: Palgrave.

McChesney, Robert W. (1997). "The global media giants: We are the world." http://fair.org/extra-online-articles/the-global-media-giants/. Accessed September 26, 2014.

McChesney, Robert W. (2001). "Global media, neoliberalism, and imperialism." *Monthly Review*. 52:10. http://monthlyreview.org/2001/03/01/global-media-neoliberalism-and-imperialism. Accessed May 28, 2014.

McChesney, Robert W. (2004a). "The political economy of international communications." *Who Owns the Media? Global Trends and Local Resistances*. Pradip N. Thomas and Zaharom Nain, Editors. New York: Zed Books. 3–22.

McChesney, Robert W. (2004b) "Making a molehill out of a mountain." *Toward a Political Economy of Culture: Capitalism and Communication in the Twenty-First Century*. Andrew Calabrese and Colin Sparks, Editors. New York: Rowman & Littlefield Publishers, Inc. 62–90.

McDougall, Andrew. (2013, June 4). "Skin lightening trend in Asia boosts global market." http://www.cosmeticsdesign-asia.com/Market-Trends/Skin-lightening-trend-in-Asia-boosts-global-market. Accessed February 24, 2015.

Medad, Batya. (2014, June 27). "Israeli media, again, humanizes Arab terrorists." JewishPress.com. Accessed June 27, 2014.

"Media reform needs wide consultations – Mandiwanzira." (May 30, 2014). *The Zimbabwean*. http://thezimbabwean.co/2014/05/media-reform-needs-wide-consultations/. Accessed February 11, 2017.

Meikle, Glendora. (2013, July 5). "Poverty porn: Is sensationalism justified if it helps those in need?" *The Guardian*. http://www.theguardian.com/global-development-professionals-network/2013/jul/05/poverty-porn-development-reporting-fistula. Accessed July 25, 2015.

Memmi, Albert. (2006). *Decolonization and the Decolonized*. Robert Bononno, Translator. Minneapolis, MN: University of Minnesota Press.

Meredith, Martin. (2005). *The Fate of Africa: From the Hopes of Freedom to the Heart of Despair*. New York: Public Affairs.

Merrill, J. (1974). *The Imperative of Freedom*. New York: Hastings House.

Meyer, Pamela. (2015, August). "How good leaders learn the truth." http://www.conversationagent.com/2015/08/how-good-leaders-learn-the-truth.html. Accessed November 29, 2016.

Mezlekia, N. (2000). *Notes from the Hyena's Belly*. New York: Picador.

Mezzofiore, Gianluca. (2011, November 18). "Benetton: A history of shocking ad campaigns." http://www.ibtimes.co.uk/benetton-history-shocking-ad-campaigns-pictures-252087. Accessed May 4, 2015.

Micó, Josep-Lluis and Casero-Ripollés, Andreu. (2014). "Political activism online: Organization and media relations in the case of 15M in Spain." *Information, Communication & Society*. **17**: 7. 858–871.

Miége, Bernard. (2004). "Capitalism and communication." *Toward a Political Economy of Culture: Capitalism and Communication in the Twenty-First Century*. Andrew Calabrese and Colin Sparks, Editors. New York: Rowman & Littlefield Publishers, Inc. 115–129.

Milton, John. (1644 /n.d.). "Areopagitica" in *Complete Poetry and Selected Prose of John Milton*. New York: The Modern Library.

Minow, Martha. (1998). *Between Vengeance and Forgiveness: Facing History after Genocide and Mass Violence*. Boston, MA: Beacon Press.

Mooney, Chris. (2014, February 14). "Internet trolls really are horrible people." *Slate*. http://www.slate.com/articles/health_and_science/climate_desk/2014/02/internet_troll_personality_study_machiavellianism_narcissism_psychopathy.html. Accessed June 24, 2015.

Moos, Julie. (2010, June 13). "5 reasons broadcasters pay licensing fees for stories and why it corrupts journalism." http://www.poynter.org/latest-news/top-stories/135226/5-reasons-broadcasters-pay-licensing-fees-for-stories-and-why-it-corrupts-journalism/. Accessed May 28, 2014.

Morano, Lou. (2002, February 26). Report filed for United Press International. http://www.propagandacritic.com/articles/examples.osi.html. Accessed August 12, 2014.

Morgenstern, Madeleine. (2014, August 11). "'That's my boy': Islamic State fighter tweets photo of his son holding a severed head." http://www.theblaze.com/stories/2014/08/11/thats-my-boy-islamic-state-fighter-tweets-photo-of-his-son-holding-a-severed-head/. Accessed August 19, 2014.

Mosco, Vincent. (2004). "Capitalism's Chernobyl?" *Toward a Political Economy of Culture: Capitalism and Communication in the Twenty-First Century*. Andrew Calabrese and Colin Sparks, Editors. New York: Rowman & Littlefield Publishers, Inc. 268–289.

Mouffe, Chantal. (2000). "Deliberative Democracy or Agonistic Pluralism?" *Reihe Politikwissenschaft 72*. Vienna, Austria: Institut für Höhere Studien (HIS).

Mpofu, Shepherd. (2013). "Social media and the politics of ethnicity in Zimbabwe." *Ecquid Novi: African Journalism Studies*. **34**: 1. 115–122.

Mujtabavī, Sayyid Jalāl al-Dīn. (2004). "Ethics in Islamic culture." *Ethics in Islam*. Behruz Rafiee, Compiler. Abolfazl Haghiri, Translator. Tehran: Al-hoda.

Munyaradzi, Mawere. (2011). "Ethical quandaries in spiritual healing and herbal medicine: A critical analysis of the morality of traditional medicine advertising in southern African urban societies." *PanAfrican Medical Journal*. http://www.panafrican-med-journal.com/content/article/10/6/full/. Accessed March 5, 2015.

Murray, C. (2014, June 30). "The trouble isn't liberals." *The Wall Street Journal*.

Murray, Senan. (2007, June 20). "Anger at deadly Nigerian drug trials." http://news.bbc.co.uk/2/hi/africa/6768799.stm. Accessed March 5, 2015.

National Film and Video Censors Board (NFVCB). (2002). *Film and Video Directory in Nigeria*. Abuja: NFVCB.

Nayak, D., *et al.* (2015, September 15). "Report landed analyst in jail." *The Wall Street Journal*. **C-1**.

Ndongmo, Kathleen. (2015, June 24). "Opinion: The rise of the African trolls." http://www.cp-africa.com/2012/04/15/opinion-the-rise-of-the-african-trolls-kathleen-ndongmo/. Accessed June 24, 2015.

Neem, J. (2015). "The common core and democratic education." *Hedgehog Review*. **17**: 2. 102–110.

New York Daily News. (2013). "'Dark is beautiful' movement takes on India's obsession with whiter skin." http://www.nydailynews.com/life-style/india-obsessed-white-skin-actress-article-1.1498783. See also http://womenofworth.in/dark-is-beautiful/. Accessed February 11, 2017.

Newslab. (2014). "Seth Rogen and James Franco's feud with North Korea over their future film 'The Interview' has reached new heights." http://newslab.us/article/north-korea-files-complaint-with-the-u-n-over-the-rogenfranco-film-the-interview/. Accessed August 12, 2014.

Ng, Marie, Freeman, Michael K., Fleming, Thomas D., *et al.* (2014). "Smoking prevalence and cigarette consumption in 187 countries, 1980–2012." *Journal of the American Medical Association*. **311**. 183–192.

Nhuyae. (n.d.). "No mud, no lotus." https://www.tumblr.com/tagged/skin-whitening. Accessed March 1, 2015.

Niebuhr, R. (1941). *Nature and Destiny of Man*. London: Nisbet.

Nisbett, Nicholas. (2007). "Friendship, consumption, morality: Practising identity, negotiating hierarchy in middle-class Bangalore." *Journal of the Royal Anthropological Institute*. **13**: 4. 935–950.

Noam, Eli. (2013). "Who Owns the World's Media?" Paper presented at the 41th Research Conference on Communication, Information and Internet Policy, September 27-29, George Mason University School of Law, Arlington, VA.

Novinite.com. (2014, May 16). "European Initiative for Media Pluralism opens Bulgarian unit." http://www.novinite.com/articles/160593/European+Initiative+for+Media+Pluralism+Opens+Bulgarian+Unit. Accessed May 18, 2014.

Odozor, Paulinus Ikechukwu. (2008). "An African moral theology of inculturation: Methodological considerations." *Theological Studies*. **69**: 3. 583+.

Okome, O. (2001). "The popular art of African video-film." http://www.nyfa.orgb/archivbe_detail_q.asp?type=3&qid+45&fid=6&year=2001&s=Summer. Accessed February 5, 2007.

Oladeji, Bayo. (2014, July 11). "Boko Haram: Western media misleading the world – Adefuye." *Leadership*. Leadership.ng. Accessed July 11, 2014.

Olinger, H.N., Britz, J.J., and Olivier, M.S. (2005). "Western privacy and Ubuntu – influences in the forthcoming Data Privacy Bill." www.psu.edu. Accessed February 22, 2011.

Ong, Aihwa. (1996). "Strategic sisterhood or sisters in solidarity? Questions of communitarianism and citizenship in Asia." *Global Legal Studies Journal*. **4**: 1. 107–135.

Ono, Sokyo. (1962). *Shinto: The Kami Way*. Boston, MA: Tuttle Publishing.

Orr, Deborah. (2014, September 26). "The internet has changed everything – and nothing." *The Guardian*. http://www.theguardian.com/technology/commentisfree/2014/sep/26/internet-changed-everything-nothing-serious-business. Accessed June 23, 2015.

Osborn, R. (2015). "The great subversion: The scandalous origins of human rights." *The Hedgehog Review*. Summer. 91.

Overdorf, Jason. (2012, December 28). "India: To stop rape, start at the top." *Globalpost*. http://www.globalpost.com/dispatch/news/regions/asia-pacific/india/121226/india-gang-rape-protests. Accessed July 9, 2015.

"Over the line, Smokey!" (2009, July 17). "'24' fictional character Jack Bauer important inspiration for Bush torture-makers." http://seesdifferent.wordpress.com/2009/07/17/24-fictional-character-jack-bauer-important-inspiration-for-bush-torture-makers/. Accessed August 14, 2014.

Oyekanmi, Lekan and Adigun, Bashir. (2014, July 14). "Activist Malala in Nigeria: 'Bring Back Our Girls.'" http://news.yahoo.com/activist-malala-nigeria-bring-back-girls-105937734.html. Accessed July 22, 2014.

Oxfam. (2014, March 20). "Is 'getting to zero' really feasible? The new Chronic Poverty Report." http://oxfamblogs.org/fp2p/is-getting-to-zero-really-feasible-the-new-chronic-poverty-report/. Accessed July 25, 2015.

Pakistan Today. (2014, June 6). "Govt constitutes committee to remove ambiguities in code of conduct for media." http://www.pakistantoday.com.pk/2014/06/06/govt-constitutes-committee-to-remove-ambiguities-in-code-of-conduct-for-media/. Accessed February 5, 2017.

Palzer, Carmen and Hilger, Caroline. (2001). "Media supervision on the threshold of the 21st century – structure and powers of regulatory authorities in the era of convergence." *IRIS plus: Legal Observations of the European Audiovisual Observatory. Issue 2001-8*. Strasbourg, France: European Audiovisual Observatory.

Pan, Elysia. (2013). "Beautiful White: An Illumination of Asian Skin-Whitening Culture." Thesis submitted in partial fulfillment of the requirements for graduation with distinction. Raleigh-Durham, NC: Duke University.

Pappu, S.S. Rama Rao. (2004). "Hindu ethics." *Contemporary Hinduism: Ritual, Culture, and Practice*. Robin Rinehart, Editor. Santa Barbara, CA: ABC-CLIO, Inc. 155–178.

Parfit, Derek. (2011). *On What Matters*. Volume 1. Samuel Scheffler, Editor. New York: Oxford University Press.

Parker, Kathleen. (2015, May 9). "Pamela Geller's abuse of free speech." *Washington Post*. http://www.washingtonpost.com/opinions/pamela-gellers-abuse-of-free-speech/2015/05/08/136f29d2-f5c3-11e4-bcc4-e8141e5eb0c9_story.html?hpid=z2. Accessed May 9, 2015.

Peperzak, Adriaan. (1993). *To the Other: An Introduction to the Philosophy of Emmanuel Levinas*. West Lafayette, IN: Purdue University Press.

Peregrino, Claudia P., Moreno, Myriam V., Miranda, Silvia V., *et al.* (2011). "Mercury levels in locally manufactured Mexican skin-lightening creams." *International Journal of Environmental Research and Public Health*. **8**. 2516–2523.

Perlroth, Nicole. (2014, August 14). "Anonymous hackers' efforts to identify Ferguson police officer create turmoil." *New York Times*. http://www.nytimes.com/2014/08/15/us/ferguson-case-roils-collective-called-anonymous.html?ref=topics&_r=0. Accessed June 23, 2015.

Perlroth, Nicole. (2015, April 10). "China is said to use powerful new weapon to censor internet." *New York Times*. http://www.nytimes.com/2015/04/11/technology/china-is-said-to-use-powerful-new-weapon-to-censor-internet.html?emc=edit_th20150411&nl=todaysheadlines&nlid=48963716&_r=0. Accessed April 11, 2015.

Perreault, G. (2014). "Islam is everywhere." *Journal of Media and Religion*. **13**: 2. 97–113.

Perrett, Roy W. (1998). *Hindu Ethics: A Philosophical Study*. Honolulu: University of Hawaii Press.

Peters, John Durham. (2005). *Courting the Abyss: Free Speech and the Liberal Tradition*. Chicago: University of Chicago Press.

Phillips, Michael. (2004). "Suicide prevention in developing countries: Where should we start?" *World Psychiatry*. **3**: 3. 156–157.

Phillips, Whitney. (2011). "Meet the trolls." *Index on Censorship*. **40**: 2. 68–76.

Polanyi, M. (1958). *Personal Knowledge*. Chicago: University of Chicago Press.

Poole, Anna K. (2015, March 11). "India bans documentary on New Delhi gang rape." *World*. http://www.worldmag.com/2015/03/india_bans_documentary_on_new_delhi_gang_rape. Accessed July 9, 2015.

Pottier, Johan. (2002). *Re-Imagining Rwanda: Conflict, Survival and Disinformation in the Late Twentieth Century*. New York: Cambridge University Press.

Preston, Ronald. (1993). "Christian ethics." *A Companion to Ethics*. Peter Singer, Editor. Malden, MA: Blackwell Publishing. 91–105.

Price, Monroe E. (2015). *Free Expression, Globalism, and the New Strategic Communication*. New York: Cambridge University Press.

PTI. (2015, July 7). "China, India played central role in global poverty reduction: UN report." *The Economic Times*. http://economictimes.indiatimes.com/news/politics-and-nation/china-india-played-central-role-in-global-poverty-reduction-un-report/articleshow/47971194.cms. Accessed July 25, 2015.

Radovic, Katarina. (2011, November 16). "Benetton's shocking UNHATE campaign." *Branding Magazine*. http://www.brandingmagazine.com/2011/11/16/benettons-shocking-unhate-campaign/. Accessed July 22, 2014.

Ramsey, Paul. (1950). *Basic Christian Ethics*. Louisville, KY: Westminster John Knox Press.

Rand, Ayn. (1964). *The Virtue of Selfishness: A New Concept of Egoism*. New York: Penguin Books.

Rapoza, Kenneth. (2012, May 29). "China official says country to top U.S. consumer market by 2015." *Forbes*. http://www.forbes.com/sites/kenrapoza/2012/05/29/china-official-says-country-to-top-u-s-consumer-market-by-2015/#1a48ae56aeba. Accessed July 17, 2016.

Rawls, John. (1971). *A Theory of Justice*. Cambridge, MA: Harvard University Press.

Razumovskaya, O. (2014, May 6). "Moscow curbs profanity." *The Wall Street Journal*. http://online.wsj.com/news/articles/SB20001424052702303417104579543933682775184. Accessed July 9, 2014.

"Reckless consumption depleting earth's natural resources." (2008, October 9). http://www.redorbit.com/news/science/1594776/reckless_consumption_depleting_earths_natural_resources/. Accessed October 3, 2014.

Recuber, Timothy. (2015). "Occupy empathy? Online politics and micro-narratives of suffering." *New Media & Society*. **17**: 1. 62–77.

Reinhart, A. Kevin. (2005). "Origins of Islamic ethics: Foundations and constructions." *Handbook of Palliative Care*. Second edition. Christina Faull, Yvonne Carter, and Lillian Daniels, Editors. Malden, MA: Blackwell Publishing. 244–253.

Reisinger, Don. (2011, October 20). "iPhone 4S parts cost $188, study finds." *c/net*. http://www.cnet.com/news/iphone-4s-parts-cost-188-study-finds/. Accessed June 10, 2015.

Research Directorate, Immigration and Refugee Board of Canada. (2008, March 6). "Rwanda: Involvement of members of the Roman Catholic clergy in the 1994 genocide." RWA102792.E. http://www.refworld.org/docid/49b92b279.html. Accessed August 12, 2015.

Reuters. (2012, September 18). "Benetton's 'UNHATE' ad campaign to target unemployed youth." Huffington Post. http://www.huffingtonpost.com/2012/09/18/benettons-unhate-unemployed-youth-unemployment_n_1892634.html. Accessed May 4, 2015.

Reuters. (2015, April 28). "ISIS kills five journalists." *The Jerusalem Post*. http://www.jpost.com/Middle-East/ISIS-kills-five-journalists-working-for-Libyan-TV-station-399379. Accessed April 29, 2015.

Richardson, Michael. (1994, November 24). "Rise in materialism prompts worry about a moral decline: With more money, fewer values?" *New York Times*. http://www.nytimes.com/1994/11/24/news/24iht-moral.html. Accessed February 1, 2015.

"Right to Communicate." (2002, April 27). https://www.article19.org/resources.php/resource/3074/en/Right%20to%20Communicate. Accessed February 5, 2017.

Riordan, Ellen. (2004). "Feminist theory and the political economy of communication." *Toward a Political Economy of Culture: Capitalism and Communication in the Twenty-First Century*. Andrew Calabrese and Colin Sparks, Editors. New York: Rowman & Littlefield Publishers, Inc. 417–433.

Rist, John M. (2002). *Real Ethics: Reconsidering the Foundations of Morality*. Cambridge, UK: Cambridge University Press.

Roberts, Dexter. (2014, May 14). "Detained Chinese journalists forced to make televised confessions." *Bloomberg Businessweek*. Mobile.businessweek.com. Accessed May 19, 2014.

Robie, David. (2014, May 20). "RSF 'information hero' fights new media law in Timor-Leste." *The Daily Blog*. thedailyblog.co.nz. Accessed May 19, 2014.

Robinson, Nick. (2014, July 18). "Noriega's beef with Call of Duty, or how US games consistently misrepresent history." http://theconversation.com/noriegas-beef-with-call-of-duty-or-how-us-games-consistently-misrepresent-history-29415. Accessed July 21, 2014.

Roman, D. (2015, July 23). "Foreign journalists go missing in Syria." *The Wall Street Journal*. A6.

Rondonuwu, Olivia and Bigg, Matthew. (2012, May 24). "Child addicts at heart of Indonesia anti-smoking suit." Reuters. http://www.reuters.com/article/2012/05/24/us-indonesia-smoking-idUSBRE84N0DF20120524. Accessed February 22, 2015.

Rooney, David. (2002, February 24). Review of "Suicide Club." *Variety*. http://variety.com/2002/film/reviews/suicide-club-1200551172/. Accessed June 26, 2015.

Rosaldo, M.Z. (1980). "The use and abuse of anthropology: Reflections on feminism and cross-cultural understanding." *Signs*. **5**: 3. 389–417.

Rosenbaum, Thane. (2005). *The Myth of Moral Justice: Why Our Legal System Fails to Do What's Right*. New York: Perennial.

Rosow, Stephen J. and George, Jim. (2015). *Globalization and Democracy*. Lanham, MD: Rowman & Littlefield Publishers, Inc.

Rothkopf, Joanna. (2014, September 4). "WHO publishes first global report on topic 'shrouded in taboo': Suicide." *Salon*. http://www.salon.com/2014/09/04/who_publishes_firstglobal_report_on_topic_shrouded_in_taboo_suicide/. Accessed June 24, 2015.

Roussinos, Aris. (2014, April 15). "Behead first, ask questions later: The disturbing social media of British jihadists." https://news.vice.com/article/behead-first-ask-questions-later-the-disturbing-social-media-of-british-jihadists. Accessed July 11, 2014.

Roy, Arundhati. (2009). *Field Notes on Democracy: Listening to Grasshoppers*. Chicago: Haymarket Books.

Rundle, Michael. (2011, November 17). "Benetton Unhate campaign: World leaders 'kiss' in new clothing adverts." *Huffington Post*. http://www.huffingtonpost.co.uk/2011/11/16/benetton-unhate-campaign-_n_1097329.html?ref=canada-living&ir=Canada%20Living#s477316title=Obama_and_Hu. Accessed July 22, 2014.

Rule, J. Editor. (1969). *Louis XIV and the Craft of Kingship*. Columbus: Ohio State University Press.

"Rwanda nun jailed over genocide." (2006, November 10). BBC News. http://news.bbc.co.uk/2/hi/6136192.stm. Accessed August 12, 2015.

Sachedina, Abdulaziz. (2005). "Islamic ethics: Differentiations." *Handbook of Palliative Care*. Second edition. Christina Faull, Yvonne Carter, and Lillian Daniels, Editors. Malden, MA: Blackwell Publishing. 254–267.

Sadig, Haydar Badawi. (2010). "Ustadh Mahmoud Mohamed Taha and Islamic reform: A story in the embodiment and communication of absolute individual freedom." *Ethics and Evil in the Public Sphere: Media, Universal Values and Global Development*. Robert S. Fortner and Mark Fackler, Editors. Cresskill, NJ: Hampton Press. 237–247.

Sagan, Aleksandra. (2015, July 2). "'Poverty porn' reality TV: Does it have the capacity to do good?" http://www.cbc.ca/news/arts/poverty-porn-reality-tv-does-it-have-the-capacity-to-do-good-1.3118791. Accessed July 25, 2015.

Said, Edward W. (1978). *Orientalism*. New York: Pantheon Books.

Said, Edward W. (1993). *Culture and Imperialism*. New York: Vintage Books.

Sandel, Michael J. (2009). *Justice: What's the Right Thing to Do?* New York: Farrar, Straus and Giroux.

Sands, Philippe. (2008). *Torture Team: Rumsfeld's Memo and the Betrayal of American Values*. New York: Palgrave Macmillan. Kindle e-book edition.

Sarkar, S.C., Lalwani, S., Rautji, R., *et al.* (circa 2003). "A Study of Victims of Sexual Offences in South India." http://medind.nic.in/jah/t05/i1/jaht05i1p60.pdf. Accessed July 9, 2015.

Scheid, Bernhard. (2002). "Shinto as a religion for the warrior class: The case of Yoshikawa Koretaru." *Japanese Journal of Religious Studies*. **29**: 3–4. 299–324.

Schmitt, John and Zipperer, Ben. (2006). "Is the U.S. a good model for reducing social exclusion in Europe?" *Post-Autistic Economics Review*. 40.

Schoenbaum, Alan. (2013, April 4). "Why Rackspace is suing the most notorious patent troll in America." http://www.rackspace.com/blog/why-rackspace-sued-the-most-notorious-patent-troll-in-america/. Accessed June 24, 2015.

Schubeck, Thomas L. (1993). *Liberation Ethics: Sources, Models, and Norms*. Minneapolis, MN: Augsburg Fortress.

Schultze, Q. and Badzinski, D. (2015). *The Essential Guide to Interpersonal Communication*. Grand Rapids, MI: Baker Academic.

Schut, K. (2013). *Of Games and God*. Grand Rapids. MI: Brazos.

Searle, John R. (1969). *Speech Acts: An Essay in the Philosophy of Language*. New York: Cambridge University Press. Kindle e-book edition. No page numbers.

Seko, Yukari. (2008). "'Suicide machine' seekers: Transgressing suicidal taboos online." *Learn Inquiry*. **2**. 181–199.

Shah, Salik. (2012). "Cinema, citizenship and the promise of the internet: A personal view from the Third World." http://jkalternativeviewpoint.com/jkalternate/?p=2657. Accessed July 16, 2014.

Shalby, Colleen. (2014, May 9). "'Bring Back Our Girls' photos on Twitter are not of missing Nigerians." http://www.pbs.org/newshour/rundown/bring-back-girls-photos-twitter-missing-nigerians/. Accessed July 22, 2014.

Shanghaiist. (2014, April 23). "Piss Gate: Mainlander toddler pees in Hong Kong street, uproar ensues." http://shanghaiist.com/2014/04/23/piss_gate_mainlander_toddler_pees_i.php. Accessed August 19, 2014.

Shankar, P. Ravi and Subish, P. (2007). "Fair skin in South Asia: An obsession?" *Journal of Pakistan Association of Dermatologists.* **17**. 100–104.

Sharma, Anuradha. (2013). "In Need of a Leveson? Journalism in India in Times of Paid News and 'Private Treaties.'" Reuters Institute Fellowship Paper, University of Oxford. https://reutersinstitute. politics.ox.ac.uk/about/news/item/article/in-need-of-a-leveson-journalism-in.html. Accessed May 28, 2014.

Shattuck, R. (1996). *Forbidden Knowledge.* San Diego: Harcourt Brace.

Shaw, Aaron and Benkler, Yochai. (2012). "A tale of two blogospheres: Discursive practices on the left and right." *American Behavioral Scientist.* **56**: 4. 459–487.

Shaw, Alison and Gray, A.L. (2009). "Quality of pharmaceutical print advertising in South Africa – assessment of reproductive health advertisements 2001–2005." *South African Family Practice.* **51**. 53–58.

Shears, Richard. (2014a, January 23). "Kangaroo court orders Indian woman to be gang-raped by 13 men for having a relationship with a man from another village . . . with 'judges' carrying out the punishment." *Daily Mail.* http://www.dailymail.co.uk/news/article-2544450/Kangaroo-court-orders-Indian-woman-gang-raped-13-men-having-relationship-man-village-judges-carrying-punishment. html. Accessed July 9, 2015.

Shears, Richard. (2014b, January 24). "'Go and enjoy yourselves': What tribal elder said before Indian gang rape victim was tied to a platform to be assaulted in view of entire village because of affair with a Muslim." *Daily Mail.* http://www.dailymail.co.uk/news/article-2545138/Go-enjoy-What-tribal-elder-told-men-latest-Indian-gang-rape-victim-tied-bamboo-platform-assaulted-view-entire-village.html. Accessed July 9, 2015.

Sherwin, Byron L. (1999). *Jewish Ethics for the Twenty-First Century: Living in the Image of God.* Syracuse, NY: Syracuse University Press.

Shibui, T. (2005). *Net Group Suicide by Seven Men and Women: Why 'Maria' Chose to Die. (Danjo Nananin Net Shinjū: Maria ha Naze Shindanoka)* Tokyo: Shinkigen-sha.

Shirky, Clay. (2011, January/February). "The political power of social media." *Foreign Affairs.* http://www. panzertruppen.org/documentos/pdf/3.pdf. Accessed May 28, 2015.

Shrader, John. (2013). "Folly of outrage: Talk radio's unethical and damaging business model." *Journal of Mass Media Ethics.* **28**. 289–292.

Silberschmidt, Margrethe. (2001). "Disempowerment of men in rural and urban east Africa: Implications for male identity and sexual behavior." *World Development.* **29**: 4. 657–671.

Simmel, Georg. (1903 /1950). "The Metropolis and Mental Life." *The Sociology of Georg Simmel.* Kurt Wolff, Translator. Adapted by D. Weinstein. New York: Free Press. 409–424. http://www.altruists.org/ static/files/The%20Metropolis%20and%20Mental%20Life%20%28Georg%20Simmel%29.htm. Accessed October 5, 2014.

Simon, P. (1994). *Freedom's Champion.* Carbondale, IL: Southern Illinois University Press.

Simons, Marlise. (2003, February 20). "Rwandan pastor and his son are convicted of genocide." *New York Times.* http://www.nytimes.com/2003/02/20/world/rwandan-pastor-and-his-son-are-convicted-of-genocide.html. Accessed August 12, 2015.

Singh, Vijai and Tanenhaus, Sam. (2013, June 12). "Leakers: Saints or villains?" *New York Times*. Timesvideo. http://www.nytimes.com/video/us/politics/100000002275534/saints-or-villains.html. Accessed June 22, 2015.

Siochrú, Seán Ó. (2004). "Global institutions and the democratization of the media." *Who Owns the Media? Global Trends and Local Resistances*. Pradip N. Thomas and Zaharom Nain, Editors. New York: Zed Books. 23–42.

Sirota, David. (2012, June 11). "Whistle-blowers vs. leakers." *Salon*. http://www.salon.com/2012/06/11/whistleblowers_v_leakers/. Accessed June 22, 2015.

Smadhi, Asma. (2014, February 12). "Journalist sanctioned after interview with terror suspect's father." *Tunisia Live*. http://www.tunisia-live.net/2014/02/12/journalist-sanctioned-after-interview-with-terror-suspects-father/. Accessed August 14, 2014.

Small, Jamie L. (2012). "Trafficking in truth: Media, sexuality, and human rights evidence." *Feminist Studies*. **38**: 2. 415–443.

Soh, Kelvin. (2010, May 26). "Apple supplier in damage control blitz after suicides." *Jakarta Globe*. http://thejakartaglobe.beritasatu.com/archive/apple-supplier-in-damage-control-blitz-after-suicides/. Accessed June 10, 2015.

South China Morning Post. (2014, July 17.) "Information gag is wrong – journalists have duty to report in the public interest." www.scmp.com. Accessed July 18, 2014.

Solzhenitsyn, Alexandr I. (2009). *In the First Circle: The First Uncensored Edition*. Harry T. Willets, Translator. New York: Harper Perennial.

"Southeast Asian journalists speak out for press freedom." (2014). https://globalvoices.org/2014/05/18/southeast-asian-journalists-speak-out-for-press-freedom/. Accessed February 5, 2017.

Sparks, Colin. (2000). "From dead trees to live wires: The internet's challenge to the traditional newspaper." *Mass Media and Society*. James Curran and Michael Gurevitch, Editors. London: Arnold. 268–292.

Speck, Sandra K. and Roy, Abhijit. (2008). "The interrelationships between television viewing, values and perceived well-being: A global perspective." *Journal of International Business Studies*. **39**: 7. 1197–1219.

Spencer, Richard. (2015, February 24). "Saudi Arabia court gives death penalty to man who renounced his Muslim faith." *The Telegraph*. http://www.telegraph.co.uk/news/worldnews/middleeast/saudiarabia/11431509/Saudi-Arabia-court-gives-death-penalty-to-man-who-renounced-his-Muslim-faith.html. Accessed November 21, 2015.

Stalk, George, Jr. (2011, June). "What the West doesn't get about China." *Harvard Business Review*. https://hbr.org/2011/06/what-the-west-doesnt-get-about-china. Accessed July 17, 2016.

Stengel, Richard. (2014, April 29). "Russia Today's disinformation campaign." Dipnote. https://blogs.state.gov/stories/2014/04/29/russia-today-s-disinformation-campaign. Accessed August 12, 2014.

Stewart, Will. (2012, April 23). "'Glorious nation of Kazakhstan salute Borat': Country ridiculed by comic now THANK him for tourist boom (after banning the film)." *MailOnline*. http://www.dailymail.co.uk/news/article-2134025/Glorious-nation-Kazakhstan-salute-Borat-After-banning-film-country-ridiculed-comic-THANK-tourist-boom.html. Accessed August 14, 2014.

Stone, Rupert. (2016, July 9.) "Chilcot lets media off hook for selling Iraq war." Al-Jazeera English. www.aljazeera.com. Accessed July 9, 2016.

Subbotovska, Iuliia. (2015, May 29). "Russia steps up propaganda push with online 'Kremlin trolls.'" *Huffington Post*. http://www.huffingtonpost.com/2015/05/29/russia-kremlin-trolls_n_7468036.html. Accessed June 24, 2015.

Suchenwirth, Lioba and Keeble, Richard Lance. (2011 /2013). "Oligarchy reloaded and pirate media: The state of peace journalism in Guatemala." *Expanding Peace Journalism: Comparative and Critical*

Approaches. Ibrahim Seaga Shaw, Jake Lynch, and Robert A. Hackett, Editors. Sydney: University of Sydney Press. 168–190.

Sudan Tribune Editorial Team. (2014, July 18). "Sudanese official says press censorship necessary for political stability." *Sudan Tribune*. www.sudantribune.com. Accessed July 18, 2014.

Sumal, Roop. (2014, April 15). "Bollywood and India's obsession with fair skin." Peter Law Group. http://peterlawgroup.com/bollywood-and-indias-obsession-with-fair-skin/. Accessed August 19, 2014.

Tan, David. (2012, September 18). "Who's the fairest of them all?" *Asian Scientist*. Editorial. http://www.asianscientist.com/2012/09/features/skin-whitening-products-asia-2012/. Accessed February 24, 2015.

Tandoh, Francis. (2015, May 16). "Ghanaian journalists urged to delve deep into oil and gas issues." https://www.newsghana.com.gh/ghanaian-journalists-urged-to-delve-deep-into-oil-and-gas-issues/. Accessed February 11, 2017.

Tang, Lu and Li, Hongmei. (2009). "Corporate social responsibility communication of Chinese and global corporations in China." *Public Relations Review*. **35**. 199–212.

Tani, Maxwell. (2015, June 4). "Here's the big problem with China's bizarre new censorship rules." *Business Insider*. http://www.businessinsider.com/china-is-censoring-new-words-2015-6?op=1. Accessed June 5, 2015.

Taylor, Charles. (1989). *Sources of the Self: The Making of Modern Identity*. Cambridge, MA: Harvard University Press.

Taylor, Charles. (2001). "A world consensus on human rights." The Philosophy of Human Rights. Patrick Hayden, Editor. Paragon Issues in Philosophy. St. Paul, MN: Paragon House. 409–422.

Taylor, John V. (1963). *The Primal Vision*. London: SCM Press.

Teasdale, Bradford A. (n.d.). "Japanese Tradition and Culture: Aid or Obstacle to Future Success?" http://www.lehigh.edu/~rfw1/courses/1999/spsring/ir163/Papers/pdf/bat5.pdf. Accessed February 18, 2011.

Telushkin, Joseph. (2006). *A Code of Jewish Ethics, vol. 1: You Shall Be Holy*. New York: Bell Tower.

Tharoor, Ishaan. (2014, April 30). "Chinese toddler pees in Hong Kong street, stirs online firestorm." Washington Post.http://www.washingtonpost.com/blogs/worldviews/wp/2014/04/30/chinese-toddler-pees-in-hong-kong-street-stirs-online-firestorm/?tid=pm_pop. Accessed August 19, 2014.

"The definition of morality." (2011, March 14). *Stanford Encyclopedia of Philosophy*. http://plato.stanford.edu/entries/morality-definition/. Accessed June 26, 2014.

"The Digital Divide, ICT and the 50x15 Initiative." (n.d.). http://www.internetworldstats.com/links10.htm. Accessed July 15, 2014.

Thera, K. Sri Dhammananada Maha. (n.d.). "Buddhist ethics." www.buddhanet.net/budas/ebud/whatbudbeliev/145.htm. Accessed February 9, 2011.

"The truth about Rupert Murdoch's new plot for world domination." (2014, July 18). PR Newswire. http://www.prnewswire.com/news-releases/top-five-global-broadcast-media-companies-performance-strategies-and-competitive-analysis-248876321.html. Accessed July 19, 2014.

Thomson, Susan. (2014, March 17). "Rwanda's Twitter-gate: The disinformation campaign of Africa's digital president." African Arguments. http://africanarguments.org/2014/03/17/rwandas-twitter-gate-the-disinformation-campaign-of-africas-digital-president-by-susan-thomson/. Accessed August 12, 2014.

Ting-Toomey, Stella. (1990). *A Face Negotiation Perspective Communicating for Peace*. Beverly Hills, CA: Sage.

Titova, Irina. (2015, April 20). "Russia's 'gay propaganda' laws are targeting teachers amidst rising anti-LGBT sentiment." *Huffington Post*. http://www.huffingtonpost.com/2015/04/02/russia-gay-law-teachers_n_6994274.html. Accessed June 5, 2015.

Today's Zaman. (2015, June 5). "Journalist Mumcu faces 5 years in jail for insulting Erdoğan." http://www.todayszaman.com/anasayfa_journalist-mumcu-faces-5-years-in-jail-for-insulting-erdogan_383304.html. Accessed June 5, 2015.

"Top five global broadcast media companies: Performance, strategies and competitive analysis." (2014, March 6). PR Newswire. http://www.prnewswire.com/news-releases/top-five-global-broadcast-media-companies-performance-strategies-and-competitive-analysis-248876321.html. Accessed July 19, 2014.

"Top 10 global media owners." (2014). http://www.marketingcharts.com/wp/traditional/the-worlds-10-largest-global-media-owners-42481/attachment/zenithoptimedia-top-10-global-media-owners-may2014/. Accessed July 19, 2014.

"Top 10 controversial United Colors of Benetton ads." (2012, March 22). http://top10buzz.com/top-ten-controversial-united-colors-of-benetton-ads/. Accessed July 22, 2014.

Tran, Mark. (2014, March 10). "Generate decent jobs 'or a billion people will remain in extreme poverty.'" *The Guardian.* http://www.theguardian.com/global-development/2014/mar/10/jobs-billion-people-extreme-poverty. Accessed July 25, 2015.

Tu, We-Ming. (1998). "Probing the 'three bonds' and 'five relationships' in Confucian humanism." *Confucianism and the Family.* Walter H. Slote and George A. De Vos, Editors. Albany, NY: State University of New York Press. 121–136.

Tuckman, Jo. (2015, March 16). "Whistleblowers wanted: Mexican journalists seek tips through website." *The Guardian.* http://www.theguardian.com/world/2015/mar/16/whistleblowers-mexico-journalists-website. Accessed June 23, 2015.

Tufekci, Zeynep and Wilson, Christopher. (2012). "Social media and the decision to participate in political protest: Observations from Tahrir Square." *Journal of Communication.* https://www.theengineroom.org/wp-content/uploads/jcom_1629_review.pdf. Accessed May 28, 2015.

Tuffs, Annette. (2004, February 28.). "Only 6% of drug advertising material is supported by evidence." http://www.ncbi.nlm.nih.gov/pmc/articles/PMC1125284/. Accessed March 5, 2015.

Turovsky, Daniil. (2015, April 7). "Meet Anonymous International, the hackers taking on the Kremlin." *The Guardian.* http://www.theguardian.com/world/2015/apr/07/anonymous-international-hackers-kremlin. Accessed June 23, 2015.

Twining, William. (2007). "Human rights: Southern voices – Francis Deng, Abdullah An-Na'im, Yash Ghai and Upendra Baxi." *Law, Social Justice and Global Development.* http://www2.warwick.ac.uk/fac/soc/law/elj/lgd/2007_1/twining/. Accessed February 15, 2017.

"TV journalist quits in protest at Kremlin's policies on Ukraine." (2014, July 17). Radio Free Europe. www.rferl.mobi. Accessed July 18, 2014.

"Two teenage girls allegedly gang raped and hanged in India." (2014, May 30). *The Telegraph.* http://www.telegraph.co.uk/news/worldnews/asia/india/10864605/Two-teenage-girls-allegedly-gang-raped-and-hanged-in-India.html. Accessed July 9, 2015.

UNDP (United Nations Development Programme). (circa 2015). "Gender Inequality Index." http://hdr.undp.org/en/content/gender-inequality-index-gii. Accessed June 11, 2015.

"United Nations and the Rule of Law." (2014). http://www.un.org/en/ruleoflaw/. Accessed May 23, 2014.

United States Department of Commerce. (2014). "The Media & Entertainment Industry in the United States." http://selectusa.commerce.gov/industry-snapshots/media-entertainment-industry-united-states. Accessed September 26, 2014.

Universal Declaration of Human Rights. (n.d.). http://www.un.org/en/documents/udhr/. Accessed July 22, 2014.

Vakis, Renos, Rigolini, Jamele, and Lucchetti, Leonardo. (2015). *Left Behind: Chronic Poverty in Latin America and the Caribbean.* Washington, DC: International Bank for Reconstruction and Development/The World Bank.

Valenti, M. (2000). *More Than a Movie*. Boulder, CO: Westview Press.

Valle, C. (1992). "Media and religion." *Media Development*. http://www.religion-online.org/showarticle. asp?title=273. Accessed September 8, 2015.

Van Couvering, Elizabeth. (2011). "Navigational media: The political economy of online traffic." *The Political Economies of Media: The Transformation of the Global Media Industries*. Dwayne Winseck and Dal Yong Jin, Editors. New York: Bloomsbury Academic. E-book. No page numbers.

Van der Wurff, Richard, Bakker, Piet, and Picard, Robert G. (2008). "Economic growth and advertising expenditures in different media in different countries." *Journal of Media Economics*. **21**. 28–52.

Van Dijk, Paul. (2000). *Anthropology in the Age of Technology: The Philosophical Contribution of Günther Anders*. Frans Kooymans, Translator. Amsterdam: Editions Rodopi B.V.

Vattimo, Giani. (2003). *Nihilism & Emancipation: Ethics, Politics, & Law*. New York: Columbia University Press.

Vitale, Ami. (2014). "Safeguarding Truth in Photojournalism: Ami Vitale's Survival Guide." *Ochre*. No. 5. http://ochre.is/tools/safeguarding-truth-in-photojournalism-ami-vitales-survival-guide/? utm_source=Ami+Vitale+Newsletter&utm_campaign=8666b0ffb4-Fall+2014&utm_medium=email&utm_term=0_4f5df3db7d-8666b0ffb4-107119981. Accessed September 27, 2014.

Volokh, Eugene. (2015, May 6). "More on the University of Minnesota Charlie Hebdo controversy: 'There are limits on free speech.'" *Washington Post*. http://www.washingtonpost.com/news/volokh-conspiracy/wp/2015/05/06/more-on-the-university-of-minnesota-charlie-hebdo-controversy-there-are-limits-on-free-speech/. Accessed June 5, 2015.

Volpp, Leti. (1994). "(Mis)Identifying culture: Asian women and the cultural defense." *Harvard Women's Law Journal*. **17**. 57–101.

Vultee, Fred. (2013). "'Spike the football': Truth-telling, the press and the Bin Laden photos." *Journal of Mass Media Ethics*. **28**. 241–254.

Wadhams, Nicholas. (2009). "Report: Drug companies violating WHO ethics on advertising in east Africa." http://www.ip-watch.org/?s=Drug+companies+violating+WHO+ethics. Accessed March 7, 2015.

Walker, Margaret Urban. (2007). *Moral Understandings: A Feminist Study in Ethics*. Second edition. New York: Oxford University Press.

Walker, Ralph. (2012). "Kant." *Ethics: The Key Thinkers*. Tom Angier, Editor. New York: Bloomsbury Academic. 144–161.

Wallerstein, Immanuel. (2006). *European Universalism: The Rhetoric of Power*. New York: The New Press.

Wang, Cheng Lu and Lin, Xiaohua. (2009). "Migration of Chinese consumption values: Traditions, modernization, and cultural renaissance." *Journal of Business Ethics*. **88**. 399–409.

Wang, Jian and Chaudhri, Vidhi. (2009). "Corporate social responsibility engagement and communication by Chinese companies." *Public Relations Review*. **35**. 247–250.

"War Report." (n.d.). http://www.comw.org/warreport/iraqarchivemedia.html. Accessed August 12, 2014.

Warungu, Joseph. (2014, July 10). "Letter from Africa: Fight back against hate." BBC News Africa. www.bbc.co.uk. Accessed July 11, 2014.

Washington Post. (2013). *NSA Secrets: Government Spying in the Internet Age*. New York: Diversion Books.

Wax, Emily. (2010, April 30). "Men buy skin-lighteners in growing numbers as a path to love, wealth." http://defence.pk/threads/skin-lightening-in-india.56145/. Accessed March 1, 2015.

"Western and Asian Ethics: Introduction." (n.d.). Chapter 9. AsiaEUniversity. www.Aeu.edu.my. Accessed February 18, 2011.

"What is the Rule of Law?" (2014). http://worldjusticeproject.org/what-rule-law. Accessed May 23, 2014.

"'Whiter skin in 15 days': fury in Dakar at skin whitening cream advert." (2012). http://observers. france24.com/content/20120914-whiter-skin-15-days-fury-dakar-advertising-skin-whitening-cream-senegal-dakar-petition. Accessed March 1, 2015.

WHO. (2014). *Preventing Suicide: A Global Imperative: Executive Summary*. Geneva, Switzerland: World Health Organization.

Wickman, Forrest. (2012, November 9). "How accurate is *Lincoln?*" http://www.slate.com/blogs/ browbeat/2012/11/09/lincoln_historical_accuracy_sorting_fact_from_fiction_in_the_steven_spielberg. html. Accessed July 21, 2014.

Wiegrefe, Klaus. (2011, March 31). "A triumph of justice: on the trail of Holocaust organizer Adolf Eichmann." *Spiegel Online International*. http://www.spiegel.de/international/germany/a-triumph-of-justice-on-the-trail-of-holocaust-organizer-adolf-eichmann-a-754133.html. Accessed September 3, 2014.

Wild, John. (1991). "Introduction." *Totality and Infinity*, by Emmanuel Levinas. Dordrecht, The Netherlands: Kluwer Academic Publishers. 11–20.

Willis, L. and Osborne, T. (2014, July 16). "Peter Greste: Egypt ambassador concedes many see case as backward step." *666 ABC News*. http://news360.com/article/248262517. Accessed July 16, 2014.

Wilson, A. (2010, January 19). "The media's trouble with religion." *The Guardian*. http://www. theguardian.com/commentisfree/belief/2010/jan/19/religion-media-bbc. Accessed September 8, 2015.

Wilson, Courtney. (2010, November 27). "The power of a war-and-peace picture – all 179 of them." http://pacific.scoop.co.nz/2010/11/the-power-of-a-war-and-peace-picture-%E2%80%93-all-179-of-them/. Accessed February 11, 2017.

Wilson, J. (1993). *The Moral Sense*. New York: The Free Press.

Winseck, Dwayne. (2011). "The political economies of media and the transformation of the global media industries." *The Political Economies of Media: The Transformation of the Global Media Industries*. Dwayne Winseck and Dal Yong Jin, Editors. New York: Bloomsbury Academic. 3–49.

Winston, Brian. (1998). *Media Technology and Society*. London: Routledge.

Wirekoh-Boateng, Kwaku. (2010, May 23). "Youth and the culture of materialism." http://www. ghanaweb.com/GhanaHomePage/NewsArchive/artikel.php?ID=182561. Accessed February 1, 2015.

"WJP Rule of Law Index." (2014). Worldjusticeproject.org/rule-of-law-index. Accessed May 23, 2014.

Wolterstoff, N. (1976). *Reason Within the Bounds of Religion*. Grand Rapids, MI: Eerdmans.

Wong, David B. (2004). "Rights and community in Confucianism." *Confucian Ethics: A Comparative Study of Self, Autonomy, and Community*. Kwong-loi Shun and David B. Wong, Editors. Cambridge, UK: Cambridge University Press. 31–48.

Wong, David. (2008, November 11). "5 ways to stop trolls from killing the internet." http://www.cracked. com/article_16765_5-ways-to-stop-trolls-from-killing-internet.html. Accessed June 24, 2015.

Woodard, William P. (1962). "Preface." *Shinto: The Kami Way*, by Sokyo Ono. Boston, MA: Tuttle Publishing. ix–xii.

World Bank Group. (n.d.). "Tobacco Control in Developing Countries: Media Information." http:// siteresources.worldbank.org/INTETC/Resources/375990-1089904539172/474683-1089904575523/ TobaccoFacts1-6.pdf. Accessed February 21, 2015.

"World's 25 largest consumer markets!" (2011, July 29). http://www.rediff.com/business/slide-show/slide-show-1-worlds-25-largest-consumer-markets/20110729.htm. Accessed October 6, 2014.

Wu, Tim. (2010). *The Master Switch: The Rise and Fall of Information Empires*. New York: Knopf. Kindle e-book edition.

Xinhua. (2010, May 27). "Another Foxconn suicide after boss apologizes." http://www.china.org.cn/ china/2010-05/27/content_20125588.htm. Accessed June 10, 2015.

Xinran. (2002). *The Good Women of China: Hidden Voices*. Esther Tyldesley, Translator. New York: Random House.

Yardley, Jim. (2013, May 22). "Report on deadly factory collapse in Bangladesh finds widespread blame." *New York Times*. http://www.nytimes.com/2013/05/23/world/asia/report-on-bangladesh-building-collapse-finds-widespread-blame.html?_r=0. Accessed June 10, 2015.

Zahriyeh, Ehab. (2015, March 2). "Top 5 ISIL parody videos." http://america.aljazeera.com/articles/2015/3/2/SNL-parody-of-isil-made-headlines-but-its-far-from-original.html. Accessed November 21, 2015.

Zhao, Yuezhi. (2004). "The state, the market, and media control in China." *Who Owns the Media? Global Trends and Local Resistances*. Pradip N. Thomas and Zaharom Nain, Editors. New York: Zed Books. 179–212.

Index

World Media Ethics: Cases and Commentary, First Edition. Robert S. Fortner and P. Mark Fackler.
© 2018 John Wiley & Sons, Inc. Published 2018 by John Wiley & Sons, Inc.